ial. The
in almost e
most critical years o
g of libraries for out-of-th
-forgotten pamphlets, and for
ve been published, he is not su
History of the French Revolutio
History of the Dutch Repub
ly give us the undigested results
esses a power of selection, an a
and something of a prophet's i
interpretation of the comm
red into and made the
sed in English litera
he beginning

ERASMUS

LIFE AND LETTERS

OF

ERASMUS

LECTURES DELIVERED AT OXFORD 1893-4

BY

J. A. FROUDE
REGIUS PROFESSOR OF MODERN HISTORY

NEW YORK
CHARLES SCRIBNER'S SONS
1894

The Riverside Press, Cambridge, Mass., U. S. A.
Electrotyped and Printed by H. O. Houghton and Company.

PREFACE

THE following Lectures are published as they were delivered. The references are to the edition of the Works of Erasmus which was brought out at Leyden in 1702.

The letters from which I quote are so numerous and so elaborate that it is impossible for me in a mere sketch to give complete translations of them. I have been obliged, as the reader will see, to abridge, compress, and epitomise. My object has been rather to lead historical readers to a study of Erasmus's own writings than to provide an abbreviated substitute for them.

Erasmus advises students to read only the best books on the subjects with which they are occupied. He cautions them against loading their memories with the errors of inferior writers which they will afterwards have to throw off and forget. The best description of the state of Europe in the age immediately preceding the Reformation will be found in the correspondence of Erasmus himself. I can promise my own readers that if they will accept Erasmus for a guide in that entangled period, they will not wander far out of the way.

J. A. FROUDE.

July, 1894.

LIFE AND LETTERS OF ERASMUS.

LECTURE I.

THE subject of these lectures was born at Rotterdam in 1467. Charles the Bold had just become Duke of Burgundy. Louis XI. was King of France. Philip de Commines will have told you about Charles and Louis. If not De Commines, you will have read about them in "Quentin Durward." Edward IV. had fought his way to the throne of England. Caxton was just setting up his printing-press, and Columbus was making adventurous voyages anywhere between Iceland and the tropics, observing the stars and meditating on the shape of the globe. The country in which Erasmus came into the world was the rival of Italy in commerce and art and learning. Antwerp was the mart of Western Europe. The towns in the Low Countries — Bruges, Ghent, Brussels, Amsterdam — were great manufacturing centres, inhabited by a dense population of industrious burghers and artisans, subjects of the Duchy of Burgundy, but tenacious of their liberties, and fierce in asserting them; governed by their own laws and their own representatives — a free people in the modern sense. If the mind of a man inherits its qualities from the stock to which he belongs, there was no likelier spot in Europe to be the birthplace of a vigorous independent thinker.

The father of Erasmus was named Gerrard, pronounced, I suppose, Gierard, from *gieren* "to *desire*," or "long passionately." In the son the word was Latinized into Desiderius, and Græcized afterwards according to the affectation of the time into Erasmus, just as Reuchlin became Capnio, and Swartzerde was turned into Melanchthon; affectionate nicknames which hardened into permanence. Legend says that Erasmus was what is called a love-child. The father was a man of some station, well educated — with a singularly interesting and even fascinating character. He fell in love, it is said, with a certain Margaret, daughter of a physician at Sieben Bergen. Margaret was equally in love with him. For some unknown reason the relations, either his or hers, opposed their marriage. They were imprudent, and the usual consequences seemed likely to follow. At this dangerous time business of some kind required Gerrard's presence at Rome. He went expecting to return immediately, when the marriage was to be completed, to save the legitimacy of the expected child. He was detained. Communications were irregular. The relations sent a story after him that Margaret was dead. He believed it, and in despair became a priest. His marriage was made thus impossible, and he discovered the trick when it was too late for remedy. Thus the child was born out of wedlock.

So ran the story. It grew up out of tradition when Erasmus had become famous, and his enemies liked to throw a slur upon his parentage. It is perhaps a lie altogether; perhaps only partly a lie. The difficulty is that Erasmus says distinctly that he was a second child, and had a brother three years older than himself. There is no suggestion of any previous marriage with another person. The connection of his father and mother must therefore have been of long continuance. Erasmus's own letters are the only trustworthy authority for his early life. From them we learn that the two children were brought up like other people's children under the joint care of their father and mother, and that the younger was his mother's special favourite, a bright clever little fellow, with flaxen hair, grey-blue eyes, and sharp clean-cut features; very pretty, it is said, and with a sweet-toned voice which seemed to say that Nature meant him for a musician. The mother thought so, and proposed to make a little angel of him, and train him as a chorister. But he had no real gift that way, and no taste for it. In his later years he came even to hate the droning of ecclesiastical music.

The chorister plan failing, he was entered when nine years old as a day boy at a school at Deventer; his mother removing there from Rotterdam to take care of him. The school had a reputation. The master was a friend of his father: among his schoolfellows were several who were afterwards distinguished, especially Adrian of Utrecht, tutor to Charles V., Cardinal Regent of Spain, and eventually pope. The little boy soon showed talent, had an extraordinary memory, learnt Horace and Terence by heart, and composed verses of his own. He showed a passionate fondness for books; devoured all that he could get hold of; got up mimic debates; challenged other boys to dispute with him on points of language or literature in approved university style. He says that he was ill-taught, that his master was illiterate, and did not understand him. He once composed what he considered an excellent Latin letter to the man, for which he expected to be complimented. The master only told him to mind his handwriting, and attend to his punctuation. There was free use of the rod besides, and

Erasmus never pardoned his tyrant as Horace pardoned his plagosus Orbilius. One can easily understand that a quick forward lad, conscious of superior abilities, may have been troublesome and insubordinate. There is a story of a pear-tree in a convent garden which the boys now and then visited at night, with Erasmus for a ringleader, when the rod may have been legitimately called into use. But he says distinctly that he was once severely flogged for a fault of which the master knew that he was innocent, merely from a general theory that a flogging would be good for him.

He could never have been the model good boy of story-books, who learnt his lessons and never did wrong. It is noticeable, however, that, in spite of this, it was early recognized that he was no common lad. He was pointed out to visitors as a boy of exceptional promise. When he was eleven years old, the famous Rudolph Agricola[1] came to Deventer to inspect the school. Erasmus was brought up to him: the great man patted his flaxen poll, and said, "This little fellow will come to something by-and-by."

Erasmus hated the master, and perhaps with some reason. We have only Erasmus's own story, however, and one would like to hear the other. It is quite certain that the man retained the confidence of Erasmus's father in spite of the boy's complaints.

Shortly after the visit of Agricola the mother died. Her husband was unable to survive her loss. Erasmus and his elder brother Peter were now orphans, and were left under the guardianship of three of his father's friends, a banker in the town, a burgher unnamed who soon died of the plague, and the master of another school at Goude. The banker was busy with

[1] Others say it was Zinthius.

his own affairs, and gave the schoolmaster the whole charge. There was some property, in ready money, bills, and land — not much, Erasmus says, but enough to launch his brother and himself respectably in the world.

What followed was related afterwards by himself in a letter to Grunnius, a high official at the Apostolic Court, and intended of course for the Pope himself.[1] Erasmus never told wilful lies. He detested lies as heartily as Achilles, but he never forgave an injury, and a fool to him was as much a criminal as a knave. The guardians, he says, made away with this property. He suggests fraud; but as he adds that it is a common fault of guardians to neglect their wards' interests, he means no more than that they were guilty of culpable negligence. The banker had left all to the schoolmaster. The schoolmaster had been careless; money, land, and bills were wasted almost to nothing, and to crown their own delinquency and get their charge off their hands, they agreed that the two boys should be sent into a monastery, and so, as the phrase went, be provided for. It was against the Canons. They were still little more than children, and the monastic vow, according to Church law, was not to be taken by anyone under age. But practice and connivance had set Church law aside. Inconvenient members were disposed of in this way by their families. The kidnapping of boys and girls who had either money, or rank, or talent, was a common method of recruiting among the religious orders in the 15th century. It is alluded to and sharply condemned by a statute of Henry IV., passed by the English Parliament. Erasmus appeals in the letter I speak of to the Papal

[1] Erasmi *Epistolæ*. Appendix ccccxlii.

Secretary's personal knowledge. The Pharisees, he says, compass sea and land to sweep in proselytes. They hang about Princes' Courts and rich men's houses. They haunt schools and colleges, playing on the credulity of children or their friends, and entangling them in meshes from which, when they are once caught, there is no escape. He does not mince his words. "The world," he says, "is full of these tricksters. When they hear of a lad of promise with wealthy parents, they lay traps for him unknown to his relations. In reality they are no better than so many thieves, but they colour their arts under the name of piety. They talk to the child himself of the workings of the Holy Spirit, of vocations which parents must not interfere with, of the wiles of the devil; as if the devil was never to be found inside a monastery. This truth comes out at last, but only when the case is past mending. The ears of all mankind are tingling with the cries of these wretched captives."

I do not condemn the religious orders as such (he continues). I do not approve of those who make the plunge, and then fly back to liberty as a license for loose living, and desert improperly what they undertook foolishly. But dispositions vary; all things do not suit all characters, and no worse misfortune can befall a lad of intellect than to be buried under conditions from which he can never after extricate himself. The world thought well of my schoolmaster guardian, because he was neither a liar, nor a scamp, nor a gambler; but he was coarse, avaricious, and ignorant; he knew nothing beyond the confused lessons which he taught to his classes. He imagined that in forcing a youth to become a monk he would be offering a sacrifice acceptable to God. He used to boast of the many victims which he devoted annually to Dominic and Francis and Benedict.

Erasmus, from his earliest years, had a passion for learning. He had no help from anyone. He tells us that he was carried away as if by some secret spontaneous impulse. He was checked, threatened, reprimanded. He was refused access to books. But they could not be wholly kept from him, and he devoured all that he could get. He wrote verses, essays, anything that came to hand. From the first (he says) he was far too precipitate, flying at the first subject which offered. Haste made him careless: and this fault always clung to him. In later life he was never able to endure the bore of correcting his books. As Plato said, he made such haste at starting that he came late to the goal. But such was his disposition. He was always at work: writing prose, writing verse — verse in preference, which came easier. He composed whole heroic poems. He addressed a Sapphic Ode to the Archangel Michael. To send such a youth as that into a monastery was a sentence of death. Into a monastery, however, the guardians had determined that go he should, and his brother Peter along with him. When they had done with grammar, were beginning logic, and were old enough to stand alone, the time had come for the first steps to be taken. If they were left longer at large it was thought that they might get a taste for the world and refuse the fate intended for them. They were, therefore, placed as a commencement in a house of Collationary Fathers. Except from this account of Erasmus, I never heard of these people, nor can I learn any more about them. Erasmus says that they were a community who had nests all over Christendom, and made their living by netting proselytes for the regular orders. Their business was to catch in some way superior lads, threaten them, frighten them, beat them, crush their spirits, tame them, as the process was called, and break them in for the cloister. They were generally very successful. They did their work so well that the Franciscans and Dominicans admitted that without the Collationaries' help their orders would die out. In no institutions were students worse taught or learnt grosser manners. In one of these Erasmus and Peter wasted two years of their youth. Erasmus knew more than his teachers of the special subjects in which they tried to instruct him, and found them models of conceit and ignorance. A member of the fraternity, less a fool than the rest and recognizing the boy's abilities, advised him to become a Collationary himself, and he says it was a pity that he did not, for he could have then remained with them or have left them at his pleasure. The Collationaries took no irrevocable vows. If wise men and not fools had the ordering of the world, he bitterly observes, no irrevocable vows would be taken anywhere except in baptism.

Well, this Collationary, Erasmus says, did contrive to get an influence over him, kissed him, caressed him, flattered him, urged him, if he would not remain with themselves, to consent to his friends' wishes. He pleaded his youth; he said that till he was older he could not decide on so grave a matter, and must take time to think about it. Collationaries sometimes employed incantations and exorcisms when they found boys hesitating and frightened. His new friend spared him such methods of conversion, and let him alone for the exhortations to work. The effect passed off. When the two years were out, Erasmus and Peter[1] returned home. Peter in a year or two would be

[1] This brother is called Anthony in the letter to Grunnius, Erasmus calling himself Florence. Peter, according to Dupin, was the brother's real name.

of age, when the guardians would have to produce their accounts. Erasmus says that they could not face the exposure, and resolved to wait no longer. Into the cloister the boys should go, and no more talk about it. The banker left all to the schoolmaster. The schoolmaster professed to think that he would please God Almighty by presenting him with a pair of lambs.

I must again remind you that all this was written for the Pope. It was not the calumny of an apostate addressed to a revolted or revolting world. It was an appeal to the Father of Christendom to interpose with his authority and end an intolerable abuse.

Erasmus was now fifteen; Peter, as I have said, being three years older. When their intended fate was communicated to them they consulted what they should do. Peter hated the prospect as heartily as Erasmus, but he was a cowardly lad and was afraid of disobeying his guardians. Erasmus had better spirit. He had not spent two years with the Collationaries for nothing. Peter, as the elder, would have to speak first. Erasmus told him it would be madness to give way; at worst the guardians could but beat them, and what signified a beating? He bade his brother pluck up his courage; they would scrape the wreck of their fortunes together and go to Paris to the university; never fear they would find friends; there would be plenty of the students in worse case than they.

One can fancy the two boys: Peter a big heavy fellow, dull and torpid; Erasmus, short, slight, and agile, with eyes flashing and heart rebelling against injustice. Peter himself caught fire so far as such damp material would kindle. He promised to stand out if Erasmus would undertake the speaking. Erasmus agreed on condition that his brother would swear to stand by him, and would not leave him to bear the brunt of the storm by himself.

The moment came; the guardian sent for them; and after a long preface about his conscience and his concern for their welfare, said that he had been fortunate enough to find them a home in a house of religion. Like enough the poor man meant it. If he was not a rogue, he had at least mismanaged his wards' property; and a monastery, as times went, and in most men's minds, was a very proper place for a pair of orphan boys. Monks, if they had talents, could rise out of monasteries, and often did rise to the high places in the Church. Erasmus on his side, however, concluded at once that the guardian was a rascal and a hypocrite. He answered politely, but not perhaps concealing his feeling, for himself and Peter, that they were obliged to the guardian for his care and kindness, but they were too young to take irrevocable vows. Neither of them had ever been inside a monastery. They did not know what they would be entering on or undertaking. They wished to be permitted to study for a few more years; they would then see their way more clearly.

It is likely that Erasmus may have dropped out other expressions which he does not record. Schoolmasters do not like to be contradicted by lads whom they have recently flogged, and the justice of what Erasmus said may not have made it more palatable. Erasmus says that the guardian flew into a rage, shook his fist at him, called him a young reprobate, a lad without a soul, foretold his eternal perdition, and declared that he would throw up his trust. Their property was gone. He would not be answerable further for them. They must now look out for themselves.

The exasperated gentleman lashed Erasmus with

his tongue so furiously that the poor lad burst into tears. But he held out stoutly, and so they parted. The schoolmaster reported to the banker, and they decided to make one more attempt. Violence would n't answer; so they must try flattery. Men are very like one another at all times when you can get a clear sight of them, and the story which Erasmus tells is very human and natural. The next meeting was in the banker's garden. The boys were told to sit down. They were given wine and cake. The banker was affectionate. He drew a delightful picture of a life devoted to religion; earthly distinctions likely enough to come of it, with Paradise certain beyond. The great man even condescended to entreaty. The foolish Peter blubbered and gave in, and Erasmus was left to fight his battle by himself. With Peter, Erasmus says in his scornful way, the monastic life answered well. Peter's mind was dull and his limbs were strong. He was cunning and greedy, a thief, a stout man at his cups, and a fair performer with loose women.[1] Angry at his desertion, he accuses Peter of treachery like Iscariot's, and says it was a pity he did not follow Iscariot's example a little further, and hang himself. In the end the wretched being ran away from the monastery, took to abandoned courses, and died miserably.

Erasmus, whose tastes were all for learning, cared nothing for the monks' enjoyments and continued obstinate. His habits were simple. His constitution was delicate. To break his spirit he was hardly treated at home. No one spoke to him. His food was cut down. He fell ill, but was still determined, and the blockhead of a guardian then set a parcel of friars upon him, with relations, male and female, per-

[1] "Illi pulchre cessit res. Erat enim ut ingenio tardus ita corpore robustus; attentus ad rem, vafer et callidus, pecuniarum furax; strenuus compotor nec scortator ignavus."

suading, threatening, beseeching — all to melt the will of a single boy. Some of the friars, he says, were such born fools that but for their dress he would have expected to see them with caps and bells. Others were seeming saints, with long, grave faces and airs of piety. He allows that perhaps they meant well, but it mattered little, he said, to a perishing soul whether it was murdered by folly or by perversity. Every imaginable weapon was made use of to batter down his resistance. One holy man described to him the sweet peace of the cloister, where all was beautiful down to the quartan agues. The brighter side was put forward in exaggerated figures. The bad was passed over as if it had no existence. Another fellow put before him in tragic colours the perils of the world, as if there were no monks who lived in the world and for the world. He described the world as a stormy ocean; the monastery as a seaworthy ship floating securely in the tempest, while those outside were buffeting with the waves and perishing, unless some friendly hand would throw them a spar or a rope. A third described the perils of hell, as if no road led to hell out of a religious house. All went to heaven who died in a monastery. If a monk's own merits were not enough, he was saved by the merits of the order, and the Franciscans kept a stock of stories ready of the established sort — how a tired traveller seated himself on a serpent which he mistook for the root of a tree; how the serpent rose up and devoured him, and how the world, serpent-like, devours those who rest upon it. How another traveller called once at a religious house; how the brethren besought him to remain and become one of them; how he would not and went his way, and how a lion met him and ate him up. Tale followed tale, absurd as old nurses' ghost stories. A monk in special favour was allowed to converse regularly with Christ at stated hours. Catherine of Sienna (mind, I am reading to you Erasmus's words to the Pope) — Catherine of Sienna had Christ for a lover. She and Christ used to walk up and down a room side by side, and repeated their Hours together.[1] The argument of arguments was the stock of good works accumulated by the fraternity and availing for all, as if there were not fraternities which had more need of Christ's mercy than the children of this world.

In short, no artifice was left untried to vanquish a sick child deserted by his treacherous brother. He was watched like a besieged city. The rival orders in the town had their emissaries clutching at him on account of his reputed talents, each wishing to secure a proselyte who they hoped would be an ornament to their community.

To cut short a long story. The persecuted Erasmus wandered about forlorn and neglected. One day, apparently by accident, though really in consequence of a preconcerted plot, he was led to call at a convent near Deventer. He found there an old acquaintance named Cantelius, whom he had known from childhood. A friend's face was pleasant to him. He suspected nothing. Cantelius was the last person whom he could have supposed likely to entangle him. Cantelius was a stupid, ignorant fellow, who had taken the vows from idleness and love of good living. He had a fine voice, sang well, and had wandered about the world as a musician. In the end he had come home, and, finding his relations unwilling to support him, he had taken to the cloister. There he found all

[1] "Cui puellæ tanta fuit cum Christo Sponso, vel Amasio potius, familiaritas, ut ultra citraque deambularent in cubiculo nonnunquam et preces horarias simul absolverent."

that he wanted. You could do as you liked — plenty to eat and drink, and no tight lacing. The brethren were all good friends and never quarrelled, and he strongly advised Erasmus to follow his example. If he wished for books there was the library and a quiet place for reading. The schoolmaster had instructed him how to bait his hook, and he did his work well.

Erasmus liked Cantelius. He heard from him the real truth. There were no airs of affected piety; and harassed, lonely, and desolate, he was half persuaded to accept a fate where freedom and books were promised him. Half persuaded, but not entirely. He still hesitated, but the chorus of priests and connections grew louder with the hopes of success. Again they put before him the desperate condition of his fortune and the hopelessness of his prospects. At last, as an experiment, he agreed to try a few months as a boarder at a house of Augustinian canons, the special attraction being a fine collection of classics. Nothing was said to him about vows or observances. He was to do as he pleased, and to leave if he did not wish to remain. His home was intolerable to him, and the temptation of books was irresistible. He went. The brethren showed their fairest side to him. They were all smiles, sang with him, joked with him, and capped verses. He was not required to fast. He was not disturbed for Nocturns. He could study as freely and as long as he chose. No one spoke a harsh word to him, and so the months ran on till the time came when he must either take the novice's dress or else leave.

He had not yet given in. Once more he addressed himself to his guardians, demanded his liberty, and such of his inheritance as was left. They produced accounts which made him out to be a beggar. He

be smothered in such a vile dung-heap. Possibly,
ay hope, the prior felt some natural remorse.
vised Erasmus to throw himself on the protection
Bishop of Cambray, and for fear the poor monk
not be listened to by so great a person, he prob-
ommunicated with the Bishop himself. The
was a man of sense. He could not interfere
y, but he had the Pope's ear. He was able to
ent at the Vatican that he wanted a secretary,
at there was a youth in a monastery in Holland
talents who would exactly suit him. Dispensa-
rom the vow altogether were given only on rare
treme occasions. Dispensations for temporary ab-
from the convent on adequate cause shown were
obtained when applied for by persons of conse-
.

smus was thus set loose from the den into which
fallen, and was given back to liberty and hope.
after, when he had become famous, the Augustin-
ied to refasten the yoke upon him. It was then
e told his story to the Pope, appealed for final
tion, and found it. For the present his freedom
nditional. The Bishop was kind, but pedantic
arrow. Erasmus had his troubles in the palace,
Blas had with the Spanish Primate. A secretary
panion to a Church dignitary was but a higher
f valet, and a mercurial genius like Erasmus
ubtless a good deal to bear. But his high patron
sentially good to him, and occasionally when he
pare his services sent him to improve himself at
in.

will ask if all monasteries were like that in which
us suffered; you will hear more of this as we go
rasmus will tell you that a great many of them
o better than *lupanaria*. If you desire partic-

still detested monkdom as heartily as ever, but he was desperate and friendless, and at length, and after a hard struggle, he agreed to go on a step further and try the noviciate. The ceremony was undergone, and seemed at first to make no great difference. He was still treated with exceptional indulgence. He passed his time in the library devouring books. But even the volumes themselves made him discontented. He was conscious of high talents. He had ambition, and was burning to distinguish himself, and the road to eminence as a monk was not such as a youth of free and true intelligence could care to rise by. The chantings and the chapel-goings wearied him. The officials might be good-natured, but they were illiterate blockheads. Intellect was not encouraged in such places. Lads of intellect were troublesome and to be kept down. The thing wanted was a robust body, and tough fellows with strong stomachs found highest favour. How, he asked, was a youth born for the Muses and the Graces to pass his life in a society like this? His health was always delicate. Fasting disagreed with him. If he tried it he suffered tortures from dyspepsia. Sturdy ruffians could laugh at such inconveniences. "They were like vultures," he said; "stuff them full one day, they could hold out over the next." Bodies organised more delicately must eat little and eat regularly. He was a bad sleeper. If he was roused once in the night he could not go off again. He could not endure salt fish. The smell of it made him sick. Had the fathers been men of ordinary sense or humanity, they would have seen how matters stood with him. They would have told him that it was useless to go on; that he was not fit for monastic life, or monastic life for him, and that he had better choose another profession before it was too late. Christ was to be found elsewhere as well as in religious houses. Piety did not depend on dress. He must not remain. This, Erasmus says, is the advice which ought to have been given to him. But the fish was in the net, and in the net they meant to keep him. One said his sufferings were a device of Satan to draw him from Christ. Let him defy Satan, and all would be well. He was mistaken in thinking his condition singular. They had all experienced the same sensation when they began. Let him persevere; he would soon find himself in Paradise. Another warned him how he displeased St. Augustine. St. Augustine was a dangerous person to provoke. Mutinous brothers had been struck by plague or by lightning, or had been bitten by snakes. For a novice to desert after having made a beginning was the worst crime that he could commit. He had put his hand to the plough; it was too late for looking back. If he threw the dress off he would be the talk of the neighbourhood; he would be branded as an apostate; the monks would curse him; the world would despise him. The poor lad could not face the thought of public disgrace. He felt he would sooner die than be held up to scorn. Guardians and friends sang the same song, and at last he was forced to yield. He was but seventeen, and the stream was too strong to struggle with further. He loathed what he was doing. The words were forced into his mouth and choked him as he spoke his assent. The halter was about his neck. He was like a handcuffed prisoner in the clutches of the police. The vow was twisted out of him as if he was on the rack, and the fatal declaration was uttered.

This is Erasmus's own account of his profession, exactly as he related it to the Pope. It was the experience of thousands besides himself, whose cries in their

ulars you will find particulars more than enough in Cardinal Morton's account of the Abbey of St. Albans at the end of the fifteenth century. Sir T. More fixes a hundred years before his time as the period at which monastic degradation began. There is no period in English history when you do not find corruption and irregularity, but in the fifteenth century the degradation had become universal.

It is said now that the stories told about the monks were calumnies invented by kings and politicians to justify spoliation. Let those who incline to think so remember that they are not entitled to calumniate without proof the actions of men otherwise honourable, and study the preamble to the English Act of Dissolution.

LECTURE II.

In the rescue of Erasmus from the monastic purgatory the Bishop of Cambray had shown sense and feeling. His action may not have been entirely disinterested. No love was lost between the secular prelates and the monastic orders. The prelates naturally wished to rule in their own dioceses. The friars were exempt from their jurisdiction, took possession of the pulpits, heard confessions, dispossessed the secular clergy of half their functions. The Bishop may have felt some human satisfaction in recovering a youth of promise out of the clutches of proud and insolent men who defied his authority, and had the youth been a docile subject he might have been glad to keep Erasmus at his side.

But Erasmus was a restless soul, ambitious of fame, conscious of brilliant capacities. He was grateful for his deliverance, but the position of dependent on a great Church dignitary could not long satisfy so aspiring a spirit. The Bishop was kind, but dry, cold, and, as appeared afterwards, inclined to suspicion. Restraint of any kind was intolerable to Erasmus; he wished to see what the world was which religious men denounced as something so terrible, and of which he was as yet only on the confines. He was hungry for knowledge; he had not been satisfied with an occasional residence at Louvain; he pined for further instruction, and more intellectual society. From his boyhood he had set his heart on Paris and the university there, and to Paris he was allowed to go.

It is uncertain how long he remained with the Bishop; several years are unaccounted for, with no light on them except from tradition. He may have been twenty when he left the convent. In 1492 he was ordained priest at Utrecht; but he still craved after Paris, and society, and learning. The Bishop consented, not, doubtless, without paternal warnings against temptations within and without. He made him an allowance rather too moderate in Erasmus's opinion; other old men besides bishops are apt to doubt the prudence of sending the young ones into the world with too much money in their pockets.

Thus furnished, Erasmus was launched on to the Parisian ocean. He still wore his monastic dress: it was a condition of the dispensation which released him from residence; but he was allowed to hide the more obvious emblems of his calamity under more ordinary garments.

At the University of Paris the students lived apparently as they now do at Edinburgh and Glasgow, in lodgings of their own, and were trusted much to their own prudence. A priest of twenty-five could not be kept in leading strings. Erasmus's fame had gone before him; his poems had been collected and circulated in private by admiring friends, and he found himself admitted into the best intellectual society. His acquaintance seems from the first to have been more secular than ecclesiastical: like seeks like. He was witty, and he sought companions among the wits of the period; an intimate favourite, if not the most intimate, was Faustus Anderlin, the poet-laureate, brilliant, indolent, but infinitely amusing. Such a circle was not what the Bishop would have preferred for him, but he was to find his own place and to make his own way. He was free for the first time in his life, like a fish in the water, and now in his proper element. He was in no danger from vulgar dissipation; he had no tastes that way; but he had an infinite capacity for enjoyment, and he got as much of it as his means allowed. Amusement never betrayed him into idleness. His craving for knowledge, his determination to distinguish himself, remained, then and always, his overruling passion. But it is clear also that his habits were expensive; he liked easy living, he saw no use in voluntary and unnecessary hardships. He went to plays, he went to parties, and go where he would the sparkle of his genius made him welcome. Naturally his patron's economical allowance was soon found inadequate. To eke out his income he took pupils, and his reputation for talent provided him with as many as he wanted. What he learnt himself he taught to others. Greek was then a rare acquisition, and was frowned on by the authorities; but the disapproval of authorities sends young ardent students hunting after the forbidden. Erasmus learnt for himself the elements of Greek, and instructed his pupils in it. Young and old came about him to be helped over the threshold of the new intellectual world. Booksellers gave him small sums for his writings; men of the highest genius — such men as Shakespeare, Cervantes, Tasso — were not above accepting presents from wealthy admirers. The purses of the richer students were freely opened to their popular teachers. Ecclesiastics were going out of fashion; Erasmus laughed at monks and monkdom, and was applauded and encouraged.

We do not know much of his early Paris adventures, but we can catch glimpses of his life and habits from occasional letters. His correspondents seem quickly to have seen their value, and preserved them as treasures or curiosities.

Here is a picture of a students' lodging-house in Paris four hundred years ago. Human nature changes little, and landladies and chambermaids were much the same as we now know them.

One day (he says [1]) I saw the mistress of the house quarrelling with the servant girl in the garden. The trumpet sounded, the tongues clashed; the battle of words swayed to and fro — I looking on from a window in the *salon.* The girl came afterwards to my room to make the bed. I praised her courage for standing up so bravely. I said I wished her hands had been as effective as her tongue, for the mistress was an athlete, and had punched the girl's head with her fists. "Have you no nails?" said I. She laughed. "I would fight her gladly enough," said she, "if I was only strong enough." "Victory is not always to the strong," said I; "cunning may do something." "What cunning?" says she. "Tear off her false curls," answer I; "and when the curls are gone seize hold of her hair." I was only joking, and thought no more about the matter. But see what came of it. While we were at supper in runs our host, breathless and panting. "Masters, masters," he cries, "come and see a bloody piece of work." We fly. We find maid and mistress struggling on the ground. We tear them apart. Ringlets lay on one side, caps on the other, handfuls of hair lying littered about the floor. After we had returned to the table, in came the landlady in a fury to tell her story. "I was going to beat the creature," she said, "when she flew at me and pulled my wig off. Then she scratched at my eyes. Then, as you see, she tore my hair. Never was a girl so small and such a spitfire." We consoled her as well as we could. We talked of the chances of mortal things, and the uncertainties of war. We contrived at last to make up the quarrel. I congratulated myself that I was not suspected, and so escaped the lash of her tongue.

[1] Erasmus Christiano, *Ep.* xix.

Very unbecoming in a student in priest's orders aspiring to fame and eminence. Well, here is a letter more in character, though this too may be thought over-lively for the future editor of the New Testament. Laurentius Valla was just then the idol of the clever young men at Paris. He was a scholar and a rationalist. He had ventured to touch with a profane hand ecclesiastical legends and the scholastic philosophy. He had stirred the Scotists in their sleep, and had provoked them to answer him at least with curses. Intellect and daring were on Valla's side. Prudence and orthodoxy shook their heads at him. A young friend of Erasmus had shaken his among the rest, and Erasmus gave him a good-natured touch of his whip.

Is it to be peace or war between us? Will you dare to speak as you do of such a man as Valla — Valla, who has been well called *Suadæ medulla.* And you to call him a chattering magpie. Oh! if he was alive he would make you skip for it. He is in his grave now, and you think that dead men do not bite, and that you can say what you please. Not quite. I will stand as his champion, and this *cartel* is my challenge. Apologise or look to your weapons. Expect no mercy. I care nothing for attacks on myself, but I will stand up for my friend; and you will have others besides me to deal with. I have no love for strife: the worst peace is better than war. But eat your words you shall and must. I insist. Instead of chattering pie, you shall speak of Valla as the Attic Muse. And, moreover, you shall let me see certain other writings of your own which you keep guard over like the dragon of the Hesperides. See them I must and will. It is no jest. I am not to be trifled with.[1]

These letters give us, as I said, certain glimpses of the young Erasmus, smart and bright, animated, full

[1] Erasmus to Cornelius Aurotinus, *Ep.* i.

of hope and spirit. Such sensitive natures are always in extremes. His enemies accused him of irregularities in his Paris life. Even his friend the Bishop, as we shall see, was uneasy at rumours which reached him. Erasmus admits himself that he was not immaculate, though vicious he never was. His constitution was generally delicate. He was overtaken by a severe illness. Always, even to the last, he shuddered at the thought of death; and, as men will do, he looked back with remorse at certain features of his conduct which were not satisfactory to him. His celebrity had been growing, and his ambition along with it. He had formed projects of going to Italy, and making acquaintance with the famous Italian scholars. Poverty was an objection. Illness threatened to be another and more fatal one. Here is a desponding letter to an English friend at Paris.

All I ask for is leisure to live wholly to God, to repent of the sins of my foolish youth, to study Holy Scripture, and to read or write something of real value. I could do nothing of this in a convent. Never was a tenderer plant. I could not bear fasts and vigils when I was at my best. Even here, where I am so well cared for, I fall sick; and how would it be with me if I was in the cloister? I had meant to go this year to Italy and study theology. My plan had been to take a degree at Bologna, go to Rome for the jubilee, and then come back and settle myself into some regular course of work. It cannot be. I am too weak to endure long journeys in hot weather. I should want money too. Life in Italy is expensive. The degree would be expensive, and his Lordship of Cambray is not lavish in his presents. He is more kind than generous, and promises more than he performs. Perhaps I ought not to expect so much, though he is liberal enough to some others that I know. I must just do the best that I can.[1]

[1] To Arnoldus, *Ep.* iii.

Erasmus, one fancies, ought to have been more grateful to a man who had rescued him from drowning. But it will go hard with most of us if we are held accountable for our impatient moods. We know too little of the relations between patron and client to be fair judges. Men of genius are apt to take what they can get as a mere instalment of the debts which society owes to them. Erasmus, if he was thinking of Rome and Bologna, must by this time have made a reputation for himself which he might fancy the Bishop ought to have recognized with more liberal assistance. The Bishop might have considered, on the other hand, that his protégé had been living in a society which a priest would have done better to avoid, and in a style for which he at least was not called on to furnish means.

The illness, however, passed off, and the sun shone again. Erasmus's pupil-room was always well attended, and those who came to him to learn became attached friends. We find among them men of high station in society: two distinguished young Englishmen, Lord Mountjoy's eldest son, who was to have so large an influence on his later life, and one of the Greys, younger son of the Marquis of Dorset and uncle of the Lady Jane that was to be. These two he liked well, as he had good reason to like them. Besides these, either as a pupil or an acquaintance, was an elderly Lord of Vere, a Flemish grandee — Erasmus calls him Prince — to whom he claims to have done important service. The chief interest in the Lord of Vere was a gifted and beautiful wife, whom Erasmus says he ill-treated and occasionally beat. "*Senex ille*" is the phrase which he uses in writing of the Lord of Vere. In a letter to young Grey he uses the same words for another old man, known to Grey, who had been also a pupil, and may possibly be the same person. His vivid description of this gentleman is valuable as a specimen of Erasmus's style.

No poet (he says) ever invented such a portent as this spiteful little wretch; setting up, too, for religion and pleading conscience to cover his villainies. I had loved him as a brother; but when he found that he was under more obligations to me than he could repay, he told lies about me worse than ever dropped from the mouth of Cerberus. Sphinx, Tisiphone, Chimæra, Gorgon were angels compared to this monster, and his person is the image of his mind. Imagine a pair of sullen eyes under shaggy eyebrows, a forehead of stone, a cheek which never knew a blush, a nose thick with bristles and swollen with a polypus, hanging jaws, livid lips, a voice like the barking of a dog, his whole face branded, like a felon's, with the stamp of deformity to warn off approach as we tie hay to the horns of a shrewd cow. To think that I should have taught classics to such a creature as this — should have wasted so much time and pains on him, when I was but sowing dragon's teeth which have sprung up and hurt me.[1]

Though it be doubtful who the person was thus described, or how far the portrait was a just one, such a letter lets in considerable light on Erasmus himself. His language when he was angry was as vigorous as Voltaire's, whom intellectually he not a little resembled. It is characteristic, too, that the next letter is strewed with passages of wise and judicious advice to Grey about his own reading, telling him to be careful what he studied, to read only the best books, to avoid loose literature as poison, to stick to Virgil, Lucan, Cicero, Lactantius, Jerome, Sallust, and Livy.

Erasmus despised the Lord of Vere, and disliked

[1] To Thomas Grey, *Ep.* xx., abridged.

him always. But this did not prevent him from accepting an invitation to visit him and his wife at his castle at Tournehem in Flanders. It was in the winter of 1496. He was now thirty. He was going into Holland to see whether it might be possible to recover some part of the wreckage of his property. He was to stay at the castle on the way and make acquaintance with the lady there, the fascinating Anna Bersala, whose function was to be a patroness of genius.

He had a friend named Jacob Battus, who was in some way connected with the Vere family. This Battus became afterwards a faithful and useful follower of Erasmus, and managed his money affairs for him as soon as he had got any money to manage. Battus was to be his companion on this northern expedition. They were to ride — the time of year February. Erasmus tells his adventures in a letter to Mountjoy, dated " Ex Arce Tournehemsi " : —

Here I am (he said), arrived safe, spite of gods and devils, after a desperate journey. I shall think less in future of Hercules and Ulysses. Juno, who hates poets, called in Æolus to help her, and Æolus beat down upon us with hail, and snow, and rain, and wind, and fog — now one — now all together. After the storm came a frost; snow and water froze into lumps and sheets of ice. The road became rough. The mud hardened into ridges. The trees were coated with ice. Some were split, others lost their branches from the weight of the water which had frozen upon them. We rode forward as we could, our horses crunching through the crust at every step, and cutting their fetlocks as if with glass. Your friend Erasmus sate bewildered on a steed as astonished as himself. I cursed my folly for entrusting my life and my learning to a dumb beast. Just when the castle came in sight we found ourselves on a frozen slope. The wind had risen again and was blowing furiously. I got off and slid down the hill, guiding myself with a spiked staff which acted as rudder. All the way we had not fallen in with a single traveller, so wild was the weather, and for three days we had not seen the sun. One comfort there was in it, that we were in no fear of robbers, and as we had money with us we had been in no small uneasiness about them. We reached the castle at last, and of the lady's graciousness I cannot say enough. Were I to say all that I thought about her you would call me extravagant. No description which I could give would approach the reality.[1]

Fine ladies have had an attraction for men of genius from Athanasius's time or Gregory VII.'s. Anna Bersala became for a time Erasmus's tutelary spirit. The husband was at the castle, and apparently not a courteous host; but for the lady herself he was running over with enthusiasm.

Never (he continues to Mountjoy) did Nature produce a creature more modest, kind, or good-humoured. Her goodness to us was as much beyond our deserts as the old man's malignity was below it. She, for whom I had done nothing, loaded me with good offices, while from him, who was under so many obligations to me, I met with nothing but impertinence. I detest such ungrateful persons, and am sorry that I served this one so long.

Very sorry, also, am I that I should have come so late to be known to yourself. Fortune did its worst to keep us apart till friendship drew us together. I write this from the castle on my way to my own country. I shall soon be in my beloved Paris again. Meanwhile believe that you have no heartier friend than Erasmus.

So pleased he was with Tournehem and its lady that his spirits were evidently at their best there,

[1] *Ep.* vi., abridged.

spite of the weather and the surly host. He writes the next day to a certain Falco who was to have travelled with him, but had been left behind. Erasmus gives Falco a Mephistophelian lecture very characteristic of his mocking humour.[1]

Vain is wisdom if a man is not wise for himself. Admire learning as much as you will, but fill your pockets as well. Always have a good opinion of yourself. Nothing more improves the appearance. Care above all things for your own skin. Let all else stand second to your own advantage. Choose your friends for the service which they do for you. Do not seek to be over-learned. Study moderately, and love ardently. Be liberal of your words and careful of your money. No time for more. I must hasten to take leave of my princess.

Two days were spent in this winter paradise. The lady offered him a present, which perhaps for the moment he declined; but he left his friend Battus behind him like another Gehazi to profit by her liberality, while he himself went on to Holland, where he tried in vain to recover his stolen inheritance. Evidently at this time he was in distress for supplies. Impecuniousness was his normal condition. His habits, his necessities, real or imagined, the indulgences which were required for his weak health demanded ampler funds than were doled out from Cambray or came in from pupils. Beyond this he had no income to depend on. Scanty driblets came in from booksellers' work. Some of his pupils paid him liberally, especially Mountjoy and Grey. With their help he kept a horse and a servant, and was clothed, and lodged, and fed on a tolerable scale. But his notions of a competence were always as of something

[1] *Ep.* vii.

more than he had. Books for one thing were indispensable, and the days had not come of cheap editions.

The visit to Holland was a failure. He recovered nothing there. Perhaps he saw his patron the Bishop, and probably the Bishop's brother, the Abbot of St. Bertin, who was always good to him. But nothing came of the journey to relieve his embarrassments save the acquaintance with the Lady of Vere; and we find him again soon after in Paris, anxious and uncomfortable. It was not in him to sleep on the poor scholar's straw pallet, and be content with the crust and water-jug. Of all the virtues, economy was the least possible to Erasmus, and he was, doubtless, often in uncertainty what was to become of him. He had elastic spirits, happily for himself. He was not one of those who whimper to the universe because Nature had given him a plain bun to eat instead of a spiced one. But after his disappointment in the Low Countries he sank into despondency. Like Rousseau, he fancied himself surrounded with enemies and betrayed by pretending friends. One of them, a certain William Gauden, with whom he had been a boon companion, had written a letter to him which had been especially irritating, and his answer shows him at the nadir of his affairs, entirely wretched.[1]

Why do you add by your reproaches to the burden of my sorrows? What may I expect from my enemies when I am thus treated by an old friend like you? What right have you to find fault with me? Someone, you say, has told you that I have spoken lightly of you. Why do you believe such stories? Why not have asked me frankly what I meant? I have remonstrated with you for wasting your time

[1] Erasmus Gulielmo Gaudeno suo, *Ep.* xv., abridged.

and producing nothing worthy of your talents. I have urged you to exert yourself, to leave trifles to poorer minds, and take up with some occupation on a level with your abilities. If this is to have injured you, I confess my fault. If it be to have shown more anxiety for your reputation than you have felt yourself, surely anger was never more displaced. It is true that I may have spoken more freely to you than was warranted by the degree of our acquaintance. If you think this, you should impute the cause to the wine, in which, as you may remember, we indulged too frequently, the state of my health having made me at that time relax my rules.

But you will say, What is all this about? what do you want? who is doing you any harm? I cannot explain in a letter. Ulysses never had such a load laid upon him as I have. You say many things are reported of me which you do not like to hear. I can keep my own innocency. I cannot help what men may say about me. I am alive. Indeed, I hardly know whether I am alive, for I am in utter wretchedness, worn out with sorrow, persecuted by enemies, deserted by my friends, and made Fortune's football. Yet I have committed no fault. You may hardly believe it; you may think I am the old Erasmus with the old loose extravagant ways. If you could see me you would know better, you could form a picture of me for yourself. I am no fool now, no diner out, no fond lover but a sad afflicted being who hates himself, who hates to live, and yet is not allowed to die; in short, a miserable wretch, but not through any fault of my own. May God change my state for the better or make an end of me. Never loved I man more than I have loved you. If others hate me, it is no wonder. But how could I fear to lose you whom I loved so dearly, and by whom I supposed that I was loved in return?

O William, my idol — would that I could say my constant consolation! Even if I had sinned against our friendship by any scandalous action, you should rather have pitied and wept for me than been angry. Now, when I have done you no wrong at all, you reproach me, you abuse me, as if I had not enemies enough without you who were aiming at my destruction. You have seen me in my lighter humours, you know how devoted I was in a certain quarter. I am cold as snow now. Those vulgar fires are all extinct. My heart is yours, and only yours. Absence has only endeared you to me. You never envied me in my prosperity; why turn your back on me in my misfortunes? It is the way, I know, with ordinary men; but you, I thought, were not an ordinary man. You used to call me your Pylades or Theseus; I was rather your Orestes or Peirithous. But a truce to complaints. This only I beseech you, dear William, by our ancient friendship, and by my afflicted fortunes, if you cannot pity me, at least do not hate me. Do not exasperate the wound by bitter words about it. Grant as much to a friend who has never injured you as to an enemy whom you had conquered in the field. The worse my case, the better yours. Commend me to your father, who has been so good to me, and to Jacob Battus, &c.

This letter suggests many speculations. Much of it is unintelligible for want of knowledge of the things and persons alluded to. Parts of it seem to justify the Bishop of Cambray's suspicions that his young friend was leading a relaxed life in Paris. One must not take too literally the passionate expressions of a sensitive, emotional, and evidently at the time distracted man of genius. But it does make clear what we might have guessed without it, that the great Erasmus was no dry pedant or professional scholar and theologian, but a very human creature, who bled if you pricked him, loving, hating, enjoying, suffering, and occupied with many things besides Greek grammar and the classics. With his poetry, his delicate wit, and his grey eyes, he was as fascinating to one sex as to the other. He may have had his love affairs — very wrong in him, as he was a priest, but not the less common, not the less natural. In another letter, written at the same time, there is an allusion to a certain Antonia, with whom he had been in some kind of passionate, if innocent, relation. His habits were confessedly not strict. He was fond of pleasure, and went in search of it, perhaps, into society which a severe moralist might disapprove. But original writers, men who do not borrow the thoughts of other authors, but have drawn their knowledge fresh from life, must have seen and known what they describe. Even the great Saint Epiphanius, the arch-denouncer of heresy, learnt the dangers of the Gnostic love feasts by personal experience of the temptation. Those who have written works which endure and take hold upon mankind have themselves struggled in the cataracts. True enough, many drown in these adventures, and Erasmus, if he had been left just then in Paris, might easily have been one of them. Happily, at that moment, his friend and pupil Mountjoy, who probably knew his circumstances, and wished to extricate him, invited Erasmus to accompany him to London and try his fortune in a new scene at an English university. The adventure was less rash than it might seem. Mountjoy, as will be seen, had distinguished friends in England, eager to welcome a distinguished scholar. Nowadays, unfortunately, a foreign teacher, however eminent, can look for only a poor reception at an English school or college. We had always a reputation for coolness to strangers; we were, and we are, a proud and insular-minded race, and our prejudices were stiffened by the Reformation. But before that great convulsion, educated men in Europe were more like citizens of a common country than they have ever been since. Among the educated there was no sharp division of language to separate mind from mind. Theologians, statesmen, lawyers, physicians, men of letters spoke Latin and used Latin as their common tongue. Erasmus, in his letters, and in his conversation on all serious subjects, used nothing else. Though he had lived in every country in Europe during his wandering existence — Flanders, France, Italy, England, Germany, Switzerland; though for the common purposes of life he must, at least, have spoken French and German patois, he yet always described himself as unable to use any language but Latin. The vernacular idioms were only beginning to shape themselves into intellectual instruments, and Latin was the universal tongue in which men of intelligence exchanged their thoughts. Language would, therefore, be no difficulty. And in England also, as everywhere else in Europe, there was a growing thirst for knowledge: the long night of narrow ecclesiasticism was drawing to an end; the old stars of learning, the scholastic divines, had ceased to interest; the saints and their biographies were fading into dreams; the shell was bursting; the dawn was drawing on of a new age, when, as Newman said of our own time, the minds of men were demanding something deeper and truer than had satisfied preceding centuries. The movement was most active in the young. Erasmus was the voice of the coming era, and Mountjoy could hold out a promise to him of meeting kindred spirits like his own who would receive him with enthusiasm.

The intellect of Erasmus was not the intellect of a philosopher. It was like Voltaire's or Lucian's, lucid, clear, sparkling, above all things witty; and wit, which is the rarest of qualities, is the surest of appreciation. He was a classical scholar when classical scholars were few and in eager demand. The classics were then the novelty, the recovering and returning voice of life and truth when theology had grown dry and threadbare — "Literæ humaniores," as they have ever since been called, the very name and the comparative degree indicating the opening of the conflict between human culture and mediæval scholasticism.

To England, therefore, Erasmus went, conducted by the young Lord Mountjoy, turning his back upon his enemies, real or imagined, in Paris, and his financial confusions, which were not imaginary. It must have been a welcome change to him, the turning over a fresh page of life.

The editors of his letters have been unable, after all the pains that they have taken with them, to fix accurately the dates at which they were written. He was himself careless of such things, especially in his earlier years, when he could not foresee the interest which would one day attach to them. As they are now arranged, they assign him movements contradictory and often impossible. One day he is represented as at Tournehem, the next in Paris, the next in London or Oxford; then in Paris once more, and then back again in London. Sometimes a whole decade of years is dropped out or added, and with the most patient efforts the confusion can be but partially disentangled. Something, however, can be done to arrange them, at least with an approach to correctness. Special dates can be fixed from independent sources when events are alluded to as having happened, or happening, the dates of which we know. I shall do the best that I can with it; and to start with, it may be taken as certain that Erasmus was in London at the beginning of December, 1497.

LECTURE III.

In introducing Erasmus to England at the close of the fifteenth century, I must say a few words on the condition of the country which he was about to visit. Henry VII., as you know, was on the throne. Of him I shall say but little. Historians make too much of kings. They fill their pages with reflections on their policy, or with anecdotes about their personal character and actions, chiefly lies. Voltaire says there is an indescribable pleasure in speaking evil of dead kings, because one cannot speak evil of them while they are alive for fear of one's ears. Henry VII. was not a sovereign on whom it is either just or possible to pass summary sentence. Rhadamanthus himself would have had to pause. Nor does it much matter what we think of him. The thing of moment to ourselves is the state of England, and the social and moral character of the English people, when they had the first of the Tudors to rule over them.

The long and desperate war of succession had ended on Bosworth field. In that furious struggle half the English peerage had been destroyed, and along with them had disappeared the whole fabric of the old aristocratically governed England. The heads of the noble families had ruled hitherto in their various districts as feudal princes. The Wars of the Roses accomplished in this country what the Wars of the League accomplished in France.

The remnant of the dukes, and earls, and barons

had to subside into the position of subjects, and take their places in reality as well as name as the king's lieges. The nation had enough of fighting, and had to set its house in order. A glance at Henry VII.'s statutes shows that violence during the long disorders had taken the place of law. The strong had oppressed the weak. Tenants had been driven from their farms. Courts of Justice had been overborne. The highways were infested with armed ruffians. Traders had learnt dishonesty: sold articles which were not what they pretended to be, and used false weights and measures. With the accession of the Tudors, honest men in all ranks of society seem to have set themselves wisely to work to repair the mischief.

With the diminution and changed position of the peerage, the middle classes had come to the front, showing superior quality. Commoners, canon lawyers who had capacity were called into the Council of State. A serious tone prevailed in the houses of the gentry. Erasmus speaks with astonishment of the conversations which he heard at the tables of leading laymen, in contrast with the ribaldry of the monastic refectories. Archbishop Morton, Cardinal and Chancellor, obtained a commission from the Pope to visit, and, if possible, reform the corruptions of the religious houses. One curious evidence can still be seen of the energy of the time in the number and beauty of the churches built and repaired all over the kingdom, which show the earnestness with which the English nation set itself to reconstruct society after the shock which it had gone through. Morton was still Primate when Erasmus first came over. Warham, who succeeded him both as Archbishop and Chancellor, was Master of the Rolls.

So then we are in London in December, 1497.

Erasmus had then been some weeks in England. Mountjoy had introduced him to Thomas More, then a lad of twenty; to Colet, afterwards the famous Dean of St. Paul's, who was born in the same year with Erasmus himself; to Grocyn, who was teaching the rudiments of Greek at Oxford, no grammars or dictionaries yet within reach, under much opposition and obloquy from old-fashioned conservatism. He had introduced his friend also to various other persons, to Mountjoy's own family among them. Obviously, the young stranger had been kindly received, while Erasmus himself was charmed with everybody and everything. He found the country beautiful, the climate (though it was midwinter) delightful, and the society the most delightful of all.

The air (he writes) is soft and delicious. The men are sensible and intelligent. Many of them are even learned, and not superficially either. They know their classics, and so accurately that I have lost little in not going to Italy. When Colet speaks I might be listening to Plato. Linacre [Henry VIII.'s famous physician afterwards] is as deep and acute a thinker as I have ever met with. Grocyn is a mine of knowledge, and Nature never formed a sweeter and happier disposition than that of Thomas More. The number of young men who are studying ancient literature here is astonishing.[1]

Mountjoy had kept his word. The men whom Erasmus mentions grew to be the most eminent of their time. What he saw was as instructive as it was surprising. His letters being dated only by the years, and that often incorrectly, it is impossible to follow his movements, and there seems to have been no hurry in introducing him at Oxford; but Colet and Grocyn

[1] To Robert Fisher, *Ep.* xiv.

were both lecturing before the University, and in the spring of 1498 he was taken down there, perhaps to stay if arrangements could be made for him, at any rate to see and be seen. Depending entirely as we do on irregular fragments of information, we have to be content with occasional pictures which accident has preserved.

Here is a picture of a scene at Oxford which he drew for a friend at Paris.[1] He was the guest of Richard Charnock, Prior of St. Mary's College, which stood on the site of what is now called Frewin Hall. Charnock had invited a party to meet him. He describes the scene for us: —

Would that you could have been present at our symposium. The guests were well selected, time and place suitable. Epicurus and Pythagoras would have been equally delighted. You will ask how our party was composed. Listen, and be sorry that you were not one of us. First there was the Prior, Richard Charnock, and a modest learned divine who had the same day preached a Latin sermon. Next him was your clever acquaintance, Philip. Colet was in the chair, on his right the Prior, on his left a young theologian, to whom I sate next, with Philip opposite, and there were several others besides. [One wonders whether Wolsey was perhaps one of them.] We talked over our wine, but not about our wine. We discoursed on many subjects. Among the rest we talked about Cain. Colet said that Cain's fault had been want of trust in his Creator: Cain had trusted to his own strength, and had gone to work upon the soil, while Abel fed his sheep, and was content with what the earth gave him of its own accord. We disagreed. The theologian was syllogistic, I was rhetorical; but Colet beat us all down. He spoke with a sacred fury. He was sublime and as if inspired.

[1] Joanni Sixtino, *Ep.* xliv., abridged.

The conversation became too serious at last for a social gathering, so I took on myself the part of a poet, and entertained the company with a story, which I asked them to believe to be true. I said I had found it in an ancient moth-eaten manuscript, of which only a page or two were legible. These pages, however, happily referred to the subject of which we were speaking.

Cain was industrious, but he was also avaricious. He had heard his parents say that splendid wheat crops grew in the garden from which they had been expelled. The stalks and ears reached to their shoulders, and there was not a tare among them, or thorn, or thistle. Cain turned it over in his mind. He contrasted this wheat of Paradise with the scanty crop which was all that he could raise with his plough. He addressed himself to the angel at the gate, and begged for a few grains from the crop in the garden. God, he said, does not look nicely into such things, and if He noticed it He would not be angry. He had only forbidden the eating of certain apples. You should not be too hard a sentry. You may even displease God by over-scruple; on such an occasion as this He might very likely wish to be deceived. He would sooner see His creatures careful and industrious than slothful and negligent. This is no pleasant office of yours. From having been an angel you have been set as a watchman at a gate, to keep us poor lost creatures out of our old home. You are used, in fact, as we use our dogs. We are miserable enough, but I think you are even worse off than we are. We have been turned out of Paradise because we had too much inclination for a pleasant fruit that grew there; but you have been turned out of Heaven to keep us from going near it, and you are not in Paradise yourself either. We can go where we please over the rest of the world, and a charming world it is. Thousands of trees grow in it whose names we have not had time to learn; we have beautiful shady groves, cascades foaming down among glens and rocks, limpid rivers gliding between grassy banks, lofty mountains, deep valleys, and seas teeming with living things. Earth, too, doubtless holds treasures in her entrails, which I and those who come after me will find a way to extract, and we have golden apples, figs, fruits of all varieties. If we might live in it for ever we should not much miss Paradise. We are sick sometimes and in pain, but with experience we shall discover remedies. I have myself found herbs already with rare virtues, and it may be that we shall learn in the end how to baffle death itself. I for one will never rest from searching. There is no difficulty which may not be conquered by obstinate determination. We have lost a single garden, and in exchange we have the wide earth to enjoy. You can enjoy neither Heaven nor Paradise, nor earth either. You have to stay fixed at these gates, waving your sword like a weathercock. If you are wise you will take our side. Give us what will cost you nothing, and accept in return what shall be common property to you and to us. We are miserable, but so are you; we are shut out from Eden, so are you; we are damned, you are worse damned.

The wickedest of mortals and the most ingenious of orators gained his abominable purpose. The angel gave Cain the wheat grains. He sowed them, and received them back with increase. He sowed again and gained more, and so from harvest to harvest. God looked down at last, and was wroth. The young thief, he said, desires to toil and sweat. He shall not be disappointed of his wish. An army of ants and caterpillars was let loose over his cornfields, with maggots, and lice, and locusts, to consume and devour. Great storms of rain came out of the sky, and wind that snapped the stalks, though they were strong as branches of oak. The angel was transformed into a man because he had been a friend of man. Cain tried to appease God by offering the fruits of the soil to Him upon an altar, but the smoke refused to ascend. He recognised the anger of God, and fell into despair.

The story of the symposium at St. Mary's College goes no further, but the rest of the party, it is likely, did not think the less of the singular stranger that had come among them. The legend which he told appears on the face of it to have been extempore. Erasmus could not have foreseen the conversation which led to it, and the improvising power is a new feature in his character. I have met with nothing of the same kind in his other writings, nor can it have been a faculty which he cared to exercise. As it stands it was a remarkable exhibition of high poetical genius, and explains the fascination which his talk is universally allowed to have possessed. Colet, More, Grocyn, Charnock, Linacre remained ever after his most devoted friends.

It is uncertain how long Erasmus remained at Oxford on this occasion. He perhaps went and came. Certainly he neither sought nor accepted any permanent situation there. His time appears to have been at his own disposal. He was sociable and curious. He had come to make acquaintance with England and the English people, perhaps at the expense of Mountjoy, and he did not neglect his opportunities. A letter to Colet, written from Oxford, belongs to this period. Colet was lecturing just then before the University on St. Paul's Epistles. His lecture-room was crowded with old and young. It seems that he had conveyed to Erasmus his high appreciation of his genius, and a desire to improve his acquaintance with him. Erasmus answers that it was pleasant *laudari a laudato.* He valued the good opinion of Colet above the applause of the Roman Forum. But he felt obliged to say that Colet thought better of him than he deserved. He would not allow a friend to be imposed on by false wares, and he proceeds to give an honest account of himself.

You will find me (he said) a man of small fortune or of none, and with no ambition to acquire one . . . but a man, too, who craves for friendship, with a slight knowledge of literature, and burning for more — a man who reverences goodness in others, but with none to boast of of his own; simple, frank, open, without pretence and without concealment; of moderate ability, but what he has good of its kind; not given to much speech — in short, one from whom you must look for nothing but goodwill. . . . This England of yours has many charms for me, most of all because it contains so many men of high intelligence, of whom I count yourself to be the chief. You are a man who, if he was not virtuous, would be admired for his genius, and if he had no genius would be venerated for his piety.[1]

There is another note,[2] written also from Oxford, to Mountjoy, who had been anxious to know how he was getting on there.

I do better every day (he says). I am delighted with Colet and Charnock. Everything is so much brighter than I looked for. Nothing could be less auspicious than my arrival in England. I have thrown off the lassitude with which you used to find me oppressed. I am now happier every day. You promised to join me here. Doubtless some good reason has kept you away. Send me some money under cover, and sealed with your ring. I am in debt to the Prior, who has been so kind and liberal that I must not encroach on his generosity.

So far we see Erasmus on his serious side in this English visit; amiable he was always, but he was a versatile mortal, given to levity when he could venture upon it. He had seen other aspects of English

[1] *Ep.* xli.
[2] *Ep.* xlii., abridged.

life besides what he found at Oxford, as at Oxford he had found acquaintances who invited him to their country houses. A letter to Faustus Anderlin at Paris gives a description of some of these experiences. Erasmus was an airy being, and enjoyed other things besides learning and learned society. He writes to Anderlin:[1] —

Your friend Erasmus gets on well in England. He can make a show in the hunting field. He is a fair horseman, and understands how to make his way. He can make a tolerable *bow*, and can smile graciously whether he means it or not. If you are a wise man you will cross the Channel yourself. A witty gentleman like you ought not to waste his life among those French *merdes*. If you knew the charms of this country your ankles would be winged, or if the gout was in your feet you would wish yourself Dædalus.

To mention but a single attraction, the English girls are divinely pretty. Soft, pleasant, gentle, and charming as the Muses. They have one custom which cannot be too much admired. When you go anywhere on a visit the girls all kiss you. They kiss you when you arrive. They kiss you when you go away; and they kiss you again when you return. Go where you will, it is all kisses; and, my dear Faustus, if you had once tasted how soft and fragrant those lips are, you would wish to spend your life here.

On this first visit of Erasmus to England there is no mention of Cambridge. His acquaintance lay chiefly among members of our own University. There was evidently, however, much curiosity to see him, and if he was treated as pleasantly as appears in his letter to Faustus he must have had a good time. From the Mountjoy family he met with special kindness. The Mountjoys had a country house near El-

[1] *Ep.* lxv.

tham, where there was a royal palace to which the princes and princesses were occasionally sent for change of air. Erasmus on one occasion[1] was a guest of Lord Mountjoy. Young Thomas More had been invited to meet him, and More one day carried him to the palace and introduced him to the royal party. Neither King nor Queen was there, nor the Prince of Wales, Arthur. But he saw the young Henry, then a boy of nine, with whose regal bearing, at once lofty and gentle, he was greatly struck. On Henry's right hand was his sister Margaret, afterwards Queen of Scotland; Mary, a little one of three, who was to be Queen of France and Duchess of Suffolk; and Edmond, the youngest, who was a child in arms.

Erasmus says that More presented Henry with some complimentary effusion which had been prepared for the occasion. He had himself come unprovided, not having been informed of the honour intended for him. They stayed to dine at the palace. In the course of dinner Henry, who had heard the fame of his visitor's brilliancy, sent him a note, challenging him, as he calls it, to give them an exhibition of it.

He could not venture to improvise in so high a presence. He sate silent, but on his return home composed a laudatory poem on Henry VII., Queen Elizabeth, and their children, which was forwarded and well received.

Nothing further came of this introduction at the time. But Henry never forgot Erasmus. Long after, he alluded to the visit to Eltham when inviting him back to England. The old king never seems to have noticed him at all, or to have thought of him merely as a vagrant man of genius, not necessary to be encouraged. Old men do not usually appreciate

[1] Apparently on a second visit to England in 1501.

brilliant young poets with new ideas. Nothing was then known about Erasmus which could induce a prudent, careful father to consent to place him about his children, if that had been the object.

Erasmus, perhaps, found himself in high quarters regarded as a brilliant adventurer, and did not like it. He had met with much kindness and much generosity, but he certainly saw no prospect of making a position in England answering to his merits and expectations. Freedom was the breath of his life: if not the freedom of a master, then the freedom of a beggar. He was a wild bird, and would not sing in a cage. He was too proud to flatter his way to promotion in bishops' palaces or in the courts of princes. Even in the universities he would never have consented to begin in an inferior position, while as yet he had done nothing with his talents to entitle him to a post of distinction. His letters to Anderlin show that he was a creature of whom official dignitaries might reasonably be shy. We don't know exactly how it was, but after a stay of some months Erasmus concluded that he could do better for himself at Paris, where he was known and had a position. There is no kind of person more difficult to provide for than a man of genius. He will not work in harness; he will not undertake work which he does not like. His silent theory about himself is that he must be left to do as he pleases, and to be provided somehow with a sufficient income to live in independent comfort. To this it had to come with Erasmus eventually. Ruling powers saw his value at last, and took him on his own terms. Meanwhile his Paris difficulties were provided for. They were chiefly financial, and his English friends had made him handsome presents of money. His mind was fixed upon the work which he intended to do. He found that he could do it better in his old quarters, and Mountjoy, with much regret, consented to part with him. Neither then nor at any time has official England encouraged novelties. Even Colet, who was trying with his lectures to improve theology, was having a hard fight for it.

Theology (Erasmus wrote to Colet before his departure) is the mother of sciences. But nowadays the good and the wise keep clear of it, and leave the field to the dull and sordid, who think themselves omniscient. You have taken arms against these people. You are trying to bring back the Christianity of the Apostles, and clear away the thorns and briars with which it is overgrown; a noble undertaking. You will find the task a hard one, but you will succeed, and will not regard the clamours of fools. You will not stand alone. The crowded rooms where you have been lecturing will have shown you how many are on your side.

Colet sarcastically answered that one of the wisest of the Bench of Bishops had censured his lectures as useless and mischievous.

The hardest part of the fighting had to be done by Erasmus himself. He hated mediæval theology as heartily as Colet. But England, at least for the moment, was not the place for him. He went, and at his departure he met with a misadventure which his friends feared would disgust him with England for ever. In money which they had contributed among them he was to take back what would amount in modern currency to two hundred pounds. An English statute forbade the exportation of specie, either gold or silver. Property transported abroad must go in the shape of English goods for the encouragement of English industries. More, who had mistaken the law, informed him that the prohibition extended only to English coin. He had changed his pounds into French currency, and supposed himself safe. It was seized and confiscated at the Dover custom-house, and Erasmus was sent on to Paris absolutely penniless. It was useless to appeal to the king, for the king meant Empson and Dudley. In the eyes of the unlucky sufferer it was pure robbery, and so he spoke and wrote about it in his letters. Mountjoy and Colet feared that he would revenge himself in a lampoon, which would close England against him for ever. He was wise enough to confine himself to private sarcasms. "Why," he said, "should I quarrel with England? England has done me no harm, and I should be mad to attack the king." His friend Battus wrote at once to relieve Mountjoy's alarms.

We are delighted (he said) to have our Erasmus back among us; not that we grudged him to you, but that we loved him ourselves so dearly. I am sorry for his misfortune, which indeed I feared might befall him; but in any condition, my dear Lord, we rejoice to have recovered what was part of our souls, torn and battered though it be. I do not mean that I would not sooner have heard that he had obtained a settled position in England than that he should have come back insulted and plundered. Great God! that even learning and the Muses cannot be safe from those harpies' clutches. Complaints, however, are idle. We must bear what cannot be helped, and we shall not cry out when he himself holds up so bravely. He says that, in spite of all, he does not regret his visit to England; that, if he has lost his money, he has gained friends who are worth more to him than all the gold of Crœsus. You should hear him talk of Charnock, and Colet, and More. Would that I knew them. You, too, he warmly praises, and is only sorry to have caused you so much expense and trouble. He charges me to write and tell you this.

The misadventure at Dover took wind, and was much talked about. Erasmus saw that something was expected from him on the subject. He determined to show that he was not occupied with his private misfortunes, and instead of writing a diatribe on English custom-houses, he put together with a few weeks' labour a work which was to be the beginning of his world-wide fame. He called it "Adagia," a compilation from his commonplace books, a collection of popular sayings, quotations, epigrams, proverbs, anecdotes, anything amusing which came to hand, with his own reflections attached to them. Light literature was not common in those days. The "Adagia" was a splendid success. Copies were sold in thousands, and helped a little to fill the emptied purse again. Light good-humoured wit is sure of an audience none the less for the crack of the lash, now heard for the first time, over the devoted heads of ecclesiastics and ecclesiasticism. It was mild compared with what was to follow, but the skins of the unreverend hierarchy were tender, and quivered at the touch.

A few specimens are all which I have time for here.

A Greek proverb says Androclides is a great man in times of confusion. This applies to theologians who make reputations by setting Christians quarrelling, and would rather be notorious by doing harm than live quietly and not be noticed.

Talking of the Cœna Pontificalis, he says it explains the phrase "Vinum Theologicum."

Priests (he observes) are said in Scripture to devour the sins of the people, and they find sins so hard of digestion that they must have the best wine to wash them down.

The mendicant friars who went about begging and carrying the sacrament he compares to Lucian's *μητραγύρται*, with their drums and fifes and the mysteries of Cybele, the greatest rascals in Lucian's world. Lucian's spirit can be traced all through the "Adagia," so like was the Europe of the fifteenth century to the Europe of the second. The clergy felt the presence of their natural enemy. The divines at Paris screamed. The divines at Cologne affected contempt. They said the Proverbs of Solomon were enough without the Proverbs of Erasmus. But rage or sneer as they would, they had to feel that there was a new man among them with whom they would have to reckon. From all the best, from Erasmus's English friends especially, the "Adagia" had an enthusiastic welcome. Warham, who was soon to be Archbishop of Canterbury, was so delighted with it that he took his copy with him wherever he went, and now, though he had met the author of the "Adagia" in England, perceived his real value for the first time. He sent him money; he offered him a benefice if he would return, and was profuse in his praises and admiration.

Erasmus was still shy of patronage: he feared becoming involved and losing his freedom. He regretted afterwards the opportunities which he had thrown away.

It is a great thing for a young man (he observed towards the end of his career) to secure powerful friends at starting. The wise way is to accept favours and show proper gratitude. I sinned in this way in my own youth. Had I then responded as I should have done to the advances of great persons who took notice of me, I should have grown perhaps to be something considerable. I was too fond of my liberty. I could not bear restraint. I chose companions whom I should have done better to avoid, and was thus involved in a long struggle with poverty.

But he was never ungrateful to Warham. He acknowledged that without Warham's help he would have gone under.

Happy was I (he said) to find such a Mæcenas. Whether he is ashamed of me now or not, I know not. I fear I made him but an ill return. All who have gathered good from my writings must thank Archbishop Warham for it.

The problem of how to live was now more intricate than ever. He was becoming a great man and was making a figure, and his patron at Cambray did not show that he was pleased with him by any increase of liberality. Warham and Mountjoy did what they could, but Mountjoy's father was not rich. Erasmus declined Warham's offer of a benefice till he had seen whether anything better might turn up. He did not mean to bury himself in an English parsonage, nor did he think it right to hold a sinecure. Meanwhile, he could not keep his expenses within the limits to which poor scholars have generally to confine themselves.

A certain style of easy living was essential to his existence. He required good, well-warmed rooms, good horses to ride, good servants to wait upon him, and good wine to drink; and to supply all this he had no regular income at all except scanty fees from pupils.

The loss at Dover was most serious to him, though he made light of it. The "Adagia" had been successful — more successful by far than he expected: —

The book is a sort of abortion (he said, in sending a copy to Anderlin), but I shall be grateful to you if you will say a good word for it for our friendship's sake. I am not so vain as to believe it worth much; but a poor article needs help, all the more when you want to make money out of it. I will try to improve it in the next edition.

The "Adagia" did not want Anderlin's help. Edition followed edition, and money did come of it, though far short of what its author needed.

His ambition was alight again. Once more he was hankering after Rome and a degree at Bologna. The ways and means must be provided somehow, and we find him now in confidential communication on the subject with his friend Battus. Battus was frequently at Tournehem Castle — held some office or other there, at any rate was on intimate terms there. The Lady Anna Bersala was rich; she was open-handed to distressed men of gifts, and proud especially of her acquaintance with Erasmus. Her fortune apparently, or a large part of it, was at her own disposition. Here was a possible resource.

Erasmus tells Battus that he has been ill, robbed of his money, and worn out by hard work over the "Adagia." For the moment he can only live by borrowing, and he hopes Battus will be able to manage better for him. The coming summer he wished to devote to writing Dialogues. In the winter, if means could be found, he proposed to go to Italy. The only sources from which he could hope to be supplied were the Lady Anna and the Bishop of Cambray, and he desired Battus, not as if he was asking a favour, but asking only what he had a right to demand, to ascertain how much either of them was prepared to give him.

The judicious Battus thought it unwise to apply to the Bishop. The Lady not unnaturally concluded, like Warham, that a Church benefice would be the most proper provision for her friend: a benefice could doubtless be found for him in her husband's principality; meanwhile he could take up his residence at the castle, where he could live without expense.

Erasmus certainly did not underrate his own deservings, and he wanted more than an invitation to Tournehem.

I am glad (he writes in reply) that the Lady is so well disposed towards me.

> "Varium et mutabile semper
> Fœmina."

— but the Lady Anna is not an ordinary woman. Her sending for me in this way will give you an opportunity of applying for some money for me. I could not even go to her on foot provided as I am at present; still less if I take a horse and two servants with me. Nor can I start off at the first whistle as if I was a fool. I must put my affairs in order in Paris, collect my MSS., and arrange them. You, meanwhile, must forward to me some decent viaticum. I am too poor to travel at my own cost, nor is it reasonable to expect me to give up my position here for nothing. I must have a better horse too. I don't want a Bucephalus, but I require a beast which I shall not be ashamed to ride. You must arrange this with the lady. If she will not pay the expenses of the journey, of course I need not expect a salary from her. Be careful and wide-awake. I also shall not sleep where I am. You know what to say to the Lady for me. Adieu, and show yourself a man.

The letters which passed about this business are only dated by the year, and they leave much unexplained as to the position which the Lady Anna designed for Erasmus. One thing only is clear, that she had money and he had none, and he felt that a person like himself had a right to be taken care of. Begging for largesses from a marchioness seems not a very worthy occupation. But if Erasmus was to do his work he had first to live, and to beg was better than to sell his soul for promotion in the Church, which appeared to be the only alternative.

LECTURE IV.

WE left Erasmus made famous by the "Adagia," and longing for Italy; but in sore straits for money and not knowing how he was to get there. He was to have gone to Tournehem on a long visit to the Lady of Vere. But the scheme broke down. The lady's views were interfered with. She seems to have fallen into some trouble of her own, and Erasmus, instead of being a guest in the castle, we find flying off again to his own Netherlands. He was two months at Antwerp and in other towns, perhaps examining libraries. He describes himself [1] "running and lapping like the dogs in Egypt." His relations wished him to return and settle among them,[2] but he disliked their heavy-headed revels, their dirt, and their ignorance. At one moment he would go back to England and study theology with Colet. He would do this and do that. The wind might blow him where it would. At last he says that he fled from Zealand as if from hell — why Zealand was so particularly hot just then being left unexplained. Italy was his point if he could but get there. If the Lady of Vere could not or would not help him, there was his first patron, the Bishop of Cambray. But the Bishop was in no good humour with his vagrant *protégé*.

I went to see him (he writes); as usual he finds the best of reasons for giving me nothing. As to the

[1] *Ep.* xxxv.
[2] *Ep.* lix.

Lady, I could neither speak to her without danger nor avoid her without creating suspicion. You know the affairs of ———, who is in prison. In that quarter I had no prospects, and as nothing is more silly than to hang on in idle expectation, I have returned to Paris, and here I am with Battus hard at work, he at Latin and I at Greek. My anchor is down for a month or two, and I shall then be off where the winds shall drive me. I had supposed that the Bishop would be glad to see me, but when I called on him he was cold as an icicle, and it is ill depending on such tidal favour (favour that ebbs and flows).[1] I encountered the Lady by accident on the road. She gave me her hand with a gracious smile. She is as well disposed towards me as ever she was, but I can look for no substantial help from her. The watch-dogs are on the lookout, and are as savage as wolves. Erasmus must feed himself and wear his own feathers.

Curiosity is set guessing. It is not impossible that the lady's husband may have discovered the terms in which Erasmus spoke and wrote about him. The Marquis, however, died soon after, and with him died the manly resolution with which this letter ended. Erasmus discovered that other scholars were partaking largely of the Lady's bounty. She was now free. He thought that she ought to have remembered her invitation and promises, and was disposed to resent her neglect of him. Battus was dispatched again to Tournehem.

She [2] has provided splendidly for William, and she has let me go away empty, when he was hastening to his cups, and I to my books. You know what women's minds are; and if the fine promises made to

[1] "Æstuariis admiratoribus," *Ep.* xxxv.

[2] *Ep.* xxxvi., abridged.

me are to be forgotten, I am glad that William has been more fortunate. But I do wish that you could persuade her to keep her engagements, and either give me some money or else some preferment, as she said she would. I am especially anxious now, because I wish to leave France and go back among my own people. It will be better for my reputation, and perhaps will be better for my health. My relations in Holland say that I stay at Paris because I can lead a libertine life there, while in Paris they say I remain there because I am not allowed to reside in my own country. I wrote to D—— at length with a copy of the "Adagia," and I sent a lad with other copies to England.

If the Lady or if Mountjoy will furnish the means, I shall get my Doctor's degree in Italy. If not, I must go without the degree. Either way I shall soon be among you, as I am sick of France. I am poor as a rat, but, as you know, I must and I will be free.

I hear the Lady goes with her sister to Rome, and proposes that I should accompany them. I cannot tell how it will be.

Free, that was it. He had but to put on harness again, take service with some great man, or take some office in the Church of which he would have had to do the duty, and patrons enough would have been found willing to promote him. If this could not be, economy was possible, and bread and water, such as other penniless students had to be content with.

But when all is said, Erasmus would not have been Erasmus if he had gone into bondage, and hardship would probably have killed him. He had no vices. It was not for any unworthy purpose, it was not that he might be idle and enjoy himself, that he begged so shamelessly of great people.

If every hour that he lived had been ten, he worked hard enough to occupy them all. He spent his time in the great libraries, devouring all the books that he could find. He toiled harder than ever at his Greek in competition with his friends in England. He studied the Greek poets and philosophers; he studied the Greek Christian Fathers; he translated Greek plays, translated Plutarch, translated Lucian — all under enormous difficulties, for printed books were scarce, and MSS. jealously guarded.

Beyond all, mixing as he did in every kind of society, living as he did among learned professors, learned theologians, Parisian poets and actors, fashionable ladies, bishops, men and women of all ranks and characters, he was studying the great book of mankind, without acquaintance with which all other knowledge is dry and unprofitable. He was observing his own fellow-mortals — observing what men were doing, thinking, saying, making of themselves. Now and then, perhaps — not often — (minds like his, which are busy with realities, do not worry themselves with abstruse speculations)— he may have stopped to ask himself what after all the extraordinary ant-heap meant, what he and his brother-insects were, whence they came, and what was his own business. Pedants, when they find such a man as this driven to shifts to keep his head above water, are free with their moral censures. But Erasmus starving in a garret might have been as dull and fusionless as they.

Often his impatience ran away with him. Though the Bishop was hard-hearted and the Lady would not open her purse strings, the unfortunate mendicant was forced to write flattering letters to both of them, and to the Bishop's brother, the Abbot of St. Bertin. It was an odious task: he writhed under the ignominious necessity.

May I die (he says to Battus [1]) if I ever wrote anything so much against the grain. You would understand and pardon my ill-humour if you knew how hard it is to bring one's mind to the production of a great book, and when one is on fire with one's subject to be dragged back into these contemptible trivialities. My Lady requires to be complimented for her munificence. You say it will not be enough if I make pretty allusions in the work which I am to publish; I must write six hundred private letters besides. The money was promised to me a year ago, but you still give me nothing but hopes, and you are as sick as I am of the whole business.

She neglects her own affairs, and you suffer for it. She trifles and plays with N—— or M——, and you are racked for it. You tell me she cannot give me anything at present, for she has not got it. If she had not this excuse she would find another. These great folks are never at a loss for reasons. What would it have been to her in the midst of such a wasteful expenditure to have given me a couple of hundred livres? She can supply those hooded whoremasters the monks, vile rascals as they are, and she can find nothing to make leisure for a man who can write books which will be read in ages to come.[2] No doubt she has had her troubles, but she brought them on herself. She should have married some strong, vigorous husband, not a wretched homunculus. She will be in trouble again unless she is more careful of her ways. I love her. I am bound to love her, for she has been very good to me. But, I beseech you, what are two hundred livres to her? She will not miss them seven hours after. I must have the money. If I cannot have it now from her, I must borrow from a Paris banker. You say that you have written to her about it again and again, hinting, suggesting,

[1] *Ep.* lii.

[2] "Habet quo cucullatos scortatores et turpissimos nebulones alat, non habet quo ejus sustineat otium qui possit etiam posteritate dignos libros conscribere."

entreating — and all in vain. You should have gone more roundly to work. You should have been peremptory, and then all would have gone well. Modesty is out of place when you have a friend to serve.

On reflection, Erasmus had to allow that the Lady might not be able to help him just then — that she might perhaps need help herself. But he was an irritable, careless mortal — negligent, and therefore always falling into misfortunes. The money which he made by his books went into wrong hands. The Dover accident was but one of many. He was robbed (or so he thought) by his publishers, robbed by his servants, robbed at country inns. He had been called out of Paris by business: his ill-luck still pursued him.

I have had an unfortunate journey. The bag fell off my saddle and was not to be found. It contained a shirt, a night-cap, my prayer-book, and ten gold crowns. The man in whose charge I left my other money in Paris has spent it. X——, to whose wife I advanced a loan, has run off to Louvain, and the woman after him. The publisher who received the payments for my books in my absence has not accounted for a *sou*. Augustine[1] is still absent. He has made nothing but confusion. He has stopped back advances which were on the way to me, and writes me a threatening letter, as if he was afraid that I should get hold of them. The capital has melted away more than you would believe. I had to sell my horse for five crowns.

Was ever scholar so hard bestead? The sorrows of Erasmus might make a fresh chapter in the "Calamities of Men of Genius." Obviously he had money enough if he had known how to take care of it. His

[1] A sort of secretary, and alternately an angel and a villain.

friends might well hesitate before they filled a purse which had no bottom to it.

Yet, if he was down one moment, he was up the next. He revived among the wits of Paris like Antæus when he touched his mother earth. "I continue intimate with Anderlin," he says, "and I have found another new poet that I like. The travelling about has not improved my health, but I stick steadily to work. My Italian expedition must be postponed to the end of the summer."

Italy was always dancing before his imagination, and an unexpected chance seemed to offer. The old Lord Mountjoy died; Erasmus's pupil succeeded to the title and the estates. He, too, purposed making a tour across the Alps. He had spoken before of a wish for Erasmus's company should he make the journey. The time seemed to have come, but the invitation was not renewed.

I suppose he will go (Erasmus said[1]) if his mother will let him, but he has written nothing of taking me with him. I was cheated with that hope once before.

P —— means to visit the Lady. I don't fancy him. He is a scab of a fellow, theology incarnate. As to you, finish what you have begun. I am ashamed to say how anxious I am. My money wastes daily, and my only trust is in my Battus. If your heart does not fail you, you can get what I want. Modesty forbids me to ask too much from one who has already been so generous to me. But do you hold out your hand, and I will hold out mine.[2]

I must repeat what I said before: we must not judge these beggings of Erasmus as we should judge of such entreaties now. Allowance must be made for the times. A rich patron was then the natural sup-

[1] To Battus, *Ep.* liii., abridged.

[2] *Ep.* liii.

port of a struggling author, and perhaps better books were produced under that system than the public are likely to get under free trade and in an open market. We shall not see another Hamlet just now, or another Don Quixote. But make what deductions we please on that score, modesty was not one of Erasmus's faults, nor gratitude on an exaggerated scale. Still dreaming of Italy, and unrepelled by his last repulse, he tried again with the Bishop of Cambray. Battus had told him that he must put on more submissiveness. He wrote to the Bishop's vicar-general describing himself as a poor *homuncio*—an insignificant insect, unworthy to approach such a lofty dignitary. He asked for nothing. He begged the vicar only to remember him to his father and patron, for whom he protested that he had the same boundless affection which he had felt for him on his first delivery from slavery. By the same messenger he wrote to the Bishop himself in an agony of grief, because he had heard that the Bishop suspected him of ingratitude. Faults he might have many, but not that one. He loved his old patron with his heart and soul.[1]

The hard-hearted Bishop was still unmoved, or worse than unmoved, for he sent someone to make private inquiries how Erasmus was going on in Paris. Naturally he felt himself responsible for the strange creature who was so much talked about.

Erasmus himself was no longer there; the plague had broken out. He was always easily alarmed, and he had fled to Orleans rather disconsolate. Augustine, who was so lately almost a thief, had been taken back into favour and wrote him comforting letters—how Faustus Anderlin had spoken of him as a shrine of learning; Erasmus mildly deprecating such praises

[1] *Ep.* liv.

as no better than irony, and wishing to hear no more of them.

A letter[1] from Orleans to Battus describes his occupations there. Battus was at Tournehem, and had wished Erasmus to join him.

I cannot go to you. The winter journey would be too much for me, and I am busy with work which I cannot give over. I want books, and must be in reach of Paris for them. But here I must stay till you send me money. I am writing a Commentary on Jerome; I am working on Plato; I am comparing Greek MSS. I am determined to master this Greek, and then to devote myself *arcanis literis*, which I burn to handle.[2] My health, thank God, is good enough, and in the coming year I shall strain every nerve to produce a book on theology. Let me have but three years of life, and I will make an end of envy and malice. If the Lady has made me a present, let me have it, with the money from England. If not, I must have the English money at any rate, to take me to Paris. No rock can be nakeder than I am at present. F—— offers me a share of his fortune, but I must not be a burden to him, and the fortune besides is more in expectation than possession. Tell me what I am to look for from the Lady, how I stand with the Bishop, how with the Abbot of St. Bertin now that he has seen his brother, who does not love me; what is said about the "Adagia;" whether there are news from England. Like Cicero, I want to hear everything about everything.

Again, a little later, also to Battus:[3]—

I must remain where I am. I have no money, and do not wish to borrow. I have been so battered this year that I am afraid of travelling far in winter, and

[1] *Ep.* lxxiii., abridged.

[2] He means the early Christian Fathers. His "burning" was to place before the world the original Christianity of the Apostles.

[3] *Ep.* lxxiv., abridged.

if I show in Paris again so soon, evil tongues will be busy with my reputation. The Abbot of St. Bertin writes to me in terms which show that he likes me best at a distance. In the Bishop I have been unlucky enough to find an *Anti-Mæcenas*, who not only will not help me, but grudges me my success. He has actually dispatched J. S—— from Louvain to hunt out all particulars of my private life in Paris, and report them to himself. I understand he has promised a large reward for information, and he says he wonders how I can show my face in Paris after being cast off by himself. If he was foolish enough to think such things, he was doubly foolish to betray himself to a needy student like J. S——. I suppose he thinks that I have neglected him, and that he has something to complain of. I have half a mind to do something outrageous in Paris, just to provoke him. Let me have such money of mine as is in your hands, and lend me a little besides. You may count on being repaid. The Lady will surely not be so cruel as to forget my birthday. Alas, for the blunder which caused me so much loss in England; but of that more hereafter, and I may have my revenge yet. I am sorry that I sent you so many copies of the "Adagia." They sell freely here, and at a good price.

Personal embarrassments did not prevent Erasmus from doing honourable actions when opportunity came in his way. His reputation was high, and he used it to his infinite credit. An instance occurred while he was at Orleans. Heresy-hunting had begun in the Low Countries. A Dominican monk had hunted out some poor free-thinking wretch, and denounced him in the Church Courts. The victim was saved from the stake by a defect of evidence, but he was sentenced to imprisonment for life, his wife for three months, and his daughter was forced into a convent. Erasmus heard of it. He knew the Dominican, knew him for a false, avaricious, insolent priest. He sent

Battus to remonstrate with the judges. He persuaded the Abbot of St. Bertin to interfere. The sentence was reversed, and the unfortunate heretic had his pardon.

Again, busy as he was, Erasmus always found time to give wise advice to anyone who consulted him. Never were truer words than those which he wrote from Orleans to a student at Lübeck, and never more to the purpose than in this present age of our own.[1]

Read first the best books on the subject which you have in hand. Why learn what you will have to unlearn? Why overload your mind with too much food, or with poisonous food? The important thing for you is not how much you know, but the quality of what you know. Divide your day, and give to each part of it a special occupation. Listen to your lecturer; commit what he tells you to memory; write it down if you will, but recollect it and make it your own. Never work at night; it dulls the brain and hurts the health. Remember above all things that nothing passes away so rapidly as youth.

Admirable advice! though he might have added a provision that the lecturer knew what he was talking about.

A few words will not be out of place about the work which Erasmus was himself busy over, and of which the "Adagia" had been but a preliminary specimen. If we are to believe the account of his intellectual history which he gives in his later writings, the Christian religion appeared to him to have been superseded by a system which differed only in name from the paganism of the old world. The saints had taken the place of the gods. Their biographies were as full of lies and as childish and absurd as the old theogonies. The Gospels were out of sight. In-

[1] *Ep.* lxxix.

stead of praying to Christ, the faithful were taught to pray to miracle-working images and relics. The Virgin, multiplied into a thousand personalities — our Lady of Loretto, our Lady of Saragossa, our Lady of Walsingham, and as many more as there were shrines devoted to her — was at once Queen of Heaven and a local goddess. Pious pilgrimages and indulgences had taken the place of moral duty. The service of God was the repeating of masses by priests, who sold them for so much a dozen. In the exuberance of their power the clergy seemed to exult in showing contempt of God and man by the licentiousness of their lives and the insolence of their dominion. They ruled with their self-made laws over soul and body. Their pope might be an Alexander VI.; their cardinals were princes, with revenues piled up out of accumulated benefices; their bishops were magnificent nobles; and one and all, from his Holiness at Rome to the lowest acolyte, were amenable to no justice save that of their own courts. This extraordinary system rested on the belief in the supernatural powers which they pretended to have received in the laying on of hands. As successors of the Apostles they held the keys of heaven and hell; their excommunications were registered by the Almighty; their absolutions could open the gates of Paradise. The spiritual food provided in school or parish church was some preposterous legend or childish superstition, varied with the unintelligible speculations of scholastic theology. An army of friars, released from residence by dispensation, were spread over Europe, taking the churches out of the hands of the secular priests, teaching what they pleased, and watching through the confessional the secret thoughts of man and woman. These friars thrust themselves into private families, working on the weakness of wife or daughter, dreaded and detested by husbands and fathers ; and Erasmus, as well as the loudest of the Protestant reformers, declared that they abused the women's confidence for the vilest purposes. Complaint was useless. Resistance was heresy, and a charge of heresy, unless a friendly hand interposed, meant submission or death. Unhappy men, unconscious of offence, were visited by a bolt out of the blue in the shape of a summons before a Church court, where their accusers were their judges.

Rebellion was in the air. Erasmus was never for rebellion, but he knew how far he might go and how much he might safely say with the certainty of finding support behind him. He had studied the New Testament. He had studied the early Fathers. He could point the contrast between past and present. The New Testament to the mass of Christians was an unknown book. He could print and publish the Gospels and the Epistles. He could add remarks and commentaries, and, if he was moderately cautious, neither monk nor bishop could charge him with heresy. He could mock superstition into contempt. He could ridicule as he pleased the theology and philosophy which had been sublimated into nonsense. With the New Testament he meant to publish the works of Jerome, because no one of the Fathers gave so lively, so vivid a picture of the fourth century, and Jerome, though a monk and a panegyrist of monkdom, had seen clearly that, if it was a road to sanctity, it was a road also to the other place. These were the "*arcanæ literæ*" which he was burning, as he said, to go to work upon, and through all these years of trial he was preparing for his vast undertaking.

The monks recognised their enemy. They were children of darkness, and they dreaded daylight like bats and owls. The revival of learning, the growing study of the classical poetry and history and philosophy, they knew instinctively would be fatal to them. They fought against it as if it were for life or death, and, by identifying knowledge with heresy, they made orthodoxy synonymous with ignorance. Erasmus sharpened his weapons for the fray; you trace his indignation through his letters.

Obedience (he says) is so taught as to hide that there is any obedience due to God. Kings are to obey the Pope. Priests are to obey their bishops. Monks are to obey their abbots. Oaths are exacted that want of submission may be punished as perjury. It may happen, it often does happen, that an abbot is a fool or a drunkard. He issues an order to the brotherhood in the name of holy obedience. And what will such order be? An order to observe chastity? An order to be sober? An order to tell no lies? Not one of these things. It will be that a brother is not to learn Greek; he is not to seek to instruct himself. He may be a sot. He may go with prostitutes. He may be full of hatred and malice. He may never look inside the Scriptures. No matter. He has not broken any oath. He is an excellent member of the community. While if he disobeys such a command as this from an insolent superior there is stake or dungeon for him instantly.

Scholastic theology had to be deposed from its place before rational teaching could get a hearing. Erasmus found that he must study it more closely than he had hitherto cared to do, and he set himself resolutely to work on his "Duns Scotus" and his "Angelical Doctor." He describes the effect upon him to his pupil Grey:[1] —

I am buried so deep in "Scotus" that Stentor could not wake me. "Wake me!" you say. "Why,

[1] *Ep.* lxxxv., abridged.

you must be awake, or you could not be writing a letter." Hush! you do not understand the theological slumber. You can write letters in it. You can debauch yourself and get drunk in it. I used to think that the story of Epimenides was a fable. I know better now. Epimenides lived to extreme old age. His skin, when he died, was found inscribed with curious characters. It is said to be preserved in Paris in the Sorbonne, that sacred shrine of Scotist divinity, and to be as great a treasure there as the Sibyl's book at Rome. Epimenides was a Scotist theologian, or perhaps he was Scotus himself. He composed mysteries which, as he was not a prophet, he could not himself understand. The Sorbonne doctors consult the skin when their syllogisms fail them. No one, however, may venture to look in it till he is a master of fifteen years' standing. If younger men try they become blind as moles.

Epimenides went out walking one day. He missed his way and wandered into a cave, which struck him as a quiet place for thinking. Even doctors of divinity do now and then wander. He sat down, he gnawed his nails, he turned over in his mind his instances, his quiddities and his quoddities. He dropped asleep, and so remained for forty-seven years. Happy Epimenides that he woke at last! Some divines never wake at all, and fancy themselves most alive when their slumber is deepest. When he came to himself he was in a changed world. The mouth of the cave was overhung with moss. Landscape, town, streets, houses, inhabitants, dress, language, all were altered; so fast mortal things pass on. He had been dreaming all the while, dreaming Scotist theology, and nothing else. Scotus was Epimenides *redivivus*, and now you may fancy your friend Erasmus sitting among his accursed volumes, yawning, knitting his brows, eyes staring into vacancy.[1] They say Scotist theology can-

[1] "Quid si videres Erasmum inter sacros illos Scotistas κεχηνότα sedentem, si cerneres frontem contractam, oculos stupentes, vultum sollicitum?" etc. — *Ep.* lxxxv.

not be understood by disciples of the Muses and the Graces. You must first forget what you have learnt elsewhere. You must vomit up the nectar which you have drunk on Helicon. I do my best. I speak bad Latin. I never use a neat expression. I never risk a jest. I am getting on. They will take Erasmus for one of themselves by-and-by. You ask what all this means. It means that when you see me next you will find nothing left of your old acquaintance. Do not mistake me. Theology itself I reverence and always have reverenced. I am speaking merely of the theologastrics of our own time, whose brains are the rottenest, intellects the dullest, doctrines the thorniest, manners the brutalest, life the foulest, speech the spitefulest, hearts the blackest that I have ever encountered in the world.[1]

Erasmus was doubtless right in saying that he was getting on; he was preparing to assail the Philistine champion; yet he had no better arms than the sling and the stone, and, while he was working himself into these divine furies, he was in absolute pecuniary low water. His books were selling faster than ever, but small profit came to him — none at all, if we believe his own account of his situation: "had but three crowns left, and those under weight." He had sent to England to borrow or beg from Mountjoy. He confessed that he was ashamed of himself, but there was no help for it.

Mountjoy (he writes to Battus[2]) may give me something. You must extract more for me from the Lady, or from somebody else. Thirty gold crowns I must have. It is not for nothing. I can stay no longer in Orleans. If I remain there will be a catas-

[1] "Quorum cerebellis nihil putidius, lingua nihil barbarius, ingenio nihil stupidius, doctrina nihil spinosius, moribus nihil asperius, vita nihil fucatius, oratione nihil virulentius, pectore nihil nigrius."

[2] *Ep.* lxxxi., abridged.

trophe, and I and all my knowledge will come to wreck. I beseech, I adjure you. If any spark still burns of your old affection for me, do what you can. The Lady promises every day, but nothing comes. The Bishop is displeased with me. The Abbot tells me to hope. But nobody gives except N——, whom, wretched being, I have so drained that he has nothing left to bestow. The plague has taken away my pupils, the sole resource I had for earning anything. What is to become of me if my health breaks down? What work can I do without books? What will literature ever do for me at all, unless I can obtain some secure position where I shall not be the butt of every blockhead? I do not write all this to vex you with my complaints, but I want to wake you if you are asleep, and stir you to exert yourself. Augustine reads the "Adagia" to large audiences. Everything is right that way. If you can dispose of any copies for me at St. Omer you will find them in my baggage.

Poets and philosophers have been often driven hard by the pinch of necessity. But poets and philosophers must eat like other men. They cannot feed on air like the chameleon. Evidently there was no hope from the Bishop: the "Adagia" must have finished matters in that quarter. His brother the Abbot was better inclined, though he hardly ventured to show it. Battus had told Erasmus that if he wanted to recover favour in those quarters he must flatter them. He did what he could. He addressed long letters to them both, pouring out streams of gratitude for their past kindness, and of admiration for their extraordinary qualities. He complimented the Bishop [1] on his majestic bearing on public occasions, and on the charm and grace of his private conversation. He told the Abbot, playing skilfully on the rivalry between the secular and regular orders, that he was a match for the shrewdest of the tyrants in purple (that is, the

[1] *Ep.* xci.

Bishops), while he could be kind and condescending to little persons like his client Erasmus. To show the Abbot how good he was, and how reverend towards the Church's mysteries, he sent him a long story of certain goblins and magicians who had been playing pranks at Orleans, with a comical affectation of seriousness. The story will perhaps interest you as an illustration of the times. The words are Erasmus's own, slightly compressed:—

A man in this town has been practising magic with his wife and daughter. He kept the adorable body of Christ (my flesh creeps as I write) in a box under his bed. He had bought it from a Mass priest for a less price than the Jews paid for Christ Himself. One night he brought the Mystery out of the straw. The girl, *a virgin* (only a virgin could venture), pointed at it with a naked sword. A head was produced, with three faces, representing the Triple Monad. The magician opened his book, adored the triad, and then prayed to the devil till Satan appeared in person, gave him some money and promised more. The magician said it was not enough for his long service. The devil answered that to find a treasure they must have the help of a scholar, and bade him apply to the prior of a monastery in the town. The prior was a bachelor of divinity, and of note as a preacher. Why the devil chose such a man is hard to say, unless he thought the Mendicants were all rascals. However, to the prior the magician went and told him he had some wonderful MSS. which he could not read, and that he wanted the prior's assistance. He produced them. One was an Old Testament in French; another a book of necromancy, which the prior rashly glanced at and said it was a work of evil. The magician swore the prior to secrecy, and then said he had more, and that if a learned man would read them for him they might both be enormously rich.

The prior pretended to be caught, and wormed out the

whole secret, even to the possession of the Holy Thing. He said he must see it. The magician took him to his house and showed him all. The prior went straight to the vicar-general, a good sensible man, and a friend of my own. The vicar called in the police. The magician and the women were arrested. The house was searched, the body of Christ was found and reverently carried away. All that day and all the next night the priests and monks prayed and chanted. Next morning a special service in the cathedral. The streets were carpeted. Bells rang in all the steeples. The clergy walked in procession, carrying their relics, and the Mystery was borne in solemn pomp to the Church of St. Cross. The prior told the story from the pulpit to a vast crowd, taking however so much credit to himself that the vicar-general had to rebuke him. Two divines and two lawyers were brought from Paris to examine the prisoners. The vicar told me the man confessed to horrors, which were perhaps not true, as they were drawn out of him on the rack. He said the devil also misused his wife at nights. The daughter said the devil also visited her. The tales of Medea and Thyestes become credible when such frightful things are possible in Christendom. No Chaldeans, no enchanters, no Pythonesses, no Thessalian witches produced the equal of this tragedy of Orleans — a portent not born of Night, the mother of the Furies, but of avarice, the mother of all evil: impiety, superstition, sacrilege, all in one. What wonder that we have wars, and famine, and pestilence, that vice has grown so common that it ceases to be called vice, when we have crimes among us worse than those which caused the Deluge! As Horace says: our sins forbid Jove to lay aside his thunderbolts.

Here ends my Iliad, most kind father. Grief and the pleasure of writing to you have made my pen run too long.

This lecture has run too long also; but Erasmus was a many-sided man, and it is well to look at him all round.

LECTURE V.

NEITHER flattery, nor eloquence, nor tales of magic and sacrilege melted the hearts of the Bishop of Cambray and the Abbot of St. Bertin. Both seem to have been inexorable. But Erasmus's heart was still bent on Italy. Modesty, or some such vice, prevented Battus from urging the Lady of Vere as vehemently as Erasmus desired. The lady, he was convinced, needed only to be judiciously pressed. There was no husband any longer to interfere with her liberality. Her son, the young Adolph, was a child, and she was absolute mistress of the revenues of the principality.

Go yourself to the Lady (Erasmus again writes to his friend [1]). Take Adolf with you to present my petition that he may touch his mother's heart, and do not let him ask too little. . . . Insist upon my delicacy. Say that my pride forbids my representing my necessities directly to herself. Tell her that I am in extreme distress, that this banishment to Orleans has taken away my only means of earning money for myself; that a Doctor's degree can only be obtained to advantage in Italy, and that a person so weak in health as I am cannot travel there with an empty purse. Tell her that I cannot degrade my profession as a man of learning by reducing my scale of living below its present level, and that Erasmus will do more credit to her liberality than the theologians whom she has taken into her favour. They can only preach sermons: I am writing books which will live for ever. They address

[1] *Ep.* xciv., abridged.

single congregations: I shall be read by all the world. Theologians there will always be in abundance: the like of me comes but once in centuries.

This sounds like vanity, but it is n't. Horace says: —

"Exegi monumentum ære perennius."

Shakespeare says: "The pyramids shall not outlive this powerful rhyme." Erasmus was right, though one could wish that he had not said it so emphatically; but perhaps it was only his humour. He goes on to Battus in the same strain: —

Do not be shy. Do not mind telling a lie or two in a friend's interest. Show her that she will be none the poorer if a few of her crowns go to restore the corrupt text of Jerome, to revive true theology, and give back to the world the works of other Fathers which have been left to perish. Enlarge on this with your utmost force. Insist on my character and my expectations, my love for the Lady, my diffidence, &c., &c. Then say that I have written to you that I absolutely must have 200 livres with a year's salary from the situation which she promised me. It is no more than truth. I cannot go to Italy with only a hundred, unless I put my head under the yoke again — go as companion to some rich man, and this I will rather die than do. To her it can matter nothing whether she gives it now or gives it a year hence. To me it matters everything. Suggest, besides, that some preferment ought to be waiting to receive me on my return, that I may have decent means of maintaining myself. Advise her, as of yourself, to promise me the first that shall fall vacant. It may not be the best in her gift, but it will be something, and I can change it afterwards when a better falls in.

Doubtless (the letter continues) she will have many applicants, but you can say that I am one of a thousand, and am not to be weighed in a balance with others. You will not mind a few good sound lies for Erasmus. See that Adolf presses her too, and dictate to him what he shall say that will be most moving. See also that whatever is promised shall be promised with Adolf's knowledge, so that, if anything happens to the mother, I may recover from the son. Add, besides, that I am losing my eyesight from overwork, as Jerome did: that you have this from me and know it to be true. Tell her that a sapphire or some other gem is good for bad eyes, and persuade her to send me one. I would myself have suggested that to her, but I have no Pliny at hand to refer to. Your own doctor, however, will confirm the fact. All will go well if you only do your part. Seize opportunity by the locks, and do not be afraid that if you can bring the Lady to do all this for me you will have exhausted your own claim, and can afterwards ask nothing for yourself. I know that you are dependent on her generosity, but consider that the two things cannot be had together. The Lady's purse will not be emptied by my small demands upon it. You can ask any day. I may never have another opportunity. Perhaps you think I ought to be satisfied if I am kept out of reach of starvation. I think, on the contrary, that I shall have to abandon literature altogether if I cannot obtain means from one quarter or another to go on with it properly.

No man can write as he should without freedom from sordid cares, and I at this moment am little better than a beggar, with scarce a livre left. How many ignorant asses roll in money! Is it a great thing to keep Erasmus from dying of hunger?

What, after all, have I received from the Lady except promises? You may say I lost my money in England. So I did. But it was no more my fault than it was yours. I did not go to England lightly. I did not leave it lightly. Accidents may befall any of us. You tell me that I ought to dedicate some complimentary work to the Lady. Trust me, I am working hard enough. I spare nothing, not even my health. To please my friends, I compose for one; I read for another; I correct for a third; while I compose, read, and correct for myself too. I toil over Greek texts, the toughest job of the whole, and yet I am to produce something more for the Lady, as if I had no more to do than yourself, or as if my wits were of adamant. Try yourself to write a book, and then complain of me for being dilatory. Your jokes, my sweet James, are foolish and not to the point. They have more of Momus in them than of wit. I have set my heart, I tell you, on compassing the whole round of literature. What I have done so far is mere trifling. I have long seen that the majority of men are fools. My writings will not fly away, and I prefer solid fame which comes late, to notoriety which grows quickly and fades so soon. How often have I not seen it so! Therefore, I beseech you, let me manage this business my own way. If you will take care of my material fortunes, do not fear that I shall spare myself my own exertions. One should not ask small favours from great people. Again, do your part prudently and all will be well. But I must not be cheated. If you despair of success tell me so plainly, and I will try elsewhere. You might do something, perhaps, if you saw a chance, with the Abbot of St. Bertin. You know the nature of the man. Invent a plausible excuse. Tell him that I really have a great work on hand — say I am restoring the text of Jerome, which careless theologians have corrupted — that I am clearing up points about Jerome which have been misunderstood — that I want books and must have help to get them. You will be telling no lies in this, for it is what I am really occupied with. If you can get a large sum out of the Lady send my servant with it. If she gives but ten or twelve crowns, or nothing at all, you can dispatch them by another hand. Any way, I must have a few crowns from you. I starve for books. Leisure I have none, and I am out of health besides.

Many a fine writer besides Erasmus has had to petition humbly for great men's superfluities. In these days of liberty we rejoice that all that is over, and that the gifted author deals directly with the reading public. I suppose we shall see fine results in time. I do not know that, so far as literature is concerned, they have been brilliant as yet. Erasmus might at any time have sold himself and his talents to the Church, and become as rich as Wolsey. He preferred literature and a patroness, and the result was that he became one of the Immortals. The Lady Anna waited perhaps to be entreated rather too long, but what might be honourably accepted might, under the circumstances of Erasmus, be legitimately asked for. Without Mæcenas we might have had no Odes or Satires from Horace; without the Duke of Lerma we should have had no Don Quixote; without the Duke of Weimar we might have had no Faust; without the Lady of Vere there would have been no New Testament, no "Moria," no "Colloquies." The patronage system may not be the best, but it is better than leaving genius to be smothered or debased by misery. And when genius is taught that life depends on pleasing the readers at the shilling bookstalls, it may be smothered that way too, for all that I can see to the contrary.

Even then, however, a certain price had to be paid in the way of compliment and flattery. Battus had told Erasmus that the Lady of Vere expected it, and since he had to do it, he did it handsomely. He wrote to her, and this is what the letter contained:[1]—

TO THE PRINCESS OF VERE.

Three Annas are mentioned by ancient writers: Dido's sister Anna, who became a goddess, the aged Anna the mother of Samuel, and Anna who was the mother of the Virgin. If my skill does not fail me, another shall be added to the list. Those three were illustrious ladies, but where in all Europe will be found a lady more illustrious than yourself? They

[1] *Ep.* xcii., abridged.

were pious, but so are you. They were tried by affliction: would that this had not been your fate as well! [Much more of these comparisons, and then:] Your kindness enables me to live and devote myself to literature. I grieve for your sufferings, but sufferings endured as you endure them lend splendour to virtue. Destiny has connected your fate with mine. Fortune's malice cannot reach to yourself on the height where you stand, but me she persecutes as if in my person she would persecute learning itself. To whom then can I lay open my calamities better than to her who can and will relieve them. This is the anniversary of the day on which my small substance on which I depended for the continuation of my studies was shipwrecked in England; and from that day to this misfortune in one form or another has never ceased to pursue me. When the British Charybdis had vomited me back to France, I was overtaken by a tempest. Then on the road I fell among thieves, and had their daggers at my throat. Then I was hunted out of Paris by the plague, and I had other things to trouble me besides.

It is unworthy of *me* (a man of letters and a philosopher) to be so cast down as I am, when you, who were born to rank and luxury, endure your trials so patiently. But let Fortune thunder as she will, I will not be crushed, and leave my work undone, while I have my Princess for a Cynosure to shine upon me. Malice cannot rob me of the learning which I have gained. A little money will enable me to make use of it, and this you can supply out of your abundance. My muse I shall owe to you, and she shall henceforth be dedicated to your service. Thee, dear Nutricia, dear nurse of my soul, I would not change for Augustus and Mæcenas, and future ages will marvel that in this far corner of the world, when learning lay prostrate from neglect and ignorance, a woman rose, who by her benevolence restored learning from dust to life. When Erasmus was mocked by promises which were not observed to him, when he had been robbed and flung out to buffet with the waves of fortune, you, Lady, did not suffer him to drown in penury. Continue the work which you have begun. My writings, your own children, reach out their suppliant hands to you. By your own fortune, whose smiles you despise, and whose frowns you defy; by those writings' fortune, malignant always, against which you alone can support them; by that admirable Queen, the Ancient Wisdom, which the Prophet places at God's right hand, not, as she now lies, in rags and squalor, but in golden raiment which I have toiled to cleanse and to restore, they beseech you not to desert them. If I am to continue this work I must visit Italy. I must show myself there to establish my personal consequence. I must acquire the absurd title of Doctor. It will not make me a hair the better, but, as times go, no man now can be counted learned, despite of all which Christ has said, unless he is styled Magister. If the world is to believe in me, I must put on the lion's skin. I have to fight with monsters, and I must wear the dress of Hercules. Help me, therefore, gracious Lady. Battus will tell you how. It goes against my habits, against my nature, against my modesty, to sue for favours. But necessity compels me and I have brazened my forehead to address you. From the time when I was a child I have been a devoted worshipper of St. Anne. I composed a hymn to her when I was young, and the hymn I now send to you, another Anne. I send to you, besides, a collection of prayers to the Holy Virgin. They are not spells to charm the moon out of the sky, but they will bring down out of Heaven her who brought forth the Sun of Righteousness. She is easy of approach. She will hear the supplication of another virgin, for as a virgin I hold you — a maiden, not a widow. You were married when a girl, to please your parents. That marriage brought no pleasure to you, it was but a discipline of patience; yet, though you are still in your prime, you cannot be tempted out of your resolution of continency. I reckon you not as one of the choir of maidens, who, the Scripture says, cannot be numbered; I place you not among the concubines of Solomon; I place you among St. Jerome's Queens, &c. &c.

Enough of this. The complimentary work had to be done, and done it was, not entirely without dignity, though it is rather melancholy reading. Nowadays, the enlightened public has to be flattered with equal sincerity or insincerity. The appeal was, of course, successful. Enough was given to set Erasmus free from squalid care, and get him the lion's skin that he was so anxious about. His biographers mention the Lady of Vere, but none as yet with the prominence which confers the immortal fame which Erasmus promised her. If Erasmus becomes popular again, the defect will perhaps be mended, and the fourth Anna will be duly canonized.

It is noticeable that during this sad time Erasmus studied and translated the greater part of Lucian's Dialogues. I wish more of us read Lucian now. He was the greatest man by far outside the Christian Church in the second century. He had human blood in him. The celestial ichor which ran in the veins of Marcus Aurelius and Epictetus belongs to ghosts rather than to living sons of Adam, and you will learn full as much from Lucian's Dialogues of what men and women were like in the Roman Empire when the Christian faith was taking root as you will learn from Justin Martyr or Irenæus or Tertullian. One of these dialogues seems particularly to have struck Erasmus, *Περὶ τῶν ἐπὶ μισθῷ συνόντων*. Young men of talent in Lucian's time were tempted by the promise of an easy life to hire themselves out as companions to wealthy Roman nobles to write their letters, correct their verses, amuse their guests, and write poems in their honour. Lucian traces one of these unfortunates through his splendid degradation, till he is supplanted by a new favourite and flung aside like a worn-out dress. Too late to return to any honest employment, he sinks from shame to shame, till he falls to the level of the groom of the chamber and the housekeeper, and finally is left in charge of my Lady's pug-dog.

To such a fate, doubtless, many a promising youth was drifting in the fifteenth century as well as in the second. A high education creates tastes for refinement, and does not provide the means of satisfying them. Erasmus had evidently felt the temptation. He perhaps actually tried such a situation when living with the Bishop of Cambray. Something like it had been offered him at Tournehem Castle, and Lucian had possibly saved him from accepting it.

A far more honourable relic remains of his connection with the Vere family in the "Encheiridion Militis Christiani," a Christian knight's manual, which he began at Tournehem, and finished afterwards at the Lady's request.

The occasion of it was this. It was like one of Goethe's "Gelegenheits-Gedichte," poems rising out of special incidents, which Goethe says are always a man's best. Erasmus came to write it in this way — the account is his own.

Battus and he, he says, had gone to Tournehem at the invitation of the Lord of the castle, who had been his pupil. "The Lord of Vere had a wife of remarkable piety. He himself was a pleasant man to live with, but the worst of profligates, and given to associating with abandoned women. He despised all religious teachers except me, and his lady, in alarm for his soul, asked me to write something which might bring him to a sense of his condition. He was not to know that it had been suggested by herself, for he was a rough soldier, and at times would even strike her. So I did what she desired." And the world was thus made the richer by the finest of Erasmus's minor compositions.

The money difficulties being got rid of, at least for a time, the Italian journey in search of the lion's skin could now come off. For some reason it was still delayed for two or three years. In the interval it is certain that Erasmus went back to England. The letters are lost which gave detailed pictures of this second visit; but the date of his introduction to the royal princes at Eltham is fixed by his mention of their ages. He was with Grocyn at Lambeth just after Warham was made Archbishop of Canterbury, so that he was undoubtedly in England in 1501 or 1502. He was a volatile, restless gentleman, and to follow him through his movements at this time is like chasing a will-o'-the-wisp. There is proof that he was lecturing on Greek at Cambridge in 1506, though again we have no particulars of what he did there, or of how long he stayed. The Italian journey must be placed between these two English visits, for it is equally certain that he was at Bologna in 1504, and saw Julius there.

Mountjoy and Grey had after all offered to take him with them to Italy, but with money in his pocket he preferred to be free. Colet had sent him as pupils the two sons of a Doctor Baptista, who was a court physician to Henry VII. The boys were to make the Italian tour in charge of another tutor. The Baptistas were rich. By attaching himself to their party, Erasmus could diminish his expenses. He agreed to accompany them as an independent friend. "I did not take charge of them," he said. "I declined to be responsible for their behaviour, but I was to act as general guide and overlooker."

The plan did not answer. The party consisted of Erasmus, the two Baptista lads, their English tutor, and a courier, who was to see them safe to Bologna. The tutor and courier quarrelled and fought. "At first," says Erasmus, "I thought only one of them was in fault, but they made friends again over a bottle, and I then disliked them both equally. Men who fall out without a cause, and then are reconciled with as little reason, do not suit me. I determined to have no more to say to them, and I amused myself in the passage of the Alps with composing a poem on old age."

From which it appears that Erasmus had no taste for what we call the sublime and beautiful. Like Socrates, he had no interest in scenery, and cared only for men and human things. The party separated; Erasmus went on by himself, preceded by his reputation, which secured him a gracious reception. He received the coveted lion's skin, and, as he foretold, was not a hair the better for it; but great men invited him to their houses as they had done in England; he was introduced to bishops and cardinals, and even to the great Julius II. himself, who was exchanging his Pope's robes for the steel cap and jacket. Julius was no sooner on the throne than he had large schemes for the unification of Italy, humbling the Venetians, and driving out the foreigner. You have seen his portrait in the National Gallery — a grand old man, sitting in his chair and looking like a slumbering volcano. He had heard of Erasmus as an accomplished writer. He asked him to set out his projects in some flourishing pamphlet, and Erasmus might have made his fortune if he had complied. He did write something, but not what his Holiness wanted. Erasmus disliked wars and disliked warlike popes, and threw away his chance, and preferred to be a spectator. The great Pope cared little whether an insignificant Dutch scribbler liked him or did n't like him. He took the field with his army, drove the French out of Lombardy, defeated the Venetians, annexed Bologna to the Papal Territory, and celebrated his victory by a triumphal entry into the city which recalled the memories of Cæsar and Pompey. Erasmus himself witnessed the extraordinary scene, and made his reflections on it, which he preserved for future use. He travelled afterwards on his own account, went to Sienna and lectured there, and had among his pupils a youth whom he described as of extraordinary promise, the young Archbishop of St. Andrews, a lad of twenty, natural son of James IV., who was killed a few years later fighting at his father's side at Flodden. You must exert your imagination to realize what popes and archbishops were like in those days.

At Rome he met with more than kindness. Italian art was at its highest point of glory. It was the Rome of Perugino and Raphael and Michael Angelo. In the College of Cardinals there was the ease and grace of intellectual cultivation exactly calculated to charm and delight Erasmus. The cardinals themselves saw his value, and wished to keep him among them. The Cardinal of St. George became an intimate friend, and remained afterwards the most trusted of his correspondents. Strange alternation of fortune! — one year begging for a few crowns, the next courted and sued to by the splendid princes of the Church. He had but to consent to stay at Rome and his rise to the highest dignities would have been certain and rapid. The temptation was strong. Long after, when the pinch of poverty came again with its attendant humiliations, he admitted that he looked back wistfully to the Roman libraries and palaces, and glorious art, and magnificent and refined society. All that might be his if he would consent to become a red-hatted lackey of the Holy See. Yet, strong as the inclination might be to yield, his love of freedom was stronger — freedom and the high purpose of his life, which must be abandoned for ever if he once consented to put on the golden chain. He might stoop to beg for alms from bishops and great ladies: he could not, would not stoop to prostitute his talents.

Thus he left Rome as he had come, carrying only with him the respect and regard of the Cardinal of St. George and the more famous Cardinal who was to succeed Julius as Leo X. He went back to Paris poor as ever, or nearly so, for the lady's supplies were spent; but he set himself stubbornly to work again. On his return he heard the pleasant news that his friend Colet had been made Dean of St. Paul's. He wrote to congratulate him; promotion coming, as it ought to do, on the deserving who had not sought for it. He hopes that Colet has not forgotten his little friend, and would spare an hour to let him know of his welfare. He then describes his own condition and occupation.[1]

I am rushing full speed into sacred literature, and look at nothing which keeps me back from it. Fortune wears her old face and is still a difficulty. I hope now that I have returned to France to put my affairs on a slightly better footing. This done, I shall

[1] *Ep.* cii., abridged.

sit down to Holy Scripture with my whole heart, and devote the rest of my life to it. Three years ago I wrote something on the Epistle to the Romans. I finished four sheets at a burst, and I should have gone on had I been able. Want of knowledge of Greek kept me back, but for all these three years I have been working entirely at Greek, and have not been playing with it. I have begun Hebrew too, but make small progress owing to the difficulty of the construction. I am not so young as I was, besides.

I have also read a great part of Origen, who opens out new fountains of thought and furnishes a complete key to theology. I send you a small composition of my own on a subject over which we argued when I was in England. It is so changed you would not know it again. I did not write to show off my knowledge. It is directed against the notion that religion consists of ceremonies and a worse than Jewish ritual. I wrote to you about the hundred copies of the "Adagia" which I sent over to England three years back. Grocyn undertook to sell them for me, and has probably done so. In this case they must have brought in money, which must be in somebody's hands. I was never in worse straits than I am now. One way or another I must get enough to secure leisure for myself and my work. A little will do. Help me as far as you can. Mountjoy too may contribute something, though I do not like to ask him. Mountjoy was always interested in me, and to him I owe my first conception of the "Adagia."

It must have been shortly after writing this letter that Erasmus went for a third time to England — about the close of the year 1505 — and resided and lectured for some months at Cambridge. He perhaps found that his finances prospered better where he had so many wealthy acquaintances. It is certain, too, that during this visit he again saw young Prince Henry, and had become personally known to him.

This can be proved by a letter addressed by Henry to him in answer to a letter of Erasmus on the death of his uncle Philip, King of Castile. Philip, the father of Charles V., had married Joanna, sister of Catherine of Aragon. He had assumed the title of King of Castile on the death of his mother-in-law Isabella. He had died suddenly in 1506, and Erasmus was on terms of sufficient intimacy with the Prince of Wales to write a letter of condolence on the occasion. Henry was then fifteen. Here is his answer.[1] It refers, as you will see, to Philip's death as having recently happened. At the head of the letter stands, "Jesus est spes mea," and it proceeds thus:—

Your letter charms me, most eloquent Erasmus. The writing shows by the care which you have taken that it is no hasty composition, while I can see from its clearness and simplicity that it has not been artificially laboured. Clever men when they wish to be concise are often affected and unintelligible. It is not for me to commend a style which all the world praises, nor if I tried could I say as much as your merit deserves. I will therefore leave all that. It is better not to praise at all than to praise inadequately. I had heard before your letter reached me that the King of Castile was dead. Would that the news had proved false. I have never been more grieved since I lost my mother, and, to confess the truth, that part of your letter pleased me less than the grace of the language deserved. Time has partially alleviated the pain of the wound. What the Gods decree mortals must learn to bear. When you have news more agreeable to communicate, do not fail to let me hear from you.

This letter, though perhaps slightly ironical, proves that Erasmus had more acquaintance with Henry

[1] *Ep.* ccccli., second series.

than can be explained by their meeting at Eltham when the Prince was a child. Erasmus could not have ventured to write to him without fuller justification. It may serve as evidence, therefore, that Erasmus had again had opportunities of making himself known to the Prince, and was regarded by him as a person of consideration.

Still it is equally clear that he had as yet gained no footing in England beyond the humble position of a Cambridge lecturer.

It is said that Wolsey did not like him; very probably the old king looked on him as an adventurer, and did not like him also. Nothing had come in his way save an offer of a benefice from Warham, which he honourably declined because he could not preach to his parishioners in English, and some sort of a tedious professorship at Cambridge, where he had to teach the elements of Greek to schoolboys. He had higher ambitions, which, it seemed, were not to be realized for him in England, and his thoughts turned once more to his friends the cardinals at Rome. At Rome he might have to submit to harness, and the sacrifice would be a bitter one. But the harness would be better gilded than at Cambridge. There were the libraries; there was appreciation from the ruling powers, which would leave him leisure for his work; and he might edit his Fathers, perhaps his New Testament, under the patronage of popes like Julius or Leo X.

This is only conjecture. The certainty is that two years before Henry VII. died Erasmus left England again, and once more joined his friend Cardinal Raphael at the Holy City. There he appears to have decided finally to remain, when his future was once more changed by two letters which reached him while Cardinal Raphael's guest.

One was from his friend Mountjoy, to announce the accession of Henry VIII., and the desire of the new king to attach Erasmus to his own Court, a desire which Henry had himself confirmed under his own hand. Nothing could be more brilliant than the prospect which Mountjoy announced to him.[1] The resolution to recall him seems to have been one of the first acts of the new reign. We remember Solon saying that no one should be counted happy before his death. You will observe that the King here described was Henry VIII.

What, my dear Erasmus, may you not look for from a prince, whose great qualities no one knows better than yourself, and who not only is no stranger to you, but esteems you so highly! He has written to you, as you will perceive, under his own hand, an honour which falls but to few. Could you but see how nobly he is bearing himself, how wise he is, his love for all that is good and right, and specially his love for men of learning, you would need no wings to fly into the light of this new risen and salutary star. Oh, Erasmus, could you but witness the universal joy, could you but see how proud our people are of their new sovereign, you would weep for pleasure. Heaven smiles, earth triumphs, and flows with milk and honey and nectar. This king of ours is no seeker after gold, or gems, or mines of silver. He desires only the fame of virtue and eternal life. I was lately in his presence. He said that he regretted that he was still so ignorant; I told him that the nation did not want him to be himself learned, the nation wanted him only to encourage learning. He replied that without knowledge life would not be worth our having.

I received your letter from Rome, and I read it with mingled grief and pleasure: pleasure, because you opened to me all your cares and anxieties; grief, because it showed me that Fortune wears her old face to you, and that you still suffer from her buffets. Be-

[1] *Ep.* x.

lieve me, an end has come now to all your distresses. You have only to accept the invitation of a prince who offers you wealth, honour, and distinction.

"Accipe divitias et vatum maximus esto." You say you owe much to myself. Mine is the obligation, my debt to you is more than I can ever pay.

I have the copy of your "Adagia," with the graceful compliment to myself. All here praise the book. Archbishop Warham is so charmed with it that I cannot get it out of his hands. He undertakes, if you will come to us, that some benefice shall be found for you. He sends you five pounds for the expenses of your journey, and I add as much more. Come quickly, therefore, and do not torture us with expectation. Never suppose that I do not prize your letters, or that I can be offended with anything which you may say or do. I am sorry that you have been unwell in Italy. I did not wish you to go there, but I regret that I was not your companion when I see how much the Romans make of you.

So far Mountjoy — Lord Mountjoy now, for his father was dead, and he had succeeded to the estate and title. The young king wrote as follows:[1] —

I am sorry, as your constant friend and admirer, to learn from the Archbishop of Canterbury that you have ill-wishers who have done you injury, and that you have been in some danger from them. Our acquaintance began when I was a boy. The regard which I then learnt to feel for you has been increased by the honourable mention which you have made of me in your writings, and by the use to which you have applied your talents in the advancement of Christian truth. So far you have borne your burden alone; give me the pleasure of assisting and protecting you as far as my power extends. It has been and is my earnest wish to restore Christ's religion to its primitive purity, and to employ whatever talents and means I have in extinguishing heresy and giving free course to

[1] *Ep.* cccel., second series, abridged.

the Word of God. We live in evil times, and the world grows worse instead of better. I am the more sorry therefore for the ill-treatment which you have met with, and which is a misfortune to Christianity itself. Your welfare is precious to us all. If you are taken away nothing can then stop the spread of heresy and impiety. I propose therefore that you abandon the thought of settling elsewhere. Come to England, and assure yourself of a hearty welcome. You shall name your own terms; they shall be as liberal and honourable as you please. I recollect that you once said that when you were tired of wandering you would make this country the home of your old age. I beseech you by all that is holy and good, carry out this purpose of yours. We have not now to learn the value either of your acquirements or your advice. We shall regard your presence among us as the most precious possession that we have. Nowhere in the world will you find safer shelter from anxiety or persecution; and you and we together, with our joint counsels and resources, will build again the Gospel of Christ. You will not be without friends; you have many already here. Our highest nobles know and appreciate you; I will myself introduce you among them. You require your leisure for yourself. We shall ask nothing of you save to make our Realm your home. You shall do as you like, your time shall be your own. Everything shall be provided for you which will ensure your comfort or assist your studies. Come to us, therefore, my dear Erasmus, and let your presence be your answer to my invitation.

The situation which the young Henry intended for Erasmus when he wrote this letter was evidently some office close about his own person. The passage about advice pointed to the Privy Council. At any rate, he was to be associated with the King in the most interesting and important duties. No wonder that so invited he needed no wings, as Mountjoy said, to fly to a court where honour and leisure seemed to be waiting for him.

LECTURE VI.

THE young Henry VIII. had invited Erasmus to England in terms which entitled him to think that a considerable position awaited him there. He was to be the King's adviser in an intended Church reform. He was to name his own terms. He was to have his leisure for himself and his work. He was no longer an adventurer. He had a world-wide reputation. He was a favourite of the Roman Cardinals. He was known to be preparing an edition of the New Testament with a fresh translation. He had been at work over the Greek MSS. for many years. The work was approaching completion, and if he had remained at Rome it would have appeared under the patronage of the Holy See. He might fairly have concluded (and he did conclude) that he would find rank and fortune in England (going there as he did at the earnest and warm entreaty of the King himself) equivalent to his present station in the world of letters. Doubtless this had been the intention. But the King's hands were full of other business. He had a rebellious Ireland on hand. He had a corrupt administration to reform, as well as the Church. He had corrupt ministers to punish. He had a war with France coming on upon him, undertaken for the defence of the Pope. You will find the objects of the war concisely and correctly stated in the preamble to the Subsidy Act, where Parliament provided the means. The French war does not concern us here further than it explains how

Henry, after having secured Erasmus's presence in his realm, was obliged to hand over the charge of him to Warham, who was now Primate and Chancellor. A Church benefice was the natural resource. Cardinals drew their revenues from benefices piled one upon another, with small thought of the duties attaching to them. If Erasmus had remained at Rome, he must have done like the rest. But his passion was to expose and correct the abuses which had crept over the Church administration. He had not come to England for an ecclesiastical sinecure. Warham had already offered him a benefice, and he had declined, because he could not preach in English. Again Warham pressed a living on him, the best that he had in his gift, Aldington in Kent, worth sixty pounds a year, or six hundred of our money. He accepted it at last, finding, I suppose, that nothing else could be done for him; but again, either the same scruple, or an unwillingness to be buried in the country far away from books, made him repent of his resolution almost as soon as he had resigned himself to his fate. He relinquished Aldington in six months, and Warham sacrificed the parish to his friendship. Instead of the living of Aldington the Archbishop settled a pension on him equivalent to the value of it, which was charged, according to the fashion of the time, on the tithes. Aldington had to content itself with an ill-paid curate, under whom, curiously enough, it produced in the next generation the famous Nun of Kent, whose imposture was to threaten Henry's throne. The pension, however, was made sure to Erasmus for the rest of his life. Warham saw it paid till he died, and it was continued afterwards by Cranmer. An assured income of sixty pounds, at a time when a country squire was counted rich who had forty, might have been thought enough to keep the wolf from a scholar's door. Lord Mountjoy, who felt himself responsible for Erasmus's return, promised as much more, and afterwards kept his word. Thus, so far as money went, he had nothing to complain of.

Evidently, however, he was not satisfied. It was not what he had looked for. He had expected, perhaps, to be admitted formally into the Privy Council. He had expected — one knows not what he had expected; but he began to look back on Rome again with a sense that he had made a mistake in leaving it. His feelings are frankly expressed in a letter to the Cardinal Grymanus. He says:[1] —

I had many friends in England. Large promises were held out to me, and the King himself seemed to be my special friend. England was my adopted country. I had meant always that it should be the home of my old age. I was invited over. I was pressed to go. I was promised rivers of gold, and, though I am generally careless of money, I had looked to find a stream of it running fuller than Pactolus. I rather flew than went. Do I repent? Well, I will be perfectly frank. When I think of Rome, and all its charms and all its advantages, yes, I do repent. Rome is the centre of the world. In Rome is liberty. In Rome are the splendid libraries. In Rome one meets and converses with men of learning. In Rome are the magnificent monuments of the past. On Rome are fastened the eyes of mankind, and in Rome are the cardinals, yourself the foremost among them, who were so wonderfully good to me. My position in England was not amiss, but it was not what I had been led to expect, and was not what had been promised to me. The cause, perhaps, lay in the misfortunes of the time. The King was kind, no one could be more so; but he was carried away by a sudden storm of war. He was young, high-minded, and

[1] *Ep.* clxvii., abridged.

strongly influenced by religion. He went into it enthusiastically, to defend the Holy See against French aggression. Mountjoy, who, except the Bishop of Cambray, was my earliest patron, became so much absorbed in military matters that, although he was willing as ever to help me, he was not then able; and, moreover, though one of the old nobility, and liberally disposed towards men of learning, he is not rich according to the standard of the English peerage. The Archbishop of Canterbury did all for me that was possible. He is one of the best of men and an honour to the realm — wise, judicious, learned above all his contemporaries, and so modest that he is unconscious of his superiority. Under a quiet manner he is witty, energetic, and laborious. He is experienced in business. He has played a distinguished part in foreign embassies. Besides being Primate, he is Lord Chancellor, the highest judicial office in the realm; yet, with all his greatness, he has been father and mother to me, and has partly made up to me what I sacrificed in leaving Rome; but . . . but —

In short, the Erasmus who was shortly to be the world-famous enemy of monks and obscurantists, the sun of a darkened world, was no longer the obscure student who had come to England thirteen years before in search of patronage and employment. He felt himself the equal of the best of those who were playing their parts in the Royal circle, and he had looked to be treated accordingly. He was disappointed. There was no Pactolus overflowing its banks for him. He was provided with a moderate income. He was left free to do as he pleased and go where he pleased, and that was all.

Liberty, however, then and always was the most precious of all possessions to him, and no one could make a better use of it. He had two friends in England between whom and himself there grew up a more than affectionate intimacy. With Dean Colet he travelled about the country, helped him to found the St. Paul's School where the late Master of Balliol was bred, went on pilgrimages, went to the shrine of our Lady of Walsingham, visited Becket's tomb at Canterbury, saw the saint's dirty shoes which were offered to the pious to kiss, and gathered the materials for the excellent pictures of England and English life which are scattered through his Colloquies. With Thomas More, who was soon to be knighted, he resided when in London, at the new house which More had built at Chelsea. And he has left portraits in words of these two remarkable men as exquisite as Holbein's drawings of them.

I shall detain you a little over these portraits. Our own great countrymen are as interesting to us as Erasmus himself, and the age and the men, and what they did and said, stand as fresh before us in Erasmus's story as if we saw and heard them ourselves.

I keep to Erasmus's own words, with a few compressions and omissions:[1]—

Colet was born in London, 1466, a few months before Erasmus himself. His father was twice Lord Mayor. He was the eldest of twenty-two children, of whom he was the only survivor, tall in stature, and well-looking in face. In youth he studied scholastic theology, then read Cicero, and Plato, and Plotinus, and made himself a first-rate mathematician. He went abroad, travelled in France and Italy, kept up his Scotus and Aquinas, but worked besides at the Early Christian Fathers, while Dante and Petrarch polished his language. Returning to England, he left London, settled at Oxford, and lectured on St. Paul. It was then that my acquaintance with him began, he being then thirty, I two or three months his

[1] *Ep.* ccccxxxv.

junior. He had no theological degree, but the whole University, doctors and all, went to hear him. Henry VII. took note of him, and made him Dean of St. Paul's. His first step was to restore discipline in the Chapter, which had all gone to wreck. He preached every saint's day to great crowds. He cut down the household expenses, and abolished suppers and evening parties. At dinner a boy reads a chapter from Scripture. Colet takes a passage from it, and discourses to the universal delight. Conversation is his chief pleasure, and he will keep it up till midnight if he finds a companion. Me he has often taken with him in his walks, and talks all the time of Christ. He hates coarse language; furniture, dress, food, books, all clean and tidy, but scrupulously plain, and he wears grey woollen when priests generally go in purple. With the large fortune which he inherited from his father he founded and endowed a school at St. Paul's entirely at his own cost — masters, houses, salaries, everything.

There is an entrance examination; no boy admitted who cannot read and write. The scholars are in four classes, a compartment in the schoolroom for each. Above the head-master's chair is a picture of the child Christ in the act of teaching; the Father in the air above, with a scroll saying "Hear ye Him." These words were introduced at my suggestion. The boys salute and sing a hymn on entering and leaving. Dormitory and dining-room are open and undivided, and each boy has his own place.

The foundation has been extremely costly, but he did it all himself, and in selecting trustees (I beg you to observe this) he chose neither bishops nor priests, nor members of his own Cathedral Chapter. He appointed a committee of married laymen of honest reputation, and being asked his reason, he said all human arrangements were uncertain, but he had observed generally that such persons were more conscientious and honest than priests.

He was a man of genuine piety. He was not born

with it. He was naturally hot, impetuous, and resentful — indolent, fond of pleasure and of women's society — disposed to make a joke of everything. He told me that he had fought against his faults with study, fasting, and prayer, and thus his whole life was, in fact, unpolluted with the world's defilements. His money he gave all to pious uses, worked incessantly, talked always on serious subjects to conquer his disposition to levity; not but what you could see traces of the old Adam when wit was flying at feast or festival. He avoided large parties for this reason. He dined on a single dish, with a draught or two of light ale. He liked good wine, but abstained on principle. I never knew a man of sunnier nature. No one ever more enjoyed cultivated society; but here, too, he denied himself, and was always thinking of the life to come.

His opinions were peculiar, and he was reserved in expressing them for fear of exciting suspicion. He knew how unfairly men judge each other, how credulous they are of evil, how much easier it is for a lying tongue to stain a reputation than for a friend to clear it. But among his friends he spoke his mind freely. He thought the Scotists, who are considered so clever, were stupid blockheads. He regarded their word-splitting, their catching at objections, their minute sub-dividings, as signs of a starved intellect. He hated Thomas Aquinas even more than Scotus. I once praised the "Catena Aurea" to him. He was silent. I repeated my words. He glanced at me to see if I was serious, and when he saw that I meant it he became really angry. Aquinas (he said) would not have laid down the law so boldly on all things in heaven and earth if he had not been an arrogant fool, and he would not have contaminated Christianity with his preposterous philosophy if he had not been a worldling at heart.

He had a bad opinion of the monasteries falsely so called. He gave them little and left them nothing. He said that morality was always purer among married laymen, and yet, though himself absolutely chaste, he was not very hard on priests and monks who only sinned with women. He did not make light of impurity, but he thought it less criminal than spite and malice, and envy and vanity and ignorance. The loose sort were at least made human and modest by their very faults, and he regarded avarice and arrogance as blacker sins in a priest than a hundred concubines.

He had a particular dislike of bishops. He said they were more like wolves than shepherds. They sold the sacraments, sold their ceremonies and absolutions. They were slaves of vanity and avarice. He did not much blame those who doubted whether a wicked priest could convey sacramental grace, and was indignant that there were so many of them as to force the question to be raised.

He disapproved of the great educational institutions in England. He thought they encouraged idleness. As little did he like the public schools. Education was spoilt, he said, when the lessons learnt were turned to worldly account and made the means of getting on. He was himself learned, but he had no respect for a mass of information gathered out of a multitude of books. Such laborious wisdom he said was fatal to sound knowledge and right feeling. He approved of a fine ritual at church, but he saw no reason why priests should be always muttering prayers at home or on their walks. He admitted privately that many things were generally taught which he did not believe, but he would not create scandal by blurting out his objections. No book could be so heretical but he would read it, and read it carefully. He learnt more from such books than he learnt from dogmatism and interested orthodoxy.

Such was the famous Colet, seen in undress among his friends. A dean who hated bishops was not likely to be on good terms with his own; and Erasmus adds a story which introduces suddenly the Court, and the

Court intrigues; shows us what Colet thought of the war with France which I spoke of just now, and how Fitzjames, the old Bishop of London, tried to bring him into disgrace with Henry.

I will say no harm of the Bishop of London (says Erasmus), except that he was a superstitious and malignant Scotist. I have known other bishops like him. I must not call them wicked, but I would not call them Christians either. Colet's discipline was not popular with the Chapter of Eastminster.[1] They complained to the old Bishop, who was past eighty. The Bishop consulted two other bishops, and they resolved to crush this troublesome Dean. Besides cutting short the Chapter's suppers, he had said in a sermon that it was wrong to worship images. He had denied that the injunction in the Gospel to feed the sheep was addressed specially to Peter. Finally, he had objected to the English practice of reading sermons, thereby reflecting on his own Diocesan, who always read his.

They laid their complaint before the Primate, who took Colet's side; so they next applied to the King. War with France was impending, and the King was busy with his preparations. The Bishop and a couple of friars came to him with a story that Colet had been preaching against it. The King knew Colet and valued him. Colet's real offence, he well understood, was his constant exposure of the corruptions and disorders of the Church. He sent for Colet, took no notice of the Peace Sermon, but bade him care nothing for the Bishop's malice, and go on with his work. He would bring the right reverend prelates to their bearings. Colet offered to resign his Deanery sooner than be an occasion of trouble. Henry would not hear of it, and a Sunday or two after the

[1] St. Paul's was called East Minster, corresponding to Westminster.

Dean preached before the Court, when the campaign in France was just about to begin. He went boldly at the dangerous subject. He preached on the victory of Christ, spoke of fighting as a savage business, intimated that it was not charity to plunge a sword into another man's bowels — that it would be better to imitate Christ than to imitate popes like Alexander or Julius.

The war was undertaken at Julius's instigation. The King himself, only twenty-one, in the enthusiasm of what was considered a crusade for the Catholic faith, was himself disturbed, afraid such a sermon would cool his army's spirits. The bishops flew on the preacher like so many sparrows on an owl. Colet was again sent for to Greenwich. It was supposed that his hour was come. The King received him in the garden, and dismissing his attendants, said quietly: "Mr. Dean, I do not mean to interfere with your good work. I approve heartily of all that you are doing, but you have raised scruples in me and I must talk with you."

The conversation lasted an hour and a half. The Bishop of London was puffing about the Court, thinking his enemy was done for. The King only wanted to know whether in Colet's opinion no war could be justifiable. Colet did not say as much as this, and the King was satisfied. They returned together to the palace. Henry sent for a cup of wine, pledged him and embraced him. The courtiers crowded round to hear the issue. The King said, "Let every man choose his own Doctor. Dean Colet shall be mine." The wolves gaped, especially the Bishop, and from this time no one attacked Colet any more.

The sermon on the victory of Christ did not prevent the war. The nation was enthusiastic for it.

The English armies were brilliantly successful. Flodden Field was a single incident in the campaign, and all causes seem just when they are triumphant. But these things do not concern us here, and I have touched the subject only for the sake of Colet.

Now for the companion picture of Sir Thomas More, which is given in a letter from Erasmus to Ulrich von Hutten.[1] You may have heard of Von Hutten — he who threatened to carry Luther off by force from Worms if the safe-conduct was not to be observed, and to make the Pope's Legate smart for it. Von Hutten, or a group of anonymous friends of his, were just producing the "Epistolæ obscurorum Virorum" as a caricature on the monks, which set all Europe laughing. The satire was as gross as Rabelais', but extremely witty, so witty that the world insisted that Erasmus must have written it, and when it was found not to be his, reported that he was convulsed with laughter over the inimitable humour. Erasmus said himself that, though he was not particular, the coarseness disgusted him, and he disowned not only all share in the work, but all interest in it. It had not that effect on his friend at Chelsea. Sir T. More, ardent Catholic as he was, loathed the monks as a disgrace to the Church, and frankly confessed himself delighted with this remarkable production. Von Hutten was anxious to know more of this English admirer of the "Epistolæ," and wrote to Erasmus for an account of More.

The task (Erasmus says) is not an easy one, for not everyone understands More, who is as difficult a subject as Alexander or Achilles. He is of middle height, well shaped, complexion pale, without a touch of colour in it save when the skin flushes. The hair

[1] *Ep.* ccccxlvii., abridged.

is black, shot with yellow, or yellow shot with black; beard scanty, eyes grey, with dark spots — an eye supposed in England to indicate genius, and to be never found except in remarkable men. The expression is pleasant and cordial, easily passing into a smile, for he has the quickest sense of the ridiculous of any man I ever met. The right shoulder is rather higher than the left, the result of a trick in walking, not from a physical defect. The rest is in keeping. The only sign of rusticity is in the hands, which are slightly coarse. From childhood he has been careless of appearance, but he has still the charm which I remember when I first knew him. His health is good, though not robust, and he is likely to be long-lived. His father, though in extreme old age, is still vigorous. He is careless in what he eats. I never saw a man more so. Like his father, he is a water-drinker. His food is beef, fresh or salt, bread, milk, fruit, and especially eggs. His voice is low and unmusical, though he loves music; but it is clear and penetrating. He articulates slowly and distinctly, and never hesitates.

He dresses plainly; no silks, or velvets, or gold chains. He has no concern for ceremony, expects none from others, and shows little himself. He holds forms and courtesies unworthy of a man of sense, and for that reason has hitherto kept clear of the Court. All Courts are full of intrigue. There is less of it in England than elsewhere, for there are no affectations in the King; but More loves freedom, and likes to have his time to himself. He is a true friend. When he finds a man to be of the wrong sort, he lets him drop, but he enjoys nothing so much as the society of those who suit him and whose character he approves. Gambling of all kinds, balls, dice, and such like, he detests. None of that sort are to be found about him. In short, he is the best type of companion.

His talk is charming, full of fun, but never scurrilous or malicious. He used to act plays when young; wit delights him, though at his own expense; he writes smart epigrams; he set me on my "Encomium Moriæ" (of which I shall speak presently). It was like setting a camel to dance, but he can make fun of anything. He is wise with the wise, and jests with fools — with women specially, and his wife among them. He is fond of animals of all kinds, and likes to watch their habits. All the birds in Chelsea come to him to be fed. He has a menagerie of tame beasts, a monkey, a fox, a ferret, and a weasel. He buys any singular thing which is brought to him. His house is a magazine of curiosities, which he delights in showing off.

He had his love affairs when young, but none that compromised him; he was entertained by the girls running after him. He studied hard also at that time at Greek and philosophy. His father wanted him to work at English law, but he didn't like it. The law in England is the high road to fame and fortune, and many peerages have risen out of that profession. But they say it requires years of labour. More had no taste that way, Nature having designed him for better things. Nevertheless, after drinking deep in literature he did make himself a lawyer, and an excellent one. No opinion is sought more eagerly than his or more highly paid for. He worked at divinity besides, and lectured to large audiences on Augustine's "De Civitate Dei." Priests and old men were not ashamed to learn from him. His original wish was to be a priest himself. He prepared for it with fast, and prayer, and vigil, unlike most, who rush into ordination without preparation of any kind. He gave it up because he fell in love, and he thought a chaste husband was better than a profligate clerk. The wife that he chose was a very young lady, well connected but wholly uneducated, who had been brought up in the country with her parents. Thus he was able to shape her character after his own pattern. He taught her books. He taught her music, and formed her into a companion for his life. Unhappily she was taken from him by death before her time. She bore him several children: three daughters, Margaret, Cecilia, and Louisa, who are still with him, and one son, John. A few months after he had buried her he married a widow to take care of them. This lady, he often said with a laugh, was neither young nor pretty; but she was a good manager, and he lived as pleasantly with her as if she had been the loveliest of maidens. He rules her with jokes and caresses better than most husbands do with sternness and authority, and though she has a sharp tongue and is a thrifty housekeeper, he has made her learn harp, cithern, and guitar, and practise before him every day.

He controls his family with the same easy hand: no tragedies, no quarrels. If a dispute begins it is promptly settled. He has never made an enemy nor become an enemy. His whole house breathes happiness, and no one enters it who is not the better for the visit. The father also made a second marriage, and More was as dutiful to his stepmother as he was to his own mother. She died, and the old man took a third wife, and More swore he had never known a better woman. He troubles neither his parents nor his children with excess of attention, but he neglects no duty to either. He is indifferent to money. He sets apart so much of his income as will make a future provision for his family; the rest he spends or gives away. It is large, and arises from his profession as an advocate, but he always advises his clients for the best, and recommends them to settle their disputes out of Court. For a time he was a judge in civil causes. The work was not severe, but the position was honourable. No judge finished off more causes or was more upright, and he often remitted the fees. He was exceedingly liked in the city. He was satisfied, and had no higher ambition. Eventually he was forced upon a foreign mission, and conducted himself so well that the King would not afterwards part with him, and dragged him into the circle of the Court. "Dragged" is the word, for no one ever struggled harder to gain admission there than More struggled to escape. But the King was bent on surrounding himself with the most capable men in his dominions. He insisted that More should make one of them, and now he values him so highly, both as a companion and as a Privy Councillor, that he will scarcely let him out of his sight.

More has been never known to accept a present. Happy the commonwealth where the magistrates are of such material! Elevation has not elated him or made him forget his humble friends, and he returns whenever he can to his beloved books. He is always kind, always generous. Some he helps with money, some with influence. When he can give nothing else he gives advice. He is Patron-General to all poor devils.

The history of his connection with me was this. In his early life he was a versifier, and he came to me to improve his style. Since that time he has written a good deal. He has written a dialogue defending Plato's community of wives. He has answered Lucian's "Tyrannicida." He wanted me to take the other side, that he might the better test his skill. His "Utopia" was written to indicate the dangers which threatened the English commonwealth. The second part was written first. The other was added afterwards. You can trace a difference in the style. He has a fine intellect and an excellent memory; information all arranged and pigeon-holed to be ready for use. He is so ready in argument that he can puzzle the best divines on their own subjects. Colet, a good judge on such points, says More has more genius than any man in England. He is religious, but without superstition. He has his hours for prayer, but he uses no forms, and prays out of his heart. He will talk with his friends about a life to come, and you can see that he means it and has real hopes. Such is More, and More is an English courtier, and people fancy that no Christians are to be found outside monasteries. The King not only admits such men into his Court, but he invites them — forces them — that they may be in a position to watch all that he does, and share his duties and his pleasures. He prefers the companionship of men like More to that of silly youths or girls, or the rich, or the dishonest, who might tempt him to foolish indulgences or injurious courses. If you were here in England, my dear Hutten, you would leave off abusing Courts. A galaxy of distinguished men now surrounds the English throne.

The subject of this beautiful picture had built himself, as I said before, a house on the Thames at Chelsea. It was of moderate and unpretentious dimensions, with a garden leading down to the river, not far from where Carlyle's statue now stands, or sits. The life there, as Erasmus elsewhere says, was like the life in Plato's Academy, and there Erasmus was a permanent guest whenever he was in London. No two men ever suited each other better, their intellectual differences only serving to give interest to their conversations, while both had that peculiar humour which means at bottom the power of seeing things as they really are, undisguised by conventional wrappings. More's mind was free and noble. Erasmus told Hutten that he was without superstition. Elsewhere, however, he allows that there was a vein of it, and that vein, as the sky blackened with the storm of the Reformation, swelled and turned him into a persecutor. Men who have been themselves reformers are the least tolerant when the movement takes forms which they dislike. Erasmus's inclination was to scepticism. He owns surprise that More was entirely satisfied with the evidence for a future life. Both, however, were united in a conviction of the seriousness of mortal existence. Both abhorred the hypocrisy of the monks, the simony and worldliness of the Church, and knew that without a root and branch alteration of things a catastrophe was not far off. Each went his way — More to reaction and Tower Hill; Erasmus to aid in precipitating the convulsion, then to regret what he had done, and to have a near escape of ending as a cardinal. Never, however, while they both lived, was their affection for one another clouded or weakened.

Pity that we know so little of their talks together on all things, human and divine, as they strolled by the side of the then Silver River. A Chelsea tradition, perhaps authentic, preserves a trace of what may have passed between them on the great central question which was about to divide the Christian world.

Erasmus was leaving Chelsea on some riding expedition. More provided him with a horse, which for some cause was not returned at the time when it was looked for. Instead of the horse came a letter, with the following lines: —

> Quod mihi dixisti
> De corpore Christi
> Crede quod edas et edis;
> Sic tibi rescribo
> De tuo palfrido
> Crede quod habeas et habes.

The controversy on the Eucharist had not yet risen into contradictory definitions; but doubt on the great mystery was in the air, and the friends had argued about it. More believed in the Real Presence; Erasmus believed in it too, though with latent misgivings. But More, without knowing it, had blundered into the Lutheran heresy, and had held that the change in the elements depended on the faith of the recipient.

LECTURE VII.

Erasmus continued to linger in England after he had discovered that the expectations which he had formed from the King's invitation were likely to be disappointed. He may have thought that the disappointment was due only to the war, and that with the return of peace his English prospects might brighten again. Julius II., besides, had set the Continent in a flame. Henry's army was on the frontier of the Netherlands, besieging towns in the glow of a successful campaign, and Paris might have been an unpleasant residence just then to a man who had become half an Englishman and was anxious to become a whole one. He was busy, too, printing his "Jerome" — printing it at his own expense, and money was again not plentiful with him. His New Testament was approaching completion, but it kept him hard at work, with clerks and secretaries whom he had to find in wages. His patron, Mountjoy, was with the King. The campaign was costly, and the pension which Mountjoy had promised could not yet be paid. Thus Erasmus had remained on in England, waiting for the turn of events, and finally, wishing to do something, he was induced by Fisher, Bishop of Rochester, and then Chancellor of the University, to go back to Cambridge and lecture for a time to classes there, not with any intention of a permanent residence, but to employ his time, and perhaps avail himself of the college libraries.

Of his earlier Cambridge experiences, in 1506, we

know nothing beyond the fact that he was some months resident and teaching Greek there. On this last occasion we have again his own letters to guide us, which give us a tolerably distinct view of his position. It is almost a matter of course that we should find him in his old straits for money.

A letter to Colet, written a few days after his arrival, describes his journey and the condition in which he found himself. Cambridge did not seem to have been conscious how great a man she was entertaining.[1]

If you can be amused at my misfortunes, I can make you laugh. After my accident in London[2] my servant's horse fell lame, and I could find no one to attend to it. Next day heavy rain till dinner-time. In the afternoon thunder, lightning, and hail. My own horse fell on his head, and my companion, after consulting the stars, informed me that Jupiter was angry. On the whole, I am well satisfied with what I find here. I have a prospect of Christian poverty. Far from making any money, I shall have to spend all that I can get from my Mæcenas.[3] We have a doctor at the University who has invented a Prophylactic of the Fifth Essence, with which he promises to make old men young, and bring dead men back to life, so that I may hope if I swallow some of it to recover my own youth. If this prove true, I came to Cambridge on a happy day. But I see no chance of fees. Nothing can be extracted from the naked. I am not myself a bad fellow, but I was surely born under an evil star. Adieu, my dear Protector. When I have started my professional work, I will let you know how I go on, and give you more amusement. Perhaps I may even—so audacious I grow—attack your Lectures on St. Paul.

War was now raging by sea and land. The Empire,

[1] *Ep.* cxvii.
[2] I don't know what that was.
[3] Archbishop Warham.

Spain and England combined with the Pope against Louis XII., Scotland declaring for Louis and threatening the English Border. Ammonius, an Italian agent of the Pope in London, was to accompany the English army abroad and attend the campaign. He was a friend of Erasmus, and had lent him money. To him also Erasmus wrote on reaching Cambridge:[1]—

I have no news for you except that my journey was detestable, and that this place does not agree with me. I have pleaded sickness so far as an excuse for postponing my lectures. Beer does not suit me either, and the wine is horrible. If you can send me a barrel of Greek wine, the best which can be had, Erasmus will bless you; only take care it is not sweet. Have no uneasiness about your loan; it will be paid before the date of the bill. Meanwhile I am being killed with thirst. Imagine the rest. Farewell.

It is quite clear that Erasmus did not mean to remain long at Cambridge. Ammonius goes to France, sees the fighting, and sends Erasmus a flourishing account of it. Erasmus answers:[2]—

The plague is in London, so I remain where I am, but I shall get away on the first opportunity. The thirty nobles which are due to me at Michaelmas have not yet arrived. My "Jerome" engages all my thoughts. I am printing it at my own cost, and the expense is heavy. You give a splendid picture of your doings in the campaign. The snorting of the horses, the galloping, the shouts of the men, the blare of the trumpets, the gasping of the sick, and the groans of the dying. I have it all before me. You will have something to talk of for the rest of your life. But remember my advice to you. Fight yourself where the

[1] *Ep.* cxviii.—The dates assigned to the letters from Cambridge to Ammonius are hopeless. They are represented as written in 1510 and 1511. There are continual references in them to the war of 1513.

[2] *Ep.* cxix.

danger is least. Keep your valour for your pen. Remember me to the Abbot of St. Bertin when you are at St. Omer.

The Cambridge letters generally are in the same tone. They show little interest in the University, or in Erasmus's occupations there, or in the eminent persons whom he must have met. We have no intellectual symposia such as had delighted him in Oxford, no more Colets or Grocyns, though one can fancy that he must at least have encountered Cranmer there, and possibly Latimer. He writes chiefly about his discomforts and on his chances of getting away for a week or two to visit Colet or More. The Greek wine was duly sent and paid for with a set of ardently grateful verses. The cask was soon emptied, and the thirsty soul had, he said, but the scent of it left to console him. Mountjoy had promised him the use of his house in London. He rode up and presented himself, but Mountjoy was at the war, and his "Cerberus," as Erasmus called the porter, refused to admit him in his master's absence. He went back to the University. There were highwaymen on the road, and though he escaped plunder, he did not escape a fright. A fresh supply of Greek wine was provided. The carriers found out its quality, drank half of it, and filled up the barrel with water. His only happiness was in his work. He lived, he said, as a cockle in his shell. Cambridge was a solitude. The plague had spread there, and the students had mostly gone down. Even if they had been in residence, he would have seen but little of them, for his lecture-room was thinly attended. The cost of living was intolerable. In the first five months of his stay he had spent sixty nobles and had received but one. When January came, and the cold weather with it, he had an attack of stone, brought on by the beer and the water in the wine, and he poured out his lamentations to Warham with more eloquence than the Archbishop thought the occasion called for.

The stone was the favourite subject for English wit. Warham trusted that, as it was the Feast of the Purification, the enemy would soon be cleared out.

What business have you (was the Archbishop's light reply [1]) with such a superfluous load as stones in your small body, or what do you propose to build *super hanc petram?* Stones are heavy carriage, as I know to my cost when I want them for building purposes. I presume you do not contemplate building a palace, so have them carted away, and I send you ten angels to help you to rid yourself of the burden. Gold is a good medicine. Use it freely, and recover your health. I would give you a great deal more to set you up again. You have work to do and more books to edit, so get well and do it, and do not cheat us of our hopes.

No wonder Erasmus loved Warham. He was proud besides to have so great a man for his patron, and he made the most of it to impress his friends in the Netherlands that he was living with creditable people in England. He tells the Abbot of St. Bertin that he has become half an Englishman, that the first men in the country had taken him under their protection, that he had found a Mæcenas in the Archbishop of Canterbury, a Mæcenas, too, with fine qualities of his own — learned, witty, gracious — so gracious that no one ever left his presence with a heavy heart, so little proud that he was himself the only person unconscious of his merits.[2]

But if Warham's ten angels had been ten legions of angels, as the Archbishop said he wished they had

[1] *Ep.* cxxxiv.

[2] *Ep.* cxxxv.

been, they would not have comforted the sensitive Erasmus for his captivity among the fogs and dons of Cambridge. He pined for Italy and Italian wine and sunshine, and cursed his folly for having left Rome.

Never can I forget your goodness to me (he writes to a member of the Sacred College [1]). Would that I could find some water of Lethe to wash Rome out of my memory. The remembrance of it tortures me. That sky, those parks, those walks and libraries, that charming companionship with men who are the lights of the world, that wealth in possession, and those hopes which gleamed before me. Alas! why did I leave them? The Archbishop of Canterbury is my only comfort. He is father and mother to me, and he is a good friend to Rome besides, as all the realm is. Pray God it so continue.

The Cambridge purgatory lasted for many months, and the pains of it did not abate. His impatience bubbled over in restlessness. Ammonius is advanced to some high dignity. Erasmus writes to congratulate him, and to relate his own condition.[2]

I was badly confined on the Conception of the Virgin Mary, and brought forth stones; consider them among the pebbles of my felicity. You ask me how you are to conduct yourself in your new elevation. I will tell you. "Sus Minervam"—the pig will teach Pallas and will drop philosophy. Make your forehead of brass, and be ashamed of nothing. Thrust rivals out of the way with your elbow. Love no one. Hate no one. Think first and always of your own advantage. Give nothing save when you know that you will receive it back with interest, and agree in words to everything which is said to you. To all this you will of course have an answer. Well, then, to be more particular. The English are a jealous race, as I need not tell you. Take advantage of this infirmity of theirs. Sit on two

[1] Cardinali Nanetensi, *Ep.* cxxxvi.

[2] *Ep.* cxlii.

chairs. Bribe suitors to pay court to you. Tell your employers that you must leave them. Show them letters intimating that you are invited elsewhere and are promised some distinguished post. Draw back out of society, that you may be missed and asked after.

An evident bitterness runs through these Cambridge letters. He regretted Rome. The Lady of Vere and her son had made some fresh proposals to him. He was sorry that he had rejected them, and hoped that it was not too late. He had been led, he said, to form extravagant expectations in England. He had looked for mountains of gold, and it had been all illusion. He was now poor as Ulysses, and, like Ulysses, he said he was longing for a sight of the smoke from his own chimney.[1] The Lord of Vere might provide for him. He even thought that his own sovereign, the Emperor Maximilian, might provide for him. At any rate, he considered himself ill off where he was.

Not (he writes to the Abbot of St. Bertin [2]) that I dislike England, or complain of my English patrons. I have many friends here among the bishops and leading men. The Archbishop of Canterbury is a father to me. He gave me a benefice. I resigned it, and he gave me a pension in exchange, with further additions from himself. Other great people have been good to me too, and I might have more if I chose to ask for it. But this war has turned the nation's head. All articles have gone up in price, and the bad wine gives me the stone. At best, too, an island is a place of banishment, and the war isolates us still worse. Letters can hardly pass in or out. I often wonder how human beings, especially Christian human beings, can be so mad as to go fighting with one another. Beasts do not fight, or only the most savage kinds of them, and they only fight for food with the weapons which Nature has given them. Men fight for ambition, for anger, for

[1] *Ep.* cxliii.
[2] *Ep.* cxliv., abridged.

lust, or other folly, and the justest war can hardly approve itself to any reasonable person. Who make up armies? Cutthroats, adulterers, gamblers, ravishers, mercenaries. And we are to receive this scum of mankind into our towns! We are to make ourselves their slaves while they commit horrid crimes, and those suffer most who have had least concern in the quarrel. The people build cities, the princes destroy them, and even victory brings more ill than good. We must not lightly blame our princes; but is the world to be convulsed because the rulers fall out? I would give all that I possess in England to see Christendom at peace. You have influence with the Archduke and the Emperor Maximilian and the politicians. I wish you would exert it.

The war was to cease in due time. Pope Julius had brought it on: with Julius's death in 1513 it ended. Leo X. succeeded, and brought peace with him. Henry married his sister Mary to King Louis, and all quarrels were made up. Meanwhile Erasmus lingered on, in financial difficulties as usual, and Colet, who did not quite approve of the carelessness which caused them, offered to relieve him, on condition that he would beg for help in a humble manner. The satire was not undeserved, and it stung.[1]

In your offer of money (Erasmus answers) I recognise the old Colet; but there is one phrase in your letter which hurts me, though you use it but in jest. You say you will give *si humiliter mendicavero*. You think me proud, perhaps, and would put me to shame. "*Si humiliter mendicavero et si inverecunde petam.*" How can humility go with impudence? A friend is not a friend who waits for the word *Rogo*. What, I beseech you, can be more undignified or more contemptible than the position in which I am placed in England of being a public beggar? I have received so much from the Archbishop that it would be wicked in

[1] *Ep.* cl., abridged.

me to take further advantage of him. I begged boldly enough of N——, and I received a point-blank refusal. Even Linacre, though he knew that I had but six angels left, that I was in bad health, and with winter coming on, admonished me to spare Mountjoy and the Archbishop, to reduce my expenses, and put up with being poor. Truly admirable advice. I concealed my condition as long as I could. I cannot conceal it longer, unless I am to be left to die. But, indeed, I am not so lost to shame as to beg, least of all to beg from you, who I know are ill-provided just now. I have no right to ask you for anything; but if you choose to have it so, I will accept what you may please to give.

The postscript of this letter contains the only glimpses which we have of Erasmus's intercourse with the Cambridge dignitaries. It is curious and characteristic.

Here (he adds) is something to amuse you. I was talking to some of the masters about the junior teachers. One of them, a great man in his way, exclaimed, "Who would spend his life in instructing boys if he could earn a living in any other way?" I said that instructing the young was an honest occupation. Christ had not despised children, and no labour was so sure of return. A man of piety would feel that he could not employ his time better than in bringing little ones to Christ. My gentleman turned up his nose, and said that if we were to give ourselves to Christ we had better join a regular order and go into a monastery. "St. Paul," I replied, "considers that religion means works of charity, and charity means helping others." He would not have this at all. Religion meant the *nos reliquimus omnia.* That was the only counsel of perfection. I told him that a man had not left everything who refused to undertake a useful calling because he thought it beneath him. And so our conversation ended. Such is the wisdom of the Scotists.

With this, too, may end the squalid period of Erasmus's life, for squalid it had been, notwithstanding the fame which he had won, and the occasional gleams of sunshine which had floated over it. Hitherto the world had known him chiefly through the "Adagia," a few poems, and light, graceful treatises like "The Knight's Manual," and had recognised in him a brilliant vagrant and probably dangerous man of letters. The vagrant's gown had a silver lining. Through all these struggling years he had been patiently labouring at his New Testament, and he was now to blaze before Europe as a new star. I must say a few words on what the appearance of that book meant.

The Christian religion as taught and practised in Western Europe consisted of the Mass and the Confessional, of elaborate ceremonials, rituals, processions, pilgrimages, prayers to the Virgin and the saints, with dispensations and indulgences for laws broken or duties left undone. Of the Gospels and Epistles so much only was known to the laity as was read in the Church services, and that intoned as if to be purposely unintelligible to the understanding. Of the rest of the Bible nothing was known at all, because nothing was supposed to be necessary, and lectures like Colet's at Oxford were considered superfluous and dangerous. Copies of the Scripture were rare, shut up in convent libraries, and studied only by professional theologians; while conventional interpretations were attached to the text which corrupted or distorted its meaning. Erasmus had undertaken to give the book to the whole world to read for itself — the original Greek of the Epistles and Gospels, with a new Latin translation — to wake up the intelligence, to show that the words had a real sense, and were not mere sounds like the dronings of a barrel-organ.

It was finished at last, text and translation printed, and the living facts of Christianity, the persons of

Christ and the Apostles, their history, their lives, their teaching were revealed to an astonished world. For the first time the laity were able to see, side by side, the Christianity which converted the world, and the Christianity of the Church with a Borgia pope, cardinal princes, ecclesiastical courts, and a mythology of lies. The effect was to be a spiritual earthquake.

Erasmus had not been left to work without encouragement. He had found friends, even at Rome itself, among the members of the Sacred College, who were weary of imposture and had half held out their hands to him. The Cardinal de Medici, who had succeeded Julius as Leo X., and aspired to shine as the patron of enlightenment, had approved Erasmus's undertaking, and was ready to give it his public sanction. Nor had Erasmus either flattered popes or flattered anyone to gain their good word. He might flatter when he wanted money out of a bishop or a fine lady: he was never false to intellectual truth. To his edition of the New Testament he had attached remarks appropriate to the time, and sent them floating with it through the world, which must have made the hair of orthodox divines stand on end,

"Like quills upon the fretful porcupine."

Each gospel, each epistle had its preface; while notes were attached to special passages to point their force upon the established usages. These notes increased in point and number as edition followed edition, and were accompanied with paraphrases to bring out the meanings with livelier intensity. A single candle shone far in the universal darkness. That a pope should have been found to allow the lighting of it is the most startling feature in Reformation history.

I shall read you some of these notes, and ask you to attend to them. Erasmus opens with a complaint of the neglect of Scripture, of a priesthood who thought more of offertory plates than of parchments, and more of gold than of books; of the degradation of spiritual life, and of the vain observances and scandalous practices of the orders specially called religious. From his criticisms on particular passages I will take specimens here and there, to show you how he directed the language of evangelists and apostles on the abuses of his own age.

Matthew xix. 12—"Eunuchs, which have made themselves eunuchs for the kingdom of heaven's sake." This text was a special favourite with the religious orders. Erasmus observes:—

Men are threatened or tempted into vows of celibacy. They can have license to go with harlots, but they must not marry wives. They may keep concubines and remain priests. If they take wives they are thrown to the flames. Parents who design their children for a celibate priesthood should emasculate them in their infancy, instead of forcing them, reluctant or ignorant, into a furnace of licentiousness.

Matthew xxiii., on the Scribes and Pharisees:—

You may find a bishop here and there who teaches the Gospel, though life and teaching have small agreement. But what shall we say of those who destroy the Gospel itself, make laws at their will, tyrannise over the laity, and measure right and wrong with rules constructed by themselves? Of those who entangle their flocks in the meshes of crafty canons, who sit not in the seat of the Gospel, but in the seat of Caiaphas and Simon Magus—prelates of evil, who bring disgrace and discredit on their worthier brethren?

Again, in the same chapter, verse 27, on whited sepulchres:—

What would Jerome say could he see the Virgin's milk exhibited for money, with as much honour paid to it as to the consecrated body of Christ; the miraculous oil; the portions of the true cross, enough if they were collected to freight a large ship? Here we have the hood of St. Francis, there Our Lady's petticoat or St. Anne's comb, or St. Thomas of Canterbury's shoes; not presented as innocent aids to religion, but as the substance of religion itself — and all through the avarice of priests and the hypocrisy of monks playing on the credulity of the people. Even bishops play their parts in these fantastic shows, and approve and dwell on them in their rescripts.

Again, Matthew xxiv. 23, on "Lo, here is Christ, or there": —

I (Erasmus says) saw with my own eyes Pope Julius II. at Bologna, and afterwards at Rome, marching at the head of a triumphal procession as if he were Pompey or Cæsar. St. Peter subdued the world with faith, not with arms or soldiers or military engines. St. Peter's successors would win as many victories as St. Peter won if they had Peter's spirit.

Ignatius Loyola once looked into Erasmus's New Testament, read a little, and could not go on. He said it checked his devotional emotions. Very likely it did.

Again, Corinthians xiv. 19, on unknown tongues: —

St. Paul says he would rather speak five words with a reasonable meaning in them than ten thousand in an unknown tongue. They chant nowadays in our churches in what is an unknown tongue and nothing else, while you will not hear a sermon once in six months telling people to amend their lives.[1] Modern church music is so constructed that the congregation cannot hear one distinct word. The choristers themselves do not understand what they are singing, yet according to priests and monks it constitutes the whole

[1] Was Erasmus writing prophetically of our own Anglo-Catholic revivalists?

of religion. Why will they not listen to St. Paul? In college or monastery it is still the same: music, nothing but music. There was no music in St. Paul's time. Words were then pronounced plainly. Words nowadays mean nothing. They are mere sounds striking upon the ear, and men are to leave their work and go to church to listen to worse noises than were ever heard in Greek or Roman theatre. Money must be raised to buy organs and train boys to squeal, and to learn no other thing that is good for them. The laity are burdened to support miserable, poisonous corybantes, when poor, starving creatures might be fed at the cost of them.

They have so much of it in England that the monks attend to nothing else. A set of creatures who ought to be lamenting their sins fancy they can please God by gurgling in their throats. Boys are kept in the English Benedictine colleges solely and simply to sing morning hymns to the Virgin. If they want music let them sing Psalms like rational beings, and not too many of those.

Again, Ephesians v. 4, on filthiness and foolish talking: —

Monks and priests have a detestable trick of burlesquing Scripture. When they wish to be specially malicious, they take the Magnificat or the Te Deum and introduce infamous words into them, making themselves as hateful when they would be witty as when they are serious.

1 Timothy i. 6, on vain disputations: —

Theologians are never tired of discussing the modes of sin, whether it be a privation in the soul or a spot on the soul. Why is it not enough simply to hate sin? Again, we have been disputing for ages whether the grace by which God loves us and the grace by which we love God are one and the same grace. We dispute how the Father differs from the Son, and both from the Holy Ghost, whether it be a difference of fact or a difference of relation, and how three can be one when neither of the three is the other. We dispute how the material fire which is to torture wicked souls can act on a substance which is not material. Entire lives are wasted on these speculations, and men quarrel and curse and come to blows about them. Then there are endless questionings about baptism, about synaxis, about penance, when no answer is possible, and the answer, if we could find one, would be useless to us.[1] Again, about God's power and the Pope's power. Can God order men to do ill? Can He order them, for instance, to hate Himself, or to abstain from doing good or from loving Him? Can God produce an infinite in all dimensions? Could He have made the world better than it is? Can He make a man incapable of sin? Can He reveal to any man whether he will be saved or damned? Can He understand anything which has no relation to Himself? Can He create a universal which has no particulars? Can He be comprehended under a predicate? Can the creating power be communicated to a creature? Can He make a thing done not to have been done? Can He make a harlot into a virgin? Can the three Persons assume the same nature at the same time? Is the proposition that God is a beetle or a pumpkin as probable antecedently as the proposition that God is man? Did God assume individual humanity or personal humanity? Are the Divine persons numerically three, or in what sense three? Or, again, of the Pope — can a Pope annul a decree of an Apostle? Can he make a decree which contradicts the Gospel? Can he add a new article to the Creed? Has he greater power than Peter, or the same power? Can he command angels? Can he abolish purgatory? Is the Pope man, or is he quasi-God, or has he both natures, like Christ? It is not recorded that Christ delivered a soul out of purgatory. Is the Pope more merciful than Christ? Can the Pope be mistaken?

Hundreds of such questions are debated by distin-

[1] Synaxis was an explanation of the Real Presence.

guished theologians, and the objects of them are better unknown than known. It is all vanity. Compared with Christ, the best of men are but worms. Do they imagine they will please Pope Leo? The schoolmen have been arguing for generations whether the proposition that Christ exists from eternity is correctly stated; whether He is compounded of two natures or consists of two natures; whether He is *conflatus*, or *commixtus*, or *conglutinatus*, or *coaugmentatus*, or *geminatus*, or *copulatus*. The present opinion is that neither of these participles is right, and we are to have a new word, *unitus*, which still is to explain nothing. If they are asked if the human nature is united to the Divine, they say it is a pious opinion. If asked whether the Divine Nature is united to the human, they hesitate and will not affirm, And all this stuff, of which we know nothing and are not required to know anything, they treat as the citadel of our faith.

They say that "person" does not signify relation of origin, but duplex negation of communicability *in genere*, that is, it connotes something positive, and in a noun of the first instance, not the second. They say the persons of the Divine Nature exist reciprocally by circumincession, and circumincession is when a thing subsists really in something else which is really distinct, by the mutual assistance of presentiality in the same essence. They define the personal or hypostatic union as the relation of a real disquiparation in one extreme, with no correspondent at the other. The union of the Word in Christ is a relation introduced from without, and this relation is not that of an effect to a cause, but of a sustentificate to a sustentificans.

Over speculations like these theologians professing to teach Christianity have been squandering their lives. One of them, an acquaintance of my own, told me that nine years of study would not enable me to understand the preface of Scotus to Peter Lombard. Another told me that to understand a single proposition of Scotus I must know the whole of his "Metaphysics."

So much on scholastic theology. We turn next to practice. 1 Timothy iii. 2, on "the husband of one wife": —

Because (says Erasmus) in an age when priests were few and widely scattered St. Paul directed that no one should be made a bishop who had been married a second time, bishops, priests, and deacons are now forbidden to marry at all. Other qualifications are laid down by St. Paul as required for a bishop's office, a long list of them. But not one at present is held essential, except this one of abstinence from marriage. Homicide, parricide, incest, piracy, sodomy, sacrilege, these can be got over, but marriage is fatal. There are priests now in vast numbers, enormous herds of them, seculars and regulars, and it is notorious that very few of them are chaste. The great proportion fall into lust and incest, and open profligacy. It would surely be better if those who cannot contain should be allowed lawful wives of their own, and so escape this foul and miserable pollution. In the world we live in the celibates are many and the chaste are few. A man is not chaste who abstains only because the law commands him, and such of our modern clergy as keep themselves out of mischief do it more from fear of the law than from conscience. They dread losing their benefices or missing their promotions.

Such are extracts from the reflections upon the doctrine and discipline of the Catholic Church which were launched upon the world in the notes to the New Testament by Erasmus, some on the first publication, some added as edition followed edition. They were not thrown out as satires, or in controversial tracts or pamphlets. They were deliberate accusations attached to the sacred text, where the religion which was taught by Christ and the Apostles and the degenerate superstition which had taken its place could be contrasted side by side. Nothing was spared; ritual and ceremony, dogmatic theology, philosophy, and personal character were tried by what all were compelled verbally to acknowledge to be the standard whose awful countenance was now practically revealed for the first time for many centuries. Bishops, seculars, monks were dragged out to judgment, and hung as on a public gibbet, in the light of the pages of the most sacred of all books, published with the leave and approbation of the Holy Father himself.

Never was volume more passionately devoured. A hundred thousand copies were soon sold in France alone. The fire spread, as it spread behind Samson's foxes in the Philistines' corn. The clergy's skins were tender from long impunity. They shrieked from pulpit and platform, and made Europe ring with their clamour. The louder they cried the more clearly Europe perceived the justice of their chastisement. The words of the Bible have been so long familiar to us that we can hardly realise what the effect must have been when the Gospel was brought out fresh and visible before the astonished eyes of mankind.

The book was not actually published till Erasmus had left England, but the fame of it had anticipated its appearance. The ruling powers of the Netherlands had determined at last to reclaim their most brilliant citizen, and to make a formal provision for him. England this time had seen the last of Erasmus. He was never to return to it again, or at least not for a protracted stay. His chief distress was at parting from his friends. Before he sailed he spent a fortnight with Bishop Fisher at Rochester. Sir Thomas More came down there to see the last of him, and the meeting and parting of these three is doubly affecting when one thinks of what Erasmus was to become and to do, and of the fate which was waiting More and Fisher in a storm which Erasmus was to do so much to raise.

Little could either they or their guest have dreamt of what was to be. Doubtless they believed that, with a liberal Pope Leo, there was an era before them of moderate reform. One would give much for a record of their talk. The spiritual world was not then draped in solemn inanities. Bishops wore no wigs, not even aprons or gaiters, and warm blood ran in the veins of the future martyrs and the scholar of Rotterdam. They could jest at the ridiculous. The condition of the Church was a comedy as well as a tragedy, a thing for laughter and a thing for tears — the laughter, it is likely, predominating. Out of this Rochester visit grew the wittiest of all Erasmus's writings, the "Encomium Moriæ," or "Praise of Folly," with a play upon More's name. It was composed at More's instigation, first sketched at Chelsea, then talked over at Rochester, cast finally into form on a ride from Calais to Brussels, where it was written down with a week's labour.

Of the "Praise of Folly" I shall speak to you in the next lecture.

LECTURE VIII.

I AM going to speak to you this evening about the "Encomium Moriæ," if not the most remarkable, yet the most effective of all Erasmus's writings. It originated, as I told you, in his conversations with More at Chelsea. It was put into form and words at intervals after Erasmus's return to the Continent, and the title is a humorous play on More's own name. It was brought out almost simultaneously with the edition of the New Testament.

Folly, *Moria*, speaks in her own name and declares herself the frankest of beings. The jester of the age was often the wisest man; the so-called wise men were often the stupidest of blockheads: and the play of wit goes on from one aspect to the other, the ape showing behind the purple and the ass under the lion's skin. Moria tells us that she is no child of Orcus or Saturn, or such antiquated dignitaries. Plutus begat her, not out of his own brain as Jupiter begat Pallas, but out of a charming creature called Youth. She was brought up in the Fortunate Islands by two seductive nymphs, Drink and Ignorance. Her companions were Self-love, Indolence, and Pleasure, and she herself was the moving principle of human existence. Neither man nor woman would ever think of marrying without Folly. Folly was the sunshine of ordinary life. From Folly sprang solemn-faced philosophers. From Folly came their successors, the monks, and kings, and priests, and popes. No goddess had so many worshippers as she, or was ever adored with more ardent devotion. Pious mortals offered candles to the Virgo Deipara in daylight, when she could see without candles. But they did not try to imitate the virgin. They kept their imitation for her rival, FOLLY. The whole world was Folly's temple, and she needed no images, for each one of her worshippers was an image of her himself.

Erasmus himself now assumes Folly's person, and proceeds to comment in character on the aspect of things around him, showing occasionally his own features behind the mask. After various observations he comes to his favourite subject, the scholastic divines.

It might be wiser for me to avoid Camarina and say nothing of theologians. They are a proud, susceptible race. They will smother me under six hundred dogmas. They will call me heretic, and bring thunderbolts out of their arsenals, where they keep whole magazines of them for their enemies. Still they are Folly's servants, though they disown their mistress. They live in the third heaven, adoring their own persons and disdaining the poor crawlers upon earth. They are surrounded with a body-guard of definitions, conclusions, corollaries, propositions explicit and propositions implicit. Vulcan's chains will not bind them. They cut the links with a distinction as with the stroke of an axe. They will tell you how the world was created. They will show you the crack where Sin crept in and corrupted mankind. They will explain to you how Christ was formed in the Virgin's womb; how accident subsists in synaxis without domicile in *place*. The most ordinary of them can do this. Those more fully initiated explain further whether there is an *instans* in Divine generation; whether in Christ there is more than a single filiation; whether "the Father hates the Son" is a possible proposition; whether God can become the substance of a woman, of an ass, of a pumpkin, or of the devil, and whether, if so, a pumpkin could preach a sermon, or work miracles, or be crucified.

And they can discover a thousand other things to you besides these. They will make you understand notions, and instants, formalities, and quiddities, things which no eyes ever saw, unless they were eyes which could see in the dark what had no existence. Like the Stoics, they have their paradoxes — whether it is a smaller crime to kill a thousand men than to mend a beggar's shoe on a Sunday; whether it is better that the whole world should perish than that a woman should tell one small lie. Then there are Realists, Nominalists, Thomists, Albertists, Occamists, Scotists — all so learned that an apostle would have no chance with them in argument. They will tell you that, although St. Paul could define what Faith is, yet he could not define it adequately as they can. An apostle might affirm the synaxis; but if an apostle was asked about the *terminus ad quem* and the *terminus a quo* of Transubstantiation, or how one body could be in two places at once, or how Christ's body in heaven differed from Christ's body on the cross or in the sacrament, neither Paul nor Peter could explain half as well as the Scotists. Doubtless Peter and the other apostles knew the Mother of Jesus, but they did not know as well as a modern divine how she escaped the taint of Adam's sin. Peter received the keys of knowledge and power, but Peter did not comprehend how he could have the key of knowledge and yet be without knowledge. Apostles baptized, but they could not lay out properly the formal material efficient and final causes of Baptism, or distinguish between the delible and the indelible effects of it upon character. They prayed to God; they did not know that to pray to a figure drawn with charcoal on a wall would be equally efficacious. They abhorred sin, but not one of them could tell what sin was unless the Scotists helped him. The head of

Jupiter was not so full of conundrums when he called for Vulcan with his axe to deliver him.

The object of "Moria" was evidently to turn the whole existing scheme of theology into ridicule. As little would Erasmus spare the theologians themselves, and, once off upon his humour, he poured in arrow upon arrow.

Our theologians (he says) require to be addressed as *Magister Noster*. You must not say *Noster Magister*, and you must be careful to write the words in capital letters. They call themselves *Religiosi et Monachi*, yet most of them have no religion at all; and it is accounted unlucky to meet a priest in the road.

They call it a sign of holiness to be unable to read. They bray out the Psalms in the churches like so many jackasses. They do not understand a word of them, but they fancy the sound is soothing to the ears of the saints. The mendicant friars howl for alms along the street. They pretend to resemble the Apostles, and they are filthy, ignorant, impudent vagabonds. They have their rules, forsooth. Yes, rules — how many knots, for instance, there may be in a shoe-string, how their petticoats should be cut or coloured, how much cloth should be used in their hoods, and how many hours they may sleep. But for all else — for conduct and character, they quarrel with each other and curse each other. They pretend to poverty, but they steal into honest men's houses and pollute them, and, wasps as they are, no one dares refuse them admittance for fear of their stings. They hold the secrets of every family through the confessional, and when they are drunk, or wish to amuse their company, they let them out to the world. If any wretched man dares to imitate them they pay him off from the pulpits, and they never stop their barking till you fling them a piece of meat.

Immortal gods, never were such stage-players as

these friars. They gesticulate. They vary their voices. They fill the air with their noise. To be a friar mendicant is a professional mystery, and brother instructs brother. I heard one of them once — *A fool?* No, a learned man — explaining the Trinity. He was an original, and took a line of his own. He went on the parts of speech. He showed how noun agreed with verb and adjective with substantive, and made out a grammatical triad as mathematicians draw triangles. Another old man — he was over eighty — might have been Scotus come to life again. He discovered the properties of Christ in the letters of the word Jesus. The three inflexions exhibited the triple nature — *Jesus*, *Jesum*, *Jesu*. That is *summus*, *medius*, *ultimus*. I felt as if I was turning to stone. They lift their theologic brows. They talk of their doctors solemn, doctors subtle and most subtle, doctors seraphic, doctors cherubic, doctors holy, doctors irrefragable. They have their syllogisms, their majors and minors, inferences, corollaries, suppositions; and, for a fifth act of the play, they tell some absurd story and interpret it allegorically, tropologically, anagogically, and make it into a chimera more extravagant than poet ever invented. They open their sermons quietly, and begin in a tone so low that they can scarcely hear themselves. Then suddenly they raise their voices and shout, when there is nothing to shout about. They are directed to be entertaining, so they crack jokes as if they were asses playing the fiddle. They practise all the tricks of the platform, and use them badly, and yet they are admired — wonderfully admired — by women who are on bad terms with their husbands.

Leaving the friars prostrate, "Moria" sets on other victims, and gives a turn to princes and courtiers; but apparently she finds less to laugh at in the laity, and goes back to give another toss with the horn to the Church and the Church's special representatives — popes, cardinals, bishops. Their splendour and worldliness are mocked at, and contrasted with the simplicity of the Galilean fishermen. Priestly and monastic absurdity of ignorance comes next.

I was lately (says Moria) at a theological discussion. I am often present, indeed, on such occasions. Someone asked what authority there was in Scripture for burning heretics. A sour-looking old man said that St. Paul had specially ordered it, and being asked where, answered in a voice of thunder, "Hæreticum hominem, post unam et secundam correptionem *devita*." The audience stared, wondering what he meant. He explained that *de vitâ* meant *de vitâ tollere* — to put away out of life. We all laughed, and a friend of the old man covered the blunder by producing "Maleficos non patieris vivere." Every heretic is *maleficus*, he said, and therefore must not be suffered to live. No one present seemed to know that the Hebrew word translated *maleficus* means a witch.

Simultaneously with "Moria" another production appeared, which divided public attention with it. Julius II., with his wars and his intrigues, had brought all Europe into war. In this preliminary witch dance the partners were combined on lines widely different from those on which they afterwards arranged themselves. Spain, England, and the Empire were allies of the Papacy. France, the special object of the Pope's fury, stood almost alone, in a position almost of open revolt against the authority of the Roman Church. Julius fought his battles as a temporal sovereign, but he used his spiritual thunderbolts to reinforce his cannon, and the Western Church was on the eve of a schism. The French Church stood by its sovereign. Julius excommunicated Louis, and placed France under an interdict. Louis called a Provincial Council, which claimed the right, asserted afterwards in England under Henry

VIII., to ecclesiastical as well as political independence. The Pope excommunicated the cardinals and prelates who took part in it, declared the King deposed, forbade his subjects to obey him, and fulminated in the old style of Gregory VII. and Innocent III. Henry VIII. and the English nation plunged into the quarrel as the allies of the Holy See. Henry VIII. stood out as the champion of Catholic unity, while France was challenging the sovereign rights of the Papacy, and insisting on ecclesiastical independence. Had the struggle gone forward, Louis would have led the revolt, and the course of European history would have been all different. The death of Julius postponed the inevitable convulsion. Leo X. succeeded to the papal throne. Interdicts and excommunications were taken off, and there was general peace. But the hurricane left the sea still agitated. The waves still heaved of the passions which had been stirred, and the name of the intriguing, fighting, insolent Julius was abhorred by the French nation. In 1513, after the peace had been concluded, there appeared in Paris a dramatic dialogue, so popular that it was brought upon the stage. Julius, attended by a familiar spirit, appears at the gate of Paradise demanding to be admitted. St. Peter questions, challenges, cross-questions, and the Pope replies in character, audacious as a Titan attempting to scale the home of the gods.

The Dialogue was anonymous. Who could have written it? Some gave it to Faustus Anderlin; but Anderlin was indolent and easy-going, not at all likely to have kindled himself into such a flame of scorn. Anderlin, too, would have claimed the authorship. He had nothing to fear, and would only have added to his popularity. Opinion rapidly settled on

Erasmus. Erasmus hated wars, hated popes especially who used the sword of the flesh as well as of the spirit for worldly ambition. Erasmus had looked on with disgust and scorn at the triumphal procession on the annexation of Bologna, and his friends in the Sacred College were no friends to Julius. The writer, whoever he was, knew France well, knew Rome well, and was acquainted with the inmost workings of the ecclesiastical mystery. The Dialogue became the talk of Europe. Erasmus must be the man. No other writer could use a pen so finely pointed or so dipped in gall. "Aut Erasmus, aut diabolus."

He denied the authorship himself; he says distinctly that he never published anything to which he did not set his name. And, again, he must have known that such a production must be fatal to any hopes of promotion or support at Rome. Leo X. might have been privately amused, but could not decently have patronised a man who had turned the Papacy itself into contempt. As long as the authorship was unproved, however, Erasmus could not be made responsible for it, and other great writers besides Erasmus have held themselves entitled to hide behind a blank title-page. Even in his denials there was latent mockery. He says, if it had been his, it would have been in better Latin; but the Latin is as good as his own. Cardinal Campegio, who believed him guilty, wrote to remonstrate. Erasmus calmly told him that he had heard persons attribute the authorship to Campegio himself. Sir Thomas More accepted the denial as sufficient to his own mind, but admitted that it was not conclusive. "If Erasmus did write it, well, what then?"[1] was More's final word about it. I have made a translation of "Julius," and

[1] See Appendix to this Lecture.

I mean to read it to you. Some of you will doubtless be taking this part of European history into the schools. You may have questions to answer about this remarkable successor of St. Peter, and nowhere else will you find so lively an account of him and his doings. It will be better worth your listening to than any lecture of mine.

But to return to the "Encomium Moriæ." Through the printing-press it flew over Western Christendom, through France, through Spain, through England and Germany, and, like an explosion of spiritual dynamite, it left monks and clergy in wreck and confusion, the objects of universal laughter. The "Epistolæ obscurorum Virorum" had been coarse and obscene, a book to be read in private if read at all, and not to be talked about. "Moria" was delicate and witty, running through the heart like a polished rapier and killing dead in the politest manner in the world. Princes and secular politicians took no offence; they were rather entertained, and delighted to see the punishment of an insolent order which had so long defied them. Leo X. read "Moria," and only observed, "Here is our old friend again." "Moria" and the New Testament were the voice and protest of the Christian laity against the parody of a Church which pretended to be their spiritual master. The clergy at first were stunned. When they collected themselves, they began in the usual way to cry Antichrist and heresy, and clamour for sword and faggot. But it was no heresy to denounce profligacy or gross superstitions; and scholastic theology, though universally accepted by the regular orders and the universities, was not yet guaranteed and guarded from question by an Œcumenical Council. Most fools and many women, however, were on the clergy's side, and a party which has the fools at its back has usually a majority of numbers. Bishops fulminated. Universities, Cambridge and Oxford among them, forbade students to read Erasmus's writings or booksellers to sell them. Erasmus himself was safe from prosecution while he was protected by the Pope and the civil governments, and hard as he had struck he had said nothing for which the Church Courts could openly punish him. His admirers were less prudent or less skilful, and were sent to stake or prison if they committed themselves. As the wrath and resentment took form, it concentrated itself on the new learning. "See what comes of Greek," the clergy cried. "Did n't we always say so? We will have no Greek, we will stick to our Scotus and Aquinas." And so the battle began between ignorance and intelligence, between the friends of darkness and the friends of light, which raged on till Luther spoke at Wittenberg, and the contest on languages was lost in larger issues.

In England, where Erasmus was personally known, the outcry was the loudest, especially at the universities. Erasmus had been at Oxford and had been at Cambridge. It was assumed that he had left poison behind him. Oxford divided itself into two bodies, calling themselves Greeks and Trojans, the Trojans enormously preponderating.

John Mill called English Conservatives the stupid party. Well, stupidity in its place is not always a bad thing. I have a high respect for Conservatism. Conservatism, at least, represents ideas which have proved themselves capable of being practically worked. The ideas of progress may be beautiful to look at and to talk about, but whether they will work or not no one knows till they are tried. Out of every hundred new ideas ninety-nine are generally nonsense. The odd one will be the egg which contains the whole future in it; but until the exceptional egg proves its vitality by breaking its shell, the wisest cannot foresee how it will develop.

The monks, as I observed to you the other day, said that Erasmus laid the egg and Luther hatched it. Yes, said Erasmus, but the egg I laid was a hen, and Luther hatched a game-cock. No wise man will lightly change the old for the new. The misfortune is that the world waits too long over the incubation, and the new creature often changes its nature in struggling to get born.

Oxford stayed thus too long incubating. Light had come into the world, and the dawn was spreading. To other eyes, if not to the eyes of Oxford dignitaries, it had become clear that it was no use to draw curtains and close shutters.

I shall now read to you two letters written on this occasion by Sir Thomas More. They are worth whole volumes of general history. You can understand the actions of men in past times only when you understand their tempers and passions. The English Court was at Abingdon on progress. As Oxford was so near, the news of what was going on there reached the King's ears, and Sir T. More, at Henry's direction, addressed thus the governing body of the University:[1] —

I heard lately that either in some fools' frolic, or from your dislike of the study of Greek, a clique had been formed among you calling themselves Trojans; that one of you, who had more years than wisdom, had styled himself Priam, another Hector, another Paris, and so forth; and that the object was to throw

[1] Jortin, vol. ii. appendix viii.

ridicule on the Greek language and literature. Grecians are to be mocked and jeered at by Trojans, whose laughter betrays their ignorance. An ancient adage says: "Sero sapiunt Phryges." This action of yours is foolish in itself, and gives an unpleasing impression of your general intelligence. I was sorry to hear that men of learning were making so poor a use of their leisure, but I had concluded that in a large number there would always be some blockheads, and that it was only a passing absurdity.

I have been informed, however, on coming to this town of Abingdon, that folly has grown into madness, and that one of these Trojans, who thinks himself a genius, has been preaching a course of sermons during Lent, denouncing not Greek classics only, but Latin classics too, and all liberal education. A fool's speech comes out of a fool's head. He did not, I understand, preach on a text from Scripture. He took some absurd English proverb, and at this most sacred season of the year, in the presence of a vast assembly, in the church of God, and within sight of the body of Christ, he turned a Lent sermon into a bacchanalian farce.

What must have been the feeling of his hearers when they saw their preacher grinning like an ape, and instead of receiving the word of God from him received only an onslaught upon learning?

If the worthy man had been a hermit, had he come out of a desert to preach that the road to life was through vigils and fasting and prayer, that all else was useless, and that learning was a snare, his simplicity might be forgiven and something might be alleged in his favour. But for a scholar in gown and hood, in the midst of an academy which exists only for the sake of learning, so to rail at it is malicious impudence. What right has he to denounce Latin, of which he knows little; Science, of which he knows less; and Greek, of which he knows nothing? He had better have confined himself to the seven deadly sins, with which perhaps he has closer acquaintance.

Of course we know that a man can be saved without secular learning. Children learn from their mothers the essential truths of Christianity. But students are sent to Oxford to receive general instruction. They do not go there merely to learn theology. Some go to learn law, some to learn human nature from poets, and orators, and historians — forms of knowledge even useful to preachers, if their congregations are not to think them fools. Others again go to universities to study natural science, and philosophy, and art; and this wonderful gentleman is to condemn the whole of it under one general sentence. He says that nothing is of importance except theology. How can he know theology if he is ignorant of Hebrew, and Greek, and Latin? He thinks, I presume, that it can all be found in the scholastic conundrums. Those I admit can be learned with no particular effort. But theology, that august Queen of Heaven, demands an ampler scope. The knowledge of God can be gathered only out of Scripture — Scripture and the early Catholic Fathers. That was where for a thousand years the searchers after truth looked for it and found it, before these modern paradoxes were heard of; and if he fancies that Scripture and the Fathers can be understood without a knowledge of the languages in which the Fathers wrote, he will not find many to agree with him.

He will pretend perhaps that he was not censuring learning in itself: he was censuring only an excessive devotion to it. I do not see so great a disposition to sin in this direction that it needs to be checked in a sermon. He calls those who study Greek heretics. The teachers of Greek, he says, are full-grown devils, the learners of Greek are little devils, and he was aiming at a certain person whom I think the devil would be sorry to see in a pulpit. He did not name him, but everyone knew to whom he alluded.[1] It is not for me, Domini Illustrissimi, to defend Greek. You know yourselves that it needs no defence. The finest

[1] Of course, Erasmus.

writings on all subjects, theology included, are in Greek. The Romans had no philosophers save Cicero and Seneca. The New Testament was written in Greek. Your Wisdoms will acknowledge that not all Greek scholars are fools, and you will not allow the study of it to be put down by sermons or private cabals.

Make these gentlemen understand that, unless they promptly cease from such factious doings, we outside will have a word to say about it. Every man who has been educated at your University has as much interest in its welfare as you who are now at its head. Your Primate and Chancellor will not permit these studies to be meddled with, or allow fools and sluggards to ridicule them from the pulpit. The Cardinal of York will not endure it. The King's Majesty our Sovereign has himself more learning than any English monarch ever possessed before him. Think you that he, prudent and pious as he is, will look on passively when worthless blockheads are interrupting the course of sound instruction in the oldest university in the Realm — a university which has produced men who have done honour to their country and the Church? With its colleges and its endowments, there is nowhere in the world a place of education so richly furnished as Oxford; and the object of these foundations is to support students in the acquirement of knowledge. Your Wisdoms, therefore, will find means to silence these foolish contentions. Useful learning, of whatever kind it be, shall be protected from ridicule, and shall receive proper honour and esteem.

Be you diligent in so doing. Improve the quality of your own lectures, and so deserve the thanks of your Prince, of your Primate, and the Cardinal. I have written thus out of the regard I feel for you. My own services you know that you can command if you need them. God keep you all in safety, and increase you daily in learning and godliness of life.

The heads of Houses were sleeping over a volcano, and required a sterner wakening than a letter from Sir Thomas More. Yet the rebuke is noteworthy, especially from the quarter from which it came. In a score of years their Duns Scotus was torn to pieces in the Quadrangles, the sacred leaves left to flutter in the November winds, they themselves erasing with trembling hands the Pope's name from their Service-books, and Sir Thomas More laying down his own life to stem a revolution which might have been prevented had they listened in time to him and to Erasmus. This letter does not mention Erasmus by name, though there is an evident allusion to him. The next which I shall read is a passionate and indignant defence of Erasmus himself, against some vain young English divine, who had written to More to remonstrate against his continued intimacy with the author of "Moria."[1] I do not know who this forward young person was. There were perhaps many Englishmen in the universities and out of them capable of similar folly. More's letter is very long, and I must abridge and condense it. The satire throughout is extremely fine.

You adjure me to beware of Erasmus. Gratitude for your concern for my soul obliges me to thank you for your alarms. It is my duty also to point out to you that you are yourself walking among precipices. Your fortress, from whose battlements you look so scornfully on Erasmus, may be less secure than you imagine.

I am in danger, forsooth, because I consider Erasmus (as a good Greek scholar) to have given a better rendering of passages in the New Testament than I find in the received translation. Where is the danger? May not I find pleasure in a work which the learned and pious admire, and which the Pope him-

[1] Jortin, vol. ii. appendix xii.

self has twice approved? Erasmus determines nothing. He gives the facts and leaves the reader to judge. I am not such a fool as to mistake the false for the true, and the danger is more to you than to me. Erasmus has published volumes more full of wisdom than any which Europe has seen for ages. You have turned to poison what to others has brought only health. I read with real sorrow your intemperate railing at such a man. You defame his character. You call him a vagabond and a pseudo-theologian. You say he is a heretic, a schismatic, a forerunner of Antichrist.

Before you were a priest you had candour and charity; now that you have become a monk some devil has possession of you. You say you do not give him these names yourself. You pretend that he is so described by Almighty God. Are you not ashamed to bring in God when you are doing the devil's work in slandering your neighbour? God has revealed it, you pretend, to someone that you know. I am not to be frightened by an idiot's dreams. Your "someone that you know" declares that Erasmus confessed his unbelief to him in private, and you say that your "someone" is a man of eminence and virtue. If it be the man I suppose, his acquaintance say he is more honoured than honourable. He has told you, forsooth, that Erasmus has more than once secretly admitted to him that he was an unbeliever. A likely story! Erasmus, when he was in England, lived with Colet, the Bishop of Rochester, the Archbishop of Canterbury, Mountjoy, Tunstall, Pace, and Grocyn. Did either of these ever hear him say that he was an infidel? They loved him, and loved him better the more they knew him. You answer that he would not betray himself to such men as they are. He chose, I presume, less reputable confidants like your friend. How is "someone" to prove his accusation? You say it was in secret. There were no witnesses. When and where was the conversation held? Why has your friend concealed it till Erasmus has left England?

Be it true or false, this gentleman is equally a traitor. But what Erasmus has done for Holy Scripture speaks for him. The best of mankind have been called heretics.

To proceed. You charge Erasmus with having said that Jerome, Ambrose, Augustine, and other Fathers made occasional mistakes. Since the Fathers admit it themselves, why do you blame Erasmus? When Augustine translates one way and Jerome another, they cannot both be right; when Augustine accepts the story of the Septuagint and the seventy cells, and Jerome treats it as a fable, one or other must be wrong. Augustine says angels have material bodies. This you deny yourself. Augustine says infants dying unbaptized go to eternal torments. No one now believes this.

You complain of the study of Greek and Hebrew. You say it leads to the neglect of Latin. Was not the New Testament written in Greek? Did not the early Fathers write in Greek? Is truth only to be found in Gothic Latin? You will have no novelties; you say the "old is better"; of course it is; the wisdom of the Fathers is better than the babbling of you moderns. You pretend that the Gospels can be understood without Greek; that there is no need of a new translation; we have the Vulgate and others besides, you say, and a new version was superfluous. I beseech you, where are these others? I have never met a man who has seen any but the Vulgate. Produce them. And for the Vulgate itself, it is nonsense to talk of the many ages for which it has been approved by the Church. It was the best or the first which the Church could get. When once in use it could not easily be changed, but to use it is not to approve it as perfect. You talk of the Septuagint translation, which you say suffices for all Scriptural truth. Do you imagine that the Seventy wrote in Latin? or wrote a Latin version of the New Testament? The Seventy wrote in Greek, and were all dead two hundred years before Christ was born.

You go next to "Moria." Solomon says, of the number of fools there is no end. Moria contains more wisdom and less folly than many books that I know, including your own. I shall not defend it. It needs no defence. I notice only one point in your attack. You say that in "Moria" Erasmus makes himself Moscus. Who was Moscus? Perhaps you mean Momus.

As to the "Dialogue of Julius," who wrote it, and whether it be good or bad, I have never cared to inquire. Opinions differ; I know that it was brought on the stage in Paris. The MS. passed through the hands of Faustus Anderlin, who was a friend of Erasmus, and Erasmus may have seen it before it was printed; but when you appeal to the style, there were plenty of clever men in Paris who could have imitated Erasmus's manner. But suppose he did write "Julius"—suppose that in his indignation at the broils and wars which that Pope had caused he went further than he could have afterwards wished, you will have small thanks from those who smarted under the satire by identifying it now with Erasmus. Proof you have none. But if books are bad, why read them? Time was when monks called the world Sodom, and read nothing, not even a letter from a friend. Now it appears they read everything—heresy, schism, anything that offers, to find material for evil speaking. What good have they from their prayers when they learn to lie and slander? I knew you once an innocent and affectionate youth—why are you now charged with spite and malice? You complain of Erasmus's satire and you yourself worry him like a dog. Take all the hard things he has said of anyone. It is a handful of dust to the pyramid of invective which you have piled over a man who was once kind to you. Is a boy like you to fall foul of what the Vicar of Christ approves? Is the head of the Christian Church, speaking from the citadel of the faith, to give a book his sanction, and is it to be befouled by the dirty tongue of an obscure little monk? Erasmus, forsooth, does not know Scripture! He has studied Scripture for more years than you have been alive. You yourself quote Scripture like a rogue in a play. Nothing is easier, nothing is viler. I heard a fellow the other day telling a story of a priest soliciting another man's wife, the woman refusing, the husband entering and chastising him, all told in Scripture language. Very ridiculous, no doubt. To use Scripture as you use it to slander your neighbour is a great deal worse. Erasmus is the dearest friend that I have.

He sneers, you exclaim, at the religious orders. Why be so sensitive? When he ridicules your ceremonies he ridicules only the superstitious use of them. Do not your orders quarrel and abuse each other, and fight over the cut and colour of their petticoats, and set up their crests as if they were seated on the sun's rays? Yet the same men who think the devil will have them if they change the shape of their frocks, are not afraid to intrigue and lie. They shudder if they have left out a verse in a Psalm, and they tell each other dirty stories longer than their prayers. They strain at a gnat; they swallow an entire elephant. They live in the third heaven, as if they were saints in council. They fancy themselves the holiest of men and commit the most abominable crimes. I knew a man belonging to a strict order — not a novice; he was prior of the house. He had gone from wickedness to wickedness. He had planned murder and sacrilege, and he hired a party of cutthroats. The deed was done. The men were caught. I saw them. They told me themselves that before they went to work the prior took them to his cell and made them pray on their knees to the Virgin there. This completed, they did their business with a clear conscience.

I am not holding good men answerable for others' sins. Wholesome plants and poisonous plants may grow on the same stem. The worship of the Virgin may do good to some people. With others it is made an encouragement to crime. This is what Erasmus denounces, and if you blame him you must blame Jerome, who says worse of monks than Erasmus says. Flattery makes friends and truth makes enemies. Erasmus has written truth, and you curse and insult him. You say, like the Pharisee, "God, I thank Thee that I am not as this publican." Erasmus needs no eulogium from me. His work speaks for him, and the world's honour. You say he has been vicious. What leisure has he had for vice? You call him a vagabond because he has moved from place to place to carry on his work. A saint, I suppose, must remain fixed like a sponge or an oyster. You forget your own mendicants. They wander wide enough, and you think them the holiest of mankind. Jerome travelled far, the Apostles travelled far.

Look into your own heart. You, forsooth, are never angry, never puffed up, never seek your own glory. My friend, the more conscious you are of your own faults, the more likely you are to be a profitable servant. This I pray you may be your care, and mine, and Erasmus's also. When we have done our best it will be nothing, and we shall do our best when we least detract from others' merits. Your admirers pretend that they have been induced by your heavenly arguments to abandon their friendship for Erasmus. How they have been affected I cannot say. For myself, I am not so dazzled but that I can still see that white is white.

You hint at the end that you are not yourself implacable: if Erasmus will correct his errors you will again take his hand. Doubtless he will bow to so great a man, and will correct them when you point them out. So far you have only exposed your own. In what you call errors he has substituted pure Latin for bad, cleared obscurities, corrected mistakes, and has pointed out blunders of copyists. To please so great a man as you he may perhaps undo all this, forfeit the respect of the wise, and console himself with the sense of your forgiveness.

But a truce to satire. You say that the blots you indicate are trifles. Well, you cannot regard heresy and schism and precursing Antichrist as trifles. I presume, therefore, that these charges are withdrawn. I will let the rest drop, and our tragedy may end as a comedy. Farewell! If the cloister is good for your soul make the best of it, but spare us for the future these effervescences of genius.

APPENDIX TO LECTURE VIII.

JULIUS II. EXCLUSUS. A DIALOGUE.

Brought on the Stage at Paris, 1514.

Persons. — JULIUS II.; FAMILIAR SPIRIT; ST. PETER.

Scene. — GATE OF HEAVEN.

Julius. What the devil is this? The gates not opened! Something is wrong with the lock.

Spirit. You have brought the wrong key perhaps. The key of your money-box will not open the door here. You should have brought both keys. This is the key of power, not of knowledge.

Julius. I never had any but this, and I don't see the use of another. Hey there, porter! I say, are you asleep or drunk?

Peter. Well that the gates are adamant, or this fellow would have broken in. He must be some giant, or conqueror. Heaven, what a stench! Who are you? What do you want here?

Julius. Open the gates, I say. Why is there no one to receive me?

Peter. Here is fine talk. Who are you, I say?

Julius. You know this key, I suppose, and the triple crown, and the pallium?

Peter. I see a key, but not the key which Christ gave to me a long time since. The crown? I don't recognise the crown. No heathen king ever wore such a thing, certainly none who expected to be let in here. The pallium is strange too. And see, there are marks on all three of that rogue and impostor Simon Magus, that I turned out of office.

Julius. Enough of this. I am Julius the Legurian, P. M., as you can see by the letters if you can read.

Peter. P. M.! What is that? Pestis Maxima?

Julius. Pontifex Maximus, you rascal.

Peter. If you are three times Maximus, if you are Mercury Trismegistus, you can't come in unless you are Optimus too.

Julius. Impertinence! You, who have been no more than Sanctus all these ages—and I Sanctissimus, Sanctissimus Dominus, Sanctitas, Holiness itself, with Bulls to show it.

Peter. Is there no difference between being Holy and being called Holy? Ask your flatterers who called you these fine names to give you admittance. Let me look at you a little closer. Hum! Signs of impiety in plenty, and none of the other thing. Who are these fellows behind you? Faugh! They smell of stews, drink-shops, and gunpowder. Have you brought goblins out of Tartarus to make war with heaven? Yourself, too, are not precisely like an apostle. Priest's cassock and bloody armour below it, eyes savage, mouth insolent, forehead brazen, body scarred with sins all over, breath loaded with wine, health broken with debauchery. Ay, threaten as you will, I will tell you what you are for all your bold looks. You are Julius the Emperor come back from hell.

Julius. Ma desi!

Peter. What does he say?

Spirit. They are words which he uses to make the cardinals fly after he has dined.

Peter. You seem to understand him; who are you?

Spirit. I am the genius of this man.

Peter. No good one, I fear.

Julius. Will you make an end of your talking and open the gates? We will break them down else. You see these followers of mine.

Peter. I see a lot of precious rogues, but they won't break in here.

Julius. Make an end, I say, or I will fling a thunderbolt at you. I will excommunicate you. I have done as much to kings before this. Here are the Bulls ready.

Peter. Thunderbolts! Bulls! I beseech you, we had no thunderbolts or Bulls from Christ.

Julius. You shall feel them if you don't behave yourself.

Peter. Do your worst. Curses won't serve your turn here. Excommunicate me! By what right, I would know?

Julius. The best of rights. You are only a priest, perhaps not that — you cannot consecrate. Open, I say.

Peter. You must show your merits first; no admission without merits.

Julius. What do you mean by merits?

Peter. Have you taught true doctrine?

Julius. Not I. I have been too busy fighting. There are monks to look after doctrine, if that is of any consequence.

Peter. Have you gained souls to Christ by pious example?

Julius. I have sent a good many to Tartarus.

Peter. Have you worked any miracles?

Julius. Pshaw! miracles are out of date.

Peter. Have you been diligent in your prayers?

Spirit. You waste your breath. This is mockery.

Peter. These are the qualities which make a respectable pope. If he has others better, let him produce them.

Julius. The invincible Julius ought not to answer a beggarly fisherman. However, you shall know who and what I am. First, I am a Ligurian, and not a Jew like you. My mother was the sister of the great Pope Sextus IV. The Pope made me a rich man out of Church property. I became a cardinal. I had my misfortunes. I had the French pox. I was banished, hunted out of my country; but I knew all along that I should come to be pope myself in the end. You were frightened at a girl's voice. A gipsy girl heartened me, and told me I should wear a crown and be king of kings and lord of lords. It came true, partly with French help, partly with money which I borrowed at interest, partly with promises. Crœsus could not have produced all the money that was wanted. The bankers will tell you about that. But I succeeded. I rose to the top, and I have done more for the Church and Christ than any pope before me.

Peter. What did you do?

Julius. I raised the revenue. I invented new offices and sold them. I invented a way to sell bishoprics without simony. When a man is made a bishop he resigns the offices which he holds already. He cannot resign what he has not got, so I made him buy something first, and in this way each promotion brought me in six or seven thousand ducats, besides the Bulls. I re-coined the currency and made a great sum that way. Nothing can be done without money. Then I annexed Bologna to the

Holy See. I beat the Venetians. I jockeyed the Duke of Ferrara. I defeated a schismatical council by a sham council of my own. I drove the French out of Italy, and I would have driven out the Spaniards, too, if the Fates had not brought me here. I have set all the princes of Europe by the ears. I have torn up treaties, kept great armies in the field. I have covered Rome with palaces, and I have left five millions in the Treasury behind me. I would have done more if my Jew doctor could have kept me alive, and I would give something if an enchanter could put me back so that I could finish my work. And here are you keeping the door shut against one who has deserved so well of Christ and the Church. And I have done it all myself, too. I owe nothing to my birth, for I don't know who my father was ; nothing to learning, for I have none ; nothing to youth, for I was old when I began ; nothing to popularity, for I was hated all round. Spite of fortune, spite of gods and men, I achieved all that I have told you in a few years, and I left work enough cut out for my successors to last ten years longer. This is the modest truth, and my friends at Rome call me more a god than a man.

Peter. Invincible warrior ! All this is quite new to me. Pardon my simplicity, who are these fair curly-haired boys that you have with you ?

Julius. Boys I took into training to improve their minds.

Peter. And those dark ones with the scars ?

Julius. Those are my soldiers and generals who were killed fighting for me. They all deserve heaven. I promised it them under hand and seal if they lost their lives in my service, no matter how wicked they might be.

Peter. Doubtless they are the same parties who came a while ago with these Bulls of yours, and tried to force their way in.

Julius. And you did not admit them ?

Peter. Not I. My orders are not to admit men who come with Bulls, but to admit those who have clothed the naked, fed the hungry, given the thirsty drink, visited the sick and those in prison. Men have cast out devils and worked miracles in Christ's name and yet have been shut out. Do you think we open for Bulls signed "Julius" ?

Julius. If I had but known.

Peter. What would you have done ? Declared war ?

Julius. I would have excommunicated you.

Peter. Nonsense. Proceed with your story. Why do you wear arms ?

Julius. Don't you know the Pope has two swords?

Peter. When I was in your place I had no sword but the sword of the Spirit.

Julius. Yes, you had. Recollect Malchus.

Peter. I do recollect, but I was then defending my Master, not myself. I was not then pope. I had not received the keys, nor the Holy Spirit either. Even so, my Master ordered me to sheathe my sword, to show that such weapons did not become Christian priests. Why do you call yourself Ligurian? Does it matter to Christ's Vicar from what family he comes?

Julius. I wish to do credit to my country.

Peter. You know your country, it seems, though you don't know your father. I thought you were going to speak of your heavenly country, the New Jerusalem. But, to go on. You say you are sister's son to Sextus—Sextus's nephew.

Julius. I call myself his nephew. Some people have said I was his son.

Peter. Is that true?

Julius. It is disrespectful to the Pope's dignity to say so.

Peter. The popes would consult better for their dignity by giving no occasion for such stories. But you have told us how you yourself became Supreme Pontiff. Is that the road generally followed?

Julius. There has been no other for several generations. It may be different in future. I myself issued a prohibition against further elections like my own. But others must look to these things now.

Peter. No one could have given a more complete description. I am surprised that such an office is so sought after. When I was pope the difficulty was to find men who would be priests or deacons.

Julius. Naturally, when bishops and priests had nothing for their reward but fasts, and vigils, and doctrines, and now and then death. Bishops nowadays are kings and lords, and such positions are worth struggling for.

Peter. Tell me, had Bologna fallen from the faith that you annexed it to the Holy See?

Julius. God forbid! Not a heretic in the whole place.

Peter. Bentivoglio perhaps was a bad ruler and the State was in disorder?

Julius. On the contrary, it was flourishing in the highest degree. That was why I wanted to have it.

Peter. I understand. Bentivoglio was a usurper, and had no right to be there.

Julius. Not at all. He had succeeded to the Government by formal arrangement.

Peter. Then the people did not like him?

Julius. They loved him, clung to him. They hated me.

Peter. Why did you take Bologna then?

Julius. Because I wanted the revenue for my own treasury, and because Bologna was otherwise convenient for me. So I used my thunderbolts, the French helped me, and now Bologna is mine, and every farthing of the taxes goes to Rome for the Church's use. If you had only seen my triumphal entry. The Church was militant with a witness.

Peter. So you turned our petition to God, that His Kingdom may come, into real fact. . . . Well, and what had the Venetians done to you?

Julius. They told scandalous stories about me.

Peter. True or false?

Julius. No matter which. To speak ill of the Pope is sacrilege. Then they appointed their own bishops and priests. They allowed no appeals to Rome and refused to buy our dispensations. They kept back part of your patrimony.

Peter. My patrimony! What patrimony do you mean? I left all to follow Christ.

Julius. They occupied certain towns which the Holy See claimed.

Peter. This was the injury, then! Well, was there impiety or immorality in Venice?

Julius. Not the least, but I wanted a few thousand ducats of them to pay my regiments.

Peter. And how about the Duke of Ferrara?

Julius. The Duke was an ungrateful wretch. He accused me of simony, called me a pæderast, and also claimed certain moneys of me. Moreover, I wanted the Duchy of Ferrara for a son of my own, who could be depended on to be true to the Church, and who had just poniarded the Cardinal of Pavia.

Peter. What! What! Popes with wives and children?

Julius. Wives! No, not wives; but why not children?

Peter. You spoke of a schismatical council. Explain.

Julius. It is a long story, but the fact was this. Certain persons had been complaining that the Court of Rome was a nest of abominations. They charged me myself with simony. They said I was a sot, a whoremaster, a son of this world, a scandal to the Christian faith. Things had become so bad that a council must be held to mend them ; and, in fact, they alleged that I had sworn at my instalment to call a council in two years, and that I had been elected on that condition.

Peter. Was it so ?

Julius. Why, yes it was ; but I absolved myself, and now mark what followed. Nine of my cardinals revolt. They require me to keep my word. I refuse. They appeal to the Emperor, and backed by the Emperor and the French king they call a council themselves, thus rending the seamless vesture of Christ.

Peter. But were you guilty of the crimes of which they accused you ?

Julius. That is nothing to the purpose. I was Pontifex Maximus, and if I was fouler than Lerna itself, so long as I hold the keys I am Christ's Vicar, and must be treated as such.

Peter. What, if you are a notorious scoundrel ?

Julius. As notorious as you please. He who is in God's place on earth is quasi-God himself, and is not to be challenged by any little bit of a manikin.

Peter. But we cannot respect a man whom we know to be worthless.

Julius. Thought is free, but speak reverently of the Pope you must. The Pope may not be censured even by a general council.

Peter. He who represents Christ ought to try to be like Christ. But, tell me, is there no way of removing a wicked pope ?

Julius. Absurd ! Who can remove the highest authority of all ?

Peter. That the Pope is the highest is a reason why he should be removed if he causes scandal. Bad princes can be removed. The Church is in a bad way if it must put up with a head who is ruining it.

Julius. A Pope can only be corrected by a general council, but no general council can be held without the Pope's consent ; otherwise it is a synod, and not a council. Let the council sit, it can determine nothing unless the Pope agrees ; and, again, a single pope having absolute power is superior to the council. Thus he cannot be deposed for any crime whatsoever.

Peter. What, not for murder ?

Julius. No, not if it be parricide.

Peter. Not for fornication ?

Julius. Not for incest.

Peter. Not for simony?

Julius. Not for six hundred acts of simony.

Peter. Not for poisoning?

Julius. No, nor for sacrilege.

Peter. Not for blasphemy?

Julius. No, I say.

Peter. Not for all these crimes collected in a single person?

Julius. Add six hundred more to them, there is no power which can depose the Pope of Rome.

Peter. A novel privilege for my successors — to be the wickedest of men, yet be safe from punishment. So much the unhappier the Church which cannot shake such a monster off its shoulders.

Julius. Some say there is one cause for which a Pope can be deposed.

Peter. When he has done a good action, I suppose, since he is not to be punished for his bad actions.

Julius. If he can be convicted publicly of heresy. But this is impossible, too. For he can cancel any canon which he does not like, and should such a charge be preferred in a council he can always recant. There are a thousand loopholes.

Peter. In the name of the papal majesty, who made these fine laws?

Julius. Who? Why, the source of all law, the Pope himself, and the power that makes a law can repeal it.

Peter. Fortunate Pope, who can cheat Christ with his laws. Quite true, the remedy in such a case is not in a council. The people ought to rise with paving stones and dash such a wretch's brains out. But, tell me, why do popes hate general councils?

Julius. Why do kings hate senates and parliaments? Councils are apt to throw the majesty of popes into the shade. There will be able men upon them, men with a conscience who will speak their minds, men who envy us and would like our power to be cut down. Scarce a council ever met which did not leave the Pope weaker than it found him. You experienced it yourself when James pulled you up, and there are some who think to this day that the primacy was in James and not in you.

Peter. Then you think the first object to be considered is not the welfare of the Church, but the supremacy of the Pope?

Julius. Everyone for himself. The Pope's interest is my interest.

Peter. If Christ had thought of His interest there would have been no Church for you to be supreme over. Why should Christ's Vicar be so unlike Him? But tell me how you broke up the schismatic council that you spoke of.

Julius. You shall hear. I first worked on Maximilian, and persuaded him to withdraw his support from France. I then forced the cardinals to deny their own oaths before witnesses.

Peter. Was that right?

Julius. Why not right, if the Pope wills it? An oath is not an oath if the Pope chooses. He can absolve when he pleases. It was a little impudent, but it was the most convenient way. Then, as I did not want to seem to be evading the council, I contrived that I should be myself invited to preside over it. I appealed to a council myself. I merely said that the time and place which had been chosen were unsuitable, and I invited the bishops to meet at Rome. I meant none to attend but my own friends who would support me. I instructed them what to do, and I created a batch of new cardinals who I knew were devoted to me.

Spirit. That is, the greatest rascals.

Julius. I did not want a crowd of abbots and bishops. There might have been honest men among them, so I bade them spare expense and send up one or two only from each province. Even so it seemed there would be too many; so, as they were preparing to start, I sent them word that the council was prorogued, and that they need not come. Then I reverted to my original day, with Rome for the meeting-place. None would be there save those whom I had prepared, and if any should by chance be among them who would not go along with me, I had no fear that, protected as I was, they would venture extremities. This being settled, I appealed against the French rival council. I set out briefs in which I called my council sacrosanct, and their schismatic one a synagogue of Satan.

Peter. Were the opposition cardinals bad men?

Julius. I know no harm of their morals. The Cardinal of Rouen, who was the head of the business, was a sanctimonious fellow, always crying for Church reform. He did reform certain things in his own province. Any way, death relieved me of him, and glad I was of it. Another of them, the Cardinal of St. Cross, a Spaniard, was also a good sort of man, but he was rigid, austere, and given to theology, a class of man always unfriendly to the popes.

Peter. Being a theologian, I presume he could defend the course which he was pursuing.

Julius. Of course he could, and did. He said the Church had never been so disordered, and a council must be held ; that I had myself sworn at my admission that there should be a council in two years ; that I could not be released from my oath without the cardinals' consent ; that I had been again and again reminded of my promise ; that the princes had remonstrated with me ; that all the world maintained that there would be no council while Julius lived ; that if I persisted, the College of Cardinals might call a council, or even the Emperor, the French king, and the other princes might call it.

Peter. Did they propose violent measures against yourself ?

Julius. Indeed, they were far too respectful to me, more so than I wished. They only entreated me to remember my oath, preside over their council, and help them to put the Church in order. This moderation of theirs brought much odium on me. They were learned men besides, men who fasted and prayed and lived within compass, with a reputation for holiness. This also was much against me.

Peter. What pretext did you give for calling your council in opposition to theirs ?

Julius. The best possible. I said I meant to begin the reform with the head of the Church — that is, with myself ; then to go to the princes, and then to the lower orders.

Peter. That is amusing. Well, what next ? What decision did the synagogue of Satan arrive at ?

Julius. Decisions which were horrible, not fit to be mentioned.

Peter. So bad as that ?

Julius. Impious, sacrilegious, worse than heretical. If I had not fought tooth and nail the Church would have been ruined.

Peter. Explain more literally.

Julius. I cannot speak of it without a shudder. They wanted to reduce me, the cardinals, the Court of Rome to the level of the Apostles. Bishops were to cut down their expenses and have fewer servants and horses. Cardinals were not to absorb bishops' sees and abbeys. No bishop to have more sees than one, and to be content with incomes which would not support a parish priest. Popes and bishops were to be only appointed for merit. Wicked popes were to be deposed. Bishops given to drink or fornication were to be suspended, felonious priests to forfeit their benefices and lose life or limb, with much more to the same purpose. Our wealth and power was to be taken from us, and we were to be made into saints.

Peter. And what said your sacrosanct council at Rome to all this?

Julius. I told it what it was to say. Our first meeting was formal. We had two masses, of the Holy Cross and the Holy Ghost, to show that we were acting under Divine inspiration, and then there was a speech in honour of myself. At the next session I cursed the schismatic cardinals. At the third I laid France under an interdict to exasperate the people against the King. The Acts were then drafted into Bulls and sent round Europe.

Peter. And that was all?

Julius. It was all I wanted. I had won. I deprived the cardinals who remained obstinate, and gave their hats to others. I delivered them to Satan. If I could have caught them I would have delivered them to the flames.

Peter. But according to you the acts of the schismatic council were better than yours. Your sacrosanct council only cursed. So it seems that Satan came nearer to Christ than the spirit which was in you.

Julius. Mind your words. My Bulls strike everyone who supports the schismatics.

Peter. You precious rascal! How did it all end?

Julius. I left things in the state I tell you. Fate will decide the rest.

Peter. So there is a schism still?

Julius. Yes, and a bad one.

Peter. And you, who were Christ's Vicar, preferred a schism to a genuine council?

Julius. Better three hundred schisms than be called myself to account.

Peter. Are you so much afraid? Which side will win?

Julius. Our side has most money. France is exhausted, and England has mountains of gold which have not yet been touched. I can only prophesy one thing. If France gets the best, which I don't like to think, there will be a shift of names. My sacrosanct council will be Satan's synod, and I not Pope, but a shadow. They will have had the Holy Spirit, and I the devil. But I left so much treasure behind me that I don't think it will come to this.

Peter. I don't understand about the French. The king of

France is called Most Christian. You say the French helped your election, helped you to take Bologna, and beat the invincible Venetians. How came your alliance to be broken?

Julius. It is a long story. I did n't change; I did what I meant to do all along. I never liked the French; they are barbarians, and no Italian likes barbarians. I used the French as long as I wanted them. I dissembled, lied, and put up with much. But things fell at last into the position I desired. I could then show my colours and drive them out.

Peter. What do you mean by barbarians? Are the French Christians?

Julius. Oh, Christians, yes, if that matters.

Peter. Peasants, I presume — illiterate Christians?

Julius. They are literate enough, and richer than we like.

Peter. Why do you call them barbarians, then? Explain.

Spirit. I will explain for him. The Italians are a conglomerate of all the barbarous nations in the world — a mere heap of dirt; yet they are absurd enough to call everyone a barbarian not born in Italy.

Peter. Perhaps so. But Christ died for all men, and does not respect persons. How can Christ's Vicar reject those whom Christ accepts?

Julius. I accept everyone who will pay me taxes — Indian, African, Arab, or Greek — if they only admit my supremacy; those who will not I cast off, Greeks especially, who are obstinate schismatics.

Peter. So Rome is to be the general treasury of the world?

Julius. May we not reap their carnal things when we sow our spiritual things?

Peter. What spiritual things? You tell me only of worldly things. I suppose you draw souls to Christ with your doctrines?

Julius. We keep preachers if they are wanted. We don't interfere as long as they say nothing against the Pope's supremacy.

Peter. What else can you do?

Julius. What else? How do kings levy revenues? They persuade the people that they owe their fortunes to them, and then they ask, and the people give. So we make the people believe that they owe to us their knowledge of God, though we sleep all our lives. Besides, we sell them indulgences in small matters at a cheap rate, dispensations for not much more, and for blessings we charge nothing.

Peter. This is all Greek to me. But why do you hate the barbarians, and move heaven and earth to get rid of them?

Julius. Because barbarians are superstitious, and the French worst of all.

Peter. Do the French worship other gods besides Christ?

Julius. No; but they have precise notions of what is due to Christ. They use hard words about certain things which we have left off.

Peter. Magical words, I presume?

Julius. No, not magical. They talk of simony and blasphemy, sodomy, poisoning, witchcraft, in language expressing abomination of such actions.

Peter. I do not wish to be personal, but can it be that such crimes are to be found among yourselves, professing Christians?

Julius. The barbarians have vices of their own. They censure ours and forget theirs. We tolerate ours and abominate theirs. Poverty, for instance, we look on as so wicked that anything is justifiable to escape from it, while the barbarians scarcely approve of wealth if innocently come by. We abhor drunkenness, though, for my own part, if time and place suit, I have not much objection to it. The Germans make light of drunkenness, and laugh at it. Barbarians forbid usury; we regard it as a necessary institution. They think looseness with women polluting and disgusting; we — well, we do not think so at all. They are shocked at simony; we never mention it. They stick to old laws and customs; we go for novelty and progress. While our views of life are so different, we don't like to have the barbarians too close to us. They have sharp eyes. They write letters about us to our friends. They say Rome is no See of Christ, but a sink of the devil. They ask whether, having acquired the Papacy as I did, I am a proper Pope at all. Thus my name is brought into discredit, while, if their spies had not been among us, it would never have been heard of, and I should have remained Christ's vicegerent and a god upon earth. Thus the Church suffers: we sell fewer dispensations, and get a worse price for them, and we receive less money for bishoprics and abbeys and colleges; worst of all, people are no longer frightened at our thunderbolts. Once let them think that a wicked Pope cannot hurt them, we shall be starved out. So we mean to keep the barbarian at a distance. He will then respect us as he used to do, and we can communicate with him through Briefs and Bulls.

Peter. Respect which rests on ignorance will not perhaps last. In our time all the world was welcome to know what we were doing. How comes it that the princes are so ready to take up arms for you, while to us they were the worst enemy that we had?

Julius. The princes are not so particularly Christian — on the contrary, they hold us in sovereign contempt. But the weaker sort among their subjects are still afraid of being excommunicated, and the princes are obliged to consider their opinions. Then we are rich, and this commands a certain deference; and there is a superstitious impression that it is unlucky to quarrel with priests. We have ceremonials which impose upon the vulgar. We give the princes grand titles, call one Catholic, another Serene Highness, another Augustus, and all of them our Beloved Sons. They in turn call us Holy Father, and now and then kiss our foot. We send them consecrated roses, cups, and swords, and Bulls confirming their rights to their crowns. They make us presents of soldiers, money, and now and then a boy or two. So it goes on — as the Proverb says, "Mule scratches mule."

Peter. I still do not understand why the princes broke their treaties and went to war on your account.

Julius. Listen then, and you will see how clever I am. First I studied the humour of each nation, which agreed with which, and which was hostile to which. There was an old grievance between the French and the Venetians. The French wanted to increase their territory. The Venetians held towns which the French claimed; again, the Venetians held positions which the Emperor wanted: so I easily brought France and the Empire into line against the Venetians. The French were too successful, so I next stirred up Spain to check them. The Spaniards were afraid for their possessions in Naples, and were jealous of the French advance in Italy. I did not love the Venetians, but I made use of them in the same way while they were sore at their defeats. I had first brought the Emperor Maximilian into alliance with the French. When the French were growing too strong, I worked on his old animosities and divided him from them. The English have an hereditary hatred of France, and also an old feud with the Scots, who are a fierce race, eager for war and plunder. The English king had just died. The people had broken loose and were ready for mischief. His successor, luckily for us, was a restless, ambitious young prince, whose dream as a child had been the recovery of the French provinces. All these cards I played in the interest of the Church, and thus easily brought on a general war. I gratified the Emperor, the Spaniards, and the English with the honest title of the Church's Protectors, to encourage them to work the more destruction among Christian nations. The Spanish king was at that moment at war with the Turks. He dropped it, left his proper business on my account, and threw his whole strength on France. Nowhere in the world is the Pope less regarded than in England. Read the story of their St. Thomas of Canterbury and their old Constitutions, and you will be in no doubt of that. They don't like parting with their money either; but they let me swallow them at a mouthful. Their clergy, generally so stingy, opened their purses. The princes paid no heed to the precedent which they were sanctioning when they let a Roman bishop depose a sovereign whom he hated. Indeed, the young king of England took up my quarrel more hotly than I desired, though of course it was well that he should err on the right side. I need not follow the story further. I, by my own cleverness, contrived a combination against a Christian State, which no one of my predecessors had been even able to form against the Turks.

Peter. You have lit a fire which may spread over the world.

Julius. Let it spread, so the Holy See keeps its supremacy and its possessions. I contrived, however, to throw the burden of the war from the Italians to the barbarians. Let them fight as they will, while we look on and make our profit of their madness.

Peter. Does this befit your position as Holy Father and Vicar of Christ?

Julius. Why did the French make a schism?

Peter. We must bear with things which we shall make worse by trying to mend them. But, if you had allowed their council, there would have been no schism.

Julius. God forbid! Better six hundred wars than a council. Suppose I had been deposed for simony! Suppose the council had looked into my life and published an account of it!

Peter. Even if you had been rightly Pope, you would have done better to resign than to have caused such a torrent of misery in defending your dignity. Fine dignity bought or stolen by a rascal! The French have been rightly punished for helping your election.

Julius. By my triple crown and by my victories, I will make you know who Julius is if you provoke me further.

Peter. Poor worldly madman — or not even worldly: Gentile and worse than Gentile — will you boast of your treaty-breaking and your accursed wars? These are Satan's arts, not a pope's. A Vicar of Christ should be like Christ. Christ has sovereign power, but He has sovereign goodness, sovereign wisdom, sovereign simplicity. Power with you is joined with madness and vanity. If Satan needed a vicar, he could find none fitter than you. What sign have you ever shown of an apostle?

Julius. Is it not apostolic to increase Christ's Church?

Peter. The Church is a community of Christians with Christ's Spirit in them. You have been a subverter of the Church.

Julius. The Church consists of cathedrals, and priests, and the Court of Rome, and myself at the head of it.

Peter. Christ is our Head, and we are His ministers. Are there two Heads? How have you increased the Church?

Julius. I found it poor: I have made it splendid.

Peter. Splendid with what? With faith?

Julius. Nonsense.

Peter. With doctrine?

Julius. A fig for doctrine.

Peter. With contempt of the world?

Julius. These are words. I have made it splendid with fact.

Peter. How?

Julius. I have filled Rome with palaces, trains of mules and horses, troops of servants, armies and officers.

Spirit. With scarlet women and the like.

Julius. With purple and gold, with revenues so vast that kings are poor beside the Roman Pontiff. Glory, luxury, hoards of treasure, these are splendours, and these all I have created.

Peter. Pray, inform me. The Church had nothing of all this when it was founded by Christ. Whence came all this splendour, as you call it?

Julius. No matter whence. We have it and we enjoy it. They say Constantine made a present to Pope Sylvester of the empire of the world. I don't believe it. None but a fool would have given away an empire. But it stops the mouths of people who ask questions.

Peter. At any rate, this is the worldly side. How about the other?

Julius. You are thinking of the old affair, when you starved as Pope, with a handful of poor hunted bishops about you. Time has changed all that, and much for the better. You had only the name of Pope. Look now at our gorgeous churches, our priests by thousands; bishops like kings, with retinues and palaces; cardinals in their purple gloriously attended, horses and mules decked with gold and jewels, and shod with gold and silver. Beyond all, myself, Supreme Pontiff, borne on soldiers' shoulders in a golden chair, and waving my hand majestically to adoring crowds. Hearken to the roar of the cannon, the bugle notes, the boom of the drums. Observe the military engines, the shouting populace, torches blazing in street and square, and the kings of the earth scarce admitted to kiss my Holiness's foot. Behold the Roman Bishop placing the crown on the head of the Emperor, who seems to be made king of kings, yet is but the shadow of a name. Look at all this, and tell me it is not magnificent!

Peter. I look at a very worldly tyrant, an enemy of Christ and a disgrace to the Church.

Julius. You would not say so had you seen me carried in state at Bologna and at Rome after the war with Venice, or when I beat the French at Ravenna. Those were spectacles. Carriages and horses, troops under arms, generals prancing and galloping, lovely boys, torches flaming, dishes steaming, pomp of bishops, glory of cardinals, trophies, spoils, shouts that rent the heavens, trumpets blaring, cannon thundering, money scattered among the mob, and I carried aloft, the head and author of it all! Scipio and Cæsar were nothing by the side of me.

Peter. Enough, enough, most valorous boaster. Those heathens were human compared to you — you, who triumphed because so many thousand Christians had been slain for your ambition; you, a Holy Father in Christ, who never did good to any single soul in word or deed — precious Father, worthy vicar of Him who spent himself that He might save all; you, who have spread desolation through the world for the sake of your own single pestilent self!

Julius. Mere envy! You perceive what a poor wretch of a bishop you were compared to me.

Peter. Insolent wretch! Dare you compare your glory with mine? — and mine was Christ's, and not my own. Christ gave to me the keys of the Kingdom of Heaven, trusted His sheep to my feeding and sealed my faith with His approval. Fraud, usury, and cunning made you Pope, if Pope you are to be called.

I gained thousands of souls to Christ: you have destroyed as many thousands. I brought heathen Rome to acknowledge Christ: you have made it heathen again. I healed the sick, cast out devils, restored the dead to life, and brought a blessing with me where I went. What blessings have you and your triumphs brought? I used my power for the good of all: you have used yours to crush and vex mankind.

Julius. You have not told the whole. You have left out of your list poverty, vigils, toils, prisons, chains, blows, and the cross to end with.

Peter. You do well to remind me. I glory in those sufferings more than in miracles. It was in them that Christ bade us rejoice, and called us blessed. Paul did not talk of the cities which he had stormed, the legions which he had slaughtered, the princes whom he had entangled in war: he talked of shipwrecks, bonds, disgraces, stripes. These were his apostolic triumphs, these were the glories of a Christian general. When he boasted, it was of the souls whom he had recovered from Satan, not of his piles of ducats. For us even the wicked had good words, while you every tongue of man has been taught to curse.

Julius. All this is news to me.

Peter. Very likely. With your treaties and your protocols, your armies and your victories, you had no time to read the Gospels. The discipline of Christ will not work on a mind absorbed in this world. Our Master did not come from heaven to teach an easy philosophy. To be a Christian is no idle profession. To be a Christian is to be careless of pleasure, to tread riches under foot as dirt, and count life as nothing. And because the rule is hard, men turn to empty forms and ceremonies, and create a spurious body of Christ for a spurious head.

Julius. Do you mean to say I am to give up money, dominion, revenues, pleasures, life? Will you leave me to misery?

Peter. Yes, if you count Christ as miserable. He who was Lord of all became the scorn of all, endured poverty, endured labour, fasting, and hunger, and ended with a death of shame.

Julius. Very admirable, no doubt. But He will not find many imitators in these times of ours.

Peter. To admire is to imitate. Christ takes nothing good from any man. He takes what is falsely called good, to give him instead eternal truth, as soon as he is purged from the taint of the world. Being Himself heavenly, He will have His

Church like Him, estranged from the world's corruption, and those who are sunk in pollution can not resemble One who is sitting in heaven. Once for all, fling away your imagined wealth, and receive instead what is far better.

Julius. What, I beseech you?

Peter. The gift of prophecy, the gift of knowledge, the gift of miracles, Christ Himself. The more a man is afflicted in the world the greater his joy in Christ, the poorer in the world the richer in Christ, the more cast down in the world the more exalted in Christ. Christ will have His followers pure, and most of all His ministers, the bishops. The higher in rank they are the more like Christ they are bound to be, and the less entangled in earthly pleasures. Yet you, the bishop next to Christ, who make yourself equal with Christ, think only of money, and arms, and treaties, to say nothing of vicious pleasures, and you abuse His name to support your own vanities. You claim the honour due to Christ, while you are Christ's enemy. You bless others, you are yourself accursed. You pretend to have the keys of heaven, and you are yourself shut out from it. You consecrate, being yourself execrable; you excommunicate, when with the saints you have no communion; you pretend to be a Christian, you are not superior to a Turk, you think like a Turk, you are as licentious as a Turk. If there is any difference, you are the worse.

Julius. All I wanted was to secure for the Church as much good as possible—goods of fortune, goods of body, and goods of soul, according to Aristotle's division. I kept the order. I began with the first, and would have gone on to the other two if death had not overtaken me before my time.

Peter. Before your time? Why you are in your seventies.

Julius. The world will not respect us, and the Church will go to pieces if we are poor and can't defend ourselves. Money is power. They may hate us while we are rich, but they can't despise us.

Peter. If the world saw the gifts of Christ in you, saw you holy, learned, charitable, virtuous, it would think more, not less, of you for being poor. If Christians had no care for riches, or pleasure, or empire, if they were not afraid of death, then the Church would flourish again. It withers now because Christians have ceased to exist except in name. Did you never reflect, you who were supreme shepherd, how the Church began in this world, how it grew, how it strengthened itself?—not by war, not by horses, not by gold ingots; but by suffering, by the blood of martyrs, my own among the rest, by imprisonments and stripes. You think you have added to the Church's greatness by troops of officials, or raised its character when you have polluted it with sumptuous expenditure, or defended its interests when you have set all nations fighting that priests may divide the spoil. You call the Church flourishing when it is drunk with luxury, and tranquil when it can enjoy its wealth and its pleasant vices with none to reprove, and when you have taught the princes to call killing and plundering by the fine name of defense of the Church.

Julius. I have heard this sort of thing before.

Peter. Did you ever hear it in your preachers' sermons?

Julius. I never heard anything in their sermons but my own praises. They exulted in what I did. They called me the Jove who shook the world with my thunder. They said I was a real god, the saviour of mankind, and such like.

Peter. No wonder none was found to speak the truth to you. Salt you were without savour, and a fool besides.

Julius. Then you won't open the gates?

Peter. Sooner to anyone than to such as you. We are not of your communion in this place. You have an army of sturdy rogues behind you, you have money, and you are a famous architect. Go build a paradise of your own, and fortify it, lest the devils break in on you.

Julius. I will do better than that. I will wait a few months till I have a larger force, and then if you don't give in I will take your place by storm. They are making fine havoc just now. I shall soon have sixty thousand ghosts behind me.

Peter. Oh, wretched man! Oh, miserable Church! You, Spirit, I must speak with you; I can say no more to this monster. Are the bishops generally like this one?

Spirit. A good part of them. But he is the top, far and away.

Peter. Was it you who tempted him to commit all these crimes?

Spirit. Not I. He went too fast. I must have had wings to keep abreast of him.

Peter. I am not surprised that so few apply here now for admission, when the Church has such rulers. Yet there must be good in the world, too, when such a sink of iniquity can be honoured, merely because he bears the name of Pope.

Spirit. That is the real truth — But my master beckons to me and lifts his stick. Adieu!

LECTURE IX.

Erasmus was not allowed to leave England without an effort in the highest quarters to detain him. When he waited on the King to take leave, Henry offered him a house, with a pension of 600 florins, if he would stay. The Cardinal of York, the second king, as Erasmus called Wolsey, was gracious and warm. Erasmus neither accepted nor declined. For the present he was in correspondence with the Court of Brussels, and thither it was necessary for him to go. The King's liberality was in promises. The Bishop of Durham presented him with six angels (angel equals ten shillings), Warham and Fisher with as much more. It was rumoured in Holland that he was returning with a fortune. This was the whole of it. Lord Mountjoy had been made Governor of Hammes Castle, in the Calais Pale. Erasmus was to be his guest there for a few days after crossing the Channel. He sailed (we have here a welcome fixed date) from Dover, July 8, 1514, with a calm sea and a fair wind, fortune otherwise being foul as usual. The Custom-house officers did not seize his money this time, but they detained his luggage with his MSS. Probably he spoke English ill, and could not explain himself. He made the air ring with his clamours, called them robbers, assured himself that they had stolen the labours of his life to sell his papers back to him at their own price. In a few hours or days he and his possessions were safe in

Hammes Castle, where another unpleasant surprise was waiting for him. He was still a monk at large from his convent under the temporary dispensation which the Bishop of Cambray had obtained for him nearly thirty years before. He was then an insignificant boy. He was now a dangerous spiritual force. To reduce Erasmus under a rule which he had deserted and ridiculed would be a triumph worth having in the contest which was now raging. A letter reached him at Hammes from Father Servatius, the prior of the convent from which he had been rescued, putting various questions prescribed by the rules of the order, as to how he had been employed in his absence, how he had lived, what sins he had committed, and inviting him to return. Erasmus replied with a courteous but peremptory refusal.[1]

HAMMES CASTLE, *July*, 1514.

Your letter, after following me about England, has just reached my hands. I have nothing to reproach myself with. Age and experience have corrected my early follies. I left my profession not because I had any fault to find with it, but because I would not be a scandal to the order. You know that I was forced into it by interested guardians. My constitution was too weak to bear your rule. I had a passion for literature. I knew that I could be happy and useful as a man of letters. But to break the vow was held a crime, and I endeavored to bear my misery. My profession was a mistake. You will say that there was the year of probation, and that I might have known my own mind. What can a boy of seventeen brought up on books know of his mind? I was released. I was left to my own will to choose such form of life as would suit me, and I was lucky enough to find friends who saved me from falling into mischief.

[1] *Ep.* viii., second series, abridged.

I say nothing of my writings. You, perhaps, despise them; though there are persons who believe them to be not without merit. But I have not sought money, and have little sought fame. Pleasures have tempted me, but I have not been their slave, and grossness I have always abhorred. What should I gain by rejoining you? I should be an object of malice, envy, and contemptuous tittle-tattle. Your festivals have no flavour of Christ, and your way of life does not edify me. My health is still weak. I should be useless to you, and to myself it would be death. I can drink nothing but wine. I have to be nice in what I eat. Too well I know your climate and the character of your food, to say nothing of your manners. I should die of it, I know. You may say I cannot die better than among my brethren. I am not so sure of that. Your religion is in your dress. You think it sin to change from a white frock to a black, or from a hood to a cap. Your religious orders, as you call them, have done the Church small service. They divided among themselves; indulgences followed, and dispensations, and nothing is worse than relaxed religion. There is no religion left in it save forms, which please the monks' vanity, and make them fancy themselves superior to the rest of mankind. You ask me if I do not wish for a quiet home, where I can rest in my old age. Solon and Pythagoras travelled. Plato travelled, and the Apostles, specially St. Paul. I do not compare myself to them. But when I have moved about it has been for my health or for my work. I have been invited to Spain, Italy, Germany, France, England, and Scotland by the most distinguished people there. I am well liked at Rome. The cardinals and the present Pope treated me like a brother. I am not rich, and I do not wish to be rich; but I have learning, which they value in Italy, though you Netherlanders care little for it. The English bishops are proud of my acquaintance. The King writes me affectionate letters; the Queen would have had me for a tutor, and have kept me at Court if I would have consented. The Archbishop of Canterbury could not have been kinder had he been my father. He gave me a benefice, and changed it at my desire for a pension. One day he gave me 150 crowns. Other bishops gave me large sums, and Lord Mountjoy a second pension. The King and the Bishop of Lincoln (Wolsey) both wish to keep me in England. Oxford and Cambridge are ready to receive me, and there is more piety and temperance in the colleges there than in any houses of religion. Dean Colet has no friend whom he values as he values me.

As to my writings, good judges say that I write better than any other man living. Were I with *you* I could do nothing at all. The climate would disagree with me. I left you a vigorous youth. I am now a grey-headed invalid. The basest of the base would despise me, and I am accustomed to the respect of the greatest. You undertake to make me comfortable. I know not what you mean. Am I to be an upper servant in a sisterhood, I who have never served either king or prelate? I want no money. I need no stipend. I have enough for health and leisure. I propose now to go to Bâle to print some books. The winter I shall perhaps spend at Rome. On my return, I shall perhaps pay you a visit.

The prior had been polite, and had not hinted at compulsion. But Erasmus knew the persons that he had to deal with. The monks were exasperated, and were formidable. He had no longer the protection of the Bishop of Cambray; and by law and custom the order might call on the civil power to arrest a brother absent without leave, or who had broken the implied conditions of non-residence. He made haste to secure himself, and it was on this occasion that he wrote the account of himself under the name of Florence of which I have already read a part to you in my description of his early years. The remainder is equally interesting, as well as the result which came of it. It was addressed, as you may remember, to the Protonotary at Rome, and was meant for the Pope's eye. Erasmus's special danger was in his having abandoned the dress of his order. Monks who had dispensations for absence were required by the canons to wear publicly some distinctive part of their costume. Julius II. had allowed Erasmus to wear this or to drop it as he pleased. Perhaps it was held that his licence had expired with the Pope's life, and he was now answerable for a breach of the law. He threw himself on the protection of Julius's successor.[1]

To continue this story, then, where I left it.

TO LAMBERT GRUNNIUS.[2]

Florence[3] went to Paris to follow up his studies. He wore his scapulary over his frock, and his life was twice in danger through it. The physicians who attended the plague patients were ordered to avoid the public streets, and to wear a white scarf that people might know them and keep out of their way. Florence was unaware of the rule. One day he was seen with his scapulary in an open thoroughfare. It was mistaken for the doctor's scarf. He was mobbed, and would have been killed had not a woman called out that he was a priest.

Another day he was hunted by a crowd, and, being unable to speak French, he could neither understand them nor explain. Someone told him that the people were excited by his scapulary, and that he would lose his life if he continued to appear in it.

After this he wore it under his cloak, to the great indignation of those who thought religion lay in dress. A Franciscan or a Dominican who conceals his profession is held an abandoned villain. The Dominican's frock, it is held, will save a dead man from hell if it is thrown over his body.

[1] See pages 5–16.

[2] *Ep.* ccccxlii., second series, abridged.

[3] The name under which Erasmus describes himself.

Nevertheless, the papal decretals permit the laying aside of the monastic dress for adequate reason. Augustine says [Erasmus had been an Augustinian] nothing about clothes, and only insists on morals. Florence knew this, but to be on the safe side he obtained a dispensation releasing him from the scapulary provided he wore some other mark of his order on some part of his person. He was told when he went to England that he must not show his scapulary in public under any condition. Forms which are required in one country may be forbidden in another. Florence moved in high society, and had to conform to usage. To change backwards and forwards created scandal; so at friends' advice, and trusting to the Pope's licence, he adopted the costume of a secular priest. The monastic vow itself he regarded as slavery. The New Testament knows nothing of monastic vows. Christ says the Sabbath was made for man, and not man for the Sabbath; and when such institutions do more harm than good there ought to be easier means of escaping from them than are now provided. The Pharisees of the Church will break the Sabbath for an ox or an ass, but will not relax an inch of their rule to save a perishing soul.

There are monasteries where there is no discipline, and which are worse than brothels — *ut præ his lupanaria sint et magis sobria et magis pudica.* There are others where religion is nothing but ritual; and these are worse than the first, for the Spirit of God is not in them, and they are inflated with self-righteousness. There are those, again, where the brethren are so sick of the imposture that they keep it up only to deceive the vulgar. The houses are rare indeed where the rule is seriously observed, and even in these few, if you look to the bottom, you will find small sincerity. But there is craft, and plenty of it — craft enough to impose on mature men, not to say innocent boys; and this is called *profession.* Suppose a house where all is as it ought to be, you have no security that it will continue so. A good superior may be followed by a fool or a tyrant, or an infected brother may introduce a moral plague. True, in extreme cases a monk may change his house, or even may change his order, but leave is rarely given. There is always a suspicion of something wrong, and on the least complaint such a person is sent back. And besides, how can he know that the house to which he goes is better than the house which he is leaving? The change is but a throw of the dice. He may find himself worse off than he was.

Young men are fooled and cheated into joining these orders. Once in the toils, they are broken in and trained into Pharisees. They may repent, but the superiors will not let them go, lest they should betray the orgies which they have witnessed. They crush them down with scourge and penance, the secular arm, chanceries and dungeons. Nor is this the worst. Cardinal Matteo[1] said at a public dinner before a large audience, naming place and persons, that the Dominicans had buried a young man alive whose father demanded his son's release. A Polish noble who had fallen asleep in a church saw two Franciscans buried alive; yet these wretches called themselves the representatives of Benedict and Basil and Jerome. A monk may be drunk every day. He may go with loose women secretly or openly. He may waste the Church's money on vicious pleasures. He may be a quack or a charlatan, and all the while be an excellent brother and fit to be made an abbot; while one who for the best of reasons lays aside his frock is howled at as an apostate.[2] Surely the true apostate is he who goes into sensuality, pomp, vanity, the lusts of the flesh, the sins which he renounced at his baptism. All of us would think him a worse man than the other if the commonness of such characters did not hide their deformity. Monks of abandoned lives notoriously swarm over Christendom.

[1] "*Matthæus Cardinalis Sedunensis*," an intimate personal acquaintance of Erasmus.

[2] "Qui in sacrâ veste indulget quotidianæ temulentiæ, qui gulæ servit et ventri, qui scortatur clam et palam, nihil enim addam obscœnius, qui luxu profundit Ecclesiæ pecuniam, probus est monachus et vocatur ad abbatiam," etc.

These are the true apostates, and on them the hated name ought to fall though they may still wear the cowl.

Is it not wicked, then, my friend, to entangle young men by false representations in such an abominable net? Monks whose lives are openly infamous draw boys after them into destruction. The convent at best is but a miserable bondage, and if there be outward decency (as among so many there must be some undepraved), a knot which cannot be loosed may be still fatal to soul and body.

It is pretended that novices are not admitted till mature age. Maturity suffices for marriage, why not for the monastic profession? Yet men have joined at thirty, and have been aghast at what they found. They had been taken in by specious words. The orders talk of purity as if they were themselves pure; of obedience, as if while obeying man they were not disobeying God; of irrevocable vows, when no vows ought to be irrevocable. They quote their Scotus to prove that a monk's vow cannot be recalled because it is made to God. These orders depend for their existence upon the Pope; yet let the Pope for cause shown set a monk at liberty, they defy him, they deny his authority, they accuse him of a crime. As long as he does what they please, he is Vicar of Christ and cannot err; when he thwarts them, they say he is but an ordinary man.

I do not condemn the regular orders as such. If there are persons for whom the rule is salutary, the vow may stand. But the more sacred the profession, the more caution must be observed in the admission to it. There must be no influencing, or violence or terror. It ought not to bind when a frightened lad has had the halter forced upon him. Shame on a law which says that a vow taken when the down is on the cheek is of perpetual obligation! Florence was goaded into it. They made him wear the dress, but they never had his consent. His oath was but an oath sworn to so many pirates. The Pope will surely disown these villains and protect their victims. What is the charge which they bring against Florence? That he does not wear the scapulary outside. Who knows that he does not wear it inside? If he does not wear it at all, who knows his reasons? The Pope gave him leave. If the Pope is absolute in other things, why not in this? What is their obedience worth when they will hear neither God nor man? They call themselves dead to the world, while unspeakable enormities are daily brought home to them.

It is hateful to taunt a man with a misfortune which the malice of others has caused. If a mule has broken a man's leg, who is brute enough to insult him for being lame? If he has lost an eye in a battle, do we ridicule his blindness? Do we sneer at a shipwrecked mariner who is reduced to beggary? or at a leper or an epileptic who has inherited his disorder from his parents? Men deserving to be called men pity and relieve the helpless; and is a wretched being who has fled from an order into which he was thrust to be reviled as an apostate? If to leave them was a fault, the guilt is with his accusers. We do not blame a man for flying from a pirates' nest, and those who rob another of his liberty are pirates to him. Or, to use a milder comparison, if a cobbler makes an ill-fitting boot for a customer, and the customer refuses to wear it, the cobbler will be a fool if he quarrels with him. The customer will say the boot may be a good boot in itself, but is not a good boot for him. An institution may be useful for one person and may be deadly to another.

To make an end, my dear friend. If I have made out a case for Florence, I entreat you to see his release dispatched to him with all possible speed. Spare no expense; I will be responsible. In the open space at the bottom I have noted a few points in cipher, to be particularly attended to in the diploma. I send the key in another letter. You must hold the paper to the fire.

Before I come to the answer of the Prothonotary, I have a few observations to make on this letter itself.

First, that Florence was undoubtedly Erasmus himself, and was so understood to be by the Roman authorities. The story of Florence corresponds exactly with what we know from the other sources to have been Erasmus's own story. Erasmus says at the beginning that Florence was intimately known to him, and that he had himself been an eye-witness of much that he was relating.

There is really no doubt about the matter, and I have made confident use of this letter as autobiographical, in common with Bayle, Jortin, and other biographers.

But the letter is of larger importance as an evidence of the condition of the religious houses at the time when Erasmus was writing. Whether Florence was or was not Erasmus himself, the account which he gives of monastic profligacy he gives deliberately as his own, and he speaks of it as something too well known to the Pope to need further proof. He quotes Cardinal Matteo as publicly accusing the Dominicans of murder, mentioning name and place. It is boldly said now that the charges against the religious houses in England were invented as an excuse for their dissolution; and in accepting this version of the suppression in our authoritative histories we not only accept the innocence of the monks, but we degrade and disgrace the English Privy Council and the English Parliament. What business have we to pass such summary sentence? Erasmus was not tempting the cupidity of kings, or appealing to the passions of mobs. He was addressing the Prothonotary of the Apostolic See. His letter was to be read in conclave to pope and cardinals. If he had lied or had exaggerated, if every word which he wrote had not been known to be the truth, he would have ruined himself and his cause. You are students of history; you know that you have no right to set evidence aside, to adapt it to your own prepossessions. Neither Thomas Cromwell nor Cromwell's visitors, nor the Act of Parliament which speaks of the manifest sin in the religious houses, spoke so harshly of them as Erasmus did to Leo X. and to the heads of the Church of Rome in this letter.

The answer of the Prothonotary is equally instructive. Leo respected Erasmus, recognised his value, admired his talents, and did not choose that he should be dragged back into a nest of infuriated rattlesnakes.

Never in my life (writes Lambert Grunnius in reply[1]) have I undertaken a commission more willingly than this with which you have now entrusted me. I have settled it in a form which I hope will be satisfactory to you. Unfortunate Florence! The cruelty of his fate has moved me even more than my affection for yourself. I read your letter aloud to the Pope from end to end; several cardinals and other great persons were present. The Holy Father was charmed with your style, and was more indignant than one could have believed to be possible. Those abominable scoundrels! The greater the respect of the Pope for genuine piety, the more displeased is he at the dishonour done to the Christian religion by the multiplication of miserable and wicked monks. He says that Christ is pleased with sacrifice when it is freely offered, but He will have no workhouses of slaves. He directs that your diploma shall be made out free of costs. I have given three ducats to the clerks and notaries to be quick with their work. You know what those fellows are—you must fling a sop or two to Cerberus. Farewell! Salute Florence for me. He is now our common friend.

Free now, and with no more to fear from vengeful monks, Erasmus went first on business to Antwerp,

[1] *Ep.* ccccxliii., second series.

and then hastened to present himself at Brussels. He called on the Chancellor of the Empire, and was received with humorous politeness. He was drawn to the front of the brilliant circle which formed the Court of the young Archduke Charles. "This fellow," the Chancellor said, introducing Erasmus to them, "does not know his value. Are you aware," he said to him before all the world, "that the Archduke wishes to make a bishop of you? He has chosen you a diocese, not a bad one, in Sicily; and, finding it was not among the sees reserved to the Crown, he has written to beg the Pope to let you have it." Erasmus had not the least intention of being made into a bishop. He was glad, he said, to find the Chancellor and the Prince so well disposed to him. More signal evidence could not have been given either by Pope or Archduke that they did not mean to be beaten by the reactionary party in the Church than the proposal to promote Erasmus to episcopal rank in the face of so furious a clamour. He implied, however, that he would be more than satisfied by a less onerous promotion; and, in fact, a considerable additional pension was promised him under the single condition that he should reside in the Archduke's dominions. Charles wished to take him into Spain in his own suite. But this, too, would not answer for the work which he had to do. Louvain was thought of for him, and it was not at first to his taste. Writing to his friend Ammonius, he says:—

At Louvain I should be the maid-of-all-work to the University. It would be "Amend this poem," "Correct this epistle," "Edit this or that edict." Not a soul in the place would do me any good. I should have the theologians on my back; and I regret to say

I do not love those gentry. One of them has begun at me already, and I have the wolf by the ears. I cannot crush him, and I cannot let him go. He flatters me to my face. He abuses me behind my back. He professes friendship. He is my enemy at heart. He belongs to a class of men who can make us neither better nor wiser, but can worry our lives out.

The edition of Jerome was being printed at Bâle by the famous Froben. Erasmus had to go there to superintend the work, which was to be dedicated to the Pope. He intended, if he could, to go on afterwards to Rome, and thank Leo in person for the service which had been rendered to him. In the midst of his printing he was making time to write an "Educational Institute" for Prince Charles. Most of all he was taken up with the battle of the languages, and the attacks, too successful, by the monastic enemies of Greek on his friend Reuchlin, which were echoing over Germany. Rome, which had protected Erasmus, might protect Reuchlin. "Proximus ardet Ucalegon." If Reuchlin was overwhelmed, Erasmus might be the next victim himself. Anxiously he wrote to the cardinals: —

What a disgrace will it be (he said) if a man so learned, so accomplished as Reuchlin, who has made the world richer by his presence in it, is to be sacrificed in the autumn of his life, when he has deserved only praise and honour. What a stir is raised about him, and all for nothing. I can only say that if a man will examine Jerome in the same spirit which they are showing about Reuchlin, the theologians will find plenty in him which they will not like the taste of. All the country is indignant. We look to you at Rome to save him.

I have mentioned Reuchlin before, but you will wish for a word or two more about him.

He was among the first of the distinguished scholars who introduced the study of Hebrew and Greek into Germany, and was thus, in fact, the father of modern Bible criticism. He was born at Baden in 1455, and was twelve years older than Erasmus. He came early under the notice of the Emperor Maximilian, who assisted and encouraged him. The jealousy of Hebrew among the clergy extended to the Hebrew race. A Jew-baiting cry was easily raised, and the orthodox German Church began to demand through the mouth of a convert (Pfeffercorn) that all Hebrew books except the Bible should be burned. Reuchlin induced Maximilian to suspend so absurd a proposal. The Dominicans, who hated Reuchlin already, turned upon him, denounced a passage in one of his writings as heretical to the Inquisition, and the Inquisition, as it could not burn the Talmud, was willing to take Reuchlin in exchange. Young Germany, led by Ulrich von Hutten, swore that if Reuchlin was burnt, the Church should smoke for it. The Emperor could not afford to quarrel with the Inquisition. Reuchlin was suspended from his office and imprisoned, while the question what was to be done with him was referred to the Pope. The Pope delayed his answer till the next year, when Reuchlin was forgotten in the storm of the Reformation. Meanwhile he was in imminent danger of the stake, and it is to Erasmus's credit that he was willing to run risks in Reuchlin's defence which he was afterwards not the least inclined to run for Luther.

In supporting Reuchlin (he wrote to Cardinal Raphael[1]) you will earn the gratitude of every man of letters in Germany. It is to him really that Germany owes such knowledge as it has of Greek and

[1] *Ep.* clxviii.

Hebrew. He is a learned, accomplished man, respected by the Emperor, honoured among his own people, and blameless in life and character. All Europe is crying shame that so excellent a person should be harrassed by a detestable prosecution, and all for a matter as absurd as the ass's shadow of the proverb. The princes are at peace again. Why should men of education and knowledge be still stabbing each other with poisoned pens? Julius II. rescued another friend of ours from a prosecution of the same kind, and silenced his accusers. Anyone who will give us Reuchlin back safe and sound will deserve all our blessings.

The Roman visit had to be abandoned. The incessant reprints of his books, the attacks upon his New Testament, and the corrections and additions found necessary obliged Erasmus to remain on the spot. He had to make Louvain his head-quarters, within easy reach of Brussels, and for several years his time was divided between Louvain and Froben's printing establishment at Bâle.

From Louvain he writes in 1517 to his friend Pirkheimer, while the Reuchlin controversy was still raging:[1]—

I live here at great expense, but I must remain for a few months longer to finish the work which I have in hand, and see what comes of the Chancellor's promises. I am busy with a new edition of my New Testament. The first was done too hastily. I am making a fresh book of it. I am delighted that you have stood up for Reuchlin. Poor Reuchlin! What a fight he is having, and with what enemies! The Pope himself is afraid to provoke the monks. Alexander VI. used to say that it was less dangerous to provoke the most powerful prince in Europe than offend the meanest of the mendicant friars. Those wretches in the disguise of poverty are the tyrants of

[1] *Ep.* cclxxiv., abridged.

the Christian world, and a precious leader they have in their assaults on Reuchlin — a fool with a forehead of brass, and himself more than half a Jew. The devil himself, the eternal enemy of Christ, could devise no fitter instrument to disturb the peace of Christendom in the name of religion than such a child of hell disguised as an angel of light. It is a shame to Europe. Here is a man who deserves immortal honour reduced to crossing swords with a monster whose name would pollute my papers. I believe the creature was only baptized that he might the better poison people's minds — a veritable Satan, Diabolus, slanderer, going among foolish women and canting about heresy and the need of defending the faith.

What is to happen if such an impure beast as this is allowed to rage against men of learning and reputation, and to force them on their defence? Believe me, it will not end here. Mischief will come of it. A small spark will kindle a large fire. The bishops ought to stir themselves. The Emperor should look to it. Such a viper ought not to be tolerated.

Reuchlin's friends were not idle. The "Epistolæ obscurorum Virorum" made Pfeffercorn the jest of Europe. Other satires followed. The air was thick with libels on the monks. The "Epistolæ" were anonymous. The monks insisted that Erasmus must have written them. Only Erasmus, the Antichrist, the heretic, the schismatic, was capable of so horrible an enormity. Erasmus, safe under the protection of the Emperor and the Holy See, left them to snarl, and finished his "Jerome," which he proceeded to lay at the feet of Leo, with a request to be allowed to dedicate his labours to him. He knew how to flatter, and he was really under deep obligations to Leo.

The greatest princes (he said) might tremble at writing to the Pope, who was as far above other men as other men were above the beasts of the field. But the kindness of Leo X. gave him courage.

Men of letters praised God for such a pastor. The Medici were the immortal patrons of culture and knowledge. Leo was the greatest of them all — the perfect man of Plato — gold tried in the fire — born to triumph over all difficulties. When Leo was raised to the throne the iron age became golden. War ceased in all lands. Princes laid down their swords. The wounds of Christendom were healed, and not a scar remained. Leo was Hercules, Ulysses, Marius, Alexander, the lion of the tribe of Judah. Literature was bound to celebrate his praises. Erasmus desired to do his part to keep such virtues perennially blooming. Too weak in himself for such a glorious task, he might hope to achieve it by connecting Leo with a name already immortal — the name of Jerome, the greatest of Latin theologians. Jerome alone of the whole of them deserved to be called a theologian; all others were dwarfed at his side, and only Greece had produced his equal. As he was the worthiest of the Latin Fathers, so his writings had been left in the worst condition; no intelligible meaning was to be had out of them.

Erasmus had compared the MSS., corrected texts, exposed and expelled interpolated passages. St. Jerome had been born again. The credit was not all due to Erasmus. Reuchlin had opened the way. But, such as it was, the work was completed, and was humbly offered to Leo's acceptance.[1]

Leo graciously complied. He had sanctioned the New Testament. He now allowed his name to appear on the title-page of the "Jerome" as Erasmus's avowed patron. He even wrote to Henry VIII., recommending Erasmus for an English bishopric. The author of "Moria," who had mocked and insulted the religious orders, appeared before the world with the Pope's name beside his own, in the sunlight of pon-

[1] *Ep.* clxxiii.

tifical favour. What wonder if Erasmus now believed that a peaceful Reformation was at hand, when such open favours had been shown to himself; that Pope and princes and the wisdom of the laity were about to make an end of ecclesiastical abuses, clear out the monks, silence the jargon of scholasticism, and restore the Church of the Apostles with Scripture for its foundation! You can trace his expectations in a letter to Fabricius Capito, a celebrated preacher at Bâle.[1]

I am now (he says) fifty-one years old, and may be expected to feel that I have lasted long enough. I am not enamoured of life, but it is worth while to continue a little longer with such a prospect of a golden age. We have a Leo X. for Pope; a French king content to make peace for the sake of religion when he had means to continue the war; a Maximilian for emperor, old and eager for peace; Henry VIII., king of England, also on the side of peace; the Archduke Charles "divinæ cujusdam indolis adolescens." Learning is springing up all round out of the soil; languages, physics, mathematics, each department thriving. Even theology is showing signs of improvment. Theology, so far, has been cultivated only by avowed enemies of knowledge. The pretence has been to protect the minds of the laity from disturbance. All looks brighter now. Three languages are publicly taught in the schools. The most learned and least malicious of the theologians themselves lend their hand to the work. I myself, insignificant I, have contributed something. I have at least stirred the bile of those who would not have the world grow wiser, and only fools now snarl at me. One of them said in a sermon lately, in a lamentable voice, that all was now over with the Christian faith. There were persons who were talking of mending religion, and even mending the Lord's Prayer. An Englishman

[1] *Ep.* ccvii., abridged.

clamours that I profess to be wiser than Jerome, and have altered his text, when all I have done has been to restore his text.

But the clouds are passing away. My share in the work must be near finished. But you are young and strong; you have the first pulpit in Bâle; your name is without spot — no one dares to reflect upon Fabricius; you are prudent, too, and know when to be silent; you have yourself experienced the disorder, and understand the treatment of it. I do not want the popular theology to be abolished. I want it enriched and enlarged from earlier sources. When the theologians know more of Holy Scripture they will find their consequence undiminished, perhaps increased. All promises well, so far as I see. My chief fear is that with the revival of Greek literature there may be a revival of paganism. There are Christians who are Christians only in name, and are Gentiles at heart; and, again, the study of Hebrew may lead to Judaism, which would be worse still. I wish there could be an end of scholastic subtleties, or, if not an end, that they could be thrust into a second place, and Christ be taught plainly and simply. The reading of the Bible and the early Fathers will have this effect. Doctrines are taught now which have no affinity with Christ and only darken our eyes.

Reform was in the air — reform, or some more dangerous change. What Erasmus wished, what Leo and the Cardinals wished, what Warham and More and Colet and Fisher wished in England, is tolerably clear. They saw popular Christianity degraded into a superstition; the clergy loose and ignorant; practical religion a blind idolatry; the laity the victims of the mendicant friars, who enslaved them through the confessional; theology, a body of dogmatic propositions developed into an unintelligible scholasticism, without practical bearing upon life.

Wise men desired to see superstition corrected, the Scriptures made the rule of faith and practice, the friars brought to their bearings and perhaps suppressed, the clergy generally disciplined and educated. They had no wish to touch the Church or diminish its splendour. The Church was, or might be, a magnificent instrument of human cultivation, and might grow with the expansion of knowledge.

Something of this kind was, or seemed then to be, possible. But the devil is not expelled by rose-water. A few months after this letter was written the sky was black with thunderclouds, and a storm had opened which raged for two long centuries. Mankind are not relieved so easily of the consequences of their own follies.

LECTURE X.

FORTUNE appeared to have changed her face to Erasmus after the publication of the New Testament and the "Encomium Moriæ." Relieved of his monastic vow, favoured by his own government, and applauded by the general voice of Europe, with sufficient money besides and with the full command of his own time, he had conquered a position for himself in which he might now pursue calmly the great objects of his life, and achieve the intellectual regeneration of the Church under the ægis of Pope Leo himself. The great powers of Europe contended for the possession of him. Henry VIII. and Wolsey made fresh efforts to recover him to England. The Pactolus which he had looked for six years before and had not found was now ready to flow: a fine house in London with a handsome income was placed at his disposition if he chose to accept it. Francis I., among his first acts on succeeding to the crown, invited Erasmus back to Paris. Leo was eager to receive him again at Rome. Minor magnates in Church and State would have secured if they could so splendid an ornament to their courts, while at Brussels he was welcomed so warmly by the young Archduke Charles and his brother Ferdinand that, if he desired preferment, it seemed that he had but to ask and to have.

In October 1516 he writes from Brussels to Peter Giles, who had been his pupil, in paternal good-humour, advising him to be regular at his work, to keep a journal, to remember that life was short, to study Plato and Seneca, love his wife, and disregard the world's opinion — advice which indicates at least the composure of mind of the adviser. For himself he says: —

> What others sweat and toil for has come to me in my sleep. The Catholic King [Charles, now king of Spain] had almost made a bishop of me, not *in partibus infidelium*, but in Sicily. There had been a mistake, however, and I am glad of it. It appeared that the nomination belonged to the Pope, and the King could do no more than write to him to confirm the appointment. This happened while I was at work in libraries at Antwerp. The Chancellor sent for me hither, and I obeyed more readily than I would have done had I known the cause of my summons. I was received with congratulations from those who were in the secret. I laughed, and told them they were losing their labours. I would not change my freedom for the best bishopric in the world.

Erasmus, however, was a thin-skinned mortal. It was the nature of him to heat the water wherever he was. Pope, kings, and bishops might throw their shield over him, but he had provoked the implacable enmity of the religious orders. In addition to his own offences, he had rushed to the front in defence of Reuchlin. They were wise in their generation. They had recognised that Erasmus was more dangerous to them than a thousand Reuchlins. If they could crush Erasmus they would make short work of Reuchlin and Von Hutten and young Germany; and the religious orders were terribly powerful. They were amenable to no authority but the Pope's, and the Popes themselves were afraid of provoking them.

Sir Thomas More had been sent across to the Low Countries to represent England at the settlement of the peace. He had not liked his occupation. Priests who had neither wives nor children he thought were the fittest persons for ambassadors. Their expenses were paid by their Governments, and if they did well they could be rewarded with bishoprics. Laymen had no such prospects. He himself had to maintain a double establishment; and though he was the most generous of masters, he had never been able to persuade his people at home to be economical in his absence. He had been able, however, to discover while at Cambray that a conspiracy had been formed among the monks at Louvain to make a general attack upon Erasmus's work, and make it impossible for his own or any other Government any longer to encourage him.

They mean (More wrote to him) to have an examination of your writings, with the worst intentions towards you. Be cautious, therefore, and correct any faults that you are conscious of. You will ask who the parties are. I fear to tell you, lest you be frightened by such antagonists. The object is to expose your mistakes. They have divided your works among them; each is to take a special part. You see your danger, so collect your forces. The resolution was taken at a supper party, where they had drunk more wine than was good for them.

Erasmus, like More, was at first rather amused than alarmed.

I hear (he writes to Ammonius) that those fellows at Louvain want to have my writings examined in the School of Theology there. They will have work cut out for them for two years, and the examiners must learn some Greek and Latin, of which at present they know nothing. I think it will go off in wind. The best people there are for me, and some, indeed, of the most distinguished of the theologians themselves.

The storm proved more angry and more dangerous than either More or Erasmus expected.

You will hardly believe (Erasmus writes a little later to Ammonius) how near I escaped being burnt, the divines at Louvain were in such a rage at me. They petitioned the King and the Pope to throw me over. I went to Louvain myself and scattered the smoke. The great people and the *literati* broke up the conspiracy at home, but I still wait for the decree of the Roman oracle. If I do not get a final decision in my favour there is an end of Erasmus, and nothing will remain but to write his epitaph. I had sooner have made two journeys to Rome than be tortured by this delay.

There was nothing to be afraid of from Rome. Leo decided all the points, whatever they were that were put before him, in Erasmus's favour, and the Louvain theologians were left to their own pens and their own voices, which, it must be allowed, they knew how to use. Erasmus found them abundant material. The edition of the New Testament was followed by paraphrases on the various books, giving life and meaning to a narrative which had been trampled into barrenness by mechanical repetition or conventional interpretation. The Paraphrases were received with enthusiasm, and were read in churches by the more enlightened clergy. Thanks, praises, congratulations rained upon their author; but, as admiration swelled on one side, fury was as loud upon the other. He had deliberately stirred a nest of hornets, and he smarted under the inevitable sting. His letters are full of complaints against the blockheads who railed at him in their sermons. Hypocrites he calls them, who slandered better men than themselves, as if their occupation was calumny and lies. Silence them he could not, for they commanded the pulpits, and they flitted and buzzed about him like bats and mosquitoes. In Louvain, where he was, his enemies swarmed the thickest. He might crush this venomous insect or that; but they were swarming in clouds, and he was dealing with a foe which was as the air, invulnerable. He knew his danger when he provoked it. He had attacked the monks, and the monks were ubiquitous, so that it would be useless to fly. There was no spot on the Continent where he could escape from their resentment. In England he had pined for Rome, or, if not for Rome, for a sight of the smoke from the chimneys of his own land. He had left England meaning never to see it again. He now looked back upon it with passionate regret.

Oh, splendid England! (he writes from Louvain to his friend Dr. Pace[1]) — Oh, splendid England, home and citadel of virtue and learning! How do I congratulate you on having such a prince to rule you, and your prince on subjects which throw such lustre on his reign! No land in all the world is like England. In no country would I love better to spend my days. Intellect and honesty thrive in England under the Prince's favour. In England there is no masked sanctimoniousness, and the empty babble of educated ignorance is driven out or put to silence. In this place I am torn by envenomed teeth. Preachers go about screaming lies about me among idiots as foolish as themselves.

Again, to Bishop Fisher:[2] —

The war is carried on *chartâ dentatâ*; each side bites in earnest with purpose to hurt, and the hooded sycophants are at the bottom of it, who call themselves the only champions of Gospel truth.

He thought of flight.

What shall I do? Whither shall I go? To Venice? To Bâle? Not to Germany; the hot rooms

[1] *Ep.* ccxli.

[2] *Ep.* cxxxiii., second series.

and stoves forbid Germany. The banditti forbid it, the plague forbids it. Distance and summer heats are against Italy. I am overwhelmed with invitations. The Archbishop of Mentz wishes for me, the Bishops of Maestricht, Liège, Bayeux wish for me. The King of England invites me back, and his Achates the Cardinal of York. I have so many adorers that I can scarce reply to their letters. I have written, as you advise me, to our Imperial Chancellor, and it is he who must decide for me.

He was still sanguine that better times were coming. He adds: —

You will soon see a new age among us. The Paraphrases are universally praised, and it is something to have written a book of which that can be said. They will have done at last with stoning Erasmus, and will take to kissing him.

Not the least of his troubles came from the violence of his own and Reuchlin's friends in Germany. The "Epistolæ obscurorum Virorum" was but one of many anonymous publications poured out by Von Hutten and the young passionate champions of light in defence of Reuchlin, and heaping ridicule on his prosecutors. Erasmus being the special object of the monks' hatred, they were all attributed to his own pen or his own instigation. He had to publish a defence of himself, which he detested doing. He tried, but tried in vain, to convince these hot-spirited youths that they were hurting their own cause by offending the civil power and the bishops, who would be their best protectors if they would keep their invectives within the limits of legitimate satire. He was stumbling over the roots of the trees which he had himself planted, and he did not like it at all.

The "Epistolæ" (he writes[1] in August, 1517) do

[1] To Cæsarius, *Ep.* clx., second series.

not please me. I might have been amused by the wit, but the example is pernicious. I love a jest, but I have no taste for ribaldry, and if play the fool they must they have no right to bring my name into the business and ruin the work of my life. They are not only ill friends to themselves, but they bring disgrace on the cause of learning. It is now said in Cologne that I wrote the libel on Pope Julius. I am amazed that such a production should be attributed to me. If it had been mine it would at least have been in better Latin. I might mock a little in "Moria," but I drew no blood and never hurt any man's good name. I satirised manners, not individuals. Do, if you can, keep such stuff out of the press. Everyone who knows me knows how I disliked the book and how unworthy I thought it.

Pfeffercorn, the conceited Jew who had led the attack on Reuchlin, had been the tool of stronger heads behind him. But he had stood forward in the front. His name alone was a butt for the satire of coarser wits. Erasmus had to notice the man, but felt disgraced in touching him.

It is right (he again writes to Cæsarius) for the defenders of learning to support Reuchlin, but there was no need for them to point their lances at that pestilent trumpeter of the Furies, that vicar of Satan, with the theologians in masks behind him. He is a fellow made of malevolence. To denounce him is not to conquer him, for he has no shame, and he counts the attacks upon him as a distinction. He pretends to defend the Gospel, and he is destroying Christianity. If his body be examined, may I be hanged if a Jew is not found inside him, or six hundred Jews. He is a bad Jew and a worse Christian. Conflicts with so vile a monster are better avoided. Conquerors or conquered, those who meddle with him will be spattered with mud. I would rather see the whole Old Testament abolished, so we preserved the New, than have the peace of the world broken for the books of the Jews.[1]

One has heard of Satan rebuking sin; Erasmus complaining of his friends' strong language was something in the same position. Two months later he writes on the same subject to Pirkheimer:[2] —

No mortal hates these quarrels more than I do. I hate even my own "Apology," which I was forced into writing. I am ashamed that men of reputation should be driven into crossing swords with such a monster, or dirting paper with the name of him. No wise man doubts that Reuchlin has been abominably used, but I would rather hold my tongue than bandy words with swarms of wasps who carry poison in their tongues. Innocence needs no defence. It was enough for Reuchlin to have all good men on his side. I wonder that the magistrates and bishops permit such a venomous wretch to rage as he does, and that no Hercules is found to drag this new Cacus into gaol. That is the way in which such ruffians ought to be dealt with.

Erasmus might deny his responsibility for "Julius" or the "Epistolæ;" but he had published "Moria" under his own name, and on "Moria" the monks fastened next — very much, it is curious to observe, to the surprise of Erasmus and even of Sir Thomas More, to whom "Moria" seemed no more than an innocent piece of satire. The monks knew better; they would have abandoned their cause if they had allowed a stab so terribly effective to pass unresented. The challenge was taken up by a Carmelite professor at Louvain named Egmondanus — Egmond, I suppose — who for many years was to be a thorn in Erasmus's side.

[1] "Malim ego incolumi Novo Testamento vel totum Vetus aboleri quam Christianorum pacem ob Judæorum libros rescindi." — *Ep.* ccii., second series, abridged.

[2] *Ep.* cciii., second series.

I am not surprised (More writes to his friend [1]) that this little black Carmelite hates you, but I could hardly have believed that he would attack "Moria," when he is himself Moria incarnate. Insolent ass, to be ashamed of his own mistress. He may hide himself in the lion's skin, but he will not be able to hide his ears.

I could not have dreamt (writes Erasmus himself) that "Moria" would have provoked so much anger. I abhor quarrels, and would have suppressed the thing could I have foreseen the effect it would produce. But why should monks and theologians think themselves so much injured? Do they recognise their portraits? The Pope read "Moria" and laughed; as he finished it, all he said was, "Here is our old friend Erasmus." And yet the Popes are handled there as freely as anyone else. I am no evil speaker. Had I seriously wished to describe monks and theologians as they really are "Moria" would seem a mild performance by the side of what I should then have written. They say it is being read in schools. I had not heard of this. There is nothing in it, however, which can injure young people. Why you should fear that it may lead to a disregard of religion is a mystery to me. Will religion vanish if I ridicule superstition? Would that what is now called religion deserved to be so called! Would that priests and congregations followed the teaching of Christ as faithfully as they now show their neglect of it! Religious houses are spread over Christendom. I do not condemn what is called a religious life in itself; but ask yourself what trace of piety is now to be found in such houses beyond forms and ceremonies, how worse than worldly almost all of them are. I have blackened no individual's name. I have mocked only at open and notorious vice.

So matters were standing with Erasmus himself and with Europe generally in the momentous year 1517. His writings were flying over Catholic Christendom

[1] *Ep.* cxlviii., second series.

and were devoured by everyone who could read. The laity, waking from the ignorance of ages, were opening their eyes to the absurdities and corruptions of irresponsible ecclesiasticism. The fatal independence of the clergy, which had been won by popes like Gregory VII. and bishops like our St. Thomas of Canterbury, had produced its inevitable effect. Popes and clergy share the infirmities of ordinary mortals, and no human being or body of human beings can be raised above the authority of law and opinion without developing into insolence, presumption and profligacy. Some vast change, as Erasmus saw, was immediately imminent. He expected, and he was entitled to expect by the favour which had been shown to himself, that it would take the shape of an orderly reform, carried out by the heads of the Church themselves and the princes who were then on the various thrones of Europe. Every sign seemed favourable to such an issue. The invectives of Orthodoxy against Erasmus had produced no effect on the Pontiff who bore the sword of St. Peter. Henry VIII. was, according to Sir Thomas More, the most deeply read and the most nobly intentioned of all the English kings. Francis I. had shown his own disposition by entreating Erasmus to live with him in Paris. The Emperor Maximilian was old, but generous and wise. His grandson Charles had shown so far symptoms of brilliant promise. The smaller German princes waited for nothing but a sign from their leaders to put their own hands to the work. Reactionary ecclesiasticism had no friends anywhere, save in the sense of the sacredness of religion and reluctance to meddle with a system which had been sanctified by the customs of ages — a reluctance which would have yielded immediately before a movement of which the Pope was to be the head.

Europe was at last at peace. The princes were all friends. It was an opportunity which might seem created specially by Providence, and to this forfeited chance Goethe alluded sadly when he said that the intellectual progress of mankind had been thrown back for centuries when the passions of the multitude were called up to decide questions which ought to have been left to the thinkers.

No time is worse wasted than in speculations over what we suppose might have been. Erasmus's hopes for a peaceful change depended on the Pope's assistance or leadership. The Roman Court was the centre and heart from which ecclesiastical corruption flowed over Europe, and he seems really to have persuaded himself that an elegant and accomplished Leo X. would consent to a genuine reform which must begin with himself and his surroundings. Providence or destiny is a stern schoolmistress, and the evil spirits of folly and iniquity do not yield so easily to the enlightened efforts of Goethe's thinkers.

Suddenly, as a bolt out of the blue, there came a flash of lightning, which scattered these fair imaginings and set the world on fire. A figure now steps out upon the scene which has made a deeper mark on the history of mankind than any one individual man has ever left, except Mahomet.

The subject of these lectures is Erasmus, and not Luther. I may presume that you are generally familiar with Luther's history, and a few words about it will be enough on this occasion.

Martin Luther was the son of a miner in Saxony. Bred up piously and wisely, he had a natural enthusiasm of his own. The Christian religion taught him that the highest duty of man was the service of God, and to this he determined to devote himself. Many young men have experienced similar emotions; they cool down with most of us as we come into practical contact with the world and its occupations. With Luther they did not cool down, they took the form of ardent resolution, and against his father's wishes, who knew better than he did that he was striking on a wrong career, he made his profession as a monk in an Augustinian convent. He was not content with the usual exercises of the rule. He prayed perpetually. He slept on the stones, fasted, watched, welcomed all the hardships which Erasmus most abhorred. In the library he found a copy of the New Testament lying dusty on the shelves. He studied it, digested it, discovered the extraordinary contrast between the Christianity which was taught in the Gospels and Epistles and the Christianity of the monasteries. He was perplexed, filled with doubts and misery, and knew not what to do or where to turn. He increased his austerities, supposing that he might be tempted by the devil. In the convent he became marked for the intensity of his earnestness, and was supposed to be maturing for a saint. The house to which he belonged had business at the Court of Rome. Luther was selected as one of the brethren who were sent thither to represent the fraternity. Erasmus went to Italy as a companion to rich young Englishmen, with horses and luxuries. Luther went too, but Luther walked there barefoot and penniless, passed on through the houses of his order from one to another. But both witnessed the same scenes and experienced the same sensations at the sight of Julius II. calling himself the successor of St. Peter. Luther, too, saw the cardinals, the hinges of Christendom, with their palaces and retinues and mistresses. He saw Papal Rome in all its magnificence of art, and wealth, and power.

He and Erasmus were alike conscious of the monstrous absurdity. But Erasmus, while he wondered, could also admire and enjoy. He found human life cultivated into intellectual grace. He found the extraordinary cardinals, Leo X. being then one of them, open-minded, liberal, learned, sceptical, and scornful as himself of the follies of the established creed, and refined even in their personal vices. He did not admire the vices, but he admired the men. Humanity, as represented in the circle which surrounded the Papacy, appeared to him infinitely superior to the barbarism and superstition of Western Christendom. He wanted Western Christendom to be educated and renovated, and he thought enlightened popes and prelates to be competent instruments for the work.

The impression formed upon Luther by the culture and magnificence was totally different. To him it seemed an impious parody. He had kissed the ground when he came in sight of Rome, expecting to find it the nursery of godliness. Of godliness he saw not a trace, or a trace of wish for such a thing. Erasmus despised superstition. If it be superstitious to believe that man is placed in this world to learn God's will and do it, that life has no other meaning, and that splendour and luxury rather hinder than help in the pursuit of duty, then Luther was as superstitious as the most ignorant hermit that ever macerated his body in a desert. He was no rebel against established authorities, he wrote no "Moria," no satires upon mendicant friars or scholastic divines. He went home bewildered, but resolved that he would do his own small bit of work faithfully, whatever it might be. The superior of his convent saw that for such a mind active occupation must be provided if it was not to prey upon itself, and Luther was removed under a dispensation to the new University of Wittenberg. There he taught classes. There he preached on Sundays and saints' days at the great town church, and soon drew crowds to hear him, who were astonished at his strange earnestness, his strange eyes which were like a lion's, and the strange things which he said.

He had no notion of making a disturbance in the world. He took no prominent part in the Reuchlin conflict. He had read voluminously, but learning in and for itself did not particularly interest him. His whole soul was turned on the will of God and what God had made known about Himself, and thus his course lay altogether apart from Erasmus and the prophets of the Renaissance. Erasmus had never heard of him. If he had heard he would not have cared to make further inquiry. Yet here, unrecognised and unthought of beyond the walls of Wittenberg, was the man who was to revolutionise the Christian Church.

The Pope was rich, but the gardens of Aladdin would have scarcely supplied the means for the splendid expenditure of Leo X. Four sources contributed the streams which supplied the papal treasury: the ordinary revenues of the States of the Church; the profits from the Roman Law Courts, to which causes were brought by appeal from every part of Europe; the annats, or first year's income from every priest, or bishop, or abbot presented to a benefice; and, lastly, the sale of pardons, dispensations, and indulgences, permissions to do things which would be wrong without them, or remissions of penalties prescribed by the canons for offences — indulgences which were extended by popular credulity to actual pardons for sins committed, and were issued whenever the Pope wanted money. Sorrowing relations, uneasy for the fate of a soul in purgatory, could buy out their friend at a fixed scale of charges. The results were calculated beforehand. Averages could be taken from repeated experience. Sometimes a capitalist contracted on speculation for the anticipated sum. Sometimes the issue was disposed of by recognised officials resident in the various countries. The price was high or low, according to the papal necessities, or according to the magnitude of the sins to which it would reach; but as no one could be held so innocent as to have no sins to be pardoned at all, every pious Christian was on all such occasions expected to provide himself with a Bull.

St. Peter's Church at Rome had been commenced, but waited its completion. Pope Leo wished to distinguish his reign by perfecting the magnificent structure. For this, and for other purposes, he required a subsidy unusually large, and an indulgence extravagantly wide was the natural expedient.

There was nothing in such a measure to suggest remark. Custom had made such things too familiar. The Pope possessed in his treasury the accumulated superfluous merits of all the saints from the beginning of the Christian Church. They were his to dispose of as he pleased to unfortunates who had none of their own. The Pope was God's vicegerent. The kingdom of God was the greatest of all kingdoms, and it was fit and right that its capital should be magnificent. The splendour of sovereigns can be maintained only by the contributions of their subjects, and indulgences were sanctified by usage as the mode in which such contributions could best be offered. The Pope did not exact taxes like secular sovereigns. He gave something in return. The "something" might not admit of precise definition. But Christ had given to the Christian priesthood the power of absolution. The Pope was supreme priest, Pontifex Maximus, and possessed that power, whatever it might be, in supreme degree. What Christ could do the Pope could do; and at any rate the grant of indulgences was a time-honoured custom in the Church. They might or they might not be of real benefit to the soul, but they were evidence of the Pope's goodwill, and at least could do no possible harm. Leo X. put out a profuse issue of these spiritual bank-notes, which the faithful were expected to purchase at their nominal value, either for themselves or for their relations who were in purgatory. The contract for Saxony was taken by the Archbishop of Mentz, a brilliant youth of twenty-eight who had been lately made cardinal, and who had a heavy bill against him still unpaid in the papal treasury as the price of his red hat.

The collector appointed by the Archbishop was a Dominican monk named Tetzel, who went about with bells and fifes, and a suite behind him like a procession of the priests and priestesses of Cybele. His method of disposing of his wares was admitted to have been injudicious. The sale of pardons for sins, however sanctioned by practice, was a form of trade which ought to have been covered by some respectable ceremonial. Tetzel travelled from town to town, advertising his patent medicines from the pulpit like a modern auctioneer, and telling his audience that as the money clinked in the box the souls of sinners flew up to heaven, no matter how mortal their offences. His progress brought him near to Wittenberg, and it was too much for Luther's patience. He entreated the Elector of Saxony to interfere. The Elector was as disgusted as himself, but did not see his way to interrupting the officials of the Holy See. Luther acted alone, and nailed up his world-famous challenge on the Wittenberg Church door — a challenge to Tetzel or any monk or priest to prove that a piece of paper signed by the Pope could put away sin.

To a question so presented the unclerical mind could return but one answer. From Wittenberg, from Saxony, from all Northern Europe — for the news spread like an electric stroke — there rose a "No!" which shook the Church to its foundations. The religious orders raved "heresy" from their pulpits. Luther replied first with moderation, then fiercely and scornfully. Pamphlet followed pamphlet, and it was soon open war, with the laity of Europe for an audience, cheering on the audacious rebel. The vibration of the shock reached Erasmus, and was received by him with very mixed feelings. At first he admitted that he felt a secret pleasure. If Luther could succeed in putting down the system of indulgences there would be one imposture the less, and he was not sorry that the Church should be made to face the danger of postponing longer the inevitable reforms. But he was in the midst of his own battle. He did not wish to be burdened with further responsibilities. Least of all could he wish that his quarrel with the monks should be complicated with an attack upon the Pope, who was his own chief support. Nor had he any particular sympathy with Luther's way of looking at things. He hated tyranny. He had an intellectual contempt for lies and ignorance, backed up by bigotry and superstition. He was ready and willing to fight angry monks and scholastics. But he had none of the passionate horror of falsehood in sacred things which inspired the new movement. He had no passionate emotions of any kind, and rather dreaded than welcomed the effervescence of religious enthusiasm. The faults of the Church, as he saw them, were oblivion and absolute neglect of ordinary morality, the tendency to substitute for obedience to the Ten Commandments an extravagant superstition chiefly built upon fiction, and a doctrinal system, hardening and stiffening with each generation, which was made the essence of religion, defined by ecclesiastical law, guarded by ecclesiastical courts, and enforced by steel and fire. His dream was a return to early Christianity as it was before councils had laid the minds of men in chains; a Christianity of practice, not of opinion, where the Church itself might consent to leave the intellect free to think as it pleased on the inscrutable mysteries; and where, as the Church would no longer insist on particular forms of belief, mankind would cease to hate and slaughter each other because they differed on points of metaphysics. In Luther he saw the same disposition to dogmatic assertion at the opposite pole of thought; an intolerance of denial as dangerous as the churchman's intolerance of affirmation. What could Luther, what could any man know of the real essence of the Divine Will and Nature? Canons of orthodoxy were but reflections of human passion and perversity. If Luther's spirit spread, dogma would be met with dogma, each calling itself the truth; reason could never end disputes which did not originate in reason, but originated in bigotry or a too eager imagination. From argument there would be a quick resort to the sword, and the whole world would be full of fury and madness. How well Erasmus judged two centuries of religious wars were to tell. The wheel has come round at last. The battle for liberty of opinion has been fought out to the bitter end. Common-sense has been taught at last that persecution for opinions must cease. After the exhaustion of the struggle the world has come round to the Erasmian view, and one asks why all that misery was necessary before the voice of moderation could be heard. I suppose because reason has so little to do with the direction of human conduct. I called Erasmus's views of reform a dream. It was a dream of the ivory gate. Reason is no match for superstition. One passion can only be encountered by another passion, and bigotry by the enthusiasm of faith.

But what was Erasmus to do in the new element which had sprung out so suddenly? Turn against Luther he would not, for he knew that Luther's denunciation of the indulgences had been as right as it was brave. Declare for him he would not. He could not commit himself to a movement which he could not control, and which for all he could see might become an unguided insurrection. Like all men of his temperament, he disbelieved in popular convulsions, and remained convinced that no good could be done except through the established authorities. He determined therefore to stand aside, stick to his own work, and watch how things went. He held aloof. He purposely abstained from reading Luther's books that he might be able to deny that he had been in communication with him. Not wishing to write to Luther himself, yet not wishing to seem to be without sympathy for him, he wrote in the summer of 1518, a few months after the scene at Wittenberg, to the rector of the school at Erfurt where Luther had been bred. He says:—

That frigid, quarrelsome old lady, Theology, had swollen herself to such a point of vanity that it was necessary to bring her back to the fountain, but I would rather have her mended than ended. I would at least have her permitted to endure till a better theology has been invented. Luther has said many things excellently well. I could wish, however, that he would be less rude in his manner. He would have stronger support behind him, and might do real good. But, at any rate, unless we stand by him when he is right, no one hereafter will dare to speak the truth. I can give no opinion about his positive doctrines; but one good thing he has done, and has been a public benefactor by doing it—he has forced the controversialists to examine the early Fathers for themselves.

The atmosphere at Louvain grew more squally than ever after Luther's business began. It gave the monks a stick to beat Erasmus with, and they used it to such purpose that he doubted whether he would be able to keep his footing there, and whether he might not be forced to fly for refuge to England again. Even there he could not be certain of his reception.

The monks said the conflagration was his doing. In a sense it is true that it was his doing. "Moria" and the New Testament had been dangerous fire-works, and every Greek scholar and every friend of learning was on Luther's side. The reactionaries in Germany and England too could point to their predictions: had not they always said how these novelties would end?

To see how the wind lay on the English side, and to prepare the way should flight from Louvain be necessary, he wrote a long and remarkable letter to Wolsey.

Considering how much we hear from Erasmus about England, there is less mention of Wolsey in the correspondence generally than might have been expected.

At first, perhaps, the great Cardinal took no notice of Erasmus; and then, finding that he was become a person of consequence, paid him some kind of attention. But there was never any kind of intimacy between them. Oil and water would sooner mix than the great pluralist Cardinal, symbol of all that was worst in ecclesiastical ascendency, half statesman, half charlatan, and the keen sarcastic Erasmus, to whom the charlatan side would be too painfully evident.

But Wolsey was now omnipotent in England. Erasmus might need his help, or at least his sanction to a return thither. The letter was sent with a due dose of flattery and incense, to assure Wolsey that he had no connection with the German movement.[1]

Stories, he says, had reached his Eminence's ears that he, Erasmus, was responsible for the German outburst. He wishes Wolsey to understand that it was not true. Luther, he heard, was a person of blameless life; this Luther's worst enemies acknowledged; but he had never seen him, he had never read his books. As to the opinions contained in them, he was not vain enough to pass a judgment on a man so remarkable. He had thought it imprudent on Luther's part to reflect on pardons and indulgences, forming as they did the chief part of the monks' revenues, but he had expressed no opinion on what Luther had published, favourable or unfavourable. He was not rash enough to praise what he had not studied, nor unprincipled enough to condemn.

As to the rest (he went on) Germany has young men of high promise, who are fighting against the Obscurantists and use the first weapon which comes to hand. I should blame their violence if I did not know how intolerably they have been provoked. The

[1] *Ep.* cccxvii., abridged.

enemies of learning denounce and slander them, and shriek and scream if they get a scratch in return. They are to cry heresy, and appeal to earth and heaven, and to the princes and the mob, and we are not to utter a disrespectful word. Von Hutten and his friends are young, they are not without wit, and they are naturally exasperated at the attacks on them. I have admonished them to be more cautious. I have advised them to keep their pens off popes, and cardinals, and bishops, who are their only protectors. What can I do more? I can control my own style: I cannot govern theirs. Everything is laid at my door. Each new work that appears must be mine, whether I wrote it or not. My works are widely read, and expressions used by me may find their way into the writings of others, even of my enemies. There is mockery in "Moria"—but only innocent mockery. No word has come from me to offend modesty or encourage sedition or impiety. I have the thanks of everyone, except of divines and monks, who do not like to have their eyes opened. I am saying perhaps more than I need. I have said so much only because I learn that certain persons are trying to prejudice your Eminence's mind against me. I trust you will not listen to such calumnies. Erasmus will always be found on the side of the Roman See, and especially of its present occupant.

LECTURE XI.

THE Court of Rome, which had survived the infamies of Alexander VI., might naturally disdain the rumours of spiritual disturbances in a remote province of Germany. The roots of the papal power had struck so deep into the spiritual and secular organisation of Europe, that it might believe itself safe from any wind that could blow. If the crimes of the Borgias had not disenchanted mankind of their belief that the popes were representatives of the Almighty, the spell was not likely to be broken by a clamour over indulgences. It was but a quarrel of noisy monks. When Luther's theses were submitted to Leo X., the infallible voice observed merely that a drunken German wrote them: "When he has slept off his wine he will know better." Erasmus, encouraged by the Pope's encouragement of art and learning, and especially by Leo's patronage of himself, had believed that they were on the eve of a general Reformation, undertaken by the Church itself. Though he had not liked Luther's tone or manners, he had been delighted with the stir in Saxony, as giving the Holy See the impulse to begin the work which he supposed alone to be needed. It was a fond imagination. Pope Leo is credited by tradition with having called the Church system a profitable fable. Fabulous or true, it was the foundation on which had been erected his own splendid dominion, and he was not likely to allow his right to his own revenues to be successfully challenged.

Roused at last into recognising that Luther's action had set tongues busy asking questions which could not be answered, he struck at first on the notable idea of a fresh crusade against the Crescent, and the recovery of Constantinople. It would divert attention, create a fresh tide of emotional piety, and lend new lustre to his own throne. How far this scheme was intended to be proceeded with it is impossible to say, but it went far enough to show Erasmus the folly of his own expectations, and in all his letters none are more scornfully bitter than those in which he denounced the sinister influences of Leo's advisers. He would as soon, he said, turn Mahometan himself as be a Christian after the type in favour at the Vatican. He writes to Sir T. More, March 5, 1518:[1] —

The Pope and the princes are at a new game. They pretend that there is to be a grand war against the Turk. The poor Turk! I hope we shall not be too savage with him. What will the women say? The whole male sex between twenty-six and fifty are to take up arms, and as the Pope will not let the ladies enjoy themselves while their husbands are in the field, they are to wear no silk or jewels, drink no wine, and fast every other day. Husbands who cannot go on the campaign are to be under the same rule. No kissing to be allowed till the war is over. Many wives will not like this. Yours I am sure will approve. But oh, immortal gods! what has come over these rulers of ours? Are popes and kings so lost to shame that they treat their subjects as cattle to be bought and sold?

Nero fiddled while Rome was burning. Leo X. trying to occupy the mind of Europe with fighting or converting Turks while Luther was setting Germany on fire was a feat not very dissimilar.

[1] *Ep.* cclxv., second series, abridged.

At greater length Erasmus poured out his disappointment and indignation to his friend Abbot Volzius, who became afterwards a Calvinist.[1]

We are not, I presume, to kill all the Turks. The survivors are to be made Christians, and we are to send them our Occams and our Scoti as missionaries. I wonder what the Turks will think when they hear about instances and causes formative, about quiddities and relativities, and see our own theologians cursing and spitting at each other, the preaching friars crying up their St. Thomas, the Minorites their Doctor Seraphicus, the Nominalists and Realists wrangling about the nature of the Second Person of the Trinity as if Christ was a malignant demon ready to destroy you if you made a mistake about His nature. While our lives and manners remain as depraved as they now are the Turks will see in us but so many rapacious and licentious vermin. How are we to make the Turks believe in Christ till we show that we believe in Him ourselves? *Reduce the Articles of Faith to the fewest and the simplest* — "*Quæ pertinent ad fidem quam paucissimis articulis absolvantur.*" Show them that Christ's yoke is easy, that we are shepherds and not robbers, and do not mean to oppress them. Send them messengers such as these instead of making war, and then we may effect some good. But, oh! what an age we live in. When were morals more corrupt? — ritual and ceremony walking hand in hand with vice, and wretched mortals caring only to fill their purses. Christ cannot be taught even among Christians. The cry is only for pardons, dispensations, and indulgences, and the trade goes on in the name of popes and princes, and even of Christ Himself. Ask a question of the scholastic divines and the casuists, and you are told of qualifications, or equivocations, and such like. Not one of them will say to you, Do this and leave that. They ought to show their faith in their works, and convert Turks by the beauty of their lives.

[1] *Ep.* cccxxix., abridged.

And dogmas were to be heaped on dogmas, and Christendom was to be turned into a bloody circus of quarrelling doctrinaires, murdering each other in the name of God, while the Turks, far away from conversion, were to hang over Europe, threatening Western Christianity with the same fate which had overwhelmed the Churches of Asia. Why would not men be reasonable? Luther's voice swelled louder. Erasmus vainly implored him to be moderate. Erasmus had no spell to command the winds not to blow. Leo's eyes were opened at last. He found his indulgences would no longer sell in the market. His revenues were seriously threatened. The troublesome monk must be silenced. He required the Elector of Saxony to arrest Luther. The Elector declined, till the objections to the indulgences had been answered. Indulgences and pardons were but one of a thousand forms in which the flock of Christ had been fleeced. Each grievance found a voice, and the movement began perilously to shape itself into a revolt of the laity against the clergy. Luther dared to say that the clergy were but as other men, that their apostolic succession was a dream, and the claim to supernatural powers on which the whole pretension of the Church to its sovereign authority rested was an illusion and imposture. Something had to be done, but what? Nuncios were sent and then legates — not to answer Luther, for no answer was possible, but to threaten him, to bribe him, any way to silence him. Luther had not meant to raise such a tempest. He had merely protested against a scandal. If the Pope would have stopped the sale of the indulgences and condemned the grossness of Tetzel and his doings, Luther, much as he disliked the teaching and practice of the Church in general, would have said no more, and his own share in the revolt would have ended. It was not for him to call to account Pope and bishops, and remodel the world. But, as Erasmus said, the whole business was mismanaged. Aleander, Miltitz, Cardinal Cajetan, who were despatched successively from Rome to quiet matters, were insolent churchmen, impatient and indignant that the majesty of the Papacy should be defied by a miserable monk. Fire and faggot were the fitting and proper remedy. A troublesome Elector of Saxony, himself half a heretic at heart, refusing to indulge them, they alternately flattered and cursed, entreated and imprecated. A Papal Bull came out formally approving the indulgences, condemning Luther's action, which Erasmus says every right-minded man in Germany approved, ordering his books to be burnt, and commanding his arrest and punishment. It might have answered a century before, but times change, and men along with them. Free Germany only asked the louder who and what the Pope was that he should claim to punish a German citizen who had only thrown into words what every honest man believed.

Erasmus, moving between Louvain and Bâle, was noting anxiously the spread of the conflagration, more and more uncertain what part to take, and breaking out, as men will do when they see things going as they do not like, into lamentations on the wickedness of the world.

Princes, he well knew, disliked and feared popular movements. Rebellion against the Pope might turn easily into rebellion against themselves. Possibly enough they might combine to put the whole thing down ; and then, as he sadly recognised, the forcible suppression of Luther would give the victory to his own enemies, and he and all that he had done or tried to do would be crushed along with this new insurgent. Or it might be that the princes might try and fail, and there would be revolution and civil war. In that case ought he not, must he not declare himself on Luther's side? He had told Wolsey that his place would be always with the Pope, but the Pope had not then gone to extremities.

As it was, the blame of what had happened was thrown upon him, and not altogether without justice. At that very moment he was doing Luther's work. His New Testament and his "Moria" were circulating in hundreds of thousands of copies, bringing the monks and theologians into scorn. Naturally enough his opponents saw their own predictions confirmed. Here is what comes of your Greek and Hebrew. Did n't we say it would be so? He could not clear himself. Would it not be safer, better, more honourable to fall into rank with the general movement? And yet the whole form of Luther's action was distasteful to him. He had no passion. He distrusted enthusiasm. He abhorred violence. To declare for Luther after Luther had been condemned at Rome was to quarrel for ever with the Vatican; and victory, if Luther succeeded, seemed to be leading to fresh dogmas as unwelcome to him as scholasticism. His position was infinitely uneasy. He was railed at in lecture-rooms, insulted in the pulpits, cursed and libelled in the press, and, except by now and then turning round and biting some specially snarling cur, he could do nothing to defend himself.

Erasmus said he disliked fighting monsters, for whether he won or lost he was always covered with venom. He writes to Marcus Laurinus:[1]—

When you find a man raging against my New Testament ask him if he has read it. If he says Yes, ask

[1] Canon of Bruges. *Ep.* ccclvi., abridged.

him to what he objects. Not one of them can tell you. Is not this Christian? Is it not "monastic" to slander a man without knowing where he is in fault? Heresy is held a deadly crime, so if you offend one of these gentlemen they all rush on you together, one grunting out "heretic," the rest grunting in chorus, and crying for stones to hurl at you. Verily, they have whetted their teeth like serpents. The poison of asps is under their lips. They have no tongue to bless with, but tongue enough for lies and slander. Nothing pleases them like blackening another man's good name. Such creatures are not to be forgotten. They must be embalmed in writing that posterity may know the malice which can conceal itself under zeal for religion. Possibly, if I try, I may be able to preserve the portraits of some of these gentry myself.

The monks and divines had no cause to love Erasmus. No wonder they returned the compliments which he had paid them. It was blow for blow and sting for sting, and he need not have cried out so loudly. Happily for him he was not chained to Louvain. Half his time was spent at Bâle with his printer, where the noises reached him less. But more than ever he looked wistfully towards England.

His English friend, Dr. Pace, who had been abroad on a diplomatic mission, had spent a few days at Bâle with him. The sight of an English face revived his longings.

TO PAULUS BOMBASIUS.[1]

July 26, 1518.

Pace is recalled. The King and Cardinal cannot do without him. I have myself avoided princes' courts, as I looked on life in such places as splendid misery; but if I had my life to begin again I would prefer to spend it at the English Court. The King

[1] Professor at Bologna. *Ep.* ccclxxvii.

is the heartiest man living (*cordatissimus*) and delights in good books. The Queen is miraculously learned for a woman, and is equally pious and excellent. Both of them like to be surrounded by the most accomplished of their subjects. Linacre is Court physician, and what he is I need not say. Thomas More is in the Privy Council. Mountjoy is in the Queen's household. Colet is Court preacher. Stokesly, a master of Greek, Hebrew, Latin and scholastic theology, is a Privy Councillor also. The Palace is full of such men, a very museum of knowledge.

Again, to Wolsey: —

Fool that I was to have rejected the King's and your kind offers. Had I accepted the hand which was held out to me I might have been living happily in a cultivated circle of friends, instead of struggling with ungrateful and insolent calumniators. Bodily torments are bad enough, but these mental torments are worse. They come one knows not whence — perhaps from the stars, perhaps from the devil. What a thing it is to cultivate literature. Better far grow cabbages in a garden. Bishops have thanked me for my work, the Pope has thanked me ; but these tyrants the mendicant friars never leave me alone with their railing.

Erasmus was ill this summer at Bâle (1518) with cough and dysentery. The worse he was the more he pined for England. He had decided to go there if his health would let him, whether invited or not.

I would like well to know whether I have anything to look for with you (he wrote to Cuthbert Tunstall[1]). I grow old. I am not as strong as I was. If I could have the additional hundred marks which the King offered me some time back I would ask no more. Here I have nothing to look for. The Chancellor, on

[1] Then Master of the Rolls, afterwards Bishop of London and of Durham.

whom I chiefly depended, is dead in Spain. His chaplain writes that if he had lived three months longer he would have provided for me. Cold comfort. Nowhere in the world is learning worse neglected than here.

Trouble enough and anxiety enough! Yet in the midst of bad health and furious monks — it is the noblest feature in him — his industry never slackened, and he drew out of his difficulties the materials which made his name immortal. He was for ever on the wing, searching libraries, visiting learned men, consulting with politicians or princes. His correspondence was enormous. His letters on literary subjects are often treatises in themselves, and go where he would his eyes were open to all things and persons. His writings were passing through edition on edition. He was always adding and correcting; while new tracts, new editions of the Fathers show an acuteness of attention and an extent of reading which to a modern student seems beyond the reach of any single intellect. Yet he was no stationary scholar confined to desk or closet. He was out in the world, travelling from city to city, gathering materials among all places and all persons, from palace to village alehouse, and missing nothing which had meaning or amusement in it. In all literary history there is no more extraordinary figure. Harassed by orthodox theologians, uncertain of his duties in the revolutionary tempest, doubtful in what country to find rest or shelter, anxious for his future, anxious for his life (for he knew how Orthodoxy hated him, and he had no wish to be a martyr in an ambiguous cause), he was putting together another work which, like "Moria," was to make his name immortal. Of his learned productions, brilliant as they were, Erasmus thought but little.

He considered them hastily and inaccurately done; he even wondered how anyone could read them. But his letters, his "Moria," and now the "Colloquies," which he was composing in his intervals of leisure, are pictures of his own mind, pictures of men and things which show the hand of an artist in the highest sense, never spiteful, never malicious, always delightful and amusing, and finished photographs of the world in which he lived and moved. The subject might be mean or high, a carver of genuis will make a work of art out of the end of a broomstick. The journey to Brindisi was a common adventure in a fly-boat; Horace has made it live for ever. Erasmus had the true artist's gift of so handling everything that he touched, vulgar or sublime, that human interest is immediately awakened, and in these "Colloquies," which are the record of what he himself saw and heard, we have the human inhabitants of Europe before us as they then were in all countries except Spain, and of all degrees and sorts; bishops and abbots, monks and parish priests, lords and commoners, French grisettes, soldiers of fortune, treasure-seekers, quacks, conjurors, tavern-keepers, there they all stand, the very image and mirror of the time. Miserable as he often considered himself, Erasmus shows nothing of it in the "Colloquies." No bitterness, no complainings, no sour austerity or would-be virtuous earnestness but everywhere a genial human sympathy which will not be too hard upon the wretchedest of rogues, with the healthy apprehension of all that is innocent and good. The "Colloquies" were not published till four years latter than the time with which we are now concerned, but they were composed at intervals during a long period — the subjects picked up as he went along, dressed into shape as he rode, and written as opportunity served, sometimes two or three in a single day.

They are a happy evidence that in the midst of his complaints and misgivings his inner spirit was lively and brilliant as ever, and that the existence of which he professed to be weary was less clouded than he would have his friends believe. The best and brightest are his pictures of England. No one who has ever read them can forget his pilgrimage with Colet to Becket's tomb at Canterbury, with Colet's scornful snorts, or his visit with Aldrich, the master of Eton, to the shrine of Our Lady of Walsingham. In the whole collection there is probably nothing which he had not himself seen and heard, and the "Colloquies," which in their own day had unbounded popularity, can still be read with delight in our own. Works of science and history, famous at their appearance and in front of advancing knowledge, fall out of date, become insipid, and are forgotten. A genuine work of art retains its flavour to the end of time.

Occasionally in his letters we find adventures of his own which might have served for an additional chapter in the "Colloquies." I mentioned his illness at Bâle in the summer of 1518. On his recovery in the autumn he had to return to Louvain. He went back with a heavy heart, expecting to find his tormentors there. He reached Louvain so ill that he was confined to his room for six weeks, and the surgeons thought his disorder had been the plague. The description of his journey which he gave to Beatus Rhenanus is a companion picture to the journey to Brindisi.[1]

Listen to the tragedy of my adventures. I left Bâle relaxed and worn out as one out of favour with

[1] *Ep.* ccclvii., abridged.

the gods. The river part of my journey was well enough, save for the heat of the sun. We dined at Breisach. Dinner abominable. Foul smells and flies in swarms. We were kept waiting half an hour while the precious banquet was preparing. There was nothing that I could eat, every dish filthy and stinking. At night we were turned out of the boat into a village — the name I forget, and I would not write it if I remembered. It nearly made an end of me. There were sixty of us to sup together in the tavern, a medley of human animals in one small heated room. It was ten o'clock, and, oh! the dirt and the noise, especially after the wine had begun to circulate. The cries of the boatmen woke us in the morning. I hurry on board unsupped and unslept. At nine we reached Strasburg, when things mended a little. Scherer, a friend, supplied us with wine, and other acquaintances called to see me. From Strasburg we went on to Speyer. We had been told that part of the army would be there, but we saw nothing of them. My English horse had broken down, a wretch of a blacksmith having burnt his foot with a hot shoe. I escaped the inn at Speyer and was entertained by my friend the Dean. Two pleasant days with him, thence in a carriage to Worms and so on to Mentz, where I was again lodged by a Cathedral canon. So far things had gone tolerably with me. The smell of the horses was disagreeable and the pace was slow, but that was the worst. At a village further on I call on my friend Christopher, the wine-merchant, to his great delight. On his table I saw the works of Erasmus. He invited a party to meet me, sent the boatmen a pitcher of wine and promised to let them off the customs duty as a reward for having brought him so great a man. Thence to Bonn, thence to Cologne, which we reached early on Sunday morning.[1]

Imagine a wine-merchant reading my books and given to the study of the Muses. Christ said the publicans and the harlots would go into the kingdom

[1] *Ep.* cccxxxix.

of heaven before the Pharisees. Priests and monks live for their bellies, and vintners take to literature. But, alas, the red wine which he sent to the boatmen took the taste of the bargeman's wife, a red-faced sot of a woman. She drank it to the last drop, and then flew to arms and almost murdered a servant wench with oyster-shells. Then she rushed on deck, tackled her husband, and tried to pitch him overboard. There is vinal energy for you.

At the hotel at Cologne I ordered breakfast at ten o'clock, with a carriage and pair to be ready immediately after. I went to church, came back to find no breakfast, and a carriage not to be had. My horse being disabled, I tried to hire another. I was told this could not be done either. I saw what it meant. I was to be kept at Cologne, and I did not choose to be kept; so I ordered my poor nag to be saddled, lame as he was, with another for my servant, and I started on a five hours' journey for the Count of New Eagle. I had five pleasant days with the Count, whom I found a young man of sense. I had meant, if the autumn was fine, to go on to England and close with the King's repeated offers to me. From this dream I was precipitated into a gulf of perdition. A carriage had been ordered for me for the next morning. The Count would not take leave of me overnight, meaning to see me before I started. The night was wild. I rose before dawn to finish off some work. At seven, the Count not appearing, I sent to call him. He came, and protested that I must not leave his house in such weather. I must have lost half my mind when I went to Cologne. My evil genius now carried off the other half. Go I would, in an open carriage, with wind enough to tear up oak-trees. It came from the south and charged with pestilence. Towards evening wind changed to rain. I reached Aix shaken to pieces by the bad roads. I should have done better on my lame horse. At Aix a canon to whom the Count had recommended me carried me off to the house of the Precentor to sup. Other

Cathedral dignitaries were also of the party. My light breakfast had sharpened my appetite, and there was nothing to eat but cold carp. I filled myself as I could, and went early to bed under plea that I had not slept the night before. Next day I was taken to the Vice-Provost, whose table usually was well provided, but on this occasion, owing to the weather, he had nothing to offer but eels. These I could not touch, and I had to fall back on salt cod, called "bacalao," from the sticks they beat it with. It was almost raw. Breakfast over, I returned to the inn and ordered a fire. The canon stayed an hour and a half talking. My stomach then went into a crisis. A finger in my mouth brought on vomiting. Up came the raw cod, and I lay down exhausted. The pain passed off. I settled with the driver about my luggage, and was then called to the *table d'hôte* supper. I tried to excuse myself. I knew by experience that I ought to touch nothing but warm sops. However, they had made their preparations for me, so attend I must. After the soup I retreated to the Precentor's to sleep. Another wild night. Breakfast in the morning, a mouthful of bread and a cup of warm beer, and then to my lame beast. I ought to have been in bed, but I disliked Aix and its ways, and longed to be off. I had been suffering from piles, and the riding increased the inflammation. After a few miles we came to the bridge over the Meuse, where I had some broth, and thence on to Tongres. The pain then grew horrible. I would have walked, but I was afraid of perspiring or being out after nightfall. I reached Tongres very ill all over. I slept, however, a little; had some warm beer again in the morning, and ordered a close carriage. The road turned out to be paved with flint. I could not bear the jolting, and mounted one of the horses. A sudden chill, and I fainted, and was put back into the carriage. After a while I recovered a little, and again tried to ride. In the evening I was sick, and told the driver I would pay him double if he would bring me early to my next stage. A miserable night —suffering dreadful. In the morning I found there was a carriage with four horses going straight through to Louvain. I engaged it and arrived the next night in an agony of pain. Fearing that my own rooms would be cold, I drove to the house of my kind friend Theodoric, the printer. An ulcer broke in the night, and I was easier. I send for a surgeon. He finds another on my back; glands swollen and boils forming all over me. He tells Theodoric's servant that I have the plague, and that he will not come near me again. Theodoric brings the message. I don't believe it. I send for a Jew doctor, who wishes his body was as sound as mine. The surgeon persists that it is the plague, and so does his father. I call in the best physician in the town, who says that he would have no objection to sleep with me. The Hebrew holds to his opinion. Another fellow makes a long face at the ulcers. I give him a gold crown, and tell him to come again the next day, which he refuses to do. I send doctors to the devil, commend myself to Christ, and am well in three days. Who could believe that this frail body of mine could have borne such a shaking? When I was young I was greatly afraid of dying. I fear it less as I grow older. Happiness does not depend on age. I am now fifty, a term of life which many do not reach, and I cannot complain that I have not lived long enough.

You will tell me, perhaps, that all this is not history. Well, if history consists of the record of the fragments of actions preserved by tradition, attributed to wooden figures called men and women, interpreted successively by philosophic writers according to their own notions of probability, and arranged to teach constitutional lessons, certainly it is not history. But if by history we mean as much as we can learn of the character and doings of past generations of real human creatures who would bleed if we pricked them, then a letter like this, bringing as it does such a crowd of figures before us in the working dress of common life, is very historical indeed. Boatmen, bargemen, drunken bargemen's wives, literary wine-merchants, taverns and tavern dinners, canons and precentors eager to recognise the great man and poison him with cold carp and bacalao, carriages, horses, bad roads, sixteenth-century surgeons — there, in a few pages, we have it all alive before us, whether philosophy can make anything out of it or not.

Unfortunate Erasmus! No sooner was he quit of his bodily tortures than his old enemies opened fire again upon him. He sent Colet a short account of his calamities on his journey, with a glimpse of the condition of his mind: —

You often call Erasmus unlucky. What would you call him if you saw him now? Who would credit me with strength to survive such a tossing, to say nothing of sycophant divines who bite at my back when to my face they dare not? The [new edition of the] New Testament will be out soon. The Comments on the Apostolic Epistles are in the press. The Paraphrases will follow. The Archbishop of Mentz, still a young man, has disgraced himself by accepting a cardinal's hat and becoming a Pope's monk. Oh, my dear Colet, what a fate for a human soul! We make tyrants out of priests and gods out of men. Princes, popes, Turks combine to make the world miserable. Christ grows obsolete, and is going the way of Moses.

Faster and faster copies of the New Testament spread over Europe, and with it the wrath of the orthodox. The Pope had refused their request for an official examination of Erasmus's work. Eager individuals rushed in with their separate complaints, and over France, England, and Germany monks and priests were denouncing the errors which they imagined themselves to have discovered. For the first time it had to be explained to them that the Bible was a book, and had a meaning like other books. Pious, ignorant men had regarded the text of the Vulgate as sacred, and probably inspired. Read it intelligently they could not, but they had made the language into an idol, and they were filled with horrified amazement when they found in page after page that Erasmus had anticipated modern criticism, correcting the text, introducing various readings, and retranslating passages from the Greek into a new version. He had altered a word in the Lord's Prayer. Horror of horrors! he had changed the translation of the mystic Λόγος from *Verbum* into *Sermo*, to make people understand what Λόγος meant. The wildest stories were set flying. Erasmus was accused of having called the Gospel an old woman's fable. He had merely rendered συλλαλοῦντες into *confabulantes*. A preacher at Louvain, cursing Luther as a heretic and Antichrist, charged Erasmus and literature with the guilt of having produced him, and said that the desire for knowledge had been the origin of all the misery in the world, as if it had not been notorious, as Erasmus observes, that Luther had been educated entirely on the schoolmen, and knew nothing of literature. His old enemy, Egmond, declared that the publication of Erasmus's New Testament was the coming of Antichrist. Erasmus asked him what he had found there to offend him. He answered that he had never looked into the book, and never would. An English divine (Erasmus himself tells the story) was one day preaching before the King. He used the occasion to denounce the new studies, and Greek especially. Dr. Pace, who was present, looked at Henry. Henry smiled, and after the sermon sent for the preacher and sent for Sir T. More to discuss the question between them. The preacher had trusted to pulpit irresponsibility. He fell on his knees, and pleaded that the Spirit had moved him. The King said it must have been a foolish spirit. The preacher had denounced Erasmus by name. Henry asked him if he had read any of Erasmus's writings. He said he had read something called "Moria." Pace observed that he was not surprised; his argument smelt of it. The man said that perhaps Greek might be innocent after all, as it was derived from Hebrew. The King sent him about his business, and ordered that he should never preach before the Court again.

A bishop, who was one of Queen Catherine's confessors, had abused Erasmus to her with similar nonsense. The Queen one day asked a friend of Erasmus whether Jerome was not a learned man, and whether he was not in heaven. "Yes, certainly," was the answer. "Why then," said she, "does Erasmus correct Jerome? Is he wiser than Jerome?"

"Such stuff," said Erasmus, commenting on these stories, "is taught seriously by pillars of the Church and champions of the Christian religion. I shall argue no more. I am a veteran and have earned my discharge, and must leave the fighting to younger men."

There was to be no discharge for Erasmus while the breath was in him. More unwelcome than the attacks of monks or bishops was a letter which next reached him. He had avoided Luther's books. He had wished to be able to say that he did not know Luther, and had held no communication with him. Luther, on the other hand, naturally thought that Erasmus, who had so far led the campaign, ought to stand his friend, and ventured to appeal to him.[1] He wrote

[1] *Ep.* cccxcix.

naturally, simply, even humbly. Erasmus's splendid qualities had filled him, he said, with admiration, and the anger which Erasmus had provoked was a sign that God was with him. He apologised for venturing to address so great a man. His life had been spent among sophists, and he knew not how to speak to a scholar. "But I trust," he said, "that you will let me look on you as a brother. My fate is a hard one. I, a poor ignorant creature, fit only to be buried in a corner out of sight of sun and sky, have been forced forward into controversy against my natural will."

Never had any request been addressed to Erasmus more entirely inconvenient to him. He had enough to do to fight his own battles. To take up Luther's was to forfeit the Pope's protection, which had hitherto been his best defence. The Pope let him say all that he wished himself. Why lose an advantage so infinitely precious to him? Luther resented his hesitation, and Protestant tradition has execrated Erasmus's cowardice. His conduct was not perhaps heroic, but heroism is not always wisdom. The Luther who was now wishing to be his brother was not the Luther of history, the liberator of Germany, the regenerator of the Christian faith. To Erasmus he was merely an honest, and perhaps imprudent monk, who had broken out single-handed into a noisy revolt. Doubtless the indulgences were preposterous, and the Church of Rome was an Augean stable which wanted all the waters of the Tiber through it; but the first beginners of revolutions are not those who usually bring them to a successful conclusion. Walter the Pennyless goes before Godfrey of Bouillon. The generous and the rash rush forward prematurely without measuring the difficulties of the enterprise, and attack often in the wrong place. The real enemy in the mind of Erasmus was not the Pope and his indulgences, absurd as they might be; but the gloomy mass of lies and ignorance which lay spread over Europe, and the tyranny of a priesthood believed to possess supernatural powers. If cultivated popes and bishops like Leo and Archbishop Warham, and hundreds more whom Erasmus knew, would lend a hand to help education and spread the knowledge of the New Testament, there might be better hopes for mankind in using their assistance than in plunging into a furious battle with popular superstition and the Roman hierarchy combined.

Erasmus may have been wrong. Times come when rough measures alone will answer, and Erasmian education might have made slight impression on the Scarlet Lady of Babylon. But Erasmus was not bound to know it, and I think it rather to his credit that he met Luther's advances as favourably as he did.

I knew various persons of high reputation a few years ago who thought at bottom very much as Bishop Colenso thought, who nevertheless turned and rent him to clear their own reputations, which they did not succeed in doing. Erasmus was no saint. He thought Luther an upright, good man, if not a wise one, and he was too intellectually honest to conceal his real convictions. How he behaved under his temptation we shall see in the next lecture.

LECTURE XII.

THE moderate reformer always resents the intrusion of the advanced Radical into work which he has been himself conducting with caution and success. He sees his own operations discredited, his supporters alienated, his enemies apparently entitled to appeal to the fulfilment of their prophecies, the leadership snatched out of his hands and passed on to more thorough going rivals. He is not to be hastily blamed if he is in a hurry to disconnect himself from hot spirits whom he cannot govern and whose objects extend beyond what he himself desires or approves. If Erasmus had publicly washed his hands of Luther and advised his suppression, he would have done no more than any ordinary party leader would have done in the same position. His real action was absolutely different. Aleander, the Papal Nuncio, had brought the Bull condemning Luther to the Elector of Saxony, had called on the Elector in the Pope's name to order Luther's works to be burnt, to seize Luther himself, and either execute the papal sentence or send his heretical subject as a prisoner to Rome. It was no easy matter for a subordinate prince of the German empire to fly in the face of the spiritual ruler of Christendom. The Elector knew Erasmus only by reputation, but to Erasmus he turned for advice, and went to Cologne to see Erasmus personally, and consult with him as to what should be done. Erasmus told the Elector that Luther had committed two unpardonable crimes — he had touched the

Pope on the crown and the monks in the belly; but however that might be, a German subject ought not to be given up to destruction till his faults had been proved against him. Luther had always professed himself willing to argue the question of the indulgences, and to submit if they were shown to be legitimate. He had been so far a quiet peaceful man, with an unblemished reputation, which was more than could be said of many of his accusers. The Pope's Bull had offended every reasonable man, and, in fact, he advised the Elector to refuse till the cause had been publicly heard. The advice was the more creditable to Erasmus, because he knew that if it came to a struggle he would be himself in danger. He was not inclined to be a martyr, and in extremity meant to imitate St. Peter. So at least he said, but perhaps he would have been better than his word. He wrote to the President of Holland, strongly deprecating the Pope's action. "I am surprised," he said, "that the Pope should have sent Commissioners on the business so violent and ignorant. Cardinal Cajetan is arrogant and overbearing; Miltitz is little better; and Aleander is a maniac" — worse indeed than a maniac, in Erasmus's secret opinion.[1] Aleander had been bred in the Court of Alexander VI. The Court of Rome had determined one way or another to rid themselves of the troublesome Saxon monk. If he could not be disposed of in the regular fashion, there were other methods. "They will now probably take Luther off by poison," Erasmus wrote, "as certain of his defenders have been removed in Paris. This possibly is among the instructions: that when the enemies of the Holy See cannot be got rid of otherwise, they may be

[1] To Nicholas Everard, President of Holland. *Ep.* cccxvii., second series, abridged.

taken off by poison with his Holiness's blessing. Everyone is an enemy of the Faith with these harpies if he will not submit to them in everything. Aleander is an old hand at such business. He asked me to dine with him at Cologne. He was so urgent that I thought it prudent to decline."[1] "The apostolic rod no longer sufficing," he says elsewhere, "they will first try prisons, chains, stake, and gallows, cannon and armies, and if these won't do they will fall back on the cup."

In the middle of the crisis the old Emperor Maximilian died. The imperial crown fell vacant. The Elector of Saxony had but to consent to be chosen to be unanimously elected. The situation seemed less dangerous, and Erasmus was able to answer Luther's letter to him. He calls him "his dearest brother in Christ." He thanked Luther for desiring his friendship, and spoke of the storm which he had caused.[2]

Had I not seen it with my own eyes (he wrote) I could not have believed that the theologians would have gone so mad. It is like the plague. All Louvain is infected. I have told them that I do not know you personally; that I neither approve nor disapprove your writings, for I have not read them, but that they ought to read them before they spoke so loudly. I suggested, too, that the subjects on which you have written were not of a sort to be declaimed on from pulpits, and that, as your character was admitted to be spotless, denouncing and cursing were not precisely in place. It was of no use. They are mad as ever. They do not argue because they cannot, and they trust entirely to evil speaking. I am myself the chief object of animosity. The bishops generally are on my side and against them, and this makes them savage.

[1] "Fortassis hoc in mandatis est, ut quoniam aliter vinci non possunt hostes Sedis Romanæ veneno tollantur cum benedictione Pontificis. Hac arte valet Aleander. Is me Coloniæ impensissime rogavit ad prandium. Ego quo magis ille instabat hoc pertinacius excusavi." *Ibid.*

[2] *Ep.* ccccxxvii., abridged.

I can only despise them. Wild beasts are tamed by gentleness; they are only made more ferocious by it.

For yourself, you have good friends in England, even among the greatest persons there. You have friends here too — one in particular. As to me, my business is with literature. I confine myself to it as far as I can, and keep aloof from other quarrels; but, generally, I think courtesy to opponents is more effective than violence. Paul abolished the Jewish law by making it into an allegory; and it might be wiser of you to denounce those who misuse the Pope's authority than to censure the Pope himself. So also with kings and princes. Old institutions cannot be rooted up in an instant. Quiet argument may do more than wholesale condemnation. Avoid all appearance of sedition. Keep cool. Do not get angry. Do not hate anybody. Do not be excited over the noise which you have made. I have looked into your "Commentary on the Psalms," and am much pleased with it. The prior of a monastery at Antwerp is devoted to you, and says he was once your pupil. He preaches Christ and Christ only. Christ give you His spirit, for His own glory and the world's good.

On the whole I think this letter extremely honourable to Erasmus. It says no more and no less than he really felt, and it was one of those many instances where truth serves a man better than the subtlest subterfuge; for the letter was immediately printed by Luther's friends, and perhaps with Luther's own consent, to force Erasmus to commit himself.

I suppose these hasty gentlemen thought that he must make the plunge sooner or later, and that they were helping him over for his own good. It did not answer. Erasmus had said no more to Luther than what he had said about him to everyone else. He could not have extricated himself out of his difficulty more simply or more sensibly.

He was himself beset with other correspondents besides Luther. His answers are always full, consistent and pointed.

A Bohemian student had written to invite him to Prague. He could not go to Prague, but was pleased to hear that he was appreciated there. He was a harmless person, he said; he had never hurt anybody, and was surprised at the outcry against him. He had perceived that theology had grown thorny and frigid; the early Fathers were neglected, and he had merely tried to recall men to the original fountain of the faith. The signs in the sky were ugly and portended a schism.

So many cardinals, bishops, princes in the world, and not one ready to take up reform in a Christian spirit. Were St. Paul Pope, he would part with some of his wealth — yes, and some of his authority too, if he could restore peace to the Church.

Cardinal Campegio told Erasmus he was suspected of having stirred the fire with anonymous books and pamphlets. He protested that he had stirred no fire, and had published nothing to which he had not set his name.

His mind was still turning to his English friends. In May 1519, he writes a remarkable letter, from Antwerp, to Sir Henry Guildford, the King's master of the horse.[1]

The world is waking out of a long deep sleep. The old ignorance is still defended with tooth and claw, but we have kings and nobles now on our side. Strange vicissitude of things. Time was when learning was only found in the religious orders. The religious orders nowadays care only for money and sensuality, while learning has passed to secular princes and

[1] *Ep.* ccccxvii., abridged.

peers and courtiers. Where in school or monastery will you find so many distinguished and accomplished men as form your English Court? Shame on us all! The tables of priests and divines run with wine and echo with drunken noise and scurrilous jest, while in princes' halls is heard only grave and modest conversation on points of morals or knowledge. Your king leads the rest by his example. In ordinary accomplishments he is above most and inferior to none. Where will you find a man so acute, so copious, so soundly judging, or so dignified in word and manner? Time was when I held off from royal courts. To such a court as yours I would transfer myself and all that belongs to me if age and health allowed. Who will say now that learning makes kings effeminate? Where is a finer soldier than your Henry VIII., where a sounder legislator? Who is keener in council, who a stricter administrator, who more careful in choosing his ministers, or more anxious for the peace of the world? That king of yours may bring back the golden age, though I shall not live to enjoy it, as my tale draws to an end.

On the same day Erasmus writes to Henry himself:[1] —

The heart of a king is in the hands of God. When God means well to any nation he gives it a king who deserves a throne. Perhaps after so many storms He now looks on us with favour, having inspired the present reigning monarchs with a desire for peace and the restoration of piety. To you is due the highest praise. No prince is better prepared for war, and none more wishes to avoid it, knowing, as you do, how deadly a scourge is war to the mass of mankind, while you have so well used your respite that you have cleared the roads of robbers — so long the scourge and reproach of England; you have suppressed vagabonds; you have strengthened your laws, repealed the bad ones, and supplied defects. You have encouraged learning.

[1] *Ep.* ccccxviii., abridged.

You have improved discipline among the monks and clergy. You have recognised that a pure and noble race of men is a finer ornament to your realm than warlike trophies or splendid edifices. You make yourself the pattern of what you prescribe for others. The king's command goes far, but the king's example goes further. Who better keeps the law than you keep it? Who less seeks unworthy objects? Who is truer to his word? Who is juster and fairer in all that he does? In what household, in what college or university will you find more wisdom and integrity than in the Court of England? The poet's golden age, if such age ever was, comes back under your Highness. What friend of England does not now congratulate her? What enemy does not envy her good fortune? By their monarchs' character realms are ennobled or depraved. Future ages will tell how England throve, how virtue flourished in the reign of Henry VIII., how the nation was born again, how piety revived, how learning grew to a height which Italy may envy, and how the prince who reigned over it was a rule and pattern for all time to come. Once I avoided kings and courts. Now I would gladly migrate to England if my infirmities allowed. I am but a graft upon her — not a native; yet, when I remember the years which I spent there, the friends I found there, the fortune, small though it be, which I owe to her, I rejoice in England's felicity as if she were my natural mother. . . . For yourself, the intelligence of your country will preserve the memory of your virtues, and scholars will tell how a king once reigned there who in his own person revived the virtues of the ancient heroes.[1]

I seriously believe that this will be the final verdict of English history on Henry VIII. What Erasmus says of him is no more after all than what Reginald

[1] "Græca pariter ac Latina facundia grata tuis erga se meritis semper loquetur apud Britannos fuisse quendam Henricum Octavum qui unus tot heroum dotes ac decora suis retulerit."

Pole said of the promise of his youth; and Pole's opinion only changed when Henry turned against the Pope. I have compressed the flow of Erasmus's eloquence, and have omitted some parts of it. One of these omissions contains what is, perhaps, the most curious passage in the whole letter. Going through the catalogue of Henry's literary excellences, Erasmus mentions with special praise a position which Henry had lately defended against an eminent divine: "Utrum laicus obligaretur ad vocalem orationem?" — Whether a layman was obliged to say his prayers in words? It is not said which side Henry took in the discussion; but the raising of such a question at all throws an interesting light on the condition of theological opinion.

The vacancy of the imperial throne for a time paralysed authority in Germany. Erasmus describes Brussels in the following month as in a state of panic; doctors of theology stirring tragedies, mining and plotting, with open war close ahead against the new learning.

Would (he said) that we had such a prince here as they have in England. The King of England is well read, has a keen intelligence, supports literature openly, and shuts the mouths of the enemy. The Cardinal of York is equally decided, and so is Campegio,[1] who is one of the best and most learned men living. The English Court contains at present more persons of real knowledge and ability than any university in Europe. The German princes are doing almost as well. It is only here in Flanders that we hang behind. The Archduke Ferdinand is an admirable youth. He delights in me and my writings, and the "Institution of a Christian Prince" is seldom out of his hands. They wanted me to be his tutor, and he

[1] Campegio held an English bishopric — Salisbury.

seemed to wish it himself. My health and my dislike of courts stand in the way. It would perhaps kill me, and I should be of no use to anyone, while as long as I keep alive I can at least use my pen.

The fate of Europe seemed to turn on the choice of Maximilian's successor. The new emperor, whoever he might be, would have to declare for Luther or declare for the Pope. According to law and custom, the civil magistrate was bound to maintain truth as well as execute justice. Truth in spiritual matters had been hitherto what Popes decreed. Rome and the Empire had quarrelled in earlier times over the limits of jurisdiction; and whether Popes might depose sovereigns was an open question. But neither Frederic II. nor Henry IV. had pretended to a voice in doctrine. Popes and Councils had managed doctrine. The Pope in issuing indulgences had followed recognised usage, and Luther was a rebel. But he was a rebel so backed by secular opinion that a mistake in dealing with him might throw Germany into civil war. How Maximilian would have acted was uncertain. He had died while he was hesitating, and a new occupant was to be found for the crown. Seven electors chose the Emperor of Germany, three Archbishops — Mentz, Trèves, and Cologne, and four princes — the Dukes of Saxony and Brandenburg, the Count Palatine, and the King of Bohemia. The strongest candidates were Francis I. of France, and Maximilian's grandson, Charles. A French sovereign was distasteful to the Germans. Charles, though a youth of promise, was but nineteen years old, the exact age of the century. He was already King of Spain and the Indies, King of Naples and Sicily, and Archduke of Flanders. There was a natural fear that, if Charles was chosen, a prince already so powerful might be dangerous to German liberty. With the Lutheran question in the very front, and with Frederick of Saxony as Luther's protector, the electoral body, bishops and princes, unanimously offered the succession to one of whose disposition, at least on that point, no doubt could be entertained. But the Elector of Saxony had other things to think of besides Luther. The Pope's crusade against the Turks, instead of terrifying the Sultan, was like to bring the Crescent into Germany. The Elector of Saxony considered that an Emperor with large resources of his own was essential to the safety of Europe against the foreign enemy. He set aside his ambition, if he had any. He proposed Charles, and Charles by his influence was chosen. What would Charles do? He was in Spain at the moment of the election, suppressing the revolt of the Comunidades. He would hurry back, of course, and Luther's affair would be the first problem to be dealt with. The Elector perhaps expected that Charles would be guided by the advice of the prince to whom he owed the throne. Erasmus at one time heard that Charles was inclined to Luther's side, but felt no confidence either way, and, perhaps, distrusted Charles's Spanish blood. Writing immediately that the matter was decided to George Spalatin, he says: —

I think the Elector of Saxony deserves more praise for refusing the crown than some deserved who sought it. He is fittest to wear a crown who best knows the weight of it. Let us pray God that all may go well. These Provinces were delighted at first that the choice had fallen on their own sovereign; but as with all human things, there is some alloy with the satisfaction.

Erasmus himself had misgivings.

In September he writes to the Archbishop of

Mentz, one of the electors, whom he had so abused for accepting a cardinal's hat, but whom, nevertheless, he trusted and liked: —

Everyone hopes that the new emperor will equal his grandfather. In late centuries the imperial crown has brought more glitter than power with it. Now, happily, there will be strength as well as name. Hitherto the title of emperor has been but a pretence of sovereignty. Charles will make the emperor into a real ruler. He is young, and Christendom may expect a happy future under him. If he chooses, he may awe into submission the barbarous enemies of Christ's Church. God grant it may so prove!

It was an odd world. Cardinal Albert was among the most guilty in the Tetzel business, yet Erasmus writes to him as if he believed him to be on the Reforming side, and recommends to him specially Ulrich von Hutten as an ornament to the Church.

So far as regarded his own prospects, Erasmus was soon relieved of anxiety. Among Charles's first acts was to name him an Imperial Councillor. It was an office like our own Right Honourable, which had no salary with it, and was only a feather; but it was a sign of goodwill, and as such was welcome. He needed comfort. His dear friend Colet had just died in England. How dear may be seen in the confessions of their sins, which he and Colet had mutually made to each other. Acquaintances hide their faults from one another, and like to appear at their best. Real friends show themselves completely as they are, and few men ever were more frank in the acknowledgment of their mutual defects than Colet and Erasmus. Erasmus wished to write his life, but perhaps he could not have improved the admirable sketch which he has left.

He had other troubles, too, just then, of the sort that never ended. The orthodox theologians, rallying from their first confusion, were falling systematically on his New Testament. Hochstrat, the Hebrew scholar, attacked him on one side; the Carmelite Egmond on another; Edward Lee, who became Archbishop of York afterwards, and was the most violent of all, on a third. He had been careless, and made various small slips, of no consequence in themselves, which critics delight to use to wound and injure the person criticised. He ought to have despised such attacks, but his skin was thin, and his letters are full of complaints. It is a pity. The world has much to occupy it, and can spare but moderate sympathy for the personal wrongs even of great men.

Most of these lamenting letters, however, contain passages of high general interest.

TO THE BISHOP OF ROCHESTER.[1]

October 17, 1519.

The Elector of Saxony has written to me twice. He tells me that in supporting Luther he is supporting rather a principle than a person. He will not permit innocent men to be borne down in his dominions by malicious persons who rather seek themselves than Christ. The other electors unanimously offered him the crown the day before Charles was chosen, nor would Charles have been chosen at all without the strong support which the Elector of Saxony gave him. On his own refusal they urged him to say who in his opinion was the fittest candidate. He said emphatically, the King of Spain. They offered him 30,000 florins as a gift. When he would not have it, they begged that at least 10,000 florins might be distributed among his household. He said his household might do as they pleased, but not one of them should remain in his service who accepted a farthing.

[1] *Ep.* ccccIxxiv.

I heard this from the Bishop of Liège, who was present. We expect our new emperor home from Spain immediately.

Almost at the same date we have another long and interesting letter to Cardinal Albert.[1] Erasmus had introduced Ulrich von Hutten to him. The Cardinal had sent him a large silver cup by Von Hutten's hands. It was called the cup of love, as binding together indissolubly those who drank out of it together. Among the promotions which Charles or his advisers had lately made in Spain, the See of Toledo, the richest in the world, had been given, with much displeasure among the Spaniards, to a young Flemish cardinal of the house of Croy.

Wishing (says Erasmus) to try the powers of your present, I experimented with it on the Cardinal of Croy, who came lately to see me. I drank out of it to him, and he drank to me. The Cardinal is a fortunate youth, and deserves his luck. I am sorry your cup did not reach me sooner. The Louvain Doctors and I had lately made a truce on condition that we should each keep in order our respective followers. It was arranged at a dinner. Nothing can be done here without eating. I would have produced it had it arrived in time; they should all have drunk out of it, and then, perhaps, our peace would have stood. Now, owing to an ill-interpreted letter of mine, the agreement is broken, and the storm is raging worse than ever. It is the malice of Satan, who will not let Christians live in harmony. The matter is this. I premise that I had nothing to do with either Reuchlin's business, or Luther's either. I cared nothing for Cabala or Talmud, and I disliked the quarrel with Hochstrat. Luther is unknown to me. I have glanced at his books, but have had no time to read them. If he has written well, it is no thanks to me; if ill, I am not responsible. I observe only that the

[1] *Ep.* cccclxxvii., abridged.

best men are those who are least offended by Luther. They may not approve entirely, but they may read him, as they read Cyprian or Jerome, and pardon much for the sake of the rest. Still I am sorry that Luther's books have been published. I tried to prevent it, as I thought they would cause disturbance. He wrote me a very Christian letter. I replied by advising him to avoid saying anything seditious, not to attack the Pope or fly in a passion with anybody, but to teach the Gospel calmly and coolly. I added that he had good friends at Louvain, hoping that he might be the more willing to listen to us. This has got abroad, and has been taken to mean that I have declared myself on Luther's side, when up to that time I was the only person who had given him any sound advice at all. I am neither Luther's accuser, nor his patron, nor his judge; I can give no opinion about him, least of all an unfavourable one.

His enemies admit that he is a person of good character. Suppose I defended him on this ground. The laws allow advocates to criminals on trial. Even suppose I said that all this storm about him is merely a covert attack on literature, where would be the harm as long as I did not personally adopt his views? It would be my duty, as a Christian, to save him, if he is innocent, from being crushed by faction, and, if he is mistaken, to recover him from his errors. A spirit which shows splendid sparks of Christian doctrine ought not to be borne down and extinguished. I would correct him that he might preach the better to Christ's glory. But certain divines that I know will neither set him right nor point out where he is wrong. They only howl and raise the mob upon him. They shout out "heresy, heretic, heresiarch, schismatic, Antichrist," and not a word besides; and their language is the more odious because most of them have never looked into his writings. He has been condemned on some points from a mere mistake of his meaning. For instance, they make him say that it is unnecessary for the penitent to confess sins which he does not himself know to be sins; he need not confess to sins which the priests are pleased to call such. This has been interpreted to mean that no sin need be confessed which is not notorious, and there has been a marvellous outcry about it.

Confession had been one of the Church's strongest and most envenomed weapons; secrets of families, secrets concerning the opinions of other people had been extorted by it, and men had found themselves accused before the Inquisition they knew not why.

Propositions (says Erasmus) taken out of Luther's writings have been condemned as heretical which are found in Bernard or Augustine, and from them are received as orthodox and edifying. I warned these Doctors at the beginning to be careful what they were about. I advised them not to clamour to the multitude, but to confine themselves to writing and argument, and above all to censure nothing publicly till they were sure that they had considered and understood it. I said it was indecorous for grave theologians to storm and rage at a person whose private life was admitted to be innocent. I said that topics like secret confession ought not to be declaimed upon before mixed audiences, where there would be many persons present who felt so strongly about it. I supposed I was speaking sense to them, but it only made them more furious. They insisted that I had prompted Luther, and that his work had been conceived and brought forth at Louvain. They stirred such a tragedy as I have never witnessed the like of.

The business of theologians is to teach the truth. These people have nothing in their mouths but violence and punishment. Augustine would not have the worst felon put to death till an effort had been made to mend him. The Louvain theologians may call themselves meek, but they are thirsting for human blood, and demand that Luther shall be arrested and executed. If they wish to deserve to be called divines, let them convert Jews, let them mend the morals of Christendom, which are worse than Turkish. How can it be right to drag a man to the scaffold who has done no more than what the theological schools themselves have always permitted? He has proposed certain subjects for discussion. He is willing to be convinced. He offers to submit to Rome or to leave his cause to be judged by the Universities. Is this a reason for handing him over to the executioners? I am not surprised that he will not trust himself to the judgment of men who would rather find him guilty than innocent. How have all these disturbances risen? The world is choked with opinions which are but human after all, with institutions and scholastic dogmas, and the despotism of the mendicant friars, who are but satellites of the Holy See, yet have become so numerous and so powerful as to be formidable to secular princes, and to the Popes themselves. As long as the Pope says what they say, these friars call him more than God. If he contradicts them, he is no more than a dream. I do not accuse them all, but I do say that too many are like this. They tyrannise over the conscience of the laity for their own purposes. They brazen their fronts. They forget Christ, and preach preposterous doctrines of their own invention. They defend indulgences in a tone which plain men cannot and will not endure.

Thus it has been that the Gospel of Christ has faded out; in a little while the last spark of Christianity would have been extinguished, and we should have been enslaved in a worse than Jewish ceremonial. There are good men even among theologians who see these things and deplore them. Nay, there are monks who will admit the truth in private conversation, and it was this I conceive which moved Luther at last to rise and speak out. What unworthy motive could Luther have had? He wants no promotion. He wants no money. I am not complaining of the fact that the Pope has censured him. I do complain of the manner and the occasion on which the censure was issued. He was imprudent enough to question the value of indulgences in which others pretended to believe. He challenged, perhaps too uncompromisingly, the authority of the Roman Pontiff in the face of an extravagant exercise of it. He ventured to reject the opinion of St. Thomas, which the Dominicans place above the Gospel, and he condemned the abuse of the confessional by the monks to ensnare the consciences of men and women. Pious souls have affected to be excruciated, while all the time no word is heard of evangelical doctrine in the schools of theology. The sacred writers are set aside as antiquated. No word of Christ is heard in the pulpits. The talk is all of the powers of the Pope and the latest development of theological dogma.

If Luther has been intemperate, this is the explanation of it. The bishops are called Christ's vicars. The chief bishop is the Pope, and our prayer for the Pope should be that he seek the glory of Christ, whose minister he professes to be. But those are no friends to the Pope who lavish higher titles on him than he claims, or than it is good for the flock of Christ that he should possess. They pretend that they are standing up in this stormy way for the Pope's honour. They are alarmed really for their own tyranny, which the Pope's power supports. The present Pontiff is, I believe, a good man, but in such a whirl of confusion he cannot know everything, and the safest advisers for him would be those who think most of Christ and least of themselves. It is plain there are persons about him who exasperate him against Luther, and against everyone who does not take their side. I could point them out, were not the truth sometimes dangerous, and I might be accused of slander. I know many of them personally. Others have shown what they are in their writings. I wish I could make your Eminence understand them as well as I do. I feel myself the more free to speak because, as I said, I have no connection either with Reuchlin or with Luther. Luther's enemies are the same persons who led the attack on literature and opposed the study of the early Christian writers. They were wise in their generation. They knew that the spread of knowledge would be fatal to their dominion. Before Luther had written a word the Dominicans and Carmelites were busy at their work. Most of them were more wicked than ignorant, and when Luther's books came out they used them as a handle to associate me with him.

Confess they must that there is not an author, ancient or modern, whose writings do not contain positions which, if challenged, would be found heretical. Why are they silent about these and fly so furiously at Luther only? He has written, rather imprudently than irreverently, things which they do not like. He is disrespectful to St. Thomas. He has spoilt the trade in indulgences. He speaks ill of the mendicant friars. He places the Gospel above scholastic dogmatism, and despises argumentative hair-splitting. Doubtless intolerable heresies. Behind the monks are crafty influential men who have the Pope's ear and urge him into dangerous courses.

In earlier times a person charged with heresy was heard in his defence; he was acquitted if his answers were satisfactory; if he persisted the worst which he had to fear was exclusion from Communion. Now heresy is the darkest of crimes, and the cry is raised on the least occasion. Nothing then was heresy, except to deny the truth of the Gospel, or the Articles of the Creed, or positive decrees of Councils. Now to dissent from St. Thomas is heresy. To reject any inference which a sophister of yesterday pretends to have drawn out of St. Thomas is heresy. Whatever the monks do not like is heresy. To know Greek is heresy. To speak grammatically is heresy. To dissent from them in the least degree in word or act is heresy.

Of course it is an offence to corrupt the truth, but everything need not be made an article of faith. The champions of orthodoxy should have no taint on them of ambition, or malice, or revenge. The world knows these friars. When their passions are up the best of men are not safe from them. They threaten the bishops. They threaten the Pope himself. Savonarola's fate can tell what the Dominicans are, or this late wickedness at Berne.[1] I do not wish to revive old stories, but I must and will point out what will happen if these people are allowed their way. It has nothing to do with Luther. The danger is real and must be exposed.

As to Luther himself, his writings are before the Universities. The decision, be it what it may, cannot affect me. I have always been cautious. I have written nothing which can be laid hold of against established order. I have started no false opinions. I have formed no party. I would rather die than cause a disturbance in the State. But the less your Eminence listens to such advisers as the monks, the better it will be for your peace.

Cardinal Albert was the most powerful churchman in Germany. He was a personal friend of Leo X., and resembled him in his splendid tastes and general liberalism. Neither he nor the Pope had any objection to satires on the monks, and the sarcasms of Erasmus they had found amusing and had probably thought useful. For himself, Erasmus had nothing to fear in such high quarters as long as he dissociated himself from Luther. But Luther had struck at the Pope himself; Cardinal Albert was personally interested in the indulgences; and that Erasmus should have come forward at such a moment with a manly protest against injustice to Luther is specially creditable to the little man. To have addressed so great a prelate at all in such a tone was to risk the loss of the

[1] *Bernense facinus*, occasioned by a dispute on the Immaculate Conception. The Franciscans asserted that Our Lady was born without original sin; the Dominicans denied it and invented a monstrous apparition to decide the question. The fraud was discovered and five of them were hanged.

high protection which alone so far had enabled him to hold his ground, and to risk it in a cause with which he had imperfect sympathy, and for a man whom he thought headstrong and unwise.

Popular opinion in Germany had at first been all on Luther's side. As the plot thickened, and as the Pope's action had widened the quarrel, many became alarmed at the magnitude of the issues which were opening, and right-minded people were doubtful how to act.

Erasmus's influence on the educated classes was enormous; his letters show how many of them wrote to him for guidance, and those letters were thought of such high importance that they were collected and printed, with or without his consent. They furnished the best evidence of his general consistency and uprightness. One advantage he and Luther both had. Printed books were scarce, and printing was costly. Publishers and compositors were all on the side of the Reformers. Anything of Luther's, anything of Erasmus's was multiplied into thousands of copies, spread everywhere, and read by everyone, while the orthodox could scarcely get their works into type.

Until it had been seen what part the young Emperor would take, and what part the German Diet would take, Erasmus uniformly protested against the violence of the Church party, and against the violence equally of Luther's passionate supporters. Philip Melanchthon, in the ardency of hero-worship and enthusiasm for the new light which had risen, was among those who went to Erasmus for advice. Erasmus warns him against rushing unnecessarily into a fray which promised to be desperate.

If you will take my counsel (he wrote, April 22, 1519) you will leave the enemy alone. They are wretches and deserve to be torn in pieces; but we shall play into their hands by striking back at them. We should show ourselves their superiors in moderation as well as in argument. Everyone here at Louvain speaks well of Luther personally. There are differences about his doctrines. I can give no opinion, for I have not yet read his books. He seems to have said some things well. I wish his manner had been as happy as his matter. I have written about him to the Elector of Saxony.

The leader of the intellect of Germany might have been expected to have marked closely the appearance of a new star which was drawing all men's eyes to it, and to have noted every word which Luther uttered. Yet Erasmus purposely abstained from reading Luther's writings. He knew that he would be pressed on both sides for his opinion, and it was obviously convenient to him to say that he had done no more than glance at them. But there was more than this. Doubtless he wrote as he had spoken to the Elector, advising him not to surrender Luther; but he was himself further from sharing Luther's opinions than he cared to explain. High-minded and gifted men naturally find the same enemies in fools and rogues. But they fall themselves under two types, the believing and enthusiastic, the sceptical and moderate. They need not oppose each other. They may be made of the same celestial material; but one blazes like a comet, perplexing nations with the fear or reality of change; the other light is fixed and steady, if less immediately dazzling, and may shine on when the comet has burnt out.

Erasmus could not attach himself to Luther, yet he was uncertain of the part which he ought to take, and the violence of the orthodox was increasingly intolerable to him. The year 1519 was waning out. The

Diet which was to decide Luther's fate was still delayed by the Emperor's absence in Spain. In November Erasmus writes to a friend:—

I thought I knew something of mankind, having had so much experience of them; but I have discovered such brutes (*belluas*) among Christians as I could not have believed to exist. Your account of the disorder in Germany is most vivid. It is due partly to the natural fierceness of the race, partly to the division into so many separate States, and partly to the tendency of the people to serve as mercenaries. As to the quarrels of religion, the misfortune would be less if those who object to the existing order of things were in agreement. But we are all at issue one with another. Strange as it may seem, there are even men among us who think, like Epicurus, that the soul dies with the body. Mankind are great fools, and will believe anything.

LECTURE XIII.

AMONG the higher clergy there were many who had welcomed and encouraged the revival of learning, but were perplexed and alarmed —alarmed partly for themselves — at the storm which had since broken out. They were the more anxious that Erasmus should not commit himself. The publication of Erasmus's letters, many of them so bitter against the monks and the scholastics, had added to their fears, and one of these moderate persons, Louis Marlianus, a bishop,[1] had written to him in distress.

Erasmus answers at length, and you can trace how his mind was working: —

March 25, 1520.

You caution me against entangling myself with Luther. I have taken your advice, and have done my utmost to keep things quiet. Luther's party have urged me to join him, and Luther's enemies have done their best to drive me to it by their furious attacks on me in their sermons. Neither have succeeded. Christ I know: Luther I know not. The Roman Church I know, and death will not part me from it till the Church departs from Christ. I abhor sedition. Would that Luther and the Germans abhorred it equally. It is strange to see how the two factions goad each other on, as if they were in collusion. Luther has hurt himself more than he has hurt his opponents by his last effusions, while the attacks on him are so absurd that many think the Pope wrong in spite of themselves. I approve of those who stand by the Pope, but

[1] Bishop of Tuy, in Gallicia. *Ep.* di., abridged.

I could wish them to be wiser then they are. They would devour Luther off hand. They may eat him boiled or roast for all that I care, but they mistake in linking him and me together, and they can finish him more easily without me than with me. I am surprised at Aleander; we were once friends. He was instructed to conciliate, when he was sent over, the Pope wishing not to push matters to extremity. He would have done better to act with me. He would have found me with him, and not against him, on the Pope's prerogative.

They pretend that Luther has borrowed from me. No lie can be more impudent. He may have borrowed from me as heretics borrow from Evangelists and Apostles, but not a syllable else. I beseech you, protect me from such calumnies. Let my letters be examined. I may have written unguardedly, but that is all. Inquire into my conversation. You will find that I have said nothing except that Luther ought to be answered and not crushed.

Even now I would prefer that things should be quietly considered and not embittered by platform railing. I would have the Church purified of evil, lest the good in it suffer by connection with what is indefensible; but in avoiding the Scylla of Luther I would have us also avoid Charybdis. If this be sin, then I own my guilt. I have sought to save the dignity of the Roman Pontiff, the honour of Catholic theology, and the welfare of Christendom. I have not defended Luther even in jest. In common with all reasonable men I have blamed the noisy bellowing of persons whom I will not name, whose real object is to prevent the spread of knowledge and to recover their own influence. Their numbers are not great, but their power is enormous. But be assured of this, if any movement is in progress injurious to the Christian religion, or dangerous to the public peace or to the supremacy of the Holy See, it does not proceed from Erasmus. Time will show it. I have not deviated in what I have written one hair's breadth from the Church's teaching. We must bear almost anything rather than throw the world into confusion. There are seasons when we must even conceal the truth. The actual facts of things are not to be blurted out at all times and places, and in all companies. But every wise man knows that doctrines and usages have been introduced into the Church which have no real sanction, partly by custom, partly through obsequious canonists, partly by scholastic definitions, partly by the tricks and arts of secular sovereigns. Such excrescences must be removed, though the medicine must be administered cautiously, lest it make the disorder worse and the patient die. Plato says that men in general cannot appreciate reasoning, and may be deceived for their good. I know not whether this be right or wrong. For myself I prefer to be silent and introduce no novelties into religion. Many great persons have entreated me to support Luther. I have answered always that I will support him when he is on the Catholic side. They have asked me to draw up a formula of faith. I reply that I know of none save the creed of the Catholic Church, and I advise everyone who consults me to submit to the Pope. I was the first to oppose the publication of Luther's books. I recommended Luther himself to publish nothing revolutionary. I feared always that revolution would be the end, and I would have done more had I not been afraid *that I might be found fighting against the Spirit of God.*

I caution everyone against reading libellous or anonymous books, books meant only to irritate; but I can advise only. I cannot compel. The world is full of poetasters and orators, and printing-presses are at work everywhere. I cannot stop them, and their extravagances ought not to be charged to me. I do not mean Ulrich von Hutten in particular, though I am sorry for him too, that with such a genius he makes no better use of his gifts. He is himself his worst enemy.

This letter is entirely honest. It shows you precisely how Erasmus was placed, how he thought, and how he acted. I presume you know generally what was going on; but I must say a few words to keep the position plain before you.

The world was changing, and the Church party would not understand it. In the first great fight between the clergy and the laity, in the twelfth century, the clergy had won. They asserted, and they made the world believe them, that they were a supernatural order trusted with the keys of heaven and hell. The future fate of every soul depended on their absolution. They only could bind and loose. They only could bring down Christ from heaven into the sacrament. They were a peculiar priesthood, amenable to no laws but their own, while the laity were amenable to theirs, and as long as this belief subsisted they were shielded by an enchanted atmosphere. By them kings reigned; all power was derived from God, and they were God's earthly representatives, and in the confidence of this assumed authority they had raised a superstructure of intolerable and irresponsible tyranny. They were men, and they might commit crimes, but they could not be punished by any secular law. They were tempted like others to vicious pleasures, but vice did not impair either their rights or their powers. Impunity had produced its natural effect, and in the centuries succeeding they had fallen into the condition which the letters of Erasmus describe.

The patience of the world was worn out. Luther's first blow was at indulgences. He followed it afterwards by striking at the heart of the imposition in treating the priesthood merely as a point of order in the Church, the supernatural power a dream and an illusion, and the Papacy an anti-Christian usurpation. Luther's words expressed the secret convictions of the laity of Northern Europe. Pardons, excommunications, dispensations, absolutions, the hated confessional, the worse hated ecclesiastical courts, the entire system of spiritual domination rocked under the blow. From Norway to the Rhine, from Vienna to the Irish Channel, German, Frank, Scandinavian, Anglo-Saxon, the vigorous and manly part of them cried with a common voice, "The clergy are but as other men. It is an imposture, we will bear it no longer." No wonder the monks raged. It was no time for Erasmus and his arguments. The fire must be put out, or they were gone. They were still, as Erasmus said, terribly powerful. They had on their side the reverence for things long established, the dread of touching the Sacred Ark, the consciences of the timid, and the passions of the fanatical, the alarm of princes and politicians at the shaking of beliefs which had been the cement of human society. To all this they were prepared to appeal to crush out the flame at its rising, to fight with it for life or death — for life or death it was to them; to burn, to kill, to set nation against nation, family against family, brother against brother, subjects against sovereigns, and sovereigns against subjects, anything to keep inviolate the ark of their own supremacy. With what fatal success a century of bloodshed was to tell.

They were not fighting, however, against an imaginary danger. Two years had not gone since Luther set up his theses, and half Germany was already at his side. Indulgences were no longer the only question. Every long-endured grievance of injured laymen against the ecclesiastical despotism sprang into light. Luther's cause was theirs. In defending Luther they were defending their own purses against priestly extortion. Erasmus saw deeper than most whither the movement was leading. He understood how deep, notwithstanding, the roots lay of the old thing, and what a struggle was impending. He hated war, civil war worst of all, and to civil war it might be coming. He could not join Luther. He dared not oppose him, lest haply, as he confessed, "he might be found fighting against the Spirit of God."

Blacker and blacker the sky grew. Leo had first ridiculed Luther, then grew frightened, wrote to the Elector of Saxony to silence him, seize him, send him prisoner to Rome. He had sent cardinal legates to threaten, to persuade, to bribe; but all ineffectually. In weak haste he issued the Bull defending the indulgences, condemning Luther's writings, and ordering every priest in Germany to preach against them. The monks' tongues were set wagging. Erasmus had been deafened with their clamours, but still to no purpose. The young Emperor was detained in Spain. The Elector of Saxony refused to surrender his subject till he had been legally condemned. Luther had been first humble, had asked only that the indulgences should be suspended, and had promised to submit if they were found to be legal. Finding that the point was not to be argued, and that for him there was to be no answer to his theses but stake or scaffold, he went on with impetuous young Germany behind him to pour out tract after tract, exposing the papal encroachments. Leo, driven forward, as Erasmus said, by headstrong advisers, put out his spiritual censures, with a formal requisition to the secular powers to see them executed. The issue of a Bull would force on a crisis. The Diet was summoned to meet at Worms in the following January. Erasmus sate at Louvain observing the gathering of the storm. His chief hope was in the Elector of Saxony, who had sent him a gold medal in acknowledgment of his services.

Writing his thanks to George Spalatin, July 6, 1520, he says: —

May Christ direct Luther's actions to God's glory, and confound those who are seeking their own interests. In Luther's enemies I perceive more of the spirit of this world than of the Spirit of God. I wish Luther himself would be quiet for a while. He injures learning, and does himself no good, while morals and manners grow worse and worse. What he says may be true, but there are times and seasons. Truth need not always be proclaimed on the house-top.

Erasmus, like all men of real genius, had a light elastic nature. He knew very well that to lose heart was the worst of losses, and a small thing made his spirits rebound. He had been ill again, and in the midst of it had been obliged to go to Bruges, where good news reached him from England.

I was nearly dead (he writes to Conrad Goclenius,[1] August 12, 1520). I could eat nothing. I tried doctor after doctor. Potions, draughts, clysters, powders, ointments, baths, plaisters, and what not. I had no leisure to be sick. Business called me to Bruges. I pack my bag, mount my horse. Servant asks me where I am going. "Going," said I, "going where there is better air than at Louvain." Scarcely had I been here for two days when my stomach does its duty again. Fever gone to the devil, and I young again, and able to digest anything. The world mends too. Lucky you, young man, to have been born in such an age as this. The louder the frogs croak the more the youths of Germany attach themselves to me. Good news from England too. More is made a knight and raised to office by the king.

His enemy, Edward Lee, is at work once more on his New Testament, and Pirkheimer has written to him about it.

[1] *Ep.* dxx.

You think (he answers,[1] September 5, from Bruges) that Lee has been bribed to do this dirty work by the monks and divines. Doubtless those birds of darkness are rejoicing; but Lee is only like himself. As a boy he was always the same, a cross, envious, malignant creature. Lee must always be first, craving for admiration, and obstinate in his own opinion. Such as he was he is now, only that his vices grow with his age. God mend him. As to me, all I have sought has been to open my contemporaries' eyes and bring them back from ritual to true Christianity. But I fear it will go the other way, and the enemy are like to get the better of us. Men, thought to be lights and the salt of the earth, hold it right to lie away their neighbours' characters from their pulpits. They don't believe what they are saying. They only want to gain great people's favour. They hate knowledge as they hate a dog or a snake. Of Luther I say only what I would say to himself. I regret that a man who promised to be a splendid instrument in the hands of God should be so exasperated by the howls at him.

A few days later Erasmus is back at Louvain, and writes to Gerard of Nimegen: [2]—

I fear what may happen to that wretched Luther. He has displeased the princes and has infuriated the Pope. Why could he not be advised by me and keep that tongue of his quiet a little? There would have been less passion, and he would have done far more good. His destruction would not in itself be of much moment, but if his enemies succeed in crushing him there will be no bearing them. They will never rest till they have made an end of learning. Hochstrat and Eck [a Dominican enemy of Luther] were to have finished him. The University of Paris was to have pronounced judgment. A furious Bull has been prepared at Rome, but I am afraid there will be only more confusion. The Pope's Council are leading their

[1] *Ep.* dxxvii., abridged.
[2] *Ep.* dcxxviii., abridged.

master along a road which they may call the road of piety, but is assuredly a dangerous one. A dirty fountain boiled over! That at first was all. The idiot monks were frightened at the spread of knowledge. They want to reign without rivals in their own darkness. I might have had a bishopric if I would have written against Luther. I refused, and stood neutral. But the end I fear will be that evangelical truth will be overthrown. We are to be driven, not taught, or taught doctrines alike against Scripture and against reason.

Evidently Erasmus thought that Luther's end was now close, and that his best hope was to save himself and his work from the general wreck. Again, a day or two after, he writes to a friend at Rome:[1]—

No one has been more distressed at this Luther business than I have been. Would that I could have stopped it at the outset. Would that now I could bring about a composition. But it has been ill managed from the first. It rose from the avarice of a party of monks, and has grown step by step to the present fury. The Pope's dignity must of course be supported, but I wish he knew how that dignity suffers from officious fools who imagine they are defending him. Their stupid screams have more recommended Luther to the multitude than any other thing. I told them they must answer him, and no one has done it. There have been a few replies, but too mild to satisfy his accusers, who have only been more furious.

Some of them hate me worse than they hate him, because I have tried to bring them back to primitive Christianity. The Pope's Bull requires all preachers to denounce Luther. Many of them said more against me than against him. One doctor thundered at me in Antwerp. A suffragan of the Bishop of Tournay at Bruges, with a pair of eyes bleared with the wine he had been drinking, stormed for a whole hour at both of us, producing nothing which we had written, but

[1] Francis Chisigat, Sept. 13. *Ep.* dxxx., abridged.

calling us beasts, blockheads, asses, geese, and such like. In a second sermon he charged me with flat heresy. A magistrate present bade him point out the heretical passages. The scoundrel dared to answer that he had not read my books. He had tried the Paraphrases, but found the Latin too much for him. Luther's revilers are of the same sort. They call themselves champions of the Holy See. If the Pope could hear them he would shut their mouths in disgust. Oh, that I could have spoken to the Pope about it! I could have shown him a better course for himself and the world than that which he has chosen. Curses and threats may beat the fire down for the moment, but it will burst out worse than ever. The Bull has lost Luther no friends, and gained none for the Pope. It makes men more cautious, but Luther's party grows stronger daily. Have no fear for me. I am no leader of a revolution. I have had applications enough, more than you would believe, and if I had listened things would not be where they are. But far from me is any such action. I have preached peace all my life, and shall not change my ways at the end of it.

I am now bringing out St. Augustine's works, corrected and annotated. This done, I shall make it known somehow that I disapprove of rebellion. The Holy See needs no support from such a worm as I am, but I shall declare that I mean to stand by it.

Erasmus imagined that if he had been consulted he could have guided matters more wisely. If he was to guide the world, the world must have been willing to follow him, and men in the fury of religious passion will never follow Laodiceans like Erasmus. The worse for them, perhaps; but such is the nature of things. Leo X. was his best hope. He respected the Pope and liked him. The Pope had more than once stood his friend in difficulties. He could not volunteer to advise, but he could explain his own feelings, and clear himself of responsibility for Luther's defiant attitude.

TO LEO X.[1]

LOUVAIN, *September* 19, 1520.

I trust your Holiness will not listen to the calumnies against me and Reuchlin. We are charged with being in confederacy with Luther. I have always protested against this. Neither of us has anything to do with Luther. I do not know him. I have not read his writings; I have barely glanced at a few pages. I gather from what I have seen that Luther rejects the modern hairsplitting and superfluous subtleties in the explanation of Scripture and inclines to the mysticism of the early Fathers. I supported him so far as I thought him right, but I was the first to scent danger. I warned Froben, the printer, against publishing his works. I wrote to Luther's friends. I bade them caution Luther himself against disturbing the peace of the Church. I did tell him in a letter, which your Holiness has seen, that he had friends in Louvain, but that he must moderate his style if he wished to keep them. I thought the knowledge might have a useful influence on him. This was two years ago, before the quarrel was so much embittered. But if anyone can prove that even in table-talk I have defended his opinions, then let me, if men so please, be called a Lutheran. I have not written against him as I have been asked to do, first, because to reply to him I must first have studied what he has said attentively, and for this I have no leisure; and next, because it would be a work beyond my powers or knowledge — the Universities had taken up the subject, and it was not for me to anticipate their verdict; and thirdly, I confess, because I hesitated to attack an eminent man when I had not been ordered to interfere. I trust, therefore, that I may rely on your Holiness's protection. I dare not oppose even my own Diocesan: I am not so mad as to fly in the face

[1] *Ep.* dxxix., abridged.

of the Vicar of Christ. I did not defend Luther when I might have lawfully done so. When I said I disapproved of the character of the attacks on him I was thinking less of the man himself than of the overbearing attitude of the theologians. Their assaults on him were carried on with malicious acerbity and dangerous appeals to popular passion, and the effect was only to give importance to his writings and provoke the world to read them. If they had first answered and confuted him they might then have burnt his books, and himself too if he had deserved it. But the minds of a free, generous nation cannot be driven. It would have been better for the theologians themselves if they had taken my advice and attended to it.

The letter ended with a hope that Erasmus might be able to go to Rome in the winter and see the Pope himself. But the stream was running too hot. The Diet was coming on. The Church party were determined that Luther should appear before it with the papal sentence already passed upon him. His books were publicly burnt. He himself was condemned, and the secular power was formally called in to support the Pope's authority. By law and custom the secular princes were bound to execute a Pope's decree against a pronounced heretic. An imperial safe-conduct had not saved John Huss or Jerome of Prague, and to stand by a rebellious monk was a novelty before which the boldest of them might hesitate. Luther himself did not expect that the laity would save him. He fully expected to be sacrificed, counting that in his death he would bring a step nearer the time of Germany's deliverance. He had made up his mind to the worst, and he determined while he was still free to strike one more blow, which all the world should hear of. The Vatican officials had burnt his own books: he himself replied with burning the Pope's Bull, with a copy of the Papal Decretals, and so defied Leo to do his worst.

So matters stood in the autumn of 1520. The young Emperor returned from Spain. The Diet was to meet at Worms in January, and Erasmus remained motionless at Louvain. The Pope, it seems, had not encouraged his wish to go to Rome. The Louvain divines were triumphing in their anticipated victory. They were confident in the Emperor. They were confident in the result of the Diet. Their enemies would now be delivered into their hand, Erasmus and his Greek as well as Luther and his theses. They were impatient to distinguish themselves by a stroke of their own before the Diet began, and involve Erasmus in Luther's fall.

Erasmus tells the story in an appeal to the Moderator of the University of Louvain.

TO GODSCHALK.[1]

October 18, 1520.

Your oath of office binds you not only to do no wrong yourself, but to see that wrong is not done to others. Nicolas Egmond may denounce Luther at your or the Pope's bidding. It is no business of mine. But it is business of mine when without any bidding he tells lies of me, and it is your duty to restrain his tongue. On St. Denys's Day, at sermon in St. Peter's Church, I myself sitting underneath him, he turned on me and called me Luther's ally. It is false. I had seen gifts in Luther which, if rightly used, might make him an ornament to Christ's Church; and when infamous libels were spread about him I said I would sooner see him corrected than destroyed. If this is to be his ally, I am his ally still, and so is the Pope, and so are you if you are a

[1] *Ep.* dxxxix., abridged.

Christian. But this Carmelite tells the people that I defend Luther on the points on which he is condemned, and he appeals to my letter to the Archbishop of Mentz. Is it to defend a man to show that his meaning has been misrepresented? He said I had not written against Luther. True, I have not. I may not censure what I have not read, specially when it is a matter of life or death, and I am not so foolish as to volunteer into a dispute when I may lawfully look on. What right has Egmond to single out me? He continued: "Luther has fallen into his terrible heresies by studying the new learning. Stand, I warn you, in the old paths, avoid novelties, keep to the ancient Vulgate." This was meant for me and my New Testament. I am accused of making a new gospel.

I had to listen to all this. His face blazed with fervour. He would never have stopped had he not seen that half his hearers were laughing, and the other half muttering or hissing. The Sunday after he preached the same sermon at Antwerp, and added that such fellows as I should be sent to the stake unless they repented. He was like a drunken orator spouting from a waggon. An ally of Luther? I have never been an ally of Luther. There are good and learned men who maintain that Luther has written nothing for which there is not sound authority; and I neither approve nor ever will approve of crushing a man before he has been confuted by reason and Scripture, and allowed an opportunity of recanting. If this be to favour him, many a wise man is on his side. Even the Pope's Bull, smacking though it does of those tyrannical mendicants, gives him time to repent. The clergy are told to preach against him, but they need not call him Antichrist or a monster of wickedness. I advised that he should be read and answered, and that there should be no appealing to the mob. You know how things have gone. There are thousands of Rabbins who are gods in their own eyes. Not one of them has attempted a real reply. Men of noble natures may be led, but cannot be forced. Tyrants drive, asses are driven. By burning Luther's books you may rid him off your bookshelves, but you will not rid him out of the minds of mankind.

My Carmelite rails about novelties and the old ways, improvements all to be suspected. He was alluding of course to the learned languages and my New Testament. The Pope himself has ordered that Greek shall be studied at Rome. He has expressly sanctioned my New Testament. If the Carmelites make so light of the Pope's judgment when it does not please them, why should we think conclusive the Pope's condemnation of Luther? He calls everything new to which he is not accustomed. Hilary, Cyprian, Jerome, Augustine, all are new, and nothing is old but the scholastic formulas and glosses. He is rash in saying Luther borrowed from me. Luther took his errors, if errors they are, from the Apostles and the Fathers, and it is unfair to denounce an innocent man from the pulpit to an ignorant mob.

Everyone was not as violent as the theologians of Louvain. A conference of moderate persons was held at Cologne, at the instance of the Imperial Council, to consider what should be done. Erasmus was invited to attend.

TO CONRAD PEUTINGER, COUNCILLOR OF THE EMPIRE.[1]

November 9, 1520.

We have been consulting how this tornado can be quieted. If not wisely handled it may wreck the Christian religion itself. Fearful consequences have come of lighter causes, and for myself I think, like Cicero, that a bad peace is better than the justest war. The quarrel has gone deeper than I like. It is not yet past cure, but the wound must be so healed that it shall not break out again. Strong measures are wanted. The Pope's authority as Christ's Vicar

[1] *Ep.* dxlii., condensed.

must be upheld, but in upholding it Gospel truth must not be sacrificed. Leo, I believe, thinks on this as we do. The question is not what Luther deserves, but what is best for the peace of the world. The persons who are to prosecute, the remedies which are to be applied, must be carefully chosen. Some are for violence, not to defend the Pope, but to keep out light, and in destroying Luther to destroy knowledge along with him. The true cause of all this passion is hatred of learning, and it is on this account that many persons now support Luther who would otherwise leave him. The contagion, we think, has spread far, and the German nation will be dangerous if provoked to active resistance. Force never answers in such cases, and other means must be found. The reports of the state of morals at Rome have caused vast numbers of men to dislike and even abhor it. On both sides there has been want of discretion. If every word had been true which Luther has said he has so said it as to grudge truth the victory. If his opponents' case had been the best possible they would have spoilt it by their wrongheadedness. Luther was advised to be more moderate. He wrote more passionately every day. His prosecutors were cautioned too, but they continued so savage that they might have seemed in collusion with him. They are of the sort that fatten on the world's misfortunes and delight in confusion. No good can come till private interests are laid aside. Human devices will come to nought. It is not for me to judge the Pope's sentence. Some regret the tone of the Bull, but impute it to his advisers, not to himself. The fear is that, if Luther's books are burnt and Luther executed, things will only grow worse. If he is removed others will take his place, and there will first be war and then a schism. Luther's conduct and the causes which led to it ought to be referred to a small committee of good learned men who will be above suspicion. The Pope need not be bound to bow to their authority. It is rather thought that this is the course which he would himself prefer as promising best for peace. Our hopes are in the approaching Diet.

The Emperor's Council were evidently in extreme perplexity. The Pope and the Sacred College were equally at a loss. In better ages they would have burnt Luther at the stake and cleared away the whole business. But these time-honoured methods had grown dangerous. The Vatican thunder and lightning had passed unheeded. The great novelty of the situation — how great we can now hardly realise — was that for the first time for many centuries a spiritual question, hitherto exclusively reserved to Church courts and councils, was to be referred to a Diet where lay barons and representatives would sit as judges and an Emperor would preside. This alone taught Rome caution. Cardinal Campegio, an old, prudent, accomplished man of the world, was despatched to see what could be done, and mend the blunders of Aleander and Cajetan. Campegio naturally applied to Erasmus for help. Erasmus replied in another extremely valuable letter. After regretting that he had been unable to go to Rome and speak in person to the Pope, he gave his own explanation of what had happened, and he attributed the whole convulsion to the religious orders, and especially to the Carmelites and Dominicans.

TO CAMPEGIO.[1]

December 6, 1520.

Jerome, who was himself a monk, was the most effective painter of monastic vices, and sketches with satiric salt the lives of the brothers and sisters. The scene is shifted, the actors are changed, but the play is the same. When the Reuchlin storm was over came these writings of Luther, and they snatched at them to finish Reuchlin, Erasmus and learning all

[1] *Ep.* dxlvii., abridged.

together. They cried that learning was producing heresies, schisms and Antichrist, and they published my private letters to the Archbishop of Mentz and to Luther. As to Luther himself, I perceived that the better a man was the less he was Luther's enemy. The world was sick of teaching which gave it nothing but glosses and formulas, and was thirsting after the water of life from the Gospels and Epistles. I approved of what seemed good in his work. I told him in a letter that if he would moderate his language he might be a shining light, and that the Pope, I did not doubt, would be his friend. What was there in this to cry out against? I gave him the truest and kindest advice. I had never seen him — I have not seen him at all. I had read little that he had written, nor had matters taken their present form. A few persons only were clamouring at him in alarm for their own pockets. They called on me to pronounce against him. The same persons had said before that I was nothing but a grammarian. How was a grammarian to decide a point of heresy? I said I could not do it till I had examined his authorities. He had taken his opinions from the early Fathers, and if he had quoted them by name he could hardly have been censured. I said I had no leisure for it, nor could I indeed properly meddle when great persons were busy in replying to him. They accused me of encouraging him by telling him that he had friends in England. I told him so to induce him to listen to advice. Not a creature hitherto has given him any friendly counsel at all. No one has yet answered him or pointed out his faults. They have merely howled out heresy and Antichrist.

I have myself simply protested against his being condemned before he has been heard in his defence. The penalty for heresy used to be only excommunication. No crime now is more cruelly punished. But how, while there are persons calling themselves bishops, and professing to be guardians of the truth, whose moral character is abominable, can it be right to persecute a man of unblemished life, in whose writings distinguished and excellent persons have found so much to admire? The object has been simply to destroy him and his books out of mind and memory, and it can only be done when he is proved wrong by argument and Scripture before a respectable commission that can be trusted. Doubtless, the Pope's authority is vast; but the vaster it is, the less it ought to be influenced by private affections. The opinions of pious, learned men should receive attention, and the Pope has no worse enemies than his foolish defenders. He can crush any man if he pleases, but empires based only on terror do not last, and the weightier the Pope's judgment and the graver the charge, the greater caution should be used. Every sensible man, secular or spiritual, even among the Dominicans themselves, thinks as I do about this. Those who wish Luther condemned disapprove of the methods now pursued against him, and what I am here saying is more for the good of the Pope and theology than in the interest of Luther. If the decrees of the Holy See and of the doctors of the Church are to carry weight they must come from men of irreproachable character, whose judgment we can feel sure will not be influenced by worldly motives.

If we want truth, every man ought to be free to say what he thinks without fear. If the advocates of one side are to be rewarded with mitres, and the advocates on the other with rope or stake, truth will not be heard. Out of the many universities in Europe, two have condemned certain propositions of Luther; but even these two did not agree. Then came the terrible Bull, with the Pope's name upon it. Luther's books were to be burnt, and he himself was denounced to the world as a heretic. Nothing could have been more invidious or unwise. The Bull itself was unlike Leo X., and those who were sent to publish it only made matters worse. It is dangerous, however, for secular princes to oppose the Papacy, and I am not likely to be braver than princes, especially when I can do nothing. The corruptions of the Roman Court may require reform extensive and immediate, but I and the like of me are not called on to take a work like that upon ourselves. I would rather see things left as they are than to see a revolution which may lead to one knows not what. Others may be martyrs if they like. I aspire to no such honour. Some hate me for being a Lutheran; some for not being a Lutheran. You may assure yourself that Erasmus has been, and always will be, a faithful subject of the Roman See. But I think, and many think with me, that there would be better chance of a settlement if there was less ferocity, if the management was placed in the hands of men of weight and learning, if the Pope would follow his own disposition and would not let himself be influenced by others.

This letter has been often quoted, among others, to prove that Erasmus was a mean creature, and had not the courage of his convictions. I do not know that a readiness to be a martyr is a very sublime quality, or that those who needlessly rush on their own destruction show any particular wisdom. Such supreme sacrifice may at times become a duty, but only when a man has no better use for his life. It is not a duty of which he need go in search. I am tempted to make a general observation. Princes, statesmen, thinkers who have played a great part in the direction of human affairs, have been men of superior character, men in whose presence ordinary persons are conscious of inferiority. Their biographers — the writers of history generally — are of commoner metal. They resent, perhaps unconsciously, the sense that they stand on a lower level, and revenge their humiliation when they come to describe great men by attributing to them the motives which influence themselves. Unable to conceive, or unwilling to admit, that men of lofty character may have had other objects than are familiar to their personal experience, they delight to show that the great were not great after all, but were very poor creatures, inferior, when the truth is known about them, to the relator of their actions; and they have thus reduced history to the dung-heap of humiliating nonsense which a large part of it has unfortunately become.

I do not wish to say more. You will take my observation for what it is worth.

LECTURE XIV.

ERASMUS, I consider, may be pardoned for not wishing to be burnt at the stake in a cause with which he had imperfect sympathy. Burning at the stake is not pleasant in itself, and there is no occasion to go in search of it. The Papacy was the only visible centre of spiritual authority. Revolution meant anarchy and consequences which none could foresee. As long as there was a hope that the Pope might take a reasonable course, a sensible person might still wish to make the best of him; and if Campegio and his master had been able to follow Erasmus's advice, I do not know that mankind would have been the worse for it. Erasmus was in sufficient danger as he stood. The monks hated him full as much as they hated Luther, and would make short work with him if they could have their way. The Diet was close approaching. They were marshalling their forces and strengthening their positions. The Louvain doctors insisted that if Erasmus did not agree with Luther he should write against him. Erasmus knew that he was refusing at his peril, but he told them that he had no intention of making enemies of the whole German nation, and he would not do it. He describes what passed in a humorous letter to Francis Cranvelt, Councillor of Bruges:[1]—

December 18, 1520.

"If you will not write," said the Carmelite Egmond to me, "then admit that we Louvainers have had the

[1] *Ep.* dl., abridged.

best of the argument." I said the Louvainers would have plenty of people to tell them that. For myself I could not give an opinion till I had seen what they had said. A victory did not amount to much which was won by Bulls and hot coals. He almost spat upon me. The monks now try to finish me with their sermons, the divines partly conniving, partly instigating. Just like them. They say nothing to my face, but slander and lie behind my back. Egmond bids his congregation pray for the conversion of Luther and Erasmus.

Erasmus again complained to the Rector of the University, and a curious scene came off shortly after in the Rector's presence, of which he sends an account to Sir Thomas More:[1] —

We met, the Rector in the chair; I on his right, my Carmelite on his left, the Rector between us, lest from words we might pass to fists and nails. The Rector stated my complaint. Egmond denied that he had injured me in his sermons, and demanded when and how. I said it was an injury to tell lies about a man in public. He was red in the face already, though it was in the forenoon. He turned purple. "Why do you slander us in your books?" said he. "I mention no names," answer I. "Nor I yours in my sermons," says he. "My books are not Scripture," say I; "I may write what I think, and I have said much less in them than I might have said. *You* have spoken a direct lie in telling the people that I support Luther, which I never have in the sense which you wished them to understand." He railed like a madman. "You — you," he said, "are the cause of all the trouble. You are a knave, a double-faced villain." His words came from him as if he was vomiting them. I grew angry. I had a word on my tongue. It was not "Raca," and had more to do with smell than sound; but I checked myself to spare the Rector's feelings.

[1] *Ep.* dliv., abridged.

"I could retort if I liked," said I. "He calls me knave: I might call him fox. He calls me 'double': I might call him 'quadruple.' But let us argue, and not scold like women. Imagine," said I. "I won't imagine" said he; "you poets imagine, and every word is a lie." "Grant, then," said I. "I won't grant," said he. "Let us assume, then," said I. "But it is not so," said he. The Rector could hardly make him listen.

"Granted," said I, "that I have written things which I had better not have written, it was no business of yours to abuse your position as a preacher to revenge what you think your wrongs. You might have remonstrated privately, or you might have brought an action." "Ah," says he, "would n't you like to have the chance?" "Of what?" said I; "of preaching?" "Yes, preaching," says he. "Well, I did preach once," said I, "and I think I could do it as well as you; but I prefer writing books. However, I should not object to your preaching if you would teach morality."

"What good have you ever done?" says he. "Written books," say I. "Bad books," says he. "I have restored the text of Scripture," say I. "Falsified it," says he. "The Pope approves," say I. "I have not seen the Pope's letter to that effect," answered he, with a sneer. "You shall see it if you like," say I. "I will see nothing belonging to you," says he. He went on to speak of the kindness which the Louvain professors had wished to show me. I said I was obliged, but I had not needed their help, and had not met with any. "Your evil offices I have experienced," I said, "and for the rest you have asked me to dinners which I do not like." I reminded him of a Wednesday dinner at the College, where he ate fish enough for four prize-fighters. I asked him if we had not pledged each other, made peace, and agreed to an amnesty. He said it was not so. The Rector, to smooth matters, said he had not understood that peace was made in direct terms. I inquired how often we must drink together to constitute a "pax theologica." "You mock," says he; "you would make out that we are a set of drunkards." I asked when I had accused him of being drunk. "You said I was *uvidus* after dinner," said he. "I did not say so," said I; "I mentioned only what others told me, viz., that you had used bad language, and your brethren excused you on the ground that you were *uvidus*."

A great deal more of this, and then: —

Egmond went on to say that he would go on denouncing Luther till he had made an end of him. I said he might denounce Luther till he burst if it gave him any satisfaction; I complained of his denouncing me. But he only made the people laugh at him. I told him it was useless to burn Luther's books unless you could burn them out of people's memories." "Yes, indeed," he said, "and it is all due to you."

We only quarrelled. The Rector interposed at last. He said it was unworthy of us to wrangle. How was the dispute to be made up?

"What am I to do," said I, "since it seems drinking together is not enough?" "You have injured our good name," Egmond answered; "undo your work." "How am I to undo it?" ask I. "Write," says he, "that there are good and honest divines at Louvain." "I never denied it," said I; "I blamed particular persons, and if you will prove me wrong I will withdraw what I said."

"You charge us with slandering you behind your back," says he; "I will tell you what you are to your face."

"I fear from your manners that you will spit in my face," say I.

The Rector brought us back to Luther.

"You have written in support of Luther," says Egmond; "now write against him."

"I have not supported Luther," said I. "I have no leisure, and it would be unfair to strike a fallen man."

"Then write," says he, "that we have beaten him."

"It is for those who win the victory to shout for triumph," said I. Besides, I was not sure they had beaten him. The arguments had not been published.

"Did I not tell you," said he, turning to the Rector, "that we should make nothing of this man? I shall continue to hold him a Lutheran till he consents to write against Luther."

"Then you are yourself a Lutheran," said I, "for *you* have written nothing against him."

We parted without an adieu. He boasted afterwards at a drinking party how he had stood up to Erasmus.

The Rector tells the story with much amusement, and wonder at my forbearance.

So passed the winter, Erasmus fighting beasts at Ephesus. They were rash in attempting to drive him to write, for he knew that he had but to declare himself on the revolutionary side to assure Luther an undisputed victory; and he felt it naturally hard

"When not to be deserved reproach of being."

Campegio, after receiving his letter, came to Louvain to consult with him. Aleander himself, who was to prosecute Luther before the Diet, came. Many eminent men begged Erasmus to give Luther open help while the Diet was assembling — one especially, *vir præpotens*, whom he calls N——, perhaps the Elector of Saxe, perhaps the Landgrave of Hesse.

This also he could not do, as he explains to N—— at length:[1] —

LOUVAIN, *January* 28, 1521.

The world is splitting into factions. I have spoken with Campegio and also with Aleander. They were both gracious and gave hopes of a peaceful settle-

[1] *Ep.* dlxiii., abridged.

ment, but my chief confidence is in the Pope's own disposition. You tell me that a few words of mine will carry more weight than papal thunderbolts. You could urge nothing more calculated to keep me silent. Who am I that I should contradict the Catholic Church? If I was sure that the Holy See was wrong I would say so on a proper occasion, but it is no duty of mine to decide. My work has been to restore a buried literature, and recall divines from their hair-splittings to a knowledge of the New Testament. I have never been a dogmatist. I think the Church has defined many points which might have been left open without hurt to the faith. The matter now in hand can be arranged if the Pope, the princes, and your Highness will refer it to a small number of learned good men.

But the busybodies who shout and rage and flatter the Holy See must be kept at a distance. None have more recommended Luther to the German people than those who have cursed him loudest, and the other side who rail and curse at the Pope must be kept out also.

I know not how Popes came by their authority. I suppose it was as the bishops came by theirs. Each Presbytery chose one of its members as president to prevent divisions. Bishops similarly found it expedient to have a chief bishop, to check rivalries and defend the Church against the secular powers. I know the charges brought against the Court of Rome, but all reports need not be true, nor, if true, need the popes be responsible for all that is done at Rome. Many wrong things escape their eye, and many are done against their will. St. Peter himself, if he now ruled, would have to connive at much. But however this be, more will be effected by moderate remonstrance than by reviling and passion. I can be no party to violence. If offences must come they shall not come through me. If Luther's books are in your people's hands let them do as I do, take the good in them and leave the bad. I will say nothing of Luther himself. But this I insist on, that the worst part of what has happened is due to the Dominican and Carmelite theologians, and if the Pope knew what they were about he would not be particularly obliged to them. Luther's style is not mine, but it is folly to call him ass, goose, blockhead, heretic, Antichrist, pest of humanity. His books are only read the more eagerly, and the Pope's Bull has failed to frighten people away from him. Divines, monkish buffoons, now and then a bishop or two, sing to the same note. The Papacy is defended by packs of barking curs. The world's eyes are opening, and unless they change their note they will effect nothing. You suggest that I should join Luther. I will join him readily if I see him on the side of the Catholic Church. I do not accuse him of having broken with it. It is not for me to pronounce. To his own Master he stands or falls. But if the worst comes and the Church is divided, I shall stand on the Rock of Peter till peace returns. Farewell.

The talk about the Rock of Peter sounds conventional and insincere, but Erasmus obviously meant it. The disease in the Church, as Erasmus saw it, lay in the propensity to dogmatic definitions. Each definition of doctrine beyond the Apostles' Creed had led to dissension and hatred, and he dreaded any fresh addition to the already too numerous formulas from whatever side it might come. Luther's mind, at white heat, was flowing into antagonistic doctrinal assertions. These would be met by counter-assertions, and the war of words would turn to a war of sword and cannon. The hope of Erasmus was that Pope and Council, if not further irritated, might be content to leave opinion free on subjects which no one could understand — be content that Christians should live together, to use the words of our own prayer in the Liturgy, "in unity of spirit" (not of definitions), "in the bond of peace" (not of strife), "in righteousness of life," the object of all religions, and that they should set themselves to reform the scandals in their own practice, which were crying to Heaven for reform.

Such a turn of things, even at that late hour, might be hoped for without insincerity, as offering the best prospect for Christendom. But it is dangerous for a man to throw himself

> "Between the pass and fell incensed points
> Of mighty opposites."

The Lutherans abused Erasmus for a coward. They insisted that he thought as they did, but dared not confess it. The Louvain doctors were of the same opinion, and struck at him from the opposite camp.

TO NICHOLAS BERALD.[1]

LOUVAIN, *February* 16, 1521.

The Dominicans pelt me daily in their sermons. I bear it for the sake of the Faith, and am a martyr like Stephen. Stephen, however, was stoned but once, and was then at rest. I am battered unceasingly with stones which are poisoned. They care not for the disgrace to themselves so long as they can injure me. Luther has discredited me and my cause. All know that the Church has been tyrannical and corrupt, and many have been busy thinking how it can be reformed. But medicines wrongly applied make the patient worse, and when attempts are made and fail the symptoms only grow more dangerous. Would that Luther had held his peace, or had gone to work more discreetly. I care nothing for the fate which may overtake him, but I do care for the cause of Christ, and I see churchmen in such a temper that, if they triumph, farewell to Gospel truth.

You know generally the story of the Diet of Worms. It was a gathering of all that was greatest in Ger-

[1] *Ep.* dlxvi.

many, the young Emperor presiding. Princes, barons, representatives of the free towns and states, bishops, abbots, cardinals, a legate from the Holy See, with his suite of divines and canon lawyers, all collected to consider what was to be done with a single poor Saxon monk. The Pope had prepared for the occasion by issuing in Passion Week his famous Bull *In Cœna Domini* against the enemies of the Church, and had included Luther by name in it. Yet you observe, as a sign of the changing times, that Luther was not brought before the Diet as a prisoner. He was invited to appear by a letter from the Emperor, promising that he should be heard in his defence, and under the protection of a safe-conduct. His friends, remembering that Sigismund's safe-conduct had not saved Huss at Constance, advised Luther not to attend. You will recollect his famous answer, that he would go to Worms if there were as many devils there as there were tiles on the housetops. You will remember how he stood alone before that stern assembly, how his books were produced, how he was required to retract them, how he said he would retract them all if he was proved wrong by Holy Scripture. To the mere sentence of the Pope he would not submit. "Ich kann nicht anders," he said: "I can do no other." He was condemned. He was placed under the ban of Empire, ordered to return home and wait till his safe-conduct was expired, when sentence would be executed on him. The Church party would have again treated the safe-conduct as a farce, have seized and burnt him on the spot. But though he was cast by a majority of votes, the Lords and Commons of Germany did not choose that there should be a second treachery of Constance. The Emperor refused to commence his reign by a breach of promise, and other questions were stirring in the Diet which forced the churchmen to be careful. The loud growl was rising — the voice of the German laity demanding redress of their grievances against ecclesiastical tyranny, soon to rise into a roar and break the fabric of the Church to pieces. In the face of such a demonstration the Emperor could not dare, if he had wished, to listen to the counsels of his spiritual advisers.

It seemed, at any rate, but a question of a few days. Luther was outlawed. His own prince could no longer lawfully protect him after his safe-conduct had expired. There was no asylum in Christian Europe where the Pope's writ would not run, or where an excommunicated fugitive could seek protection. Protestant nations there were as yet none, and Luther's speedy destruction seemed still inevitable. You know what happened. How Luther, on his way home to Wittenberg, was seized in a forest by a company of the Elector's horse, disguised as banditti. How he was spirited away to the Castle of Wartburg, and lay concealed there till war broke out between France and the Empire, when Charles could no longer afford to affront or exasperate his German subjects. It is not impossible that the plot was arranged privately between the Elector and the Emperor, to save Charles from making himself hated, as he would have been had Luther been burnt.

Meanwhile the secret was well kept. Erasmus thought that all was over with him. Luther's friends, Melanchthon and Jonas, had stood gallantly by him at Worms. Erasmus considered that the best which they could now do was to separate themselves from a lost cause.

TO JODOCUS JONAS.[1]

LOUVAIN, *May* 18, 1521.

In pleading for moderation at Worms you acted as I should have done had I been there. I am sorry that things have turned so badly. What is religion, save peace in the Holy Ghost? The corruption of the Church, the degeneracy of the Holy See are universally admitted. Reform has been loudly asked for, and I doubt whether in the whole history of Christianity the heads of the Church have been so grossly worldly as at the present moment. It was on this account that Luther's popularity at the outset was so extraordinary. We believe what we wish. A man was supposed to have risen up, with no objects of his own to gain, to set his hand to the work. I had hopes myself, though from the first I was alarmed at Luther's tone. What could have induced him to rail as he did at popes and doctors and mendicant friars? If all he said was true, what could he expect? Things were bad enough in themselves without making them worse. Did he wish to set the world on fire? This was not Christ's way, or the Apostles' way, or Augustine's. He should have looked forward. It is foolish to undertake what you cannot carry through, and doubly foolish when failure may be disastrous. Why did he refuse to submit to the Pope and the Emperor? He was ill advised, they say. But why did he let himself be ill advised? He had many friends well disposed towards him, partly because they thought he was doing good, partly because they had a common enemy. It was unfair to drag our names into the controversy. Why have I and Reuchlin been mentioned so often? They have taken passages which I wrote before Luther's movement was dreamt of, and have translated them into German, where I seem to say what Luther says. Likely enough I have insisted that vows should not be hastily taken, that men had better stay at home

[1] *Ep.* dlxxii., abridged.

and take care of their families, instead of running off to Compostella or Jerusalem. But this is not to say there should be no vows and no confessional. It is not my fault if my writings are misused. So were Paul's, if we are to believe Peter. Had I known what was coming, I might have written differently on some points. But I have done my best, and at all events have not encouraged rebellion. There was a hope at Cologne that the Pope would graciously forgive and Luther would graciously obey, the princes generally approving. But out comes the "Babylonish Captivity," and the burning of the Decretals, and the wound becomes past cure. Luther has wilfully provoked his fate.

"The Lutheran drama is over," Erasmus writes to another correspondent a week later (May 24); "would that it had never been brought on the stage." And again, in June, to Archbishop Warham: —

Luther has made a prodigious stir. Would that he had held his tongue, or had written in a better tone. I fear that in shunning Scylla we shall now fall into Charybdis. There is some slight hope from Pope Leo; but if the enemies of light are to have their way, we may write on the tomb of a ruined world, "Christ did not rise again."

Again, July 5,[1] with confidential frankness to Dr. Pace: —

Luther has given himself away; and the theologians, I fear, will make an ill use of their victory. The Louvainers hate me, and will find a ready instrument in Aleander, who is violent enough in himself, and needs no prompting. He lays the whole blame on me. I am responsible even for the "Babylonish Captivity." The Germans were always trying to drag me in; but what help could I have given Luther? There would have been two lives for one. That would

[1] *Ep.* dlxxxiii., abridged.

have been all. I was not called on to venture mine. We have not all strength for martyrdom, and I fear if trouble comes I shall do like Peter. The Pope and the Emperor must decide. If they decide wisely, I shall go with them of my own will. If unwisely, I shall take the safe side. There will be no dishonesty in this when one can do no good. Now that Luther has gone to ashes, the preaching friars and the divines congratulate each other, not, however, with much sincerity. We must look to the princes to see that the innocent and deserving are not made responsible for Luther's sins.

By the middle of the summer confused rumours were spreading that Luther had not gone to ashes, that he had been carried off, and some said murdered. The real truth was not guessed at.

"An idle tale" has reached us (he wrote,[1] July 5) that Luther has been waylaid and killed. All means were used at Worms to recover him. Threats, promises, entreaties, but nothing could be done with him. He was reconducted to Wittenberg by the Imperial herald, with twenty days allowed of respite. Then all was to end. The Emperor is incensed against him, partly by others, partly through personal resentment. Luther's books were burnt at Worms, and a fierce edict has been issued at Louvain, insisting that the Emperor shall be obeyed.

Erasmus was not, as he said, called on to be a martyr, but he was a little over-eager to wash his hands of Luther. There was no denying that his writings generally, especially his New Testament, had given the first impulse. It was he who had made the Scripture, to which Luther appealed, first accessible to the laity, garnished with notes and commentaries as stinging as Luther's own. The Louvain Carmelites

[1] *Ep.* dlxxxiv.

owed him a long debt, and they thought their time was come to pay it. He had gone to Bruges to escape them.

TO PETER BARBIRIUS.[1]

BRUGES, *August* 13, 1521.

The Louvain friars will not be reconciled to me, and they catch at anything, true or false, to bring me into odium. True, my tongue runs away with me. I jest too much, and measure other men by myself. Why should an edition of the New Testament infuriate them so? I settled at Louvain, as you know, at the Emperor's order. We set up our college for the three languages [Greek, Latin, and Hebrew]. The Carmelites did not like it, and would have stopped us had not Cardinal Adrian interfered.[2] I did my best with the New Testament, but it provoked endless quarrels. Edward Lee pretended to have discovered 300 errors. They appointed a commission, which professed to have found bushels of them. Every dinner-table rang with the blunders of Erasmus. I required particulars, and could not have them. At length a truce was patched up. They were to admit that my work had merit. I was to stop the wits who were mocking at Louvain theology. Then out came Luther's business. It grew hot. I was accused on one side from the pulpits of being in a conspiracy with Luther, on the other I was entreated to join him. I saw the peril of neutrality, but I cannot and will not be a rebel. Luther's friends quote, "I came not to send peace on earth, but a sword." Of course the Church requires reform, but violence is not the way to it. Both parties behaved like maniacs. You may ask me why I have not written against Luther. Because I had no leisure, because I was not qualified, because I would sooner face the lances of the Switzers than the pens of enraged theologians. There are plenty to do it besides me — bishops, cardinals, kings, with

[1] *Ep.* dlxxxvii., abridged.

[2] Charles V.'s tutor, and afterwards Pope.

stakes and edicts as many as they please. Besides, it is not true that I have done nothing. Luther's friends (who were once mine also) do not think so. They have deserted me and call me a Pelagian. But if severity is to be the course, someone else, and not I, must use the rod. God will provide a Nebuchadnezzar to scourge us if we need scourging.

It would be well for us if we thought less of our dogmas and more about the Gospel; but whatever is done ought to be done quietly, with no appeals to passion. The opinions of the leading men should be given in writing and under seal. The point is to learn the cause of all these disturbances, and stop the stream at the fountain. The princes must begin, and then I will try what I can do. My position at present is odious. In Flanders I am abused as a Lutheran. In Germany I am cried out against as an anti-Lutheran. I would forfeit life, fame, and all to find a means to compose the strife.

Once more to Archbishop Warham, August 24:[1] —

The condition of things is extremely dangerous. I have to steer my own course, so as not to desert the truth of Christ through fear of man, and to avoid unnecessary risks. Luther has been sent into the world by the Genius of discord. Every corner of it has been disturbed by him. All admit that the corruptions of the Church required a drastic medicine. But drugs wrongly given make the sick man worse. I said this to the King of Denmark lately. He laughed, and answered that small doses would be of no use. The whole system needed purging. For myself I am a man of peace, and hate quarrels. Luther's movement was not connected with learning, but it has brought learning into ill-repute, and the lean and barren dogmatists, who used to be my enemies, have now fastened on Luther, like the Greeks on Hector. I suppose I must write something about him. I will read his books, and see what can be done.

[1] *Ep.* dxc.

There was joy at Rome and among the Roman satellites over the sentence at Worms. For some months the Church was triumphant. Wise men and fools alike believed that all was over with Luther. The Emperor, the Archduke of Austria, half the German princes, France, Spain, even England, appeared to have agreed that the spiritual insurrection must be put down with fire. It was not blind bigotry. It was a conviction shared, as you will do well to observe, by such a man as Sir Thomas More, who was as little inclined as Erasmus himself to allow the old creed to be supplanted by a new. You cannot understand the sixteenth century till you recognise the immense difference then present in the minds of men between a change of doctrine and a reformation of the Church's manners and morals.

Luther was not dead, as Erasmus and the rest of the world believed. He had been spirited away by the Elector of Saxony, probably enough with the Emperor's connivance. The public execution of such a man would have shocked the sense of all the laity in Europe. But the meteor which had blazed across the firmament was supposed to have burnt out, and the best hope of honest men was that the Emperor would now himself take up the work, and insist on a reform of the Church by the Church itself. Unfortunately other forces, besides religion, were disturbing the peace of Christendom. The Pope was the spiritual head of the world, but he was also an Italian prince, with schemes and ambitions like other mortals. The traditions of Charles VIII. and of Julius II. were still smouldering. The Italians resented the Spanish occupation of Naples and Sicily. The French wanted Lombardy and Piedmont. Behind all was Solyman, ravaging the Mediterranean with his fleet, advancing on Hungary, and threatening to place the Crescent on the spire of St. Stephen's at Venice. A crusade against heresy required peace. Church courts and inquisitions were abhorred by the secular mind, and councils could not sit while armies were on the move. The young Emperor Charles and the young Francis I. showed both of them that they meant to try which was stronger before other questions could be attended to; and Providence, or accident, or the ambitions and passions of mankind, were preparing thus a respite for spiritual freedom till it could take root and be too strong to be destroyed.

The politics of Europe do not concern us here. We must continue to look through the eyes of Erasmus at events as they rose, with the future course of things concealed from him. This is the way to understand history. We know what happened, and we judge the actors on the stage by the light of it. They did not know. They had to play their parts in the present, and so we misjudge them always. The experience of every one of us whose lives reach a normal period might have taught us better. Let any man of seventy look back over what he has witnessed in his own time. Let him remember what was hoped for from political changes or wars, or from each step in his personal life, and compare what has really resulted from those things with what he once expected; how, when good has come, it has not been the good which he looked for; how difficulties have shown themselves which no one foresaw; how his calculations have been mocked by incidents which the wisest never dreamt of; and he will plead to be judged, if his conduct comes under historical review, by his intentions and not by the event.

This is a lesson which historians ought never to

forget, and they seem to me rarely to remember it. To understand the past we must look at it always, when we can, through the eyes of contemporaries.

After the supposed collapse of Luther, Erasmus had to gather himself together to consider what he should himself do, and advise his own party to do. He had gone to Bruges again to escape Louvain and its doctors. From Bruges he went to Anderlac for the rest of the summer, and among his letters from Anderlac is one to a literary youth, who wished to throw himself into the war of creeds.

TO JOHN SCHUDELIN.[1]

ANDERLAC, *September* 4, 1521.

Stick to your teaching work. Do not be crossing swords with the champions of the old ignorance. Try rather to sow better seed in the minds of the young. If princes are blind, if the heads of the Church prefer the rewards of this world to the rewards promised by Christ, if divines and monks choose to stick to their synagogues, if the world generally chooses to preserve the forms to which men are accustomed, well, then, we must put new wine in old bottles. The seed will grow in the end, and the opposition is more from ignorance than ill-will. Teach your boys carefully, edit the writings of the Fathers, and irreligious religion and unlearned learning will pass away in due time.

Erasmus could be calm for others. It was very hard for him to be calm for himself. The Louvainers got hold of more of his letters, and published them with alterations in the text. He had written "Lutherus"; they changed it into "Lutherus Noster," to make him out Luther's friend. They reprinted his "Colloquies," imitated his style, and made him say the contradictory of what he had really said. He

[1] *Ep.* dxcii.

had denounced extorted confessions, he had laughed at pilgrimages and ridiculed indulgences. His new editors reproduced his real language, but they attached paragraphs in his name where he was represented as declaring that he had once thought all that, but had perceived his error. He had written that "the best confession was confession to God"; his editor changed it into "the best confession is confession to a priest."

"Wonderful Atlases of a tottering faith," he might well call such people. "Once," he says, "it was held a crime to publish anything in another man's name; now it is the special game of divines, and they are proud of it."

At Anderlac he was safe at any rate from the sound of their tongues while he watched the gathering of the war storm. He hated war, but under the circumstances even war might have its value. Persecution, at least, would be impossible as long as it lasted.

But oh, what a world! (he wrote). Christendom split in two and committed to a deadly struggle; two young princes, each fierce and ardent, each bent on the destruction of the other. Immortal God! Where is the Pope? When anything is to be got for the Church he can command angels and devils, but he can do nothing to prevent his children from cutting each other's throats. Where are the eloquent preachers? Have they lost their tongues, or can they only use them to flatter? Luther is done with — I trust well done with; and for my own part I return to my studies.

Luther was not done with. Luther had risen from the dead, or, rather, the truth came out, while Erasmus was still at Anderlac, that he had never died at all, that he was alive under the Elector's protection, and would soon be heard of again under the shelter of the war. Violence had failed after all. There was nothing now for it but for Erasmus to step forward and put Luther down by argument. Statesmen, bishops, privy councillors, even friends like Lord Mountjoy in England, wrote to him that he must do it. Erasmus must speak. Germany would listen to Erasmus when it would listen to no one else. He did not choose to be at once used and abused.

TO THE SECRETARY OF THE PRINCE OF NASSAU.[1]

ANDERLAC, *November* 19, 1521.

I have no more to do with Luther than with any other Christian. I would sooner have him mended than ended; but if he has been sowing poison, the hand that sowed it must gather it up again. They may boil or roast Luther if they like. It will be but one individual the less; but mankind must be considered too. The papal party have acted like fools. The whole affair has been mismanaged by a parcel of stupid monks. The Pope's Bull directed them to preach against Luther, that is, to answer him out of Scripture. They have not answered him. They have only cursed him and lied about him. A Jacobite at Antwerp accused him of having said that Christ worked His miracles by magic. A Carmelite said at the French Court that Luther was Antichrist, and Erasmus his precursor. A Minorite raged at us from a pulpit for an hour, only to call us geese, asses, beasts, and blockheads. The magistrates at Antwerp told him to leave Luther and preach the Gospel. Another Minorite, named Matthias, said that if the people wanted the Gospel they must take it from their pastor, though he had slept the night before with a harlot. The Emperor must take order for the peace of Christendom and silence both parties. Would that all were well

[1] *Ep.* cccxiv., second series, abridged.

ended. No one would believe how widely Luther has moved men. His books are everywhere and in every language. I hear there is to be some frightful edict. I hope it may prosper, but things will not go as many seem to expect. I care nothing what is done to Luther, but I care for peace, and, as you know, when peace is broken the worst men come to the front. I had rather be a Turk than under some of these friars. If the Pope and princes are wise, they will not place good men at the mercy of such as they are.

LECTURE XV.

EUROPE was at pause, waiting for the outbreak of the war. Luther was known to be alive, but had not yet shown himself. The cry was still that Erasmus must write. Erasmus must tell Germany how to act. Even his English friends, who had stood by him so heartily in his fight with the monks, were urging him to clear himself of complicity with the rebellion against Rome. Lord Mountjoy, his oldest patron and supporter, had written to him, and Mountjoy spoke for More, and Fisher and Warham. Erasmus began to feel that he might be obliged to comply.

TO LORD MOUNTJOY.[1]

ANDERLAC.

You, too, tell me I am suspected of favouring Luther, and that I must prove my innocence by writing against him. I had nothing to do with Luther. I objected only to the outcry against him. All allow that Church discipline had gone to pieces, that the laity were oppressed, and their consciences entangled in trickery. Men both good and learned thought Luther might help to mend something of this. I looked for no more. I never thought of quarrelling with the ruling powers. If the course they take is for Christ's honour, I obey gladly. If they decide ill, we must endure what is not directly impious. When we can do no good, we have a right to be silent. A worm like me must not dispute with our lawful rulers. If they ask my advice, I will give it. Such an uproar is not

[1] *Ep.* dcvi., abridged.

for nothing, and they may wish to cleanse the wound before they close it. If they do not, I shall hold my peace, and pray Christ to enlighten them. You say I can settle it all. Would that I could. It is easy to call Luther a fungus: it is not easy to answer him. I might try, if I was sure that those at the head of things would use my victory to honest purpose. I do not see what business it is of mine. However, I will think of it.

"I will think of it" — so he had said before. But the more he thought the less he saw his way. He was afraid, as he had admitted, that he might be fighting against the Spirit of God. He explains his difficulties in an elaborate letter to the Archbishop of Palermo.[1] In the eyes of Erasmus the disorders of Christendom had risen from the dogmas which the Church and the priests had forced upon the people. Piety was held to be the acceptance of these dogmas, impiety to be doubt or disagreement. Hence had come the inevitable consequences: religion was confounded with ritual or creed, and morals were forgotten or went to ruin. Erasmus enters at length into the history of heresy and the early disputes on the Trinity, which he deprecated and condemned. It is very dangerous, he says, to define subjects above human comprehension. There was an excuse for the early Fathers, as they could not help themselves. But nothing was to be said in defence of the curious and blasphemous questions now raised, on which men might be left to think for themselves without hurt to their souls. "May not a man," he asks, "be a Christian who cannot explain philosophically how the nativity of the Son differs from the procession of the Holy Spirit? If I believe in the Trinity in Unity, I want

[1] January 5, 1522. *Ep.* dcxiii.

no arguments. If I do not believe, I shall not be convinced by reason. The sum of religion is peace, which can only be when definitions are as few as possible, and opinion is left free on many subjects.[1] Our present problems are said to be waiting for the next Œcumenical Council. Better let them wait till the veil is removed and we see God face to face."

The whole of Erasmus's thought is in these words, and they explain his difference with Luther, who was constructing a new Protestant theology, which might be as intolerant and dangerous as the Catholic. We can well understand why, if this was his view of things, he was so unwilling to publish it to the world. His uncertainty irritated him, and irritation in Erasmus always ran over into mockery. When things were at the worst with him, he wrote a characteristic letter of advice to a friend who had been attached to the Emperor's Court.

Be careful to keep sober at meals. This will ensure your espect. Assume no airs either in speech or dress. The Court soon finds out what men are. When you argue do not dispute like the schoolmen, and do not argue at all with casual persons, or on any subject which turns up. You will then be better liked and escape annoyance. Cultivate men in power. Be polite to all, and never abject. Respect your own position — an affectation of holiness will not be amiss. Never speak your mind openly about what goes on round you. Never blurt out your thoughts hastily. Be fair to everyone, and if you must take a side, take the side which is most in favour. Keep clear of Lutheranism and stand up for knowledge and learn-

[1] "Ea vix constare poterit nisi de quam potest paucissimis definiamus et in multis liberum relinquamus suum cuique judicium, propterea quod ingens sit rerum plurimarum obscuritas, et hoc morbi fere innatum sit hominum ingeniis ut cedere nesciant simul atque res in contentionem vocata est," etc.

ing. Egmond and Co. hate both worse than they hate Luther. This will make you popular with the young. The present tempest will not last long.

Louvain, as a residence, has become intolerable. He has gone thither at the Emperor's command. The divinity and the climate alike disagreed with him, and on leaving Anderlac he was allowed to remove altogether to Bâle, where he could print his books with his friend Froben. The bitter humour of the last letter continued to cling to him. Another friend had been summoned into the Imperial circle. He writes:[1]—

You tell me that you are going into court life, and that you do not like it. I trust it may be for your good. Up to the time when I was fifty I saw something of princes' courts, so you may profit by my experience. Trust no one who pretends to be your friend, let him smile, promise, embrace, swear as many oaths as he will. Do not believe that anyone is really attached to you, and do not be hasty in giving your own confidence. Be civil to all. Politeness costs nothing. Salute, give the road, and do not forget to give men their titles. Praise warmly, promise freely. Choose the part which you mean to play, and never betray your real feelings. Fit your features to your words, and your words to your features. This is the philosophy of court life, for which none are qualified till they have put away shame and trained themselves to lie. Watch how parties are divided and join neither. If man or woman falls out of favour, keep you to the sunny side of the ship. Observe the prince's likes and dislikes. Smile when he speaks, and if you can say nothing, look admiringly. Praise him to others. Your words will get round. A small offering to him now and then will do no harm, only it must not be too valuable, as if you were fishing for a

[1] *Ep.* dx., second series.

return. If there be game in sight, trust neither to God nor man, but look out for yourself. Court winds are changeable. Watch your chances, and let no good thing slip out of your hands. Keep with the winning party, but give no mortal offence to the other till you are sure of your ground. When you ask a favour, do as loose women do with their lovers, ask for what the prince can give without loss to himself — benefices, provostships, and such like. This will do to begin with. As I see you benefit by my advice, I will initiate you in the deeper mysteries.

At all times, I suppose, court atmosphere is apt to breed a halo round the sun. We have to pay for the luxury of a monarchy, and this was why Erasmus always, for himself, kept clear of those high regions. The scorn, however, may be set down to a specially uncomfortable state of mind. Must he write? If there was no escape, what was he to write? The names of Luther and Erasmus were about to be coupled closer than ever by their joint service to mankind. Erasmus had edited the Greek New Testament and made a fresh translation. Luther, in the Castle of Wartburg, was translating it into vernacular German, with the Old Testament to follow. Together, these two men had made accessible the rock, stronger than the rock of Peter, on which the faith of mankind was to be rebuilt. Less than ever could Erasmus tell how to act. At this moment Leo X. died, and the Emperor's tutor, Erasmus's old schoolfellow, Cardinal Adrian, was called to be the Church's sovereign. The rule of the Conclave was to choose only Italian Popes. That it was broken at the present crisis was due to the resolution of Charles V. to clear out the abominations of the Roman Court. But there was no likelihood of finding in Adrian any disposition to compromise with heresy. Erasmus, at their last meeting, had found him sour and cold, a severe, stern, and strictly orthodox old man, not even disposed to continue to himself the favour which he had always found from Leo. Erasmus had now left Louvain and its doctors, and was living at Bâle with his publisher Froben. From Bâle, as soon as he was settled there, he wrote to Pirkheimer, still in a bitter tone: —

I have been ill, but am better. I watch earnestly how the Lutheran tragedy is to end. Some spirit is in it, but whether God's Spirit or the other one I know not. I never helped Luther, unless it be to help a man to exhort him to mend his ways; yet I am called a heretic by both parties. My ill friends, who dislike me on other grounds, persuade the Emperor that I am the cause of all that is wrong, because I do not write against Luther. The Lutherans call me a Pelagian because I believe in free will. A pleasant situation, is it not?

In the pause we find Erasmus studying his old friend Lucian over again. Lucian had more to say to him which fitted to the time than even the Christian Fathers. The enormous fabric of false legends and forged miracles with which the monks had cajoled or frightened their flocks had brought back to him the curious dialogue called Φιλοψεύδης, in which Lucian had moralised over the fondness of mankind for lies — lies related, as Lucian says, so circumstantially and by such grave authorities, with evidence of eye-witnesses, place, and time all accurately given, that the strongest mind could hardly resist conviction unless fortified with the certainty that such things could not be. Erasmus turns to the familiar page, and finds the same phenomena repeated after twelve hundred years.

This dialogue (he says[1]) teaches us the folly of superstition, which creeps in under the name of religion. When lies are told us Lucian bids us not disturb ourselves, however complete the authority which may be produced for them. Even Augustine, an honest man and a lover of truth, can repeat a tale as authentic which Lucian had ridiculed under other names so many years before Augustine was born. What wonder, therefore, that fools can be found to listen to the legends of the saints or to stories about hell, such as frighten cowards or old women. There is not a martyr, there is not a virgin, whose biographies have not been disfigured by these monstrous absurdities. Augustine says that lies when exposed always injure truth. One might fancy they were invented by knaves or unbelievers to destroy the credibility of Christianity itself.

In the same mood is a letter to Pirkheimer,[2] evidently intended for the Emperor's eyes. Adrian is now Pope.

The Pope's satellites daily draw the meshes tighter of the old tyranny. Instead of relaxing the bonds, they tie the knots harder. The friends of liberty who call themselves Lutherans are possessed by some spirit, of what kind I know not, while both sorts have a finger in the management of things, which neither of them should touch if I could have my way. Conscience has run wild; abandoned profligates quote Luther's books as an excuse for licentiousness, while the quiet and the good are between the shrine and the stone. On one side they see reason and good sense, on the other the princes and the mob; and what the issue is to be I know not. I have small belief in submission extorted by Bulls and Imperial edicts. They may chain the tongues of men: they cannot touch their minds. Would that God would move the princes to

[1] *Ep.* ccccIxxv., second series, abridged.
[2] *Ep.* dcxviii., abridged.

set other respects aside, consider only Christ's glory, and look to the sources of the disorders which convulse the commonwealth. Some effort must and will be made for Christian liberty. New customs, new rules have been introduced into the Church, which have acquired the force of law. The schoolmen will have their dogmas received as articles of faith. The spiritual pedlars who trade under the Pope's shadow have become insolent and grasping. They cannot be torn out all at once by force. Violent remedies are mischievous and dangerous. But what can be done? On one side we have Bulls, edicts, and menaces; on the other revolutionary pamphlets which set the world in flames. If the princes' hands are full of other business, can they find no reasonable men whom they can trust to consider these things? It does not concern me. My time is nearly out. But I wish for the salvation of Christianity. If there was any right belief in Christ as the Eternal Head of the Church! But now one man is thinking what he can get, another is afraid of losing what he has, a third sees trouble coming and shrinks into his hole, and so the conflagration spreads. I myself am denounced as a Lutheran. The Nuncio (Aleander) is poisoned against me, and if the late Pope had not died I was to have been censured at Rome; and meanwhile the Lutherans abuse me, and the Emperor is half persuaded that I am to blame for everything that has gone wrong. I had thought of writing something, not as an attack on Luther, but to urge peace and moderation. Both sides, however, are so embittered that I had better not attempt it. If the Lutherans would but have fallen out with me two years ago they would have saved me a load of odium. Learned theologians whom I have consulted as to my remarks on the ninth of Romans tell me my fault is that I have attached the faintest possible power to man's free-will!

There were more hopes from Adrian than Erasmus had allowed himself to feel. He learnt from distinguished correspondents that the new Pope and the Emperor did mean after all to set their hands to the reform of the Roman Curia. He learnt too, to his relief, that he was himself less out of favour than he had feared in those high quarters, bitter as was the offence which he had given by not providing the answer to Luther. At the bottom Charles V. thought much as Erasmus did about dogmas and dogmatism. The Emperor had resented Luther's defiance of authority, but when Luther was known to be alive he had taken no steps to find or arrest him. The approaching war with France obliged him to keep on good terms with his German subjects, especially with the most powerful of them, Luther's own sovereign, the Elector of Saxony, and if fire and sword were to be used for heresy a more convenient season must be waited for. The Bishop of Palencia, who had defended Erasmus to the Emperor, wrote him a letter which restored his spirits. With Charles and Adrian working together at Roman reform all might yet go well. He thanked the Bishop for his support.[1] He hoped that "the wisdom of the new Pope and the almost divine mind of Cæsar might find a way to extirpate the disease. The roots, however," he said, "must be cut out effectually, or they would shoot again." One of these roots was the tyranny and avarice of the Roman Court. The Pope and the Emperor together might set all right without a revolution. He himself, though he was nobody, was willing to contribute his part.

They call me a Lutheran (he writes the same day to another friend[2]). Had I but held out a little finger to Luther, Germany would have seen what

[1] Bâle, April 21, 1522. *Ep.* dcxxi.
[2] Ludovico Coronello, *Ep.* dcxxii.

I could do. But I would rather die ten times over than make a schism. I have acted honestly throughout. Germany knows it now, and I will make all men know it.

Again, to the President of the Senate at Mechlin:[1] —

July 14, 1552.

Egmond may hate me, but I have kept many persons from joining Luther, and my announcement that I mean to stand by the Pope has been an obstacle in Luther's way. Had I joined him there would have been princes enough to protect me; nor is the love of the people for Luther as dead as some fancy. Here at Bâle we have a hundred thousand men who detest Rome, and are Luther's friends. I have been hardly dealt with. I have lost the confidence of Germany. The reactionaries abuse the victory for which they owe after all to me, and call me a heretic. The Emperor, however, the Archbishop of Palermo, the Bishop of Palencia, the Chancellor of the Empire, the Cardinals of Sedan and Mentz know their obligations to me, and are grateful. The Cardinal of Sedan offers me a handsome income if I will reside at Rome. Is it not preposterous that, hated as I am by the Lutherans and possessing the confidence of the greatest men in Christendom, I should be torn to pieces by a wretched little Carmelite? There are thousands in the world who have no ill-will towards Erasmus. I can make noise enough if I please.

Encouraged by the knowledge that he was in better favour, Erasmus had written at length to the Pope, giving his own views of what should be done. The Pope sent no answer, and the Dominicans at Rome reported that the letter had been ill received. The more moderate of the German princes, however, began to consult him, in a tone which showed that his

[1] *Ep.* dcxxix., abridged.

pretensions to influence were not an idle boast. Among the rest Duke George of Saxony, who had no love for Luther, but less for monks and bishops, had written to Erasmus to urge him to exert himself. He replies: —

TO DUKE GEORGE.[1]

No wonder you are displeased at the aspect of things. None can deny that Luther had an excellent cause. Christ had almost disappeared, and when Luther began he had the world at his back. He was imprudent afterwards, but his disciples were more in fault than he. The fury is now so great that I fear the victors will exact terms which none who love Christ will endure, and which will destroy the Christian faith. You are a wise prince, and I will speak my mind freely. Christendom was being asphyxiated with formulas and human inventions. Nothing was heard of but dispensations, indulgences, and the powers of the Pope. The administration was carried on by men who, like Demas, loved the life that now is. Men needed waking. The Gospel light had to be rekindled. Would that more wisdom had been shown when the moment came. Stupid monks and sottish divines filled the air with outcries, and made bad worse. Nothing was in danger but the indulgences; but they replied in language disgraceful to Christian men. They would not admit that Luther was right, and only cursed.

Seeing how the stream was running, I kept out of it, merely showing that I did not wholly go with Luther. They wanted me to answer. I had thought from the first that the best answer would be silence. The wisest men, cardinals and others, agreed with me. The Pope's furious Bull only made the flame burn hotter. The Emperor followed with an equally savage edict. Edicts cannot alter minds. We may approve the Emperor's piety, but those who advised that measure were not his best councillors. The King of Eng-

[1] *Ep.* dcxxxv., abridged.

land's book[1] was justly admired by you. It was, no doubt, his own composition. He has fine talents, and he studied style as a boy. A few years since he wrote a tract, "An Laicus obligaretur ad vocalem Orationem?" He has studied theology, and often speaks about it. Your Highness sends me two books of Luther's, which you wish me to answer. I cannot read the language in which they are written. It might be useful to admonish prelates of their duties. There are always bishops who love their dignities so well that they forget all else. But the mischief has grown from worldly men, who have despotised in the name of Christ, and, instead of being respected as fathers, are abhorred as tyrants.

It was rumoured that Charles meant to try force after all. Erasmus warned the Duke of the inevitable consequences.

The Carmelites will hear of nothing but severity. Let them try it if they will. The abhorrence of the monks and of the Roman See has gained Luther so much favour with people, princes, and nobles, that if violence is used 200,000 men need only a leader to rise and defend him. They have an honest pretext. They have their own wrongs to avenge, and like enough may have an eye to churchmen's lands and goods.

Adrian VI. now comes upon the scene. Adrian's life had lain apart from Rome. He had been the Emperor's tutor. He had been Regent in Spain during Charles's minority, and with Rome itself he had personally been little connected. He had accepted the Papacy with an honest intention of examining into the charges of simony, corruption, and profligacy in the Roman Court with which the world was ringing. He had himself seen little of it. He, perhaps, be-

[1] Henry VIII.'s answer to Luther, which brought him from a grateful Pope the title of Defender of the Faith.

lieved, as we believe now, that the stories which had reached him were invented or exaggerated. No imagination could invent, no malice could exaggerate, what the Papal Court had really become under Alexander, and Julius, and Leo X. A second Hercules would be required to drive sewers under the mass of corruption and personal profligacy which surrounded the throne of St. Peter. The general government, the courts of law, the household administration, the public treasury were all equally infected; legal justice and spiritual privileges, promotions, dispensations, pardons, indulgences, licences, all sold without attempt at disguise; the very revenue of the Holy See depending upon simony; while all officials, from the highest cardinal to the lowest clerk on the rota, who throve upon the system were combined to thwart inquiry and prevent alteration.

Adrian might well quail at the task which was laid upon him. Erasmus, on learning his accession, had, as we have seen, volunteered a letter to him, which had not been answered. Erasmus and he had been schoolfellows at Deventer, and acquaintances afterwards at Louvain, where Adrian had not been unfriendly to him. But life and temperament divided them. Adrian, a strict official person, could not have wholly liked what he heard of his old acquaintance. He may have appreciated his learning, but Erasmus had described him, in a slight communication which had passed between them, as having been cold and bitter. To Adrian he may well have seemed a dangerous person — a renegade monk who had thrown up his profession, as Luther had done; who had wandered about the world with no fixed occupation, showing brilliant talents, but light, careless, given too much to mockery at things which he, at least, pretended to consider sacred. Orthodox Catholics throughout Europe accused Erasmus of having set the convulsion going with his "Moria," his New Testament, and the satires which the monks insisted on ascribing to him. Yet he in some way had immense influence. He had a reputation, which detraction could not take from him, of being the most learned and the clearest-sighted of living men. He had kept aloof from Luther when his support would have ensured Luther victory at Worms. To him Adrian found himself obliged to apply after all for assistance, and after looking round him at Rome, and finding what he had to deal with, he wrote to invite Erasmus to help him in his difficulties.

ADRIAN VI. TO ERASMUS.[1]

December 1, 1522.

God may be trusted to stand by His Spouse. The Prophet says, "I beheld the wicked man exalted above the cedars of Lebanon. I went by, and lo he was not. I sought him, but his place could nowhere be found." The same fate doubtless awaits Luther and those who go after him, unless they repent. They are carnal and despise authority, and they would make others like themselves. Put out your strength therefore. Rise up in the cause of the Lord, and use in His service the gifts which the Lord has bestowed on you.

It lies with you, God helping, to recover those who have been seduced by Luther from the right road, and to hold up those who still stand. Remember the words of St. James: "He that recalls a sinner from the error of his ways shall save him from death, and cover the multitude of his sins." I need not tell you with what joy I shall receive back these heretics without need to smite them with the rod of the Imperial

[1] *Ep.* dcxxxix., abridged.

law. You know how far are such rough methods from my own nature. I am still as you knew me when we were students together. Come to me to Rome. You will find here the books which you will need. You will have myself and other learned men to consult with, and if you will do what I ask you shall have no cause for regret.

This letter found Erasmus at Bâle. It meant, "Crush Luther for me, and you have a bishopric or a red hat." Erasmus was not to be tempted. He replies: —

ERASMUS TO ADRIAN VI.[1]

December 22, 1522.

This is no ordinary storm. Earth and air are convulsed — arms, opinions, authorities, factions, hatreds, jarring one against the other. If your Holiness would hear from me what I think you should do to make a real cure, I will tell you in a secret letter. If you approve my advice you can adopt it. If not, let it remain private between you and me. We common men see and hear things which escape the ears of the great. But, above all, let no private animosities or private interests influence your judgment. We little dreamt when we jested together in our early years what times were coming. With the Faith itself in peril, we must beware of personal affections. I am sorry to be a prophet of evil, but I see worse perils approaching than I like to think of, or than anyone seems to look for.

The messenger sped back to Rome. In a month he had returned to Bâle with another anxious note[2] from Adrian.

January 23, 1523.

Open your mind to me. Speak freely. How are these foul disorders to be cured while there is still

[1] *Ep.* dcxxxix., abridged.
[2] *Ep.* dcxlviii., abridged.

time? I am not alarmed for myself. I am not alarmed for the Holy See, frightful as the perils which menace it. I am distressed for the myriads of souls who are going to perdition. Be swift and silent. Come to me if you can, and come quickly. You shall not be sorry for it.

ERASMUS TO ADRIAN VI.[1]

BÂLE, *February*, 1523.

Your Holiness requires my advice, and you wish to see me. I would go to you with pleasure if my health allowed. But the road over the Alps is long. The lodgings on the way are dirty and inconvenient. The smell from the stoves is intolerable. The wine is sour and disagrees with me. For all that I would like well to speak with your Holiness, if it can be made possible. Meanwhile you shall have my honest heart in writing. Your eyes and mine will alone see my letter. If you like it — well. If not, let it be regarded as unwritten. As to writing against Luther, I have not learning enough. You think my words will have authority. Alas, my popularity, such as I had, is turned to hatred. Once I was Prince of Letters, Star of Germany, Sun of Studies, High Priest of Learning, Champion of a Purer Theology. The note is altered now. One party says I agree with Luther because I do not oppose him. The other finds fault with me because I do oppose him. I did what I could. I advised him to be moderate, and I only made his friends my enemies. At Rome and in Brabant I am called heretic, heresiarch, schismatic. I entirely disagree with Luther. They quote this and that to show we are alike. I could find a hundred passages where St. Paul seems to teach the doctrines which they condemn in Luther. I did not anticipate what a time was coming. I did, I admit, help to bring it on, but I was always willing to submit what I

[1] *Ep.* dcxlix., abridged. The dates imply that these letters were sent by special courier, from the rapidity with which they were exchanged.

wrote to the Church. I asked my friends to point out anything which they thought wrong. They found nothing. They encouraged me to persevere; and now they find a scorpion under every stone, and would drive me to rebellion, as they drove Arius and Tertullian.

Those counsel you best who advise gentle measures. The monks — Atlases, as they call themselves, of a tottering Church — estrange those who would be its supporters. Alas, that I in my old age should have fallen into such a mess, like a mouse into a pitch-pot. Your Holiness wishes to set things right, and you say to me, "Come to Rome. Write a book against Luther. Declare war against his party." Come to Rome? Tell a crab to fly. The crab will say, "Give me wings." I say, "Give me back my youth and strength." I beseech you let the poor sheep speak to his shepherd. What good can I do at Rome? It was said in Germany that I was sent for; that I was hurrying to you for a share in the spoils. If I write anything at Rome, it will be thought that I am bribed. If I write temperately, I shall seem trifling. If I copy Luther's style, I shall stir a hornets' nest.

But you ask me what you are to do. Well, some think there is no remedy but force. That is not my opinion; for I think there would be frightful bloodshed. The question is not what heresy deserves, but how to deal with it wisely. Things have gone too far for cautery. Wickliff and his followers were put down by the English kings; but they were only crushed, not extinguished; and besides, England is one country under a single sovereign. Germany is an aggregate of separate principalities, and I do not see how force is to be applied in Germany. However that be, if you mean to try prisons, lashes, confiscations, stake, and scaffold, you need no help from me. You yourself, I know, are for mild measures; but you have no one about you who cares for anything but himself; and if divines only think of their authority, monks of their luxuries, princes of their politics, and all take the bit between their teeth, what can we expect? For myself I should say, discover the roots of the disease. Clean out those to begin with. Punish no one. Let what has taken place be regarded as a chastisement sent by Providence, and grant a universal amnesty. If God forgives so many sins, God's vicar may forgive. The magistrates may prevent revolutionary violence. If possible, there should be a check on the printing presses. Then let the world know and see that you mean in earnest to reform the abuses which are justly cried out against, and if your Holiness desires to know what the roots are to which I refer, send persons whom you can trust to every part of Latin Christendom. Let them consult the wisest men that they can find in the different countries, and you will soon know.

It has been often observed that the policy of the papacy is little affected by the personal character of the Popes. Had Adrian been able to act for himself, he would perhaps have taken Erasmus's advice; but without a single honest official to help him he could do nothing. He inquired into such roots as could be seen at Rome; he found that if he abolished indulgences, reformed the law courts, and gave up simony and extortion, he would sacrifice two-thirds of his revenues. He wrote no more to Erasmus; he perhaps resented his refusal to help him in the way that he had asked. He silenced the barking of the Carmelite Louvainers, but nothing further passed between them. Adrian soon died — helped out of life, perhaps, by the hopelessness of his task. He was succeeded by an Italian of the old school, bred in the Court of Alexander VI. and Julius II., who became known to the world as Clement VII., and the papacy went on upon its predestined and fatal road.

Meanwhile the German population burst through control, and all was confusion. The Emperor could not move a single man-at-arms without the consent of the Diet and the free towns, and the majority of the princes either took the Lutheran side or refused to lend the Emperor a hand. Bishops were suspended from office, and their lands sequestered. Church courts, with their summoners and apparitors, were swept away. Religious houses were dissolved, their property seized to the State, and monks and nuns, many of them too happy to be free, were sent out with trifling pensions to work for their living and to marry. The images were removed from the churches; the saints' shrines were burnt, and the relics which had worked so many miracles for others could work none to protect themselves. The overthrow of idolatry was so universal and so spontaneous that it was found necessary to restore order of some kind. Luther only had sufficient influence to control the storm. The Elector of Saxony recalled him from Wartburg, as he was no longer in personal danger, to take command in reorganising the Church. The Germans were essentially an orderly people. They had destroyed the nests of what they regarded as vermin. They had deprived unjust persons of tyrannical authority, but they did not want anarchy and atheism. Luther had brought back with him his translation of the Bible, to be immediately completed and printed. A communion service something like our own was substituted for the mass, bishops only and episcopal ordination being dispensed with as an occasion of superstition. A catechism of doctrine was introduced for schools, and as a guide for Church ministers; and the Lutheran religion became by spontaneous impulse the established creed of two-thirds of the German nation.

The Emperor, for the time, was powerless; but Erasmus knew that however smoothly the stream might run for the moment, there would be rocks enough ahead. His dread from the first had been of civil war, and civil war embittered with the malignity which only religion could inspire. Though the majority had been for the change, there were still multitudes in every State who clung to their old creed and resented its overthrow. The danger in the mind of Erasmus was infinitely enhanced by the construction of a new theology. The Church had burdened the consciences of men with too many dogmas already. Were wretched mortals to be further bound to particular opinions on free will, on predestination, on original sin? Each new definition was a symbol of war, an emblem of division, an impulse to quarrel. Dogmas which did not touch moral conduct were a gratuitous trial of faith. From the nature of the case dogmatic propositions did not admit of proof; and the appeal was immediately to passion. The Catholic Church had been brought to its present state by these exaggerated refinements. If out of the present controversies there was to rise a new body of doctrine, a rival *symbolum fidei*, as a criterion of Christianity, there was nothing to be looked for but an age of hatred and fury. To Erasmus religion was a rule of life, a perpetual reminder to mankind of their responsibility to their Maker, a spiritual authority under which individuals could learn their duties to God and to their neighbour. Definitions on mysterious subjects which could not be understood were the growth of intellectual vanity. The hope of his life had been to see the dogmatic system slackened, the articles essential to be believed reduced to the Apostles' Creed, the declaration that God was a reality, and the future judgment a fact and a certainty. On all else he wished to see opinion free. The name of heresy was a terror, but so long as the

Church abstained from deciding there could be no heresy. Men would tolerate each other's differences and live in peace together. The new movement would provoke antagonistic decrees, multiply occasions of quarrel, and lead once more to the confusion of piety of life with the holding this or that form of belief.

While Luther was under the ban of the empire, excommunicated by the Pope, under sentence of death, with the Elector unable to defend him save by concealing his existence, Erasmus had refused to set upon a fallen man. Luther brought back to life, and the leader of a powerful schism, actually busy in creating and organising an opposition Church, was another person altogether. Christendom was about to split into factions. Each nation might perhaps become a separate burning crater, and while the metal was still hot and malleable Erasmus felt that speak he must. He wrote privately to the German princes. From all save those who had definitely taken Luther's side came the same answer — that he must himself take an open part. Luther had at first desired nothing beyond a reform of scandal and immorality, and it was still possible for reasonable men of both parties to combine on a practical principle. It was represented to Erasmus that by continuing silent he was allowing things to crystallise into a form which would make reconciliation impossible. Clement VII. wrote to entreat him to do what he could. Cardinal Campegio was sent again to Germany to restore peace, if peace could be had. Campegio found Erasmus specially provoked by a fresh and violent attack upon himself from the Lutheran side. The sting was poisoned by the hand from which it came. Ulrich von Hutten had been the most brilliant and the wittiest of the band who had followed Erasmus and Reuchlin into the land of light.

He had attached himself afterwards passionately to Luther, had sworn at Worms that if Luther's life was touched he would have the Legate's in return. He could not understand the hesitation of Erasmus. He despised it as cowardice, and tried to gall him by satire into taking what Hutten considered his proper place. During Luther's eclipse at Wartburg, Hutten had led the party of revolution and iconoclasm. He had always been to the front when a sisterhood had to be scattered or a reluctant abbot expelled from his nest, while Hutten's own character, unless fame had done him injustice, was not as pure as it might be.

Erasmus was obliged to demolish Hutten's invectives, and effectually he did it in a pamphlet which he called "Spongia" (Wipe it up and say no more about it). "Spongia" was called cruelty to an old friend. Erasmus appealed to the conscience of those who knew Hutten's character. Hutten himself died shortly after, and the bright, witty, wayward, not wise career was burnt out and ended.

Erasmus gives a brief account of all this to a friend, and then adds: —

If we curse the Church of Rome, and the Church of Rome curses us, what is to be looked for but a bloody civil war? I had tried to bring about peace, and the evangelicals called me Balaam. My crime was that I showed the princes how I thought this quarrel could be ended with least injury to Gospel liberty. The new Pope professes willingness to reform what is wrong. He has sent Cardinal Campegio as legate to Germany. Campegio is one of the most just and reasonable of men. Yet they cry out at him as if they would make the confusion worse confounded. It will be their own fault if the princes become angry by-and-by, and make many of them smart for it, and then they will wish that they had listened more patiently to me. Some of them have grown past bearing. They profess the Gospel, and they will obey neither prince nor bishop — not Luther himself, unless what he says approves itself to them. Am I to be treated as a criminal if I desire to see reforms carried out decently under constituted authority, instead of leaving them to violence and mob law? They speak of me as if they were trying to put a fire out, and I was interfering with them. They would cure the diseases of a thousand years' standing with medicines which will be fatal to the whole body. The Apostles were patient with the Jews who were reluctant to part with their law. Can these New Gospellers have no patience with men who cling to doctrines sanctioned by ages and taught by popes and councils and saints, and cannot gulp down the new wine? Suppose them right. Suppose all that they say is true. Let them do Christ's work in Christ's spirit, and then I may try if I can help them.

The Pope, the princes, his own personal friends, all were urging Erasmus to step into the arena. His own clear perception of the certain consequences of Luther's action, his hatred of fanatics, and his constitutional dread of enthusiasm, alike invited him to write before it was too late, not to support or defend the Church while it was still unreformed, but to protest against the final crystallising of a new scheme of doctrine to entangle weak consciences and make reconciliation fór ever impossible.

My design (he said) was to compose three colloquies; Thrasymachus to represent Luther, Eubulus the Catholic Church, with Philalethes for arbiter. In the first they were to discuss whether if Luther had been right in substance he had been wise in the manner in which he had put the truth forward. In the second they would examine his particular doctrines. The third would suggest how the wound could be healed so that it should not break out again. The two advocates would argue calmly, without personal reflections, and nothing would be alleged which was not notoriously true. Extreme partisans clamoured for severity. My plan was to leave each party to keep their own opinions. Severity would be easiest, but toleration seemed to me most expedient. When a single limb only is injured, cautery or the knife may be successful. When the disease has spread over the whole body, and gone into the veins and nerves, the poison can only be drawn out of the system by degrees. I undertook the task at the request of Alexander Glapio and several others. Glapio had written often to me about it, and was speaking for the Emperor. Mountjoy also had pressed me. I was busy at the moment with other things, and the plan is rather conceived than begun. I dislike work of this kind. I hate disputing, and prefer harmless play. Moreover, to execute it properly is work for a Hercules, and I am but a pigmy. I cannot say how it will be. Each party is now so incensed that it will conquer or perish. The defeat of Luther will destroy evangelical truth and Christian liberty, while Luther's enemies will not be crushed without a deperate fight. I would have the strife so ended that each side shall yield the victory to Christ. The princes know my opinion. They may adopt it or not as they please. But I would have no sentence given either way. If my book was published it would be seen whether I was right. No one ought to be offended with what I have written hitherto. The evangelicals, however, will allow no dissent from Luther, and will stone a man who thinks for himself. I had been working for peace. I had hoped that both parties would have used my help. The Emperor had been consulted, and had approved. Unhappily, each side was so obstinate in its own conviction that I found my "Eirenicon" would only make me hated all round, so I hesitated to go on with it. I can but pray now that God, who alone can, may allay this tempest.

LECTURE XVI.

THE worst enemy that Erasmus had, the Carmelite Egmond himself, could not accuse him of interested motives. Rank and wealth had long been within his reach had he cared to sell his services either to prince or pope. He had refused to part with his liberty, and we have seen the straits to which he was sometimes driven to recruit his finances. He had now pensions from the Emperor, from Archbishop Warham, and Lord Mountjoy, amounting together to 400 gold florins a year. It ought to have been more than enough. Luther's income was perhaps a tenth of that, and Luther counted himself rich. But Erasmus was not Luther. His habits had always been expensive, and supplies still occasionally fell short. Friends made up the deficiency. Presents of money were made to him, more often presents of plate, of which he had at times a cupboard full; but he gave away to poor scholars as much as he received. His books had a vast circulation; he had just published his "Colloquies." Twenty-four thousand copies were sold immediately, and he was supposed to have received large sums for them. But the book trade was not then as it is now, and then, and for two centuries later, works which went deepest into the minds of mankind brought small reward to their authors. Shakespeare never cared to see his plays through the press. Milton had five pounds for "Paradise Lost." Even Voltaire and Goethe, with all Europe for a public, were poorly paid in money.

I am thought (Erasmus said) to receive a harvest from Froben; he has made more reputation than profit out of me. I have not been persuaded to take as much as he offered me, and he will himself admit that what I have accepted has been but very little. Nor would I have accepted what I did unless it had been forced upon me, and unless he had proved to me that it came from his firm and not from himself.

Thus, the 400 florins were all on which Erasmus had to depend. They came, as I said, from the Emperor, Lord Mountjoy, and Archbishop Warham. All three, with More and Fisher and the Pope, the moderate party everywhere, were alike earnest with him to answer Luther in some way or other. The "Eirenicon" would not do; some fuller expression of opinion was wanted of him, and in the position in which he stood it was peculiarly difficult for him to refuse. He consented at last, and perhaps with less reluctance than might have been expected from his past hesitation. The subject which he chose was the freedom of the will. He is supposed to have selected what was apparently a point of obscure metaphysics, on which he could maintain his own view without provoking a too violent conflict. I do not think myself that this was his reason. What he most disliked, what he most feared from Luther, was the construction of a new dogmatic theology, of which the denial of the freedom of the human will was the corner-stone. It was one of those problems which he particularly desired to see left alone, because it is insoluble by argument. Shallow men, says a wise philosopher, all fancy that they are free to do as they please. All deep thinkers know that their wills are conditioned by nature and circumstance, and that we learn to live and act as we learn everything else. All trades, all arts, from the cobbling of a shoe to the painting of a picture, must be learned before they can be practised. The cobbler does not tell the apprentice, when for the first time he puts a piece of leather in his hand, that his will is free, that he can make a shoe out of it if he pleases, and that he will be wicked if he makes it badly. The schoolmaster does not tell a boy he is wicked if he brings up a bad Latin exercise. Cobbler and schoolmaster show their pupil how things ought to be done, correct his faults, bear patiently with many shortcomings, and are content with gradual improvement. It is practically the same with human life. The child has many falls, bodily and spiritual, before he learns to walk. He is naturally wilful, selfish, ignorant, violent, or timid. Education means the curing of all that. You do not call the child wicked because he is not perfect all at once. The will, if you can get at it, may do something, but it cannot do everything. In this sense we are obliged to act on the principle that the will is not by itself sufficient to direct and control conduct. Guidance is wanted, and help and instruction; and when all is done we must still make allowances for an imperfect result. Perfection, or even excellence, is rare in any art or occupation. First-rate artists are rare. Saints and heroes are rare. Special gifts are needed, which are the privilege of the few. To tell an ordinary man that if he will use his free will he can paint a first-rate picture, or become a Socrates or a St. Paul, is to tell him what is not true.

So looked at, the subject presents no difficulty. We have but to assume that right moral action is learnt by teaching and practice like everything else, and there is no more perplexity in one than in the other. Some persons are more gifted than others, some have happier dispositions, some are better educated, some are placed in more favourable circumstances. The pains which we take in training children; the allowances which we make and are compelled to make, for inherited vicious tendencies, for the environment of vice and ignorance in which so many are brought up, prove that in practice we act, and must act, on this hypothesis.

Catholic theologians, however, step in on the other side with an absolute rule of right, to which they insist that everyone, young and old, wise and ignorant, is bound to conform, and is able to conform. Each act of child or man, they say, is a choice between two courses, one right, the other wrong; that the Maker of us expects everyone to do right, holds him guilty and liable to punishment if he falls short, and gives him originally a free will which enables him, if he pleases, to do what he is required to do. It does not avail him that after he has fallen he recovers himself, profits by knowledge and experience, and improves as he grows older. Even so he will always fall short of the best, while his failures, even the errors of his youth, are all recorded against him. His Maker gives him free will. He uses it to choose the evil and refuse the good. He has a conscience which might have guided him right if he had attended to it. He prefers his own pleasure, and falls into sin. Such is the theological doctrine of free will; but the boldest theologian is obliged to acknowledge that in no single instance since man was created has it availed for the purpose. All have sinned, all have fallen short, is the cry from the beginning. Theologians have accounted for it, not by doubting their hypothesis, but by assuming a taint in the nature derived from our first ancestors. The natural man, they say, is born with a preponderance towards evil. It does not excuse his faults that he cannot help them: the sin remains, entailing future vengeance. But he is not left without a remedy. Extraordinary means have been provided, by which the past can be pardoned and strength obtained for the more effectual resistance of temptation. The Catholic Church finds it in the sacraments. The child is regenerated in baptism. His regenerate nature is mysteriously supported by the Eucharist. He is then made able to keep the Commandments. He does keep them. He may become a saint so preeminently holy that he can become meritorious beyond his own needs. The mass of mankind will continue to fall short; but they may confess, they may repent, and a priest may absolve them in virtue of those supererogatory merits. Hence came the doctrine that over and above what the saints needed for their own salvation they had left behind a store of good works in the Church's treasure-house, of which the Church had the distribution; and out of this had grown by the natural laws of corruption the extraordinary system of masses, pardons, and indulgences which had outraged the conscience of Europe, and against which Luther had risen up to protest. Luther answered that human nature remained after sacraments as before, equally unable to keep God's law. He retained the theological conception of sin. He admitted that absolute and complete obedience was required by the law; that failure to obey incurred Divine wrath. Yet, in Luther's view, man, baptized or unbaptized, was equally incapable of such complete obedience. Merit there could be none, even among the saints. The best were still imperfect, unable by their own works even to save themselves, and the stock of good works accumulated and distributed by the Church was a fiction and a fraud. The only hope of salvation lay in the acknowledgment by everyone of his lost condition, and a casting himself by faith on the merits of Christ, not on the merits of the saints or priestly absolutions. Inequality of character and conduct were facts of experience, and could be explained only by the pleasure and purpose of God. It was not true that man of himself by his free will could please his Maker. His free will was bound under sin, and the difference between man and man meant only that to some grace was given sufficient for inadequate obedience; to others it was refused. Some were vessels made to honour, some to dishonour, predestinated by a purpose which was certain, though none could understand it; and thus was arising that body of Protestant dogma with which we are all familiar: partly negative, that the priesthood is an illusion and the sacraments merely symbols; partly positive, the dogmas of the bondage of the will, of election, reprobation, predestination, the universal sinfulness, the inefficacy of good works, justification by faith as the canon of a standing or falling Church.

I cannot go into all this. Luther's theory of the will is the same as that which philosophers like Spinoza and Schopenhauer arrive at by another road. It contradicts superficial experience, as the astronomic explanation of the movements of the stars appears to contradict the evidence of our senses; but is perhaps the most consistent at bottom with the actual facts which we observe.

But religion addresses the vulgar, and must speak in language commonly intelligible. The conclusions of Protestant theology may be held, and have been held, by powerful and intensely devotional thinkers, and the same may be said of Catholic theology. Catholic mysteries, however, among the vulgar degenerate into idolatry; while predestination, the bondage of the will, the denial of human merit, justification by faith only, serve in ordinary minds occupied with worldly interests as an excuse for the neglect of duty. What use could there be, men asked, in struggling to obey the law when the law could not be obeyed, and the salvation of the soul was to be secured, if secured at all, independently of efforts of our own? Mankind are always willing to find a substitute for moral obedience, whether in sacrifices and rituals or in doctrinal formulas. At a time when thinkers like Erasmus or statesmen like Charles V. or Granvelle were trying to restore peace to Christendom by relaxing the doctrinal bonds, by leaving men to think for themselves on matters not affecting moral conduct, and setting heartily to work to reform corrupted manners, they were naturally irritated and dismayed when they saw a rival system of doctrine crystallising into shape and splitting Christendom into new lines of cleavage. Erasmus, More, Fisher, Warham, Charles V., George of Saxony, and many besides them who had been eager and active in urging practical reform, fell off, indignant at this new move of Luther's. Like enough it was inevitable. Like enough the Romish Church would have proved too strong for reason and moderation, and could be encountered only by a spiritual force as aggressive as its own. I am here only trying to explain to you how a man like Sir T. More, a bishop like Fisher of Rochester, came, as they said, to hate Luther and burn Lutherans; how Henry VIII. came to write against Luther; how Erasmus consented at last to take pen in hand to strike at the heart of Luther's system, and produce his book "De Libero Arbitrio." It has been supposed that, having been worried into compliance with a demand that he should write something, he chose an abstruse metaphysical subject, on which temper would be least aroused. I should rather say that he aimed his lance at the heart of Luther's doctrinal system, which, if once fixed in men's minds, would lead to interminable wars.

The book produced no effect further than as it was a public intimation that Erasmus did not agree with Luther. It was unsatisfactory, for the condition of public opinion would not allow him to tell the real truth. The subject was too deep for the multitude. His friends at Rome had looked for something which could be turned to their own purposes. Luther scornfully advised him to remain a spectator in a game for which he lacked courage to play a manly part. To the "De Libero Arbitrio" Luther replied with an equally contemptuous "De Servo Arbitrio," to the delight of his followers, though it was an odd matter to be delighted about. Erasmus answered with "Hyperaspistes," which charmed Sir Thomas More; but attack and defence alike are wearying, like all controversies, to later readers.

The mud volcanoes of the day burst into furious eruption. Erasmus refused to be provoked. It was then that he spoke of the innocent hen's egg which he had laid, and the cock which Luther had hatched.

But at any rate he had done what his moderate friends required of him, and, having done it, we find him working more strenuously than ever to bring about a peace, corresponding with the Emperor, the Chancellor, the King of France, the German princes, Catholic bishops, and reforming divines, working, too, all the time with superhuman industry at his special work of editing the Fathers. He had not broken with the reformers, nor even with Luther himself, except so far as Luther insisted. His letters on public affairs become more interesting than ever: —

TO PHILIP MELANCHTHON.[1]

BÂLE, *December* 10, 1524.

The Pope's advocates have been the Pope's worst friends, and the extravagant Lutherans have most hurt Luther. I would have held aloof had it been possible. I am no judge of other men's consciences or master of other men's beliefs. There are actors enough on the stage, and none can say how all will end. I do not object generally to the evangelical doctrines, but there is much in Luther's teaching which I dislike. He runs everything which he touches into extravagance. True, Christendom is corrupt and needs the rod, but it would be better, in my opinion, if we could have the Pope and the princes on our side. Campegio was gentle enough, but could do nothing. Clement was not opposed to reform, but when I urged that we should meet him half-way nobody listened. The violent party carries all before it. They tear the hoods off monks who might as well have been left in their cells. Priests are married, and images are torn down. I would have had religion purified without destroying authority. Licence need not be given to sin. Practices grown corrupt by long usage might be gradually corrected without throwing everything into confusion. Luther sees certain things to be wrong, and in flying blindly at them causes more harm than he cures. Order human things as you will, there will still be faults enough, and there are remedies worse than the disease. Is it so great a thing to have removed images and changed the canon of the mass? What good is done by telling foolish lads that the Pope is Antichrist, that confession carries the plague, that they cannot do right if they try, that good works and merits are a vain imagination, that free will is an

[1] *Ep.* dccxiv., abridged.

illusion, that all things hold together by necessity, and that man can do nothing of himself? Such things are said. You will tell me that Luther does not say them — that only idiots say them. Yes, but Luther encourages men who say them, and if I had a contract to make I would rather deal with a Papist than with some evangelicals that I have known. It is not always safe to remove the Camarinas of this world, and Plato says you cannot guide the multitude without deceiving them. Christians must not lie, but they need not tell the whole truth. Would that Luther had tried as hard to improve popes and princes as to expose their faults. He speaks bitterly of me. He may say what he pleases. Carlstadt has been here. He has published a book in German maintaining that the Eucharist is only a sign. All Berne has been in an uproar, and the printer imprisoned.

You are anxious that Luther shall answer me with moderation. Unless he writes in his own style, the world will say we are in connivance. Do not fear that I shall oppose evangelical truth. I left many faults in him unnoticed lest I should injure the Gospel. I hope mankind will be the better for the acrid medicines with which he has dosed them. Perhaps we needed a surgeon who would use knife and cautery. Carlstadt and he are going so fast that Luther himself may come to regret popes and bishops. His genius is vehement. We recognise in him the *Pelidæ stomachum cedere nescii.* The devil is a clever fellow. Success like Luther's might spoil the most modest of men.

Erasmus persuaded himself that there was still hope both from Rome and the princes. Clement sent him two hundred florins and a complimentary diploma in return for his book. George of Saxony had complained that he had not done enough, and must go to work more thoroughly. Erasmus answers: —

TO DUKE GEORGE.[1]

BÂLE, *December* 12, 1524.

When Luther first spoke the whole world applauded, and your Highness among the rest. Divines who are now his bitterest opponents were then on his side. Cardinals, even monks, encouraged him. He had taken up an excellent cause. He was attacking practices which every honest man condemned, and contending with a set of harpies, under whose tyranny Christendom was groaning. Who could then dream how far the movement would go? Had Daniel foretold it to me, I would not have believed him. Luther himself never expected to produce such an effect. After his Theses had come out I persuaded him to go no further. I doubted if he had learning enough. I was afraid of riots. I urged the printers to set in type no more books of his. He wrote to me. I cautioned him to be moderate. The Emperor was then well inclined to him. He had no enemies save a few monks and papal commissioners, whose trade he had spoilt. These people, fools that they were, kindled a fire, and it was then said to be all my fault — I ought to have silenced Luther! I thought no one could be less fit. My old enemies took up the cry, and told the Emperor that I was the person to do it. They only wanted to throw me among the wolves. What could I have done? They required me to revoke what I had said at first in Luther's favour. A pretty condition! I was to lie against my own soul, make myself the hangman of a set of prostitute wretches, and draw the hatred on myself of all Luther's supporters. I have or had some popularity in Europe. I should have lost it all, and have been left naked to be torn in pieces by the wild beasts. You say the Emperor and the Pope will stand up for me. How can the Emperor and the Pope help me when they can hardly help themselves? To call on me to put myself for-

[1] *Ep.* dccxviii., abridged.

ward is to saddle an ox or overload a broken-down horse. I am to sacrifice myself for the Catholic Faith! It is not for everyone to uphold the Ark. Even Jerome, when he attacks heresy, becomes almost a heretic. I do it! Are there no bishops, no college dignitaries, no hosts of divines? Surely among so many there were fitter persons than I. Some really tried. Great persons declared war. The Pope put out a Bull, the Emperor put out an edict, and there were prisons, faggots, and burnings. Yet all was in vain. The mischief only grew. What could a pigmy like Erasmus do against a champion who had beaten so many giants? There were men of intellect on Luther's side to whom I had looked up with respect. I wondered what they found in him to impress them; but so it was. I thought I must be growing blind. I did see, however, that the world was besotted with ritual. Scandalous monks were ensnaring and strangling consciences. Theology had become sophistry. Dogmatism had grown to madness, and, besides, there were the unspeakable priests, and bishops, and Roman officials. Perhaps I thought that such disorders required the surgeon, and that God was using Luther as he used Pharaoh and Nebuchadnezzar. Luther could not have succeeded so signally if God had not been with him, especially when he had such a crew of admirers behind him. I considered that it was a case for compromise and agreement. Had I been at Worms, I believe I could have brought it to that. The Emperor was not unwilling. Adrian, Clement, Campegio have not been unwilling. The difficulty lay elsewhere. Luther's patrons were stubborn and would not yield a step. The Catholic divines breathed only fire and fury. If that was to be the way, there was no need of me. I conceived, moreover, that if it was fit and right to burn a man for contradicting articles decreed by the Church, there was no law to burn him for holding mistaken opinions on other subjects, as long as he defended them quietly and was otherwise of blameless life. The Paris divines do not think on the papal power as the Italian divines think, but they do not burn each other. Thomists and Scotists differ, but they can work in the same schools. Stakes and prisons are vulgar remedies. Two poor creatures have been burnt at Brussels, and the whole city has turned Lutheran. If the infection had touched only a few it might be stamped out, but it has gone so far that kings may catch it. I do not say let it alone, but do not make it worse by bad treatment. Fear will alter nothing, and spasmodic severity exasperates. If you put the fire out by force, it will burst up again. I trust, I hope that Luther will make a few concessions and that Pope and princes may still consent to peace.

May Christ's dove come among us, or else Minerva's owl. Luther has administered an acrid dose to a diseased body. God grant it prove salutary. Your Highness would not have written as you have done if you knew all that I could tell you. The Pope, the Emperor, his brother Ferdinand, the King of England wrote to me in a far different tone. Your freedom does not offend me. It rises only out of your zeal for the Faith. I risked the loss of my best friends by refusing to join Luther, but I did not break off my connection with them because they did join him, and Adrian and Campegio, and the King of England, and the Cardinal of York all say that I did right. I vex Luther more by continuing my intimacy with them than I could do with the most violent abuse.

The eager Catholics were disappointed, of course, with Erasmus's "Free Will." The mountain had brought forth a mouse. If that was all that he could do, he might as well have held his peace. The Prince of Carpi wrote to him as Duke George had done, telling him he was still under suspicion of favouring Luther. He answers:—

TO ALBERTUS PIUS, PRINCE OF CARPI.[1]

October 10, 1525.

When the Lutheran drama opened, and all the world applauded, I advised my friends to stand aloof. I thought it would end in bloodshed, and had I taken a part made enemies of the Swiss and Germans, who had stood by me in the fight for learning. Certain theologians left no stone unturned to drive me to join a party which they expected would be condemned. The Lutherans alternately courted me and menaced me. For all this, I do not move a finger's breadth from the teaching of the Roman Church. You would think more of this if you knew the Germans, and what a tempest I could raise if I chose to lead the fray. Instead of leading, I have stood naked and unarmed between the javelins of two angry foes. It is said that Luther has borrowed much from me. He denies it himself and says I do not understand theology. But suppose it is so. Has he borrowed nothing from Augustine and St. Paul? You ask me why I did not speak out at once. Because I regarded Luther as a good man, raised up by Providence to correct the depravity of the age. Whence have all these troubles risen? From the audacious and open immorality of the priesthood, from the arrogance of the theologians and the tyranny of the monks. These began the battle by attacking learning. I did not wish to expel the old studies. I wished only to give Greek and Hebrew a place among them which I thought would minister to the glory of Christ. The monks turned the question on points of faith where they thought they would have stronger ground. You remember Reuchlin. The conflict was raging between the Muses and their enemies, when up sprang Luther, and the object thenceforward was to entangle the friends of literature in the Lutheran business so as to destroy both them and him together. So things have gone on ever

[1] *Ep.* cccxxxiii., second series.

since, the clamour growing louder and the spirit of the contest worse. This is the naked fact. If what I hear is true, I must call on your highness to check the slanders spread about me. If I am mistaken, you will pardon my complaints.

The English friends of Erasmus were more eager than even the German princes that he should strike again at Luther, and strike in earnest. Beyond all others, Sir Thomas More, who wished him to silence for ever the charge of having been Luther's confederate. More had understood and valued the tract upon "Free Will." But it was not enough. He must enlarge his reply and make a final end of Luther. He must do it. No excuse would serve him for deserting the cause of God.

SIR T. MORE TO ERASMUS.[1]

GREENWICH, *December* 18, 1525.

Do it (More said), you have nothing to fear. Had the Lutherans meant to try conclusions with you in earnest, they would have done it when your first part appeared. You have drawn a picture there of a beast and the enemy of souls. You have dragged up the smoky demon of Tartarus like another Cerberus out of hell, and have shown him in visible form. You cannot increase your danger by following up your argument. Go on, therefore. Luther himself is not so cowardly as to hope, or so wicked as to wish, that you should be silent. I cannot say how foolish and inflated I think his letter to you. He knows well how the wretched glosses with which he has darkened Scripture turn to ice at your touch. They were cold enough already. If for some inexplicable reason you cannot make a public rejoinder, at least set down your private thoughts in writing and send the MS. to me. The Bishop of London and I will take charge of it.

[1] *Ep.* cccxxxiv., second series, abridged.

Alas, Erasmus could not do it. His private thought, which indeed he had spoken freely enough, was that, in the negative part of his teaching, Luther was right, and he would not be found fighting against God. He poured out his sorrows and his perplexities in a letter to the Dominican Faber, who, like More, had been urging him to write more fully.

TO FABER.[1]

You see how fiercely Luther strikes at me, moderate though I was. What would he have said had I provoked him in earnest? He means his book to live with my crimes embalmed in it. Ten editions of his reply have been published already. The great men in the Church are afraid to touch him, and you want poor me to do it again, me who am too weak to make myself feared, and too little of a saint in my life not to dread what may be said of me. Luther pretends to wish to be friendly, yet he calls me another Lucian, says that I do not believe in God, or believe, like Epicurus, that God has no care for man. He accuses me of laughing at the Bible and of being an enemy to Christianity, and yet expects me to thank him for his gentle handling. Faction spares none, and calumny sticks and cannot be washed off. The grosser the charge the more credit it receives. I wrote my book to please the princes and to show that I was not a Lutheran, but when I pointed out how the mischief was to be met which the monks and theologians were doing, no one listened. I wrote to Pope Adrian. I suppose my letter did not please him, for he took no notice of it, and now you see what has come. In France they are at work with gibbet and dungeon. It won't answer. The other side cry "Liberty!" and have the printers with them, while the Church has only monks, Epicurean priests, and rabid Divines. The nobles favour the movement with an eye to the churchmen's lands and offices. The princes like to fish in troubled

[1] *Ep.* dcccxliii., abridged.

waters and plunder the wrecks which drive ashore. Go on with your stakes and prisons and you will have universal chaos. As yet we are only at the beginning. The Pope has ordered the Italians to be quiet. He is wise. They will look on and chuckle while we cut each other's throats. Why cannot we be wise too? We are all embarked in the same ship. If the ship sinks, we shall sink with it, and the mischief is spread too widely to be cured by ordinary remedies. The princes, you say, want my opinion. They shall have it if they wish, but it must be kept secret. Ferocious writing ought to be checked on both sides. One is as bad as the other. Preachers and orators should be silenced, and quiet men put in their places who will leave alone dogmas and teach piety and morals. The Catholics are now persecuting innocent men and are driving into Luther's camp those whom they should most wish to attract. Rage if you will against rebellion, but do not hurt those who have done no harm. Do not close the schools, but see that they have fit masters. The Lutherans are strong in the towns. Bid them tolerate their opponents. Leave each man to his own conscience and put down riots. Let Catholics meanwhile reform the abuses which have provoked the revolt, and leave the rest to a general council. Stir no more hornets' nests, unless you wish to ruin Erasmus.

One more curious letter, without date or address, belongs to the present period, and was probably meant for the Emperor's eye.

TO ——[1]

The two parties are dragging at the opposite ends of a rope. When it breaks they will both fall on their backs. The reformers turn the images out of the churches, which originally were useful and ornamental. They might have been content to forbid the worship of images and to have removed only the superflu-

[1] *Ep.* dxii., second series, abridged.

ous. They will have no more priests. It would be better to have priests of learning and piety, and to provide that orders are not hastily entered into. There would be fewer of them, but better three good than three hundred bad. They do not like so much ritual. True, but it would be enough to abolish the absurd. Debauched priests who do nothing but mumble masses are generally hated. Do away with these hirelings, and allow but one celebration a day in the churches. Indulgences, with which the monks so long fooled the world with the connivance of the theologians, are now exploded. Well, then, let those who have no faith in saints' merits pray to Father, Son and Holy Ghost, imitate Christ in their lives, and leave those alone who do believe in saints. If the saints do not hear them, Christ may hear them. Confession is an ancient custom. Let those who deny that it is a sacrament observe it till the Church decides otherwise. No great harm can come of confession so long as men confess only their own mortal sins. Let men think as they please of purgatory, without quarrelling with others who do not think as they do. Theologians may argue about free will in the Sorbonne. Laymen need not puzzle themselves with conundrums. Whether works justify or faith justifies matters little, since all allow that faith will not save without works. In Baptism let the old rule be kept. Parents may perhaps be left to decide whether it shall be administered in infancy or delayed to maturity. Anabaptists must not be tolerated. The Apostles bade their people obey the magistrates, though the magistrates were heathens. Anabaptists will not obey even Christian princes. Community of goods is a chimera. Charity is a duty, but property must be upheld. As to the Eucharist, let the old opinion stand till a council has proved a new revelation. The Eucharist is only adored so far as Christ is supposed to be present there as God. The human nature is not adored, but the Divine Nature, which is Omnipresent. The thing to be corrected is the abuse of the administration. In primitive times the Eucharist was not carried about by priests on horseback, or exhibited to be made a jest of. In England at this present time there is neither house nor tavern, I had almost said brothel, where the sacrifice is not offered and money paid for it.[1] For the rest, let there be moderation in all things, and then we may hope for peace. The experiment has been tried with good success in the Duchy of Cleves. It will succeed everywhere if the clergy will only consent.

This advice was probably meant, as I said, for Charles V., who had often pressed for Erasmus's opinion. It corresponded entirely with Charles's own private views. Unfortunately, his hands were tied by the necessity of pleasing Spaniards, Italians, bigots of all kinds throughout his dominions. Least of all could he afford to offend his own subjects when the French had invaded Lombardy and were threatening Naples, with the Pope in secret alliance with them. The Emperor's own sentiments were clearly expressed to Erasmus in a letter from Gattinarius, the Imperial secretary.[2] Erasmus had told him that he would die happy if he could see the storm composed. Gattinarius answered that if the Pope and the other princes were as well disposed as his master, Erasmus would not wish in vain. As things were, he still did not despair that the schism might be healed, and the vicious practices in the Church which had led to it might be looked into and reformed.

[1] "Nunc in Angliâ nulla est domus, nulla caupona, pene dixeram lupanar, ubi non sacrificetur."

[2] February 10, 1527. *Ep.* dcccl.

LECTURE XVII.

WILDER and wilder grew the world, as if the bags of Æolus had been untied. I can but touch the outside of the political history. Francis I. had gone careering into Lombardy, and had got himself taken prisoner at Pavia, all lost but honour. France, England, and the Pope, fearing that Charles would restore the throne of the Cæsars, or perhaps make himself Pope also — for that was thought a possibility — made a frightened league together: Henry VIII. to be the special protector of the Apostolic See, the Pope in turn to do him a small service, relieve him of his old Spanish wife, and let him marry a younger woman to raise up children to succeed him. The King's request was not in itself unreasonable. Henry had married his brother's widow under a dispensation of doubtful legality. The legitimacy of the Princess Mary had been challenged, and if he died without a son there would be a disputed succession and a fresh War of the Roses. Catherine was past child-bearing. It was just one of those situations in which the dispensing powers of the Pope might be usefully exerted, and Clement, so far as he was himself concerned, would have made no objection at all. The Emperor, too, it is likely, in the distracted state of Europe, would have hesitated in raising obstacles to a natural demand, and flinging a fresh poisoned ingredient into the witches' caldron; but Catherine's consent was needed if there was to be an amicable separation, and

Catherine would not give it, and Charles, like a gentleman as he was, found himself obliged, against his own interest, to support his aunt.

The divorce of Catherine was at first but a small matter, though it grew to be a large one. Political events went their way, and, if Charles wished to reform the Church of Rome, were opening the road for him. Clement, as an Italian prince, became the ally of France, and at war with Charles.

Charles's army, a motley of Catholic Spaniards and Lutheran landknechts, stormed Rome, caged the Pope in St. Angelo, sacked convents, outraged nuns, and carried cardinals in mock procession round the sacred city, naked on the backs of asses. Castilian and German had plundered churches side by side, carried off the consecrated plate equally careless of sacrilege, while the unfortunate head of Christendom looked on helpless from the battlements of his prison. It seemed as if Charles had but to stretch out his hand, place the papal crown in commission, if he did not take it himself, and reform with sovereign power the abuses which he had acknowledged and deplored. So, and only so, he could have restored peace to Germany and saved the unity of Christendom, in which the rents were each day growing wider, for behind Luther had come Carlstadt and Zwingle, going where Luther could not follow, denying the sacraments, denying the Real Presence in the Eucharist, breaking into Anabaptism and social anarchy; while behind Zwingle, again, was rising the keen, clear, powerful Calvin, carrying the Swiss and French reformers along with him.

Erasmus was still at Bâle observing the gathering whirlwinds, his own worst fears far exceeded by the reality, determined for his own part to throw no fresh fuel on the flames, and to hold himself clear from connection with all extreme factions — Lutheran, Zwinglian, or Catholic. Charles, it seems, continued to consult him indirectly, through secretaries or other correspondents, as to what the nature of Church authority really was, evidently as if he was considering in what way it could best be dealt with. To one of such inquiries Erasmus answers: [1] —

I have always observed my allegiance to the Church, but I distinguish between the Church's decrees; some are canons of councils, some are papal rescripts, some decisions of particular bishops, some like plebiscites, some temporary and liable to recall. When the present storm began I thought it would be enough to change a few constitutions. But corruption under the name of religion has gone so far as almost to extinguish the Christian faith. Neither party will yield. Many cry for coercion; such a method might succeed for a time, but if it succeeded permanently there would still be numerous and uneasy consciences. I do not say I am neutral; I mean that I am not bound to either side. The question is not of opinions, but of morals and character, and these are worst among the loudest of the Church's champions. Church authority, however, may be preserved with a few alterations. I would give the cup to the laity. I would not have priests marry or monks abandon their vows without their bishop's consent. Boys and girls, however, who have been tempted into religious houses ought to be set free, as having been taken in by fraud. It would be well if priests and monks could be chaste; but the age is corrupt, and of two evils we must choose the least. The licence of which you complain has found no encouragement from me; I have checked it always when I could. You are afraid of Paganism; my fear is of Judaism, which I see everywhere. Anyway, you may assure the Emperor that from me he has nothing to fear.

Ep. dcccxlviii., abridged.

The capture of Rome might have been expected to have pleased Erasmus, as giving the Emperor a free hand. The world thought that the breach between the Empire and the Papacy was now final and irreparable. Erasmus was keener-sighted than his contemporaries. His hope had been to see Charles and Clement work together as friends and equals. He was afraid that the Emperor would now use and maintain the Pope for his own political objects, and would be led away with secular ambition, in which the Pope would be his creature. His anxiety appears in a letter to Warham.

TO ARCHBISHOP WARHAM.[1]

Revolution is in the air. I fear bloodshed, for the roots have gone deep. No one who has not seen Germany can believe in what condition we are. I cannot leave the Church and join the reformers. But the people are all on their side, in consequence of the raging of the monks, who are working their own ruin. At Rome all is confusion. Letters cannot enter. It is supposed that the Pope and the Emperor will be reconciled, and that the Pope will take the Emperor's side. In that case there will be no peace. The Pope ought to be indifferent.

In these later anxious years we have lost sight of the old brilliant witty Erasmus. The times had grown serious, and his humour when it showed was bitter, but the bright nature was still there, and now and then a gleam breaks out among the clouds. The letter to Warham was sent by the hand of a disciple, Nicholas Cann, who was paying England a visit. Erasmus gave him an introduction to the Archbishop, and a few hints to Cann himself.

[1] *Ep.* dccclxx.

TO NICHOLAS CANN.[1]

May 17, 1527.

You will enjoy your visit. You will meet many of the English nobles and men of learning. They will be infinitely kind to you, but be careful not to presume upon it: when they condescend, be you modest. Great men do not always mean what their faces promise, so treat them reverendly, as if they were gods. They are generous and will offer you presents, but recollect the proverb, Not everything everywhere and from everyone. Accept gratefully what real friends give you. To mere acquaintances excuse yourself lightly; more art is needed in refusing graciously than in receiving. An awkward rejection often makes enemies. Imitate the polypus and you have no difficulties. Put out your head, give your right hand, and yield the wall; smile on as many as you please, but trust only those you know, and be specially careful to find no fault with English things or customs. They are proud of their country, as well they may be.

So much for the character of our ancestors, which has altered less than one might have expected. Erasmus had other things to make him anxious, and was soon absorbed again in the German confusions. He seems to have been specially confidential with Duke George of Saxony.

TO DUKE GEORGE.[2]

September 2, 1527.

Luther amazes me. If the spirit which is in him be an evil one, no more fatal monster was ever born. If it be a good spirit, much of the fruit of the Gospel is wanting in him. If a mixed one, how can two spirits so strong exist in the same person? Intolerable corruptions have crept into Christian life which custom makes appear like virtues, and there are other

[1] *Ep.* dcccl xviii.

[2] *Ep.* dcccxci., abridged.

changes besides which wise men would gladly see if they can be had without a convulsion. This I know to be the opinion of the Emperor. But nothing will satisfy Luther, and his party is so divided, and their gospel is generating so much licence, that it may fall to pieces, even if the Pope and the Emperor combine. The hope is that the Princes may have influence enough to keep the Lutherans within bounds, or a worse fire may break out on the other side through those wretched monks and divines.

The folly of the monks and theologians made the real danger. On the same day he writes to another correspondent:[1]—

Frightful storms spring from small beginnings. The Lutheran cyclone rose out of a trifle. The Dominicans paraded their indulgences too ostentatiously. Luther objected. The Dominicans set up a clamour. I tried to stop them, but could not do it, and you see the result. The Pope should have left matters alone. No one dreads the monks more than the Pope does, and none treat the Pope with more contempt than the monks do when it suits their purpose.

Invariably Erasmus speaks of the monks as the cause of all that had happened. His especial bitterness was due, perhaps, to his early experience; and undoubtedly they returned his hatred. They had been forbidden to abuse him in their pulpits. They were working underground to prevent the circulation of his books and induce the Church to censure them. Luther's writings, being chiefly in German, were unread save where German was spoken. The writings of Erasmus had spread over Europe. His controversy with Luther had not earned his pardon. He was a subject of the Spanish crown; a party favour-

[1] *Ep.* dcccxciv.

able to him had begun to grow in the Peninsula, which roused the regulars there to fury. The sacred soil of Spain should at least be kept free from heresy. Juan Maldonado writes to him from Burgos:[1] —

September 1, 1527.

The theologians here are working with the monks, and will be counted the only wise ones. They impose on noble ladies with their pretence of holiness. They tell them that they cannot have their sins pardoned unless they go on their knees to some sophisticated friar — only friars, they say, can distinguish the qualities of sins. Not a man, from the meanest pot-boy to the Emperor, will they count a Christian unless he takes a monk for a director, and many a pretty tale is told by poor women of the shameless doings of these philosophasters. They hate you, but do not you be disturbed. You have torn the masks from their faces, and shown them to the world as they are. I need not say what curses they have imprecated on you. They are now appealing to the bishops and magistrates to prohibit the sale of your books. The hooded masters know well enough the difference between your teaching and their hypocrisy. They know that if your writings are read there will be an end of them. But their abuse does not hurt you. We love you the better for it. A Spanish translation of the "Colloquies" is in the hands of every man and woman.

The Emperor was now himself in Spain. The Spanish authorities appealed to him to support them. He had so long corresponded with Erasmus on the great questions of the day, had seemed so entirely to agree with him, had so peremptorily silenced the attacks upon him in the Low Countries, that Erasmus looked confidently for a continuance of his countenance; but it was not without reason that Erasmus

[1] *Ep.* cccxxxviii., second series, abridged.

had been alarmed at the possible consequences of the capture of Rome in a change of attitude on Charles's part. The Emperor did, indeed, order the Spanish monks to hold their tongues; but there were symptoms which Erasmus's friends did not like, and the monks were dangerous.

Your enemies (wrote another of these friends) are now mute, and dare not crow even on their own dunghills. But they mutter still in private, and I fear the beast with 700 heads may win in the end. You, though long may you live, must die at last; but a religious order never dies. It has good men in it as well as bad, but good and bad alike stand by their profession, and the worse part drags the better after it.

A religious order never dies. Charles V. could not just then afford to quarrel with the leaders of the Church in Spain. It was necessary for him to pacify the suspicions which had risen out of the imprisonment of the Pope, and though he refused to allow Erasmus's writings to be suppressed, he could not resist a demand that those writings should be examined by the Inquisition. Erasmus had appealed to him. He replied in a curious letter, half an apology, though in terms of the utmost personal esteem.

CHARLES V. TO ERASMUS.[1]

BURGOS, *December* 13, 1527.

Dear and Honoured Sir, — Two things make your letter welcome to me. The receipt of any communication from a person whom I regard with so much affection is itself a pleasure, and your news that the Lutheran fever is abating gratifies me exceedingly. The whole Church of Christ is your debtor as much as I am. You have done for it what emperors, popes,

[1] *Ep.* dccccxv., abridged.

princes, and academies have tried in vain to do. I congratulate you from my heart. You must now complete the work which you have begun so successfully, and you may rely on all possible support from me. I am sorry to find you complain of the treatment which your writings meet with here. You appear to distrust our goodwill, and to fear that the Erasmus whose Christian character it so well known to the world may be unfairly dealt with. It is true that we have allowed your works to be examined, but in this you have no reason for alarm. Human errors may be discovered in them, but the worst that can befall you will be an affectionate admonition. You will then be able to correct or explain, and Christ's little ones will not be offended. You will establish your immortal reputation, and shut the mouths of your detractors; or it may be that no faults at all will be detected, and your honour will be yet more effectually vindicated. Take courage, therefore. Be assured that I shall never cease to respect and esteem you. I do my best for the commonwealth. My work must speak for me now and hereafter. Remember me in your prayers.

This letter, gracious though it was, did not satisfy Erasmus. He knew that in all which he had written about the corruption of the Church the Emperor agreed with him. But his mind had misgiven him from the moment when he heard of the capture of Rome. Two alternatives, in fact, then lay before Charles: either to sequester the Pope and put himself at the head of Reform — the course which some, at least, of the secular statesmen of Spain and Italy urgently recommended, or to make up his quarrel with Clement, with a show of generosity, and support his failing authority. To take up reform would mean a quarrel with the Church, which was still dangerously powerful in every part of his personal dominions.

France and England were already arming in the Pope's defence. The Pope would throw himself into their arms, divorce Catherine — a small matter, but one which touched Charles's honour. The Turks had taken Rhodes, had overrun Hungary, killed the Emperor's brother-in-law, and were threatening Vienna. He would have to face a desperate war, with no allies but the Germans, who were rushing into a spiritual revolution which would then be beyond control. He could not do it. He must detach the Pope from Francis and Henry, secure the support of the Church, and leave reform till the sky brightened again. Anabaptism had spread over Germany. It was now passing into his own Netherlands, carrying anarchy and insurrection along with it. He must rally all the forces of Conservatism, recover the confidence of the leading Churchmen, and deserve it by showing the agitators that they had nothing to hope from him. He made peace with Clement, a condition of it being that Henry VIII. should have no divorce without his own consent. In return he issued an edict for the suppression of spiritual rebellion severe enough even to content the monks themselves, whose business it was to be to see the edict executed. Erasmus was dismayed. He had long satisfied himself that fire and sword would never answer, and never believed the Emperor would try it. He was not alarmed for himself; he was alarmed for Christendom. A letter to Duke George shows what he was feeling: —

TO DUKE GEORGE.[1]

The Emperor and his brother are for trying severity, and encouraging those who mistake their own passions for devotion to the Gospel. Severity will do no good. The innocent will suffer. The threatened

[1] *Ep.* dccccxix.

confiscation will be an excuse for plunder; all will be in danger who have anything to lose. Beggars and rogues will fatten, and there will be universal confusion. Knife and cautery are bad instruments when the whole frame is sick. If the princes could but combine and restrain both parties with moderation and authority there might still be hope for peace.

An extremely interesting letter follows to the Elector Herman, Archbishop of Cologne, who afterwards joined the Lutherans, and was deposed for it:[1] —

March 18, 1528.

Is there not misery enough in the world already, that the jealousies and passions of sovereigns must be making it worse? The disorder grows daily, and unless some god appears *ex machinâ* and ends the tragedy, chaos lies straight ahead. I am not hopeless. The Lord, in whose hands are the hearts of kings, may yet show these two princes (Charles and Francis) that a conquest over themselves is more glorious than a victory in the field. Gentleness is a stronger bond than force, and moral authority goes further than Imperial edicts. Peace may not be possible, but there might be a truce for a term of years, and a breathing-time. I fear now a Cadmean victory, as fatal to the victors as to the vanquished, and all that I can do is to pray. Often, very often, I have urged the Emperor to peace. He says in his last letter to me: "I have done the best I can; now and hereafter my work must speak for me." This does not sound like peace. A great war means infinite horror and wretchedness, and the wild opinions now spreading, which steal our peace of mind, are worse than war. The factions in Germany are more fatal than even the quarrels of kings, and I know not how it is, none hurt a good cause worse than those who think they are defending it. The rival parties drag at the

[1] *Ep.* dccccxlv., abridged.

two ends of a rope; when the rope breaks both go to the ground. What is the use of all these questionings and definings and dogmatisings? Let schoolmen argue if they so please. It is enough for common people if they are taught how to rule their own conduct. The mass has been made a trade for illiterate and sordid priests, and a contrivance to quiet the consciences of reprobates. So the cry is raised, "Abolish the mass, put it away, make an end of it." Is there no middle course? Cannot the mass be purified? Saint-worship has been carried so far that Christ has been forgotten. Therefore, respect for saints is idolatry, and orders founded in their names must be dissolved. Why so violent a remedy? Too much has been made of rituals and vestments, but we might save, if we would, the useful part of such things. Confession has been abused, but it could be regulated more strictly. We might have fewer priests and fewer monks, and those we keep might be better of their kind. If the bishops will only be moderate, things may end well after all. But we must not hurt the corn in clearing out the tares. We must forget ourselves, and think first of Christ's glory, cease our recriminations, and regard all these calamities as a call to each of us to amend his own life.

And to Duke George again:[1]—

March 24, 1528.

Far be it from me to accuse the Emperor and Ferdinand of cruelty. Both of them have stood my firm friends when my enemies wanted to destroy me. But I had rather the plague could be stayed by quiet remedies than by the deaths of thousands of human creatures, and in this I do but say what Augustine said, and Jerome, and other champions of the faith. I am not pleading for heretics. I speak in the interests of the princes themselves and of Catholic truth. The poison has gone deep. If the sword is to be the cure, good and bad will fall alike by it, and none can tell what

[1] *Ep.* dccccliii., abridged.

the end will be. Charity and humanity recommend milder courses. It is not what heretics deserve, but what is most expedient for Christendom. The Donatists were worse than heretics, yet Augustine did not wish them killed. I blame neither Charles nor Ferdinand. The heretics challenged them, and have earned what they may get, but I wish this war would end, as I have told the Emperor again and again; and as to heresy, it is better to cure a sick man than to kill him. To say that severity will fail to cure heresy is not to defend it, but to point out how it could be dealt with better.

One more, to the Bishop of Augsburg:[1] —

August 26, 1528.

The state of the Church distracts me. My own conscience is easy; I was alone in saying from the first that the disorder must be encountered in its germs; I was too true a prophet; the play, which opened with universal hand-clapping, is ending as I foresaw that it must. The kings are fighting among themselves for objects of their own. The monks, instead of looking for a reign of Christ, want only to reign themselves. The theologians curse Luther, and in cursing him curse the truth delivered by Christ and the Apostles, and, idiots that they are, alienate with their foul speeches many who would have returned to the Church, or but for them would have never left it.

No fact is plainer than that this tempest has been sent from heaven by God's anger, as the frogs and locusts and the rest were sent on the Egyptians; but no one remembers his own faults, and each blames the other. It is easy to see who sowed the seed and who ripened the crop. The Dominicans accuse me. They will find no heresy in work of mine. I am not so thought of by greater men then they.

The Emperor wants me in Spain, Ferdinand wants me at Vienna, the Regent Margaret invites me to Brabant, the King of England to London. Each offers

[1] *Ep.* dccccl xxi., abridged.

me an ample salary, and this they can give. Alas! they cannot give me back my youth and strength. Would they could!

Yet more important is a letter written at the same time to an unnamed English bishop,[1] who had complained of passages in the "Colloquies" reflecting on the monks and the confessional. Erasmus goes at length into the whole question.

What I have said (he writes) is not to discourage confession, but to check the abuse of it. Confessions are notoriously betrayed. The aim of the monks is not to benefit men's souls but to gather harvests out of their purses, learn their secrets, rule in their houses; and everyone who knows the facts will understand why these confessors need to be controlled. I have not condemned ceremonies. I have only insisted on the proper use of them. Christ did the same, so why find fault with me? I have complained of the extravagant importance attached to fasting. I have just heard that two poor creatures are to be murdered in France because they have eaten meat in Lent. I have said there are too many holidays; others have said so besides me. More sins are committed on holidays than on any other day in the week. I have spoken of miracles. The Christian religion nowadays does not require miracles, and there are none; but you know what lying stories are set about by crafty knaves.

After giving various instances of monastic knavery, he goes on:—

To rascals like these the Pope and the princes are now entrusting power to suppress heresy, and they abuse it to revenge their own wrongs. The monastic profession may be honourable in itself. Genuine monks we can respect; but where are they? What monastic character have those we see except the dress and the tonsure? It would be wrong to say that

[1] *Ep.* dcccclxxiv.

there are no exceptions. But I beseech you — you who are a pure good man — go round the religious houses in your own diocese; how much will you find of Christian piety? The mendicant orders are the worst; and are they to be allowed to tyrannise over us? I do not say this to injure any individual. I say it of those who disgrace their calling. They are hated, and they know why; but they will not mend their lives, and think to bear down opposition with insolence and force. Augustine says that there were nowhere better men than in monasteries, and nowhere worse. What would he say now — if he was to see so many of these houses both of men and women public brothels? [Quid nunc Augustinus diceret si videret multa monasteria quæ nihil differunt a publicis lupanaribus? Quid de monacharum multis collegiis in quibus nihil minus reperias quam castitatem?]

I speak of these places as they exist now among ourselves. Immortal Gods! how small is the number where you will find Christianity of any kind! The malice and ignorance of these creatures will breed a revolution worse than Luther's unless the princes and bishops see to them. The Dominicans and Franciscans have been lighting their fagots in France. These are but the first droppings of the storm, the preludes of what we are to expect from monastic despotism, and if their hands are not held, the rage of the people will burst out in a tornado. The mendicants are at the bottom of the mischief, and there will be no peace till they are made to know their places. It will be for their own security. The most respectable, if not the largest part of these communities, desire it themselves. To abolish them is a rude remedy. It has been done in some places, but they ought to be brought back to their original purpose as schools of piety, and it will be a good day for the monks when they are reformed. They must not be allowed to live longer in idleness. Their exemptions must be cancelled, and they must be placed under the bishops; and as to their images, the people must be taught that they are no more than signs. It would be better if there were none at all, and if prayer was only addressed to Christ. But in all things let there be moderation. The storm has come upon us by the will of God, who is plaguing us as he plagued the Egyptians. Let us confess our sins and pray for mercy.

If the Emperor meant to try persecution, the religious orders, and especially the mendicant orders, would necessarily be the most active in it, through the immense powers of the confessional. Erasmus was in terror at the prospect, and persisted, wherever his voice could reach, in exposing their real character. Had he been a Lutheran writing to Lutherans, his evidence might be suspected, but he addresses his protests to bishops, statesmen, cardinals, princes, to whose personal experience he appeals. It was dangerous to tell the truth. It would have been doubly dangerous — entirely fatal to him — to lie or exaggerate. He mentions, on his own personal knowledge, several specially disgusting features of monastic life. Part of a monk's duties was to read aloud in the refectory some edifying story. It would be begun and ended in the usual way; in the intervals the reader would introduce licentious anecdotes of adventures in brothels. Others would baptize and hear confessions when they were drunk. He tells a case where a father, who was far gone this way, fell asleep in the box when hearing a confession. The penitent, finding he was not attended to, broke off and went away; another penitent came, and the father again slept; the second sinner, less patient than the other, roused him, and asked him if he was listening. The father confounded the two. "Yes, yes," he said, "you told me you had broken open your neighbour's desk. Very good. Go on." The man said he had broken open no desk and went off in a rage.

Erasmus gives extraordinary instances of the ignorance of the clergy. One was connected with himself, and is described in a letter to Martin Lipsius.[1]

September 5, 1528.

Not long ago a physician of my acquaintance happened to say something in my favour in a public assembly. A Dominican prior present, reputed learned, said my work was worthless, full of obscenities, and unfit to be read by decent people. The physician asked for an example. The Dominican said that in my treatise on marriage I had accused the bishops of unnatural crimes, and had charged them besides with keeping four or five concubines. The book was produced, and he pointed out a passage where I say that as the rule now stands a priest cannot be a married man, but may keep mistresses and yet be *putus* or τέλειος and hold four or five *episcopas*. *Putus*, which means *pure*, he had taken to be the masculine of *puta* (a whore), and to mean a *cinædus*. *Episcopas*, St. Paul's word for bishops' sees, he had construed into bishops' wives.

Exposed to the attacks of such enemies as these, and threatened by the Spanish Inquisition, Erasmus had a bad time of it — cursed on one side by the Lutherans, who charged him with sinning against light; cursed by the theologians of the old school as the cause of all the disturbance; and both sides, and especially the Catholics, clamouring to him to speak a decisive word. His books were selling faster than ever, and the injury to the Church, if injury they were doing, was continually growing. An orthodox champion urged him to clear himself from the suspicion of favouring a falling cause. He answers:[2] —

The confusion spreads, and may grow to worse than you think. Luther's first protest was hardly

[1] *Ep.* dcccclxxix.

[2] *Ep.* cccxlv., second series.

more than a jest. The monks shrieked. Bulls and edicts followed. What have they effected? It may be that parts of my writings need correction; but there is a time for everything. You think Luther prostrate. Would that he was! He has been pierced often enough, but he lives yet — lives in the minds of men to whom he is commended by the wickedness of the monks. You and your friends think that when you have finished Luther you will settle accounts with Erasmus. You have not finished Luther, and while Luther lives you will hide like nails in your shells. I encountered him at the request of the Pope and the Emperor in his strongest position. I was victorious; but I was wounded in the fight, and you took the opportunity to fall on me from behind.

All this was hard to bear; Erasmus was growing old (past sixty), suffering besides from gout and stone, and heavy laden with his editions of the fathers, which, in spite of his troubles, he still steadily laboured at. He was thin-skinned as ever, and writhed under the darts which were flung at him. The Emperor remained personally kind, and the threatened inquiry into his works in Spain was silenced. But the public attitude of Charles was ambiguous and menacing. The edicts were being enforced in the Low Countries against Anabaptists. Peasant wars had broken out. Anabaptism meant anarchy and social ruin, and must be suppressed at all hazards. Both the Pope and Charles, however, seemed to have determined on a general policy of repression, and the victory of the Church party would mean the victory of darkness and superstition, against which he had been fighting all his life. His energy never slackened, his letters to contemporary scholars on learned subjects through this anxious time were as elaborate as if he thought of nothing save the rendering of Greek texts. But the aspect of things grew blacker and blacker, and he sickened at the thought of what was coming.

TO LEWIS BER.[1]

April 1, 1529.

God knows what the end will be. Like enough He is punishing us for our sins. Sad indeed has been the fall, specially among those who were pillars of the Church. Read the Gospels, read the constitutions of the early popes. Read what Gerson says of the priests and monks in one of his works, and see how we have degenerated. But never will I be tempted or exasperated into deserting the true communion. I have at times been provoked into a desire of revenge. But the prick goes no deeper than the skin. The ill-will of some wretched fellow-creature shall not tempt me to lay hands on the mother who washed me at the font, fed me with the word of God, and quickened me with the sacraments. I will not lose my immortal soul to avenge a worldly wrong. I resist the weakness, though I cannot choose but feel my injuries. I understand now how Arius and Tertullian and Wickliff were driven into schism by malicious clergy and wicked monks. I will not forsake the Church myself, I would forfeit life and reputation sooner; but how unprovoked was the conspiracy to ruin me! My crime was my effort to promote learning. That was the whole of it. For the rest I have been rather their friend than their enemy. I advised divines to leave scholastic subtleties and study Scripture and the fathers. I bade monks remember their profession, forsake the world, and live for God. Was this to hate the divines and the monks? Doubtless I have wished that popes and cardinals and bishops were more like the Apostles, but never in thought have I desired those offices abolished. There may be arguments about the Real Presence, but I will never believe that Christ would have allowed His Church to remain so long in such an error (if error it be) as to worship a wafer

[1] *Ep.* mxxxv., abridged.

for God. The Lutheran notion that any Christian may consecrate or absolve or ordain I think pure insanity. But if monks fancy that by screaming and shrieking they can recover their old tyranny, or that popes and prelates can put the fire out with a high hand, they are greatly mistaken. It may be smothered for a moment, but surely it will break out again. A disease can only be cured by removing the causes of it. We need not give up our belief in the Church because men are wicked. But if fresh shoots are not to sprout, the evil must be torn out by the roots.

And again, to the same correspondent: —

See what the world is coming to — rapine, murder, plague, famine, rebellion; no one trying to mend his own life; God scourging us, and we taking no heed, and hardening our hearts against Him. What can be before us but the deluge?

Anabaptism was a new and ugly phenomenon. Like the modern Socialists, the Anabaptists threatened to destroy society and remake it on a new pattern, and Luther and even Erasmus excluded these poor wretches from toleration. Yet Erasmus would have had a pitying word for the devil himself.

This sect (he says) is peculiarly obnoxious because they teach community of goods, and will not obey magistrates. They have no churches. They do not aim at power, and do not resist when arrested. They are said to be moral in their conduct, if anything can be moral with so corrupt a faith.

Erasmus was against burning even Anabaptists, and each poor victim that he heard of gave him a pang. The Sorbonne was just then active in Paris; Francis wanting to establish a reputation for orthodoxy. They had found an unhappy wretch of this persuasion preaching repentance. Erasmus observes that it was no such terrible crime, mankind being supposed to require repentance; but they seized and roasted him for all that.

The accident of date introduces another letter, written simultaneously with those which I have just quoted. It has no reference to his alarms at the state of Europe, but it relates to a subject which may have an interest for you in itself, and I may close this lecture with it.

You will all have heard of Henry VIII.'s book against Luther; a question rose at the time, and has continued ever since, whether Henry wrote it himself. Here is what Erasmus says on the subject.[1] Cochlæus, who was going fiercely into the divorce question, was among the doubters. Erasmus writes to him: —

April 1, 1539.

The German Catholics refuse to believe that a king can write a book. I will not say the King of England had no help. The most learned men now and then are helped by friends. But I am quite sure the work is essentially his own. His father was a man of strong sense. His mother was brilliant, witty, and pious. The King himself studied hard in his youth. He was quick, prompt, skilful in all that he undertook, and never took up anything which he did not go through with. He made himself a fine shot, a good rider, a fair musician besides, and was well grounded in mathematics. His intellectual pursuits he has always kept up. He spends his leisure in reading and conversation. He argues so pleasantly that you forget you are speaking with a Prince. He has studied the schoolmen, Aquinas, Scotus, and the rest. Mountjoy, who saw that I was suspicious about the book, showed me one day a number of the King's letters to himself and to others. They were obviously his own, corrected and altered in his own hand. I had no answer to make.

[1] *Ep.* mxxxviii., abridged.

LECTURE XVIII.

AGE and ill-health had tamed Erasmus's wandering propensities. He had now for several years been stationary at Bâle, by the side of his friend Froben's printing establishment, where his work was carried on. Bâle was a self-governed city with popular institutions, and had so far remained Catholic. The reformers, however, had been annually increasing. They found themselves at length with a clear majority, and he was to witness an ecclesiastical revolution immediately under his own eyes. The scene as Erasmus described it to Pirkheimer is curious in itself, and was a specimen of what had been going on in most of the free cities of Germany. He expected disorder; there was none. The Catholic members of the Senate were expelled to prevent opposition, and the people went to work methodically to abolish the mass and establish Lutheranism.

TO PIRKHEIMER.[1]

Smiths and carpenters were sent to remove the images from the churches. The roods and the unfortunate saints were cruelly handled. Strange that none of them worked a miracle to avenge their dignity, when before they had worked so many at the slightest invitation. Not a statue was left in church, niche, or monastery. The paintings on the walls were whitewashed. Everything combustible was burnt. What would not burn was broken to pieces. Nothing was spared, however precious or beautiful; and mass was prohibited even in private houses.

[1] *Ep.* mxlviii.

And in another letter:[1] —

The affair was less violent than we feared it might be. No houses were broken into, and no one was hurt. They would have hanged my neighbour, the Consul, if they had caught him, but he slipped off in the night; not like St. Paul in a basket, but down the river in a boat. His crime had been that he had so long obstructed the Gospel. As it was, no blood was shed; but there was a cruel assault on altars, images, and pictures. We are told that St. Francis used to resent light remarks about his five wounds, and several other saints are said to have shown displeasure on similar occasions. It was strange that at Bâle not a saint stirred a finger. I am not so much surprised at the patience of Christ and the Virgin Mary.

Erasmus had seen the storm coming and had prepared for it. He had perceived that a reformed Bâle could no longer be a home for him — go he must, if the Catholic world was not to reproach him with being an accomplice. He had feared that if he tried to escape, the revolutionary party might keep him by force. He procured a safe-conduct, and an invitation from the Archduke Ferdinand. His books, plate, and property he despatched privately to Freyburg, within the Austrian frontier. The magistrates, he thought, would hesitate to interfere with him when protected with a pass in the Archduke's hand.

Money (he tells Pirkheimer), with plate, jewels, and anything which would tempt robbers, had been sent on first, and afterward two waggon loads of books and furniture. I called on Œcolampadius; we had some talk, and did not quarrel. He wanted me to remain at Bâle. I said I was sorry to leave it, but if I stayed I should seem to approve of what had been done; and my baggage, besides, had been all despatched to Freyburg. He said he hoped I should

[1] *Ep.* mlxix.

return; we shook hands and parted. In fact, I had no choice. I could not stay in a place where I should be at the mercy of the rabble, and where I could not expect the protection of the magistrates. I had some difficulty in getting on board my boat. I wanted to start from a private landing-place. The Senate said that Bâle was free for everyone to come and go. There was no need of secrecy, and it could not be allowed. I submitted, and embarked with a few friends at the bridge. At Freyburg I found the officials most hospitable, even before they had received the Archduke's letter. They have allotted me as a residence the unfinished palace which was begun by Maximilian.

At Freyburg Erasmus was personally safe, but the ill-look of public affairs more and more disturbed him. "War is coming," he wrote. "The Emperor thunders from Italy, and revolution rushes forward among the Germans. I have wished myself at Cracow." He had a personal sorrow, too, in the loss of a distinguished young French friend, Louis Berquin, who was seized and burnt by the Church authorities at Paris for speaking his mind too freely.

All error is not heresy (he says, writing about it to Utenhovius [1]), and a man who is honestly mistaken, and has merely adopted a wrong opinion, is not to be confounded with ill-dispositioned rebels and disturbers of public peace. It is a new thing to burn a man for a mistake, and I wonder how the practice began. If the piety of the French kept pace with their superstition, one might approve of this new-born zeal of theirs. It is matched on the other side: in some German States the Pope is Antichrist, the bishops are hobgoblins, the priests swine, the princes tyrants, the monasteries Satan's conventicles; and the power is in the hands of Gospel mobs, who are readier to fight than reason. Happy Berquin if he has died with a

[1] *Ep.* mlx., abridged.

good conscience, for good and bad are now sent the same road — hanged, burnt, or dismembered. Decent magistrates will crucify you as readily as the savagest despot. Human courts of justice are not worth much nowadays, and those are fortunate who stand acquitted at the great tribunal.

Another letter: —

TO ÆMILIUS AB ÆMILIO.[1]

May 29, 1529.

All grows wilder and wilder. Men talk of heresy and orthdoxy, of Antichrists and Catholics, but none speak of Christ. The world is in labour. Good may come if Christ directs the birth. There is no help else. Paganism comes to life again; Pharisees fight against the Gospel; in such a monstrous tempest we need skilful pilots. Christ has been sleeping so far. I trust the prayers of the faithful will wake Him. He may then command sea and waves, and they will obey Him. The monks have howled. The theologians have made articles of belief. We have had prisons, informations, bulls, and burnings; and what has come of them? Outcries enough; but no crying to Christ. Christ will not wake till we call to Him in sincerity of heart. Then He will arise and bid the sea be still, and there will be a great calm.

The confusion in Germany and the straitened state of Charles's finances had made the payment of Erasmus's Imperial pension somewhat irregular; and beyond this he had still no settled income save what he received from Warham and Mountjoy. He had been always careless in his expenses, and failing health had not promoted economy. Lavish presents from great people, lay and ecclesiastic, plate, jewels, and money, had spared him so far from anxiety, even when Charles's treasurer forgot him. But the move from

[1] *Ep.* ml., abridged.

Bâle to Freyburg and the starting a new establishment had proved a costly business, and he might have been in difficulties again but for the generosity of the Fuggers, the great banking firm at Augsburg. The head of the house, however, came to his assistance with unbounded liberality; and Freyburg otherwise suited him well. It was within the Austrian boundary, and under Ferdinand's immediate authority. The only danger would be if the European war rolled that way, or the Turks took Vienna, either of which was possible. The country might then be overrun with vagabond soldiers, who were Erasmus's special horror and the curse of the age. He could not execrate too loudly the madness of the two monarchs for whose rivalry the world was too narrow. Francis had accepted a dispensation from the Pope from the oath which he had sworn at the Treaty of Madrid. Charles insisted on his bond; and at a time when Europe most needed the ruling hand of secular authority the Turks were left to fasten themselves on Hungary, the free cities of Germany to revolt from the Church, and frantic theologians, Catholic, Lutheran, Zwinglian, and Calvinist, to tear and rend each other.

It was a mad world.

TO BOTZEMUS.[1]

FREYBURG, *August* 13, 1529.

In such times as ours it is better to call on the Lord than to trust in princes and armies. We must pray to Him to shorten these days. Alas! Christianity has sunk so low that scarce a man knows now what calling on the Lord means. One looks to cardinals and bishops, another to kings, another to the black battalions of monks and divines. What do they want? What do they expect from protectors, who care

[1] *Ep.* mlxxii., abridged.

nothing for Catholic piety, and care only to recover their old power and enjoyments? We were drunk or asleep, and God has sent these stern schoolmasters to wake us up. The rope has been overstrained. It might have stood if they had slackened it a little, but they would rather have it break than save it by concession. The Pope is head of the Church, and as such deserves to be honoured. He stretched his authority too far, and so the first strand of the rope parted. Pardons and indulgences were tolerable within limits. Monks and commissaries filled the world with them to line their own pockets. In every Church were the red boxes and the crosses and the papal arms, and the people were forced to buy. So the second strand went. Then there was the invocation of saints. The images in churches at first served for ornaments and examples. By-and-by the walls were covered with scandalous pictures. The cult ran to idolatry; so parted a third. The singing of hymns was an ancient and pious custom, but when music was introduced fitter for weddings and banquets than for God's service, and the sacred words were lost in affected intonations, so that no word in the Liturgy was spoken plainly, away went another. What is more solemn than the mass? But when stupid vagabond priests learn up two or three masses and repeat them over and over as a cobbler makes shoes; when notorious profligates officiate at the Lord's table, and the sacredest of mysteries is sold for money — well, this strand is almost gone too. Secret confession may be useful; but when it is employed to extort money out of the terrors of fools, when an institution designed as medicine for the soul is made an instrument of priestly villany, this part of the cord will not last much longer either.

Priests who are loose in their lives and yet demand to be honoured as superior beings have brought their order into contempt. Careless of purity, careless what they do or how they live, the monks have trusted to their wealth and numbers to crush those whom they can no longer deceive. They pretended that their clothes would work miracles, that they could bring good luck into houses and keep the devil out. How is it at present? They used to be thought gods. They are now scarcely thought honest men.

I do not say that practices good in themselves should be condemned because they are abused. But I do say that we have ourselves given the occasion. We have no right to be surprised or angry, and we ought to consider quietly how best to meet the storm. As things go now there will be no improvement, let the dice fall which way they will. The Gospellers go for anarchy; the Catholics, instead of repenting of their sins, pile superstition on superstition; while Luther's disciples, if such they be, neglect prayers, neglect the fasts of the Church, and eat more on fast days than on common days. Papal constitutions, clerical privileges, are scorned and trampled on; and our wonderful champions of the Church do more than anyone to bring the Holy See into contempt. There are rumours of peace. God grant they prove true. If the Emperor, the Pope, and the Kings of France and England can compose their differences and agree on some common course of action, evangelical religion may be restored. But we must deserve our blessings if we are to enjoy them. When princes go mad, the fault is often in ourselves.

As to me, my worst enemies used to be the Dominicans and Carmelites. Now I am best hated by the Franciscans, and especially by the observant branch of them. They have long railed at me inside their walls. Lately one of them stormed at me for an hour in St Peter's Church, and in such terms that many of the people went out before the sermon was finished. Cavajal Salamanca has brought out a book worthy of a child of St. Francis; when it appeared it was nailed to a gibbet.

Cardinal Newman said that Protestant tradition on the state of the Church before the Reformation is built on wholesale, unscrupulous lying. Erasmus was as true to the Holy See as Cardinal Newman himself. I do not know whether he is included among these unscrupulous liars. It is an easy way to get rid of an unpleasant witness.

The rumours of peace proved true. Where statesmen had failed, the ladies were successful. The Queen Regent of the Netherlands and the Queen of France met at Cambray and arranged preliminaries. A conference followed, where England was again represented by Sir T. More ; and the war which had so horrified Erasmus came for a time to an end. It had begun in defence of the Pope against the Emperor. Partners had changed in the course of it, and before it was over the Emperor and the Pope had become close allies, and the future position of England towards both of them was depending on the decision which was to be given on the divorce of Catherine of Aragon. " The peace is made, " Henry said to her when the business at Cambray was concluded. " It depends on you whether it is to last. "

A few words to explain Henry's meaning.

Germany being divided and distracted, the military power in Europe was partitioned between the Emperor and the Kings of France and England. The resources of Charles and Francis I. were so nearly balanced that the accession of England to either party turned the scale. France was the hereditary enemy of England; Spain and Burgundy England's hereditary ally; and, if the old alliance could be re-established, France was unlikely to break the peace again. The only obstacle was the proposed divorce of Queen Catherine. I need not enter here into the rights and wrongs of that much-agitated question; but it is quite certain that the Emperor, the Pope, every responsible statesman in Europe, except perhaps the King of France, desired to see it honourably and amicably arranged. Marriages contracted by princes for political purposes are under other conditions than voluntary contracts between private persons. The marriage of Henry and Catherine had been arranged for a political purpose; it had failed in the primary object of providing a male heir to the crown, and in the absence of a male heir it was notorious that a fresh war of succession would follow on the King's death. Catherine was past the age when she could hope for another child. As she was Prince Arthur's widow, her marriage with Henry had been made possible only by a papal dispensation, and it was uncertain whether the dispensation itself had been lawfully granted. The dissolution of such a marriage when the interest of a great nation was at stake would have been simple and unobjectionable. No decision needed to be made on the validity of the marriage, and Catherine could retain her title and establishment, and thus would lose nothing. She had but to retire into what was called lax religion and to take a formal vow of celibacy. The King could then be easily enabled to marry again. This was the solution of the difficulty which the Pope himself desired and urged, having admitted that Henry's demand was a just one. Charles, though not pleased with the slight upon his family, would have sacrificed his pride to preserve the English alliance and the peace of Europe. The only difficulty lay with Catherine. Consent she would not, and the Emperor, as her natural protector, insisted that her marriage should not be judicially declared null against her will. The question was hanging in abeyance at the time of the Peace of Cambray, and no mention was made of it among the articles considered. Cardinal Campegio, Erasmus's friend, was on his way to England as legate with a commission to settle the dispute, and Clement had secretly promised Henry that Campegio should give judgment in his favour. But promises went for little with a Pope who had powers to bind and to loose; and Charles, on the other hand, had extorted another secret promise from him that till Catherine agreed no judgment should be given at all. Henry was a dangerous person to trifle with. Another question now naturally rose — whether a Pope who refused deliberately to do what he acknowledged to be right, who was sacrificing the interests of England at the bidding of another sovereign, could be allowed to retain any authority at all in England; whether England was not competent to settle her own problems in her own way. All turned on Catherine, and that was the meaning of Henry's words to her. If she would consent, Charles and Henry would remain friends, and they two with the Pope could restore order to Europe. Singular that so much should have hung on the will of a single woman! Erasmus was unable to believe that interests so enormous could be interfered with by so slight an obstacle. When he heard that the business was trusted to Campegio he ceased to feel even uneasiness, so confident was he of a satisfactory result. Little did he foresee, sharp-sighted though he was, that out of this small cloud would grow a storm which would cost the lives of the dearest friends that he had.

On the conclusion of the peace Charles went to Italy to be crowned by the Pope. Sir T. More, as I said, had represented England at Cambray. Erasmus wrote him a letter full of congratulations, full of admiration of Henry and the services which the King of

England has rendered and would again render to Christendom. Erasmus's chief anxiety was for Ferdinand, who was being ground between the Turks and the German Protestants.

TO SIR T. MORE.[1]

FREYBURG, *September* 5, 1529.

Would that Ferdinand's affairs were in as good condition as his kindness deserves. He had been my best friend. Two years back he wanted me to go and live with him at Vienna. Fortune deals cruelly with him now. He applied for help to the Diet of Speyer, and they offered him so little that he would not take it. The Emperor is in Italy, staying longer than I like with the Pope. This colloguing between popes and princes bodes no good to Christianity. . . . The theologians say I ran away from Bâle because I was afraid. If I went back they would say I was joining the rebels. Everyone, even my opponents, wanted me to stay, and my going was entirely against my will. Bâle had been a nest for me so many years, and there was a risk in moving with such health as I now suffer from. But I preferred to venture my life rather than appear by remaining to approve of what had been done. With common prudence the revolution might have been prevented. But a couple of monks set the fire blazing — one by a sermon in the cathedral, and the other by a similar performance in his convent.

George of Saxony talks of encountering Luther. I might as well encounter Thraso. I advised him to let Luther alone. My health is good, and the summer has been charming, but I fear for the autumn. This place is half surrounded by mountains, and scarce a day passes without rain.

Erasmus's expectations from the peace were disappointed. The Emperor's hands were now free. The Church party were clamouring to him to lose no more

[1] *Ep.* mlxxiv., abridged.

time and to interfere with a high hand in Germany, and the Emperor seemed inclined to gratify them. The Lutheran States were arming for defence, and war seemed only to have ceased with France to be followed by a furious conflict in Germany.

September 8, 1529.

I fear (Erasmus writes to Mountjoy [1]) that the Gospel will lead to a desperate struggle. Germany is preparing for it, and the theologians are inflaming the wound. I could wish them a better mind. I myself seem doomed like Hercules to be fighting monsters all my life, and weary I am of it. Never since the world began was such an age; everywhere smoke and steam. I trust Cardinal Campegio has dispersed that small cloud you wot of.[2]

Campegio, as you know, did not disperse that small cloud, and the news from England became so interesting as to make Erasmus forget for a moment the sins of the theologians. Wolsey was dismissed from the chancellorship. The seals were given to Sir Thomas More, and Parliament was summoned to begin the movement which was to sever England from the Roman communion. Campegio had argued, implored, entreated; Catherine had remained inexorable. The Emperor, relying, perhaps, on the assurances of the ambassador that the English nation would stand by the Queen, forbade the Pope to keep his promise to Henry; and the question rose whether a supreme judge of Christendom, who was allowing himself to be controlled by an earthly monarch in a cause of political importance, could be permitted to retain a power which he could no longer use impartially. At all events, respect for such a pope was no longer to delay the reform in England of the abuses which had thrown

[1] *Ep.* mlxxvii. [2] The divorce.

Germany into revolution. In England there was the same simony, the same papal exactions, the same pluralism, fortified by purchased dispensations from Rome. Wolsey held three bishoprics and the wealthiest of the English abbeys. In England there were the same convocations, passing laws, without consent of Parliament, to bind the laity; the same Church courts to enforce such laws, the same arbitrary imprisonments, the same complicated plunder in the name of religion, the same sales of pardons and indulgences, the same ruinous appeals to Rome in every cause which could be construed as spiritual, the same extortions supported by excommunication, which, if disobeyed, passed into a charge of heresy; the same exemption from the control of the common law, which the clergy claimed in virtue of their order; the same unblushing disregard of the common duties of morality, encouraged by impunity for vice.

The endurance of the laity had been long exhausted, and the quarrel with the Pope gave an opportunity for Parliament to take in hand a reform for which the whole nation clamoured. The German Diet had drawn up a list of wrongs, their *Centum Gravamina* against the clergy, and had demanded redress. Erasmus, Sir T. More, Charles V. himself, every open-minded layman in Europe, knew reform to be necessary. The fall of Wolsey, who had been the embodiment of the detested system, was a signal for the fall also of the temporal power of the clergy. Lord Darcy, the most Catholic noble in England, the special friend of Charles V., the future leader of the Pilgrimage of Grace, took the lead in drawing up Wolsey's attainder, and the famous Parliament of 1529 began its work of legal revolution amidst the shrieks of the hierarchy.

Henry VIII., with the help of his people, was doing precisely what Erasmus had himself urged on Adrian and Clement as necessary and inevitable; and it was no little joy to Erasmus to see his friend More elected to preside over such a work in the House of Lords. Unfortunately, his own best friends in England were divided. The Duke of Norfolk succeeded Wolsey as Prime Minister, Sir Thomas More was Chancellor, and both were strong for moderate reform. Fisher, Warham, Tunstall, the bishops generally, felt instinctively that far-reaching changes lay behind these beginnings, and resisted to the utmost of their power. The opposition to Church reform combined by degrees with the opposition to the divorce. Catherine's cause became identified with the Church. Other elements of discontent soon swelled her party, and Catherine herself became a secret centre of political disaffection. A vast conspiracy sprung up, organised by Erasmus's old antagonists the monks and theologians, and, as the quarrel with the Church developed into a quarrel with the Pope, it took definite and dangerous shape. Henry was to be excommunicated and deposed; the peers of the old faction of the White Rose were to take the field again. Every monastery in England became a nest of mutiny, and every friar a preacher of sedition.

The King knew what was going on, but did not choose to be frightened by it. Parliament proceeded with its work session after session. Conspiracy went on simultaneously — Catherine acquiescent and at last encouraging. A Spanish army was to be landed with the Pope's blessing in the eastern counties. The peers and gentry were to take arms. The monasteries were to find the money. Sir T. More fell back to the Catholic side in his hatred of Lutheranism, and the danger grew like the prophet's gourd. Henry armed the English Commons, built a fleet, and passed the statutes which still remain as the charter of the spiritual liberties of the English laity.

Events moved fast. In six years the authority of Rome was abolished. The Crown of England was declared independent of all foreign power, supreme in all causes, ecclesiastical and civil, within its own dominions. Warham died of grief; More and Fisher fell on the scaffold; the monasteries were peremptorily abolished and the rebellion crushed.

Erasmus lived to see all this beginning. He hoped as it proceeded that each step would be the last; that the Pope would be wise in time; that England, which he had loved so well, might be spared the convulsions which he saw hanging over Germany. On the divorce case itself he thought that Henry was justified in demanding a separation; or at any rate that the will of a single woman ought not to stand in the way of the interests of Europe. England, however, was far away. In England he could neither act nor advise. His own immediate concern was with the coming crisis in Germany.

Charles, having consulted with the Pope, seemed to have resolved on decisive action. He summoned the Diet to meet at Augsburg to take into consideration the condition of the country. Both sides had armed, and were prepared to fight if the Diet failed. Among the Germans the Lutheran party were the strongest; but behind the Catholics was the Spanish army, if Charles pleased to use it. Erasmus regretted that he had been unable to be present at Worms. He perhaps felt that he ought to make a stronger effort to attend at Augsburg, but he found an excuse in failing health.

TO CUTHBERT TUNSTALL.[1]

January 31, 1530.

So far the battle has been fought with books and pamphlets. We are coming now to guns and halberts. If I cared less for my soul than my body I would rather be with the Lutherans; but I will not forsake the one Church with death now close on me in the shape of a stone in my bladder. Were Augustine to preach here now as he preached in Africa, he would be as ill-spoken of as Erasmus. I could find 600 passages in Augustine, and quite as many in St. Paul, which would now be called heretical. I am but a sheep; but a sheep may bleat when the Gospel is being destroyed. Theologians, schoolmen, and monks fancy that in what they are doing they strengthen the Church. They are mistaken. Fire is not quenched by fire. The tyranny of the Court of Rome and a set of scandalous friars set the pile alight, and they are pouring on oil to put it out. As to More, I am pleased to hear of his promotion. I do not congratulate him personally, but I congratulate Britain and, indirectly, myself. It is hoped that the Emperor's authority will end the German schism. I trust, at any rate, that there will be no bloodshed, that the victory will be to Christ's honour, and that we shall not have papal officials and monks in power again. The clergy are thinking only of revenge, and not the least of amending their lives.

The excitement grew as the Augsburg Diet drew near. The extreme faction was in power at Rome; Erasmus's friends there were in the shade; and he himself, as he heard to his alarm and sorrow, was out of favour in the highest quarter. He could not understand why. He thought himself peculiarly meritorious in having held aloof from Luther, and now the Pope was listening to people who told him that Erasmus

[1] *Ep.* mxcii., abridged.

was at the bottom of all that had gone wrong. He wrote at great length to the Papal Secretary to complain.

TO SADOLET.[1]

March 7, 1530.

Do you think (he said) that I could ever have connected myself with a miserable mob? I have been a better friend to the Church than those who are for stamping the fire out by force. I name no one. Some of them are friends of my own, but they have done no good that I can see. The result so far is to add to the number of their enemies and to drive the Germans into a league. God grant I prove a false prophet; but if you see the Catholic Church brought to wreck in Germany, remember that Erasmus foretold it. The first mistake was to neglect Luther's protest against indulgences; the next, when things grew serious, to appeal to popular clamour and leave the defence to monks — men *orbi fere invisos*, hated of all the world. Luther's books were burnt when they ought to have been read and studied by earnest and serious persons. There was too much haste to persecute; we tolerate Jews and Bohemians, we might have borne with Luther. Time cures disorders which nothing else will cure. I said all this, but no one attended to me. I was called the friend of schismatics. Then came Aleander with the Pope's bull. He thought wonders of himself — burnt more books, filled the air with smoke, and went about with the Emperor threatening right and left. He would have laid hold on *me* if the Emperor had not protected me. Another eminent person declared war on me at Rome — said I had no learning and no judgment. When I complained, it appeared he had read nothing that I had written. I have still hopes. These trials may be for our good in the end and turn to the glory of the Church. Other countries are in the same condition as Germany, only the disorder has not yet broken

[1] *Ep.* mxciv., abridged.

out. The fever is fed by the ferocity of an interested faction.

The battle was now raging round the Real Presence. Luther on this point had remained orthodox, but it was challenged by the Swiss reformers, and every tongue was busy with it. Again we listen to Erasmus: —

TO THE BISHOP OF HILDESHEIM.[1]

FREYBURG, *March* 15, 1530.

Innumerable questions are asked — how the elements are transubstantiated; how accidents can subsist without a subject; how the colour, smell, taste, quality, which are in the bread and wine before it is consecrated can remain when the substance is changed; at what moment the miracle takes place, and what has happened when the bread and wine corrupts; how the same body can be in many places at once, &c. Such problems may be discussed among the learned. For the vulgar it is enough to believe that the real body and blood of our Lord are actually present. It is a mystery to be approached reverentially. Men should not be allowed to march up and down the aisles or chatter at the doors during the ceremony. You stay out a play till the *Valete et plaudite;* can you not wait for the completion of a miracle. In earlier times there was but one celebration in a day. Now, partly from superstition, partly from avarice, the saying of masses has become a trade, like shoemaking or bricklaying — a mere means of making a livelihood. And again, some attention should be paid to the priest's character; dress and office are not enough, the life must answer to the function. Nowadays, when the celebration is over, the man who has offered the sacrifice adjourns to drinking parties and loose talk, or to cards or dice, or goes hunting, or lounges in idleness. While he is at the altar angels wait upon him; when he leaves it he seeks the refuse of mankind. It is not

[1] *Ep.* mxcv.

decent. Priests should not by their loose living teach heretics to despise the ineffable mystery.

Two young Franciscans in Spain had been denouncing Erasmus again. An enthusiastic friend named Mexia had been fighting his battles for him. Erasmus often complained of his loneliness, of his unhappy condition between the points of the two angry factions, of the inattention which was paid by both to his advice and warnings. If the letter which he wrote to Mexia to thank him for his exertions is a faithful picture of his actual position, he ought to have been better satisfied; for whether they took his advice or not, the great people of the world seem to have been particularly anxious to hear his opinions.

TO MEXIA.[1]

FREYBURG, *March* 30, 1530.

Great lords, bishops, abbots, learned men of whom I have never heard, write daily to me, to say nothing of kings and princes and high prelates who are known to all mankind. With their communications come magnificent presents. To the Emperor Charles I owe the best part of my fortune, and his loving letters are more precious than his gifts. His brother Ferdinand writes equally often to me and with equal warmth. The French king invites me to Paris. The King of England writes to me often also. The Bishops of Durham and Lincoln send me gems of epistles, so do other bishops and archbishops and princes and dukes. Antony Fugger sent me a hundred gold florins when he heard that I was leaving Bâle, and promised me as much more annually if I would settle at Augsburg. Only a few days since the Bishop of Augsburg brought me two hundred florins and two princely drinking cups.

I have a room full of letters from men of learning,

[1] *Ep.* mciii., abridged.

nobles, princes, and cardinals. I have a chest full of gold and silver plate, cups, clocks, and rings which have been presented to me, and I had many more which I have given away to other students. Of the givers, some are sages; some are saints, like the Archbishop of Canterbury and the Bishops of London and Rochester. I have not sought their liberality; I have always said that I had enough; yet if I had no pension from the Emperor these alone would suffice for my support. Some call me, as you say, a sower of heresies, and deny that I have been of service to literature. If this be so, how came I by the favours of so many distinguished men? Compare the world as it was thirty years ago with the world as it is now, and then ask what it owes to Erasmus. Then, not a prince would spend a farthing on his son's education; now every one of them has a paid tutor in his family. The elder theologians were against me always, but the younger are on my side. Even among the monks, some who began with cursing are now taking my part; and finally here is yourself championing me against those impertinent Franciscans. But, my dear friend, do not make the monks your enemies. They are Dodona's cauldrons; if you stir one you stir all. I am sorry the Observants have so degenerated. Those two loquacious lads would not have ventured so far without encouragement from their elders. The problem before us is how to heal this fatal schism without rivers of blood; and these youths are spreading the fire. Such as they are past mending. Let them alone. I have still confidence in the Emperor; he has authority; he is pious and wise; he has even genius of a certain kind, and an Imperial objection to cruelty.

LECTURE XIX.

We have arrived at the famous Diet which met at Augsburg in the summer of 1530. The Emperor was present in person, with his brother Ferdinand, the German princes, the deputies from the free cities, the legate Campegio fresh from failure in England, with his train of ecclesiastical warriors to defend the cause of Holy Church. Luther being under the ban of the empire could not be received. The confession of the reformed faith was drawn and presented by Philip Melanchthon, and was accepted by more than half the Diet as representing their belief. What would the Emperor do? Had there been no English problem, no Catherine to perplex his action, it is likely that he would have insisted, as he afterwards did at Trent, on a practical reform of the Court of Rome and the ecclesiastical system, and have allowed the Confession of Augsburg to stand as an interim till the dirty sewers had been cleared out. But his hands were tied. The Church party required him to put the Lutherans down with fire and sword. The Pope had not forgiven the storm of Rome and his own imprisonment. If Charles refused, the Pope it was too probable would declare for the divorce and so try to recover the allegiance of England. Even had there been no Catherine, however, his situation was infinitely difficult. As emperor he was head of Germany, but he had neither revenue nor army save what he could raise in his own hereditary dominions; and these by his coronation oath he was bound not to employ without the Diet's consent inside the limits of the empire. He hated the very thought of a religious civil war, yet he was responsible for order. The reforming States had set aside the old laws, altered the religious services, abolished bishops and bishops' courts, suppressed the monasteries, seized and confiscated the inviolable property of the Church. When the Church appealed to him for protection, how was he to refuse?

He was received immediately on his arrival at Augsburg with a silent intimation of what lay before him. He was sitting at dinner with his brother Ferdinand when he was informed that a company of players wished to perform before him. They were admitted. The action was in dumb show. A man in a doctor's dress brought in a bundle of sticks, some straight, some crooked, laid them on the hearth, and retired. On his back was written "Reuchlin." Another followed who tried to arrange the sticks side by side, could not do it, grew impatient, and retired also. He was called Erasmus. An Augustinian monk came next with a burning chafing-dish, flung the crooked sticks into the fire, and blew into it to make it blaze. This was Luther. A fourth came robed as an emperor; he, seeing the fire spreading, tried to put it out with his sword, and made it flame the faster. He, too, went off, and then appeared a figure in pontifical robe and with triple crown, who started at the sight of the fire, looked about, saw two cans in the room, one full of water the other of oil, snatched the oil by mistake, poured it on, and raised such a blaze that he fled in terror. This was Leo X.

Erasmus was not present at the Diet; perhaps he could not be; but the Emperor knew what he thought; and the mummers had given a sufficiently just representation of his attitude. Erasmus wished the sticks to lie side by side. He was for toleration and concession, the Church rules for uniformity to be relaxed, the demands of the laity to be satisfied as far as might be without a schism, the clergy to be allowed to marry, the Church land question to be settled by a compromise; while, as to doctrine, the ancient Articles of Faith, on which all parties were agreed, were a sufficient basis for communion. On the new questions over which the world was quarrelling — the Real Presence, the priesthood, justification, predestination, free will, grace, merits, and the rest of it, men might be allowed to think as they pleased without ceasing to be Christians or splitting into separate communities. Time and moderation would settle these problems, as they settled all others; the worst possible course would be for one party to thrust its own opinions by force down the throat of the other.

A few wise men, the Emperor among them, thought as Erasmus did. Alas, it required two centuries of fighting, and another century of jealousy and suspicion, before mankind generally could be brought to accept what seems now so obvious a truth. Erasmus watched the Diet from his sick bed, and wrote his thoughts about it to his friends.

TO PHILIP MELANCHTHON.[1]

FREYBURG, *July* 7, 1530.

You may hold ten Diets, but only God can ravel out these complications. I can do nothing. Anyone who proposes a reasonable composition is called a Lutheran, and that is all which he gains. I have been ill these three months — suffering, sick, and miserable. Medicine made me worse. First I had a violent pain; then came a hard swelling down my right side

[1] *Ep.* mcxvii.

to the groin, gathering at last at the pit of my stomach, as if a snake had my navel in his teeth and was coiled round the umbilicus. Shooting pangs continued so that I could neither eat nor sleep, nor write nor dictate. The surgeon nearly blistered me to death; at length the tumour was cut open, sleep returned, and I was relieved. Now I crawl about feebly, but am not out of the doctor's hands.

TO RINCKIUS.[1]

I hear that three points have been proposed at the Diet: the Germans to help in driving back the Turks; the religious quarrel to be made up peaceably; and the injuries to the Catholics to be examined into and redressed. I cannot guess what will come of it, and unless the reformed States hold together there will be fighting yet. Some think terms will be made. The Lutheran demands are moderate, and the Pope is ready to make concessions. Campegio is for mild measures, and has thrice written to me from Augsburg. The Bishop of Augsburg is also for yielding something, and is of course reviled as a heretic, though one of the best of men. Melanchthon writes that he does not despair. Many think I ought to be there; but the Emperor has not sent for me, and if he does I am too ill to go. Some say the Emperor will merely ask for money, refer the doctrines to the next general council, and put off the priests and bishops and monks and abbots who have been plundered with *bona verba*. You will have seen the Lutheran libels against myself and recognized the author. Who would have thought the drunken scamp had so much venom in him! This sort of thing sets me against the whole party. They will not allow that man has a free will, and yet they hate those who do not agree with them. Some tell me not to read these things; others about the Emperor say I ought to answer, and sharply. I know not how it will be. I am ill and old and worn out, and want to be at rest.

[1] *Ep.* mcxxiv., abridged.

MELANCHTHON TO ERASMUS.[1]

August 1, 1530.

You would not believe there was such fury in man as is shown by the papal advocates. They see the Emperor and his brother are for moderation, and they want to force them into violence. You, I understand, warn him against listening to them, and I hope your words will weigh with him. Continue your good work, and deserve the thanks of posterity; you cannot use your influence to better purpose. We have given in our own views without condemning others. We are told our concessions are too late; but we wish to show that we desire peace if we can have it on fair conditions. Great changes are plainly imminent. God grant our rulers may be so guided that the Church is not wrecked in the process. Again I beseech you, for Christ's sake, do not let the Emperor declare war against quiet citizens who are willing to accept fair conditions.

The Bishop of Augsburg exerted himself for peace, and was, of course, execrated by the Church party. Erasmus advised him to pay no heed to the bite of reptiles. But, on the whole, the news from Augsburg was not encouraging. Clement, if he was ever moderate, was now urging extremities, and Charles could not break with him. It became clear that he meant to insist on submission, and the reforming leaders let him see that they were in earnest on their side. They drew together in a bond for mutual defence, *protesting* (hence the name Protestant) that they would have no lies forced on them at the sword's point. Erasmus tried his eloquence on Campegio:[2]—

August 18, 1530.

If the Emperor is only putting on a brag, well and good; if he means war in earnest, I am sorry to be a

[1] *Ep.* mcxxv. [2] *Ep.* mcxix.

bird of ill omen, but I am in consternation at the thought of it. The spirit of revolt has gone far. I myself admit the Emperor's supremacy in Germany, but others do not, save under conditions where they rather command than obey. His own dominions are exhausted. Friesland is now disturbed, and they say the Duke has turned Lutheran. The free cities are Lutheran, and the chain reaches from Denmark to Switzerland. If the Emperor becomes the servant of the Pope he will not find many to go along with him, and we are looking daily for an invasion of Turks whom we can barely resist when united. I know that the Emperor is personally for peace; yet it seems his fate to be always fighting. The fire is breaking out again in Italy, as if the world was to be drowned in blood; and as if the whole Church might be ruined in the process. The people generally regard the dispute as if it affected merely the interests of Popes, bishops, and abbots. The question is not what the sectarians deserve, but what course with them is expedient for Europe. Toleration may be a misfortune, yet a less misfortune than war. For myself, I would gladly be beyond the Alps. The Emperor has those about him who bear me no good will.

Again, to another great person:[1] —

September 1, 1530.

Unless I am far mistaken, there will be blood shed in Germany. The Lutherans have given in their Articles. The Emperor will do as the Pope wishes, and forbid all change in what has been once decreed. He does indeed promise reform, but the property taken from the bishops and priests is to be restored. It is possible, if the Pope is moderate, that things may not turn out as I fear. But just now the Pope is busy making new cardinals for his body-guard, and I doubt if that will much advantage him. There were cardinals enough already, swallowing bishoprics and abbeys.

[1] *Ep.* mcxxvii.

Alas! however, when the Emperor shows a wish to be moderate, the Evangelicals cry the louder for war. They spatter him and the Catholic princes with libels. They threaten retaliation if the professors of the Gospel are persecuted. A scandalous caricature of the Emperor has been published with seven heads.

Again:[1]—

September 6, 1530.

You would think they were celebrating the mysteries of Bona Dea at the Diet. No one knows what is doing there. If the Emperor gives way the others will cry that they have beaten him, and there will be no bearing them, while the monks will be equally intolerable if they have the Emperor on their side.

And once more to Campegio:[2]—

September 7, 1530.

Peace was rather a wish than a hope. Now there is nothing left but to pray Christ to wake and still the waves. God may yet prevent the Emperor from making war on Christians. The Turks are in the field, and will be too many for us if we fight among ourselves. Once let a civil war begin and none can guess what will come of it. I would have been present at the Diet could I have been of use there, though I have good friends who would stab me in the back were I engaged with an enemy. If trouble comes I shall be the first victim; but I will bear anything before I forsake the Church. I never made a party or gathered disciples about me, and I have deserved better treatment than I have met with. I can acknowledge this to you, in whom I have always found a kind friend and patron. The past cannot be recalled, but you may do something in future to save me from scandalous accusations.

And, the same day, to the Bishop of Trent:[3]—

I am at the last act of the play, and have now only to say, *Valete et plaudite*. I can leave the stage with

[1] *Ep.* mcxxvi. [2] *Ep.* mcxxxvii. [3] *Ep.* mcxxxix.

a quiet mind if the Emperor and the princes and bishops can still this storm without spilling blood. The worst side often wins in the field, and to kill one's fellow-creatures needs no great genius; but to calm a tempest by prudence and judgment is a worthy achievement indeed.

It was not without reason that Erasmus was heavy at heart. He was worried by the attacks of the Lutherans. The Catholics meant to be revenged on him when their time came. He had prophesied that he would be the first victim, and the prophecy seemed likely to be fulfilled. While the Diet was still sitting an edict was announced, commanding the restoration of the Catholic services through Germany, the restoration of the Church property, and the reversal of all that had been done. The Dominican Eck, Luther's first and most violent antagonist, wrote, in the glow of triumph, an exulting and insolent letter to Erasmus, telling him that he ought to be ashamed of himself, but offering to be again his friend if he would recant his sins. Eck's impertinence was too intolerable. If the Protestant League meant to fight, there would be a bloody struggle before the edict could be executed, and Erasmus feared that he might be in the centre of the storm. He thought of flying to France, and would have gone had not a letter from the Emperor recommended, and almost commanded, him to remain at Freyburg.

Others (he writes to the Abbot of Barbara [1]) give me the same advice, and I reluctantly obey. Winter is coming on. The plague is raging, and it is uncertain how long the Diet will last. The Zwinglians were refused a hearing. The Lutherans presented their Articles, which were briefly replied to. The

[1] *Ep.* mcxlvii., abridged.

Diet being unable to decide, representatives of both sides were chosen to arrange a concordat. The numbers being too large, a small committee was selected of the most distinguished men to try what they could do. They might have succeeded, but the Lutheran princes refused to restore the Church lands or to force their clergy to abandon their wives. The Emperor then said that the cities which had adopted the new opinions must conform within six months, and he used two expressions which offended the princes of the religion. He called the Lutherans a sect, and he added that their arguments had been refuted out of Scripture. This they fiercely denied. They said, in the Emperor's presence, that they not only believed, but *knew* their doctrine to be both Scriptural and Apostolic.

The Emperor was angry; the princes withdrew. The edict came out immediately after.

The Emperor's award (Erasmus writes) will lead to war. He is powerful — we know that. But the people everywhere are for the new doctrines, and will rise at the first signal. There might still be hope if the Pope trusted in Christ. Alas! he trusts more in his cardinals and the Emperor's armies, and in those wicked monks whose depravity has caused the whole disturbance.

He evidently thought that the Lutherans had been too exacting. Knowing Charles's real inclinations, he believed that, if they had shown more forbearance, his own scheme for a reconciliation might have been gradually allowed. Why that could not be, why proposals so sensible and reasonable were nevertheless entirely impossible, may be explained by Luther himself, who, it is to be remembered, was always opposed to armed resistance: —

Concord of faith is one thing, and concord of

charity is another. In charity we have not been wanting. We have been ready to do and suffer anything except renounce our faith. We have not thirsted for the blood of our opponents. We stood by them in the peasant wars against rebels and fanatics. We did more to protect them than they did for themselves; and the anarchists hate us worse than they hate the Papists. Yet the Papists wish to kill us because we will not place human tradition on a level with God's Word. God judge between us and them! It is vain for Erasmus to argue for concord in faith on the principle that each party shall make concessions. In the first place, our enemies will concede nothing. They defend every point of their position, and insist now on doctrines which they condemned themselves before the movement began. But, once for all, we can allow nothing which contradicts Scripture. Charity may yield, for charity aims at correcting faults which may be amended, and wrestles only with flesh and blood. Faith wrestles with spirits of evil, desperately wicked, of whose conversion there is no hope. There can be no peace between the truth of God and the doctrine of devils. It is said the Papists profess Christ's Gospel, and deny that their doctrine is of the devil. Yes, they *profess;* but the tree is known by its fruits. They cry, "The Church, the Church!" and by the Church they mean a body presumed to have divine authority, while the members of it lead impious and wicked lives. Erasmus must think as they do of the Church, for he says he will submit to what the Church shall decide. If the Church is what they say, where is the use of Scripture? Why do we risk our lives for what we believe to be Truth when we may be all saved compendiously in a single ship by receiving what the Papists teach? What will you do with pious souls who take Scripture as the Word of God, and cannot believe what contradicts Scripture? Will you say, "We want peace, and therefore you must submit to the Pope"? or, "The Pope has not decided on this point or that, and therefore opinion is free"? A man who fears God, who seeks life eternal, and fears eternal death, cannot rest on undecided or dubious doctrines. In my work on "The Bondage of the Will" I condemned the scepticism of Erasmian theology. Christians require certainty, definite dogmas, a sure Word of God which they can trust to live and die by. For such certainty Erasmus cares not. The Papists do not teach it. They cannot teach what they cannot understand. Therefore we can have no agreement with them. No Church can stand without the anchor of faith, and faith stands on the Word of God. The Papists and Erasmus may consult. It will avail nothing. Human devices will not serve. The pious soul listens for the voice of the Bridegroom, their Shepherd and their Master. Controversies may rise where the meaning of Scripture is uncertain. I speak not of those. I speak of doctrines and practices which are outside Scripture or against Scripture, yet are insisted on by our adversaries. They are not heresies, which are perversions of Scripture. They are profane, and therefore of the devil. Erasmus should leave theology alone, and give his mind to other subjects. Theology demands seriousness and sincerity of heart, and love for God's Word. We have suffered enough under the Papacy, driven about with shifting winds of doctrine, believing in lies, coming at last to adore the monk's hood and to be worse idolaters than the heathen. Those who pretend that the Church may decree Articles of Faith not found in Scripture make the Church a synagogue of Satan, and set up a devil's harlot for the Virgin Bride of Christ. If God gives me strength, I trust to deal more fully with all this; but while the devil's kingdom stands it is idle to look for concord in doctrine.

Compromise with such a spirit was obviously impossible. "Certainty," no doubt, is the pearl of price for which a man will sell all that he has. Those who have it have it, and, as Cardinal Newman tells us, cannot doubt that they have it. Unfortunately, of two honest disputants each is often equally without doubt. Cardinal Newman finds his "certainty" where Luther finds a synagogue of Satan. Newman finds heresy where Luther has his sure Word of Christ. Between such opposites the only argument which will convince is a broken head; and the reformers needed swords tempered in a hotter furnace than Erasmian toleration if they were to hold their own in the fight now approaching. You can tolerate what will tolerate you. Popery demanded submission at the sword's point, and could only be encountered with the sword. Reason is no match for convictions which do not rise out of reason; and Rome would have trampled opposition under its foot if it had not been met with a conviction passionate as its own.

Erasmus could but remain on his solitary watch-tower, a spectator of a struggle which he was powerless to influence. Happily for him, the circumstances of the time postponed for his own lifetime the inevitable collision, and permitted him to hope till his death. The Protestant League closed their ranks: rather death than submission to a lie. The armies of the Crescent hung over Vienna. The Turkish fleet swept the Mediterranean. France, though nominally at peace, was on the watch to revenge Pavia; and Henry of England, in his present humour, might lend France a hand if the Emperor became the armed champion of the Pope. The Emperor's resolution failed. Clement might pray; bishops and monks might clamour; but he himself had no heart for a war of religion, and as soon as it became clear that the Lutherans were really in earnest, the necessities of his position gave him an excuse for disappointing orthodox eagerness. Stake and faggot must wait for more favourable times.

Erasmus was not so destitute of religious conviction as Luther thought him. But to Erasmus religion meant purity and justice and mercy, with the keeping of the moral commandments, and to him these Graces were not the privilege of any peculiar creed. So long as men believed in duty and responsibility to their Maker, he supposed that they might be left to think for themselves on theological mysteries without ceasing to be human, and it shocked him to see half the world preparing to destroy one another on points which no one could understand, and on which both sides were probably wrong. When the Diet rose the worst seemed inevitable.

TO KRETZER.[1]

FREYBURG, *March* 11, 1531.

I fear this fine city is in danger. The Emperor is exasperated and Ferdinand is in no better humour. They say there will be a truce with the Turks, and there will be plenty of persons who will then pour oil on the fire. You know what I mean. The Duke of Bavaria covets a wider frontier, and will plead zeal for the Catholic faith: and there are cardinals willing to help him. They know that the whole storm has risen from the pride and self-indulgence of the ecclesiastical order, yet they go on spending, feasting, gambling night after night. The people see it all, yet the clergy think that the revolt can be crushed by force. The only remedy is for the heads of the Church to mend their ways, but this is the last thing in their thoughts. They regard the revolution as a mere outbreak of licence, and they look to human means to protect themselves. Their pride, their tyranny, their luxury, their profligacy daily grow

[1] *Ep.* mclxiii., abridged.

worse. It is not for me to condemn the Pope, but the news which I hear from Italy fills me with sorrow. He dreams that he can put down opposition by getting the Emperor to help him and by making more cardinals. It is to defy God Almighty. The world cannot overcome the world. They blow their trumpets, and say they are making war on heresy. The war will be only for their own revenues and power and idle pleasures. Between one faction and the other the whole country will be laid waste, and the Church and Germany be alike ruined. God grant I prove mistaken, but I have been a true prophet so far.

TO EGNATIUS.[1]

March 13, 1531.

No one had more friends than I before the battle of the dogmas. I tried to keep out of the fray, but into the arena I had to go, though nothing was more abhorrent to my nature. Had I but a single set of enemies to contend with, I might bear it. But I am no sooner engaged with one faction than the other whose cause I am defending stabs me in the back. I need to be Geryon with the hundred hands, or one of Plato's men with two faces, four arms, and four legs. You remember the fight between the scholars and the Rabbins who would mix sea and land rather than admit that there was anything which they did not know. I was in the thick of it, when out came this war of opinions by which the world is still convulsed, and almost all those who were then with me went over to the new sect. I could not go with them and I found myself deserted. They were patient with me for a time. They thought I was hiding my real views and would be with them in the end. At last I had to enter the lists against their leader, and those who had been my sworn allies became my bitterest foes. I was in no better case with my old opponents, who tried to persuade the world that the religious revolt

[1] *Ep.* mclxv., abridged.

could not be ended till learning was put down, and specially Erasmus. Thus I was shot at from all sides, and was only saved by the Emperor. Even this fate, however, is better than either to give a name to a new schism or to flatter tyrants parading themselves in the name of Christ. These last have found blood so sweet that they leave no stone unturned to bring on a civil war, which now seems impending. Had I been attended to at first, the quarrel might have been composed, and now we are to be trampled down by contending armies.

In times of excitement news vary from hour to hour. The day after he had written this desponding letter he heard reports which gave him hope again, and his fine natural spirits revived.

TO DUKE GEORGE.[1]

March 15, 1531.

The Gospellers libel me as usual, but I should care little if I could see the Church as I would have it. Italy seems quiet. France, they say, is now really friendly with the Emperor. There is no danger from Spain. And I hear the English divorce case is to be rationally and peacefully settled. I know how well disposed the King is. Also a truce is to be made with the Turk, which is like to be of infinite benefit. If this German fever would but abate we might expect a golden age.

It was a broken gleam of sunshine. The English divorce was not settled; a truce was not made with the Turk; and a fortnight later all was again black as midnight.

TO ALBERT DALBON.[2]

April 1, 1531.

I do not like the look of things. God knows what is coming. They say the Turk is putting three

[1] *Ep.* mclxix. [2] *Ep.*, mclxviii., abridged.

armies in the field — one for Austria, one for Poland, the other to land in Naples with a blessing from the Pope. This is bad enough, and a civil war in Germany will be worse. You may tell me a desperate disease requires desperate remedies. I love not remedies worse than the disease itself. When fighting begins the worst sufferers are the innocent. Spain is full of concealed Jews and Germany is full of robbers. These will supply the ranks of the regiments. Religion will be the plea, and the lava stream will first deluge Germany and then the rest of Europe. No emperor was ever stronger than our present ruler. He, it appears, will do what the Pope orders. This will be well enough if Christ's vicar will be like his master, but I fear the Pope in his eagerness for revenge will fare as the horse fared who took the man on his back to drive off the stag. We must be a wicked race when with such princes we are still so miserable. Why do we not repent and mend? They make laws against drink and extravagance, laws for priests to keep their tonsures open, wear longer clothes, and sleep without companions, but only God can cleanse the fountain of such things. May God teach the heads of the Church to prefer His glory to their own pleasures, teach princes to seek wisdom from on high, and monks and priests to despise the world and study holy Scripture.

It is interesting to observe that in the midst of his anxieties Erasmus was not neglecting his proper work. Harassed by theological mosquitoes, alarmed, and justly so, by the thunder-cloud which was hanging over Germany, we find by the dates of his letters that he was corresponding at length and elaborately with the learned men of his time on technical points of scholarship, Bible criticism or the teaching of the early Fathers. This, too, when he was past sixty, and with health shattered by gout and stone. He might complain, and complain he did loudly enough, but he had a tough elastic spirit underneath it all, and complaint did not mean weakness. It is well to mention these things if I am to make you respect him, as I hope you will. But I must leave them on one side. We have to do here with the relations of Erasmus to the great events of his time.

The reformed States had been allowed six months to comply with the Augsburg edict. They had not complied, and did not mean to comply, and Charles seemed to be getting ready to force them. Erasmus writes: —

TO LEONARDI.[1]

April 6, 1531.

All these preparations are made in the interest of the priests, yet the priests may find themselves worse off than they are now. The Emperor and his brother mean well, yet they are about to let loose a scum of ruffians over Germany — most of them half Lutherans at heart or men of no religion at all. It is said the princes will keep them in order. Will they? Look at Rome, look at Vienna, which suffered worse from its garrison than from the Turks. Our two sovereigns are good and pious, but they are young, and the greater their piety the worse they may be led astray. The Emperor will do as Clement tells him. If Clement tells him what Christ will approve, well and good; but — I will not add the rest; and what is to become of sick old creatures like me? From a movable I am become a fixture. I am one of those animals they call adhesive. I cannot fly. I must sit still and wait for my fate. Fugger invites me to Augsburg, but I should only change one dangerous place for another.

TO CARDINAL AUGUSTINE.[2]

April 12, 1531.

I have done my best to stop these German troubles. I have sacrificed my popularity and broken my

[1] *Ep.* mclxxxi. [2] *Ep.* mclxxxiii.

health, and small thanks I have met with from those whose part I have taken. The Lutherans had some right to be angry with me, but I did not look to be so venomously libelled by the Catholics. I had ill friends at Rome who tried to set the Pope against me. Happily, they did not succeed. If the Pope knew all he would see that Erasmus had been his truest adviser. Tell the Pope from me that I have encountered trials for Christ's sake which I would not have faced to be created Pope myself. I have made enemies of all the men of learning who were once warmly attached to me, and old friends are the most dangerous of foes, because they know our secrets.

Again: —

TO ANDOMAR.[1]

April 10, 1531.

I am sick of Germany. If I do not know where I should go, I know where I should not go. I have thought of Flanders. Queen Mary, who is to succeed Margaret as Regent, is a good friend to me; but if I go there the Catholics will fall upon me, and as they would have the Pope and the Emperor with them, she could not protect me. I trust things are better where you are. The factions here will leave no one alone. Where the Evangelicals are in power they do as they please, and the rest must submit; we are already Lutherans, Zwinglians, and Anabaptists; the next thing will be we shall turn Turks.

The Evangelicals were not all so savage with Erasmus or so obstinate as Luther; some of them still looked to him as the wisest guide to follow and as the best able to help them. Julius Pflug, a young influential Protestant, writes to him from Leipzig: [2] —

May 12, 1531.

To you alone all friends of peace are looking. You, by God's grace, have influence; you, and only

[1] *Ep.* mclxxxv. [2] *Ep.* mclxxxvi.

you, can convince the princes that if the controversies are to be ended, human laws and institutions must change with the times, and the Church must relax such rules as are not of divine obligation. Do you move the Emperor and his brother, and Melanchthon's party will then submit to much which they do not like. A little yielding on both sides, and peace may be preserved.

Erasmus answers at length:[1]—

August 20, 1531.

Never was so wild an age as ours; one would think six hundred Furies had broken loose from hell. Laity and clergy are all mad together. I have not the power you think. I can work no miracles. I do not know what the Pope intends. As burning heretics at the stake has failed, the priests now wish to try the sword. It is not for me to say if they are right. The Turks perhaps will not leave them leisure for the experiment. The better way would be to restore the Gospel as a rule of life, and then choose a hundred and fifty learned men from all parts of Christendom to settle the points in dispute. Opinions on special subjects need not be made Articles of Faith. Some laws of the Church may require to be changed, and clergy should be appointed fitter for their duties. At present the revenues of the Church go to support a parcel of satraps, and the people are left to the new teachers, who would abolish the whole Church organisation. Had Adrian lived and reigned ten years, Rome might perhaps have been purified. He sought my advice. I gave it, but received no answer. I suppose it did not please him. Melanchthon is a man of gentle nature. Even his enemies speak well of him. He tried your plan at Augsburg, and had my health allowed I would have been there to support him. You know what came of it. Excellent eminent men were denounced as heretics merely for having spoken to him. Suppose that he and I were to

[1] *Ep*. mcxcv., abridged.

compose a scheme of agreement, neither side would accept it—leaders or followers. Remember Monk John in the theatre. John, being country-bred, had never seen a theatre. Two prize-fighters were showing off on the boards. John rushed in to part them, and was of course killed.

The Pope, after all, had to wait for his revenge. The Turks were guardian angels to the infant Gospel. If they were not to take Vienna, Charles and Ferdinand required the help of Germany; and not a man nor a florin would the Diet vote unless religion was let alone. The English cloud grew blacker. Catherine was still obstinate. The Pope censured the King. The King replied with Acts of Parliament and fitted out his fleet. The Catholic nobles and the monks and abbots prepared to rebel, entreated the Pope to excommunicate the King, and entreated Charles to send across an army from Ostend. The Pope declined to thunder unless Charles would promise to execute the sentence; and Charles knew perfectly well that if he stirred a finger, France and England would both be in the field against him, and civil war would break out in Germany.

The Edicts of Augsburg slept. It was impossible to enforce them, and men began to talk of a General Council as the only remedy. Erasmus could breathe more freely again. Charles and Ferdinand, who had been cold while the war fever was on them, were again polite and complimentary. The Pope grew civil. Cardinals remembered their old friendship and became once more gracious and affectionate. Conciliation was to be the order of the day, and the help of Erasmus might be needed after all.

LECTURE XX.

THIS will be my last lecture, for the life of Erasmus was drawing to an end. He did not feel it. His health was shattered. He was sixty-five years old, but his indomitable spirit was rising with the apparent improvement of the prospect. The Emperor was gracious again; Clement was propitious. Ferdinand offered him some high post in the Church, and directed the Cardinal of Trent to make a formal proposal to him. He was, of course, pleased, though obliged to refuse.

May 19, 1532.

I am much gratified (he writes in acknowledgment to the Cardinal[1]), and I regret that I am not able to thank the Prince in person. You bid me ask some favour of him, which you undertake that he will grant. Would that King Christ had sent me such a message. Of Him I should have much to ask — especially a mind more worthy of His service. From the King of the Romans I can desire nothing beyond what his goodness already supplies. I am fit for nothing but study. High office would be a fresh burden on the back of a broken-down old hôrse. Wealth at the end of life is but fresh luggage when the journey is over. Neither Pope nor Emperor can delay the advance of years or make bad health into good. Both call themselves my friends, but they cannot stop the barking curs. Would they could!

Cardinal Cajetan also wrote that the Pope wished to show Erasmus some mark of esteem. This was

[1] *Ep.* mccxxi., abridged.

well enough now when his help was again needed. He was pleased, but did not choose to appear too effusively grateful. He thought Clement might have done more to stop the "barking curs," considering the service which Erasmus had done the Church by refusing to join Luther.

July 23, 1532.

Had I a grain of heresy in me (he said[1]), I should have been driven wild long ago by those snarling wretches, and have gone into the heretic camp. As it is, I never made a sect; anyone who came to me I handed back to the Church; I have no need of honours and benefices — ephemeral little mortal that I am! — but I will gladly do what I can to please the Pope, and will welcome any token of approbation from him.

Conciliation was now to be the order of the day, but Erasmus had no intention of forwarding an arrangement which was to give back their power to the monks. There could be no peace till those dogs were muzzled. The monks had been at the bottom of the whole mischief.

The champions of the Franciscans (he writes to Charles Utenhove[2]) must be more hateful to St. Francis than to any other mortal. St. Francis came lately to me in a dream and thanked me for chastising them. He was not dressed as they now paint him. His frock was brown, the wool undyed as it came from the sheep; the hood was not peaked, but hung behind to cover the head in bad weather. The cord was a piece of rope from a farmyard; the frock itself did not reach his ankles. He had no fine shoes. His feet were bare. Of the five wounds I saw not a trace. He gave me his hand on departing, called me his brave soldier, and said I should soon be with him. I would complain less of the dress of these people if they copied their founder's virtues, the seraph's six wings

[1] *Ep.* mccxxvii. [2] *Ep.* mccxxx.

as they call them — obedience, poverty, chastity, humility, simplicity, charity. If they possessed these, honest men as well as silly women would then welcome them as angels of peace. They ought to be preaching the Gospel; you find them instead haunting princes' courts and rich men's houses. Their morals — but of this I say nothing; silence is more emphatic than speech. Would that silence was not necessary! They go about begging with forged testimonials, which serve for a passport, and now they have made the notable discovery that a rich man, alarmed for his sins, may buy a share in the merits of the order if he is buried in the Franciscan habit. They demand admission at private houses, to come and go as they please, invited or uninvited, and the owner dares not refuse. What slavery is this? A man with young sons and daughters and a wife not past her prime must take a stranger into his family whether he likes it or not — Spaniard, Italian, French, English, Irish, Scotch, German, or Indian — and the secrets of his household are exposed to all the world. Wise men know that in such a multitude not all are pure. Monks are often sent on their travels because they have misconducted themselves; and, even supposing them sober and chaste, they are made of the same flesh as other men. I have heard many stories of what has happened in such circumstances. They pretend that they have no other means of living. Why should they live at all? What is the use of these mendicant vagabonds? Not many of them teach the Gospel, and, if they must needs travel, they have houses of their own order to go to.

There would be no more mendicant monks if Erasmus could have his way, and when priests took the law into their own hands and married wives he did not find particular fault with them. A humorous letter to one of these is interesting for an anecdote which it contains of Sir Thomas More.[1]

[1] *Ep.* mccxxxvii.

October 31, 1532.

Do not repent of having married a widow. If you buy a horse, you buy one already broken in. Sir T. More often said to me that if he was to marry a hundred wives he would never take a maid. He has an old one now who has lived a little too long.

Sir Thomas More was just then much in Erasmus's mind. As the prospect seemed to be clearing in Germany, the English cloud was growing darker. He had been proud of his friend's elevation to the Chancellorship, and delighted to see him engaged in the practical reforming work with which Parliament had been busy. But events were running now in a direction little pleasing to an earnest Catholic. The Act of Appeals broke up the spiritual constitution. An English court was about to settle the divorce question at home. Clement himself would have made terms, but the Imperial party at the Vatican compelled him to issue censure upon censure, which Henry continued to defy. More could no longer take a part in measures which he disapproved. He made his health an excuse, and resigned the Great Seal. He had been willing enough to use the knife in paring down the assumptions of the clergy, but, like Erasmus, he did not wish to break with the papacy or make a schism in the Church. Like Erasmus, also, he disliked the new doctrines, and disliked still more the persons by whom they were advocated — men, ignorant and uneducated, who were railing at the beliefs of fifteen hundred years. Moderate reformers always hate those who go beyond them. More confessed that he detested the Lutheran demagogues, and he had distinguished his Chancellorship by the severity with which he had punished them. Their friends in Germany heard of it, and there was an outcry which Erasmus, not very successfully, undertook to answer.

TO JOHN FABER.[1]

1533.

Report says that More has been dismissed from office, and that a number of persons have been released by his successor whom More had imprisoned for heresy. The story has flashed over Europe like lightning. I was sure it was false. I know how unwillingly the King parts with a servant whom he has once trusted, even for a real fault. More's retirement was by his own wish. The Chancellorship is a great office, next to the Crown. The Chancellor is the King's right eye and the King's right hand. More was appointed because the King loved and respected him. The Cardinal of York, when he found he could not himself return to office, admitted that More was the fittest man to succeed him; and this is the more noticeable because the Cardinal when in power had not been just to More, and had more feared than liked him. All were pleased when he accepted the Great Seal; and he lays it down to the universal regret. Who succeeds him I know not. As to what is said of the release of prisoners, I am certain that a man so merciful would have punished no one who after warning was ready to recant his heresies. Is it meant that the highest judge in the realm is not to imprison anyone? More detests the seditious doctrines with which the world is now convulsed. He makes no secret of it. He is profoundly religious, and if he inclines either way it is towards superstition. Yet during his tenure of office not one person has been punished capitally for his opinions [a large mistake of Erasmus]. But is the King's deputy to show favour to seditious novelties against the judgment of the bishops and the King? Had he been so disposed, had he not abhorred the new doctrines, he must have concealed his sympathies or resigned his office. Who does not know that behind the shield of religion crowds of rascals are ready to break into crime unless restrained by the magistrate? Yet men are angry because the Chief

[1] *Ep.* cccxxvi., second series, abridged.

Judge of England has only done what the senates of the reformed free cities have been obliged to do, if the pseudo-Gospellers were not to break into their tills. The English Chancellor, forsooth, was to sit still while a torrent of villainy overflowed the realm! The meaning of all this clamour is that England is to be a city of refuge for scoundrels; and the King will not have it so.

A generous defence, and partly sound. The laws of a great kingdom cannot be set aside in a moment to relieve the consciences of individuals. But it is not true that no heretics were sent to the stake during More's term of office, and those who suffered under him were not the rogues whom Erasmus describes. More himself repudiates the suspicion of leniency as an insult.

My epitaph shall record (he says) that I have been an enemy to heretics. I say it deliberately. I do so detest that class of men that unless they repent I am the worst enemy they have. Every day I see increasing reason to fear what mischief they may produce in the world.

Before two years were over Erasmus had himself to regret that More had not left theology alone. More, too, had to pay for excess of zeal. But it is to be remembered that he was in the centre of a hurricane, blown up, as he thought, by vanity and ignorance. He had to act according to his light, and it is not for us historians in our easy-chairs to talk glibly of bigotry and superstition. Before we censure, we must try to understand. On his resignation of the Great Seal, More wrote an interesting letter to Erasmus.[1]

CHELSEA, *June* 14, 1533.

By the grace of God and the King I am at last free, though I am not as well off as I could wish. Some

[1] *Ep.* mccxxiii., abridged.

disease, I know not what, hangs heavily about my heart. It is not pain; it is distress and alarm at what lies before us. Doctors told me I must rest, and be careful of my diet. I found I must either resign or do my duty badly and risk my life. If life went, my office would go along with it; so I thought it best to save one of them at any rate, and the King was pleased to release me. I am good for nothing when I am ill. We are not all Erasmuses. Here are you, in a condition which would break the spirit of a vigorous youth, still bringing out book on book, for the instruction and admiration of the world. What matter the attacks upon you? No great writer ever escaped malignity. But the stone which these slanderers have been rolling so many years is like the stone of Sisyphus, and will recoil on their own heads, and you will stand out more grandly than ever. You allow frankly that if you could have foreseen these pestilent heresies you would have been less outspoken on certain points. Doubtless the Fathers, had they expected such times as ours, would have been more cautious in their utterances. They had their own disorders to attend to, and did not think of the future. Thus it has been with them as with you, and heretics can quote passages from the Fathers which seem to make for their view; but so they can quote Apostles and Evangelists and even Christ Himself. The bishops and the King try to check these new doctrines, but they spread wonderfully. The teachers of them retreat into the Low Countries, as into a safe harbour, and send over their works written in English. Our people read them partly in thoughtlessness, partly from a malicious disposition. They enjoy them, not because they think them true, but because they wish them to be true. Such persons are past mending; but I try to help those who do not go wrong from bad will, and are led astray by clever rogues.

Death meanwhile had carried off Warham. He was expected to leave Erasmus a legacy, but he died so poor that there was scarce enough left to bury him. In Warham Erasmus had lost the dearest of his English friends. There was a doubt also whether he might not lose his pension, but for this there was no occasion; it continued to be paid while he lived. Who would succeed Warham was an anxious question to him.

FREYBURG, *May* 14, 1533.

I cannot guess (he writes to a correspondent)[1] who the new archbishop is. I hope it is William Knight. I am sorry things look so threatening over there. The Pope orders the King to live with his wife till the cause is decided at Rome. At the rate at which it proceeds it never will be decided while the parties are alive. It has already lasted eight years;[2] and now that two hundred doctors have proved by Scripture and argument that the marriage with Catherine cannot stand either by human law or divine, the King may fairly plead his conscience; while, on the other hand, if the Pope pronounces against the marriage, he will offend the Emperor and compromise the Holy See, which granted the original dispensation. Causes which bring so much money to Rome and the princes under the power of the Holy Father are not apt to be finished, and perhaps there is something besides that touches the King which he does not care to expose to the world.[3]

Cranmer, as we all know, was the new primate, once adored as a Protestant saint and martyr, now as passionately reviled. We are not concerned with Cranmer here, but before this letter of Erasmus was written the King and the English Parliament had

[1] *Ep.* ccclxxii., second series.

[2] *Jam octo sunt anni quod agitur hoc negotium.* The date is important as it takes us back to 1525, long before Anne Boleyn had been heard of in connection with the King.

[3] "Et fortassis aliud quiddam est quod urit Regis animum, quod efferri non vult."

taken care that the suit should not linger any longer at Rome. The Act of Appeals had been passed. Cranmer had held his court at Dunstable and had given final sentence. On the birth of Elizabeth an Act of Succession became necessary, declaring the marriage with Catherine to have been illegal from the first, and requiring all subjects to acknowledge Elizabeth as lawful heir to the Crown. Catholic Europe shrieked. The doctors at Louvain, who insisted that Erasmus was at the bottom of all that went wrong, accused him here, too, of having encouraged Henry in shaking off the Pope's authority. His friend Damian à Goes wrote to him for leave to contradict these charges. His answer contains the fullest account of his views on the divorce itself.[1]

FREYBURG, *July* 25, 1533.

You ask me, my dear Damian, what you are to answer to those who accuse me. Answer that their teeth are spears and arrows, and their tongue a sharp sword. No mortal ever heard me speak against the divorce or for it. I have said it was unfortunate that a prince otherwise so happy should have been entangled in such a labyrinth, and should have been estranged from the Emperor when their friendship was of such importance to the world. But I should have been mad to volunteer an opinion on a subject where learned prelates and legates could not see their way to a decision. I love the King, who has been always good to me. I love the Queen, too, as all good men do, and as the King, I think, also does. The Emperor is my sovereign. I am sworn of his council, and if I forgot my duty to him I should be the most ungrateful of mankind. How, then, could I thrust myself unasked into a dispute so invidious? Had I been consulted, I should have endeavoured not to answer; but neither the Emperor nor Ferdinand

[1] *Ep.* mcclii., abridged.

ever did consult me. Two years ago two gentlemen from the Imperial Court came to me and asked me what I thought. I said I had not given my mind to the subject and could therefore say nothing; the most learned men disagreed; I could tell them, if they liked, what I wished; but to say what human or divine law would permit or forbid in such a matter required more knowledge than I possessed. They assured me that they had come of their own accord, and had no commission from the Emperor; and except these, no mortal has ever questioned me on the subject. The fools you speak of have told an impudent lie. It is true that many years ago I dedicated the twenty-second Psalm to the new lady's father at his own request. He is one of the most accomplished peers in England, and is a man of wisdom and judgment. But this is nothing to the divorce, which I hear he has neither advised nor approves.

English affairs concern us here only indirectly, but the long connection of Erasmus with Sir T. More requires a few words about them. The King's marriage with Anne Boleyn was a signal for an Irish rebellion in the Pope's name. The English Catholic armed, and waited only for the landing of arms and men from Holland to rise also, perhaps with Catherine and her daughter at their head. The clergy, monks and regular, were the most active in promoting insurrection, and Bishop Fisher, unhappily for himself, had gone into the worst kind of treason (there is no doubt of it now since the publication of Chapuys's despatches), urging the introduction of an invading Catholic force as the only means of saving England for the Church. The Catholic preparations were well known to Henry, if not the names of the actual leaders. English kings had no armies at their personal command. They depended on the allegiance of their subjects, and they had to be wary what they did.

But the King could not sit still to let the storm break on him. In passing the Act of Succession, Parliament had empowered him to require his subjects to swear to observe it. The oath was generally taken without resistance. Sir T. More and Bishop Fisher refused, and were committed to the Tower. The conspiracy darkened and deepened. The Pope gave his own sentence, declaring the marriage with Catherine valid, and excommunicating the King if he refused to take her back. The King and Parliament replied with the famous Act of Supremacy, declaring that the Pope of Rome had no power or right in England at all. To refuse to acknowledge the supremacy of the Crown was to admit the superior right of the Pope, and was declared high treason. Thus the two parties stood face to face — the party of national independence and the party for a foreign ruler. The Supremacy Act was the test of loyalty. In the dangerous situation of the country every subject might be legitimately required to say on which side he stood.

So matters went on in England during these years. We must return to Erasmus. Over all the disturbed part of Europe the cry was now rising for a general free council — a council where the laity should have a voice. The confusion had become intolerable. All reasonable men, and even the wild and violent, declared themselves ready to submit to a council really free. Henry himself was ready to refer his own actions to such a council. But the question was how it was to be got together. The Pope, if it was left to him, would call only his own creatures to meet somewhere in the Papal States, and make another Council of the Lateran of it. For the Emperor to call a council would itself be an ecclesiastical revolution. To the Pope even a council of bishops meeting anywhere was sufficiently unwelcome; a council where laymen were present would probably turn the Tiber into the Vatican, and make a clean sweep of cardinals and Curia. Letters on the subject from all sorts and conditions of men poured in upon Erasmus. Here is one from an earnest moderate Catholic, expressing, perhaps, the thoughts of millions: —

GEORGE WICELIUS TO ERASMUS.[1]

March 30, 1533.

I can think of nothing but the council. Our miseries will never end till the cause of them is removed. War will settle nothing, and will leave an incurable ulcer. Germany is rent in two; Christianity itself is in peril. Oh, ears of Rome! oh, heart of Rome! deaf and dead to the one thing needful, and buried in the pleasures of the world! Have not Catholics waited long enough? Will you do nothing for the poor flock of Christ? Will not our cries move you at last? Our hope is that the Emperor will lay demands before the Court of Rome which it will be ashamed to refuse, and persuade or weary it into compliance. What Luther's party will do I know not. Some think they will never agree to any equitable settlement. I think they will agree if they are approached in a friendly spirit, and if the council, when it meets, is wise and moderate. Some are tired of the struggle already. Some I have heard say in plain words they wish their scheme of doctrine had never been formulated, so many are the inconveniences which have risen from it. Luther himself will be less violent when he hears how other learned men think of him. His haughty crest will droop and his horns drop off when he is no longer on his own dunghill, and has to defend his theories of yesterday against the sages of Christendom. But you, Erasmus, you of all men must be there. You plead age and

[1] *Ep.* ccclxxi., second series, abridged.

illness. Were I emperor I would take no excuses from you. I would have Old Appius carried thither in men's arms. It is not Hannibal who is now at the gate; it is the devil, who is trying to destroy the Christian faith. You can prove — you can answer — you can explain as no other living man can do. You can silence the rival fanatics. We will not listen to Luther; we will not listen to the sophists of the schools. We will listen to Erasmus, and to those who think like Erasmus — to those who love Christianity better than they love a faction.

As a council seemed approaching, and a council which Erasmus might guide, the louder clamoured the Ultra-Catholics. Clement himself wavered, dreading the thought of it — now flattering the Emperor, now defying him under the supposed shelter of France: weak, wavering, passionate, determined at any rate that there should be no Erasmian reforms in the Church of Rome; while monks and priests fired off their vicious letters at Erasmus himself.

December 24, 1533.

I have so many letters daily (he writes to Mexia[1]) that I can scarcely read, much less answer them. Silence is the highest wisdom. Hercules himself could not do battle with so many ants, wasps, frogs, magpies, cranes, gulls, and geese. If they had neither stings nor beaks nor claws, the very noise they make would drive him mad. How often have I answered them! yet they still sing the old song. Erasmus laughs at the saints, despises the sacraments, denies the faith, is against clerical celibacy, monks' vows, and human institutions. Erasmus paved the way for Luther. So they gabble; and it is all lies. These dead-to-the-world creatures are such a set of spitfires that it would be safer to be fighting cardinals and kings.

[1] *Ep.* mcclxv.

It soon became evident that there would be no council as long as Clement lived. He had lost England to please the Emperor, and the Emperor was refusing or neglecting to burn heretics to please him. He turned spitefully on everyone who had advised a council. Erasmus fell again out of his favour further than ever. The "dead-to-the-world" gentry received a hint that they might attack Erasmus again when they pleased. A Franciscan monk high in favour at Rome, named Nicholas Herborn, published a volume of sermons in which Erasmus was included among the heretic leaders, and a friend at Rome, the Provost of the Curia, sent him word of it. He was ill again, not with podagra, as he said in his humorous way, but with penagra, and wanted no aggravation of his sufferings. "Herborn's book," he said in reply, "has neither eloquence nor learning. There is only venom in it. He says Luther has drawn away one part of the church, Zwinglius and Œcolampadius another, and Erasmus the largest of all. He thinks it would have been better if Erasmus had never been born."

Happily for his peace, Clement died soon after, and with the succession of Paul III. better prospects seemed to open. Paul, while cardinal, had been urgent for reform, had entreated the Emperor to give way about Catherine, and had been strongly in favour of a council. His first act on his accession had been to make advances to Henry VIII. He spoke of calling a council immediately. He sent the Cardinal of St. Angelo to Germany to feel his way towards a reconciliation. In Clement's time Erasmus had been denounced, as he complained, in every church and at every dinner as only fit for a Phalaris's bull. The Cardinal of St. Angelo now sent him profuse compliments along with a handsome present.

January 9, 1535.

The Cardinal (he wrote[1]) has given me a magnificent gold cup as a sign of his good will. I produced it for my friends Glareanus and Rhenanus, who were dining with me. Rhenanus insisted that I should take my medicine as well as my wine out of it — that, in fact, I should never drink from anything else.

Erasmus describes his cup as a work worthy of Praxiteles. The Cardinal had added besides that Paul, at his election, had given him hopes of a peaceful solution of the German quarrel and particularly desired Erasmus's assistance.

This was cheering news for his old age. He might yet hope to see peace before he died, and be of use in bringing it about. Paul himself soon after confirmed the Cardinal's message under his own hands, and wrote himself to Erasmus.[2] He told him that he trusted to distinguish his reign by bringing St. Peter's boat back into harbour; that Erasmus must give him his help at the council, and so nobly end his long life, silence his detractors, and gain immortal honour.

Erasmus at this time had been seriously ill. The physicians ordered him change of air. He was too weak to ride, and was carried back from Freyburg in a woman's litter to Bâle, where the climate suited him. He meant only to stay there till he had recovered strength. He was never to leave it again. He became better at first, the Pope's letter no doubt helping his convalescence. Paul was perhaps in earnest in what he had said; but events are too strong even for popes. The first misfortune was the rising of the Anabaptists at Münster, where, as Erasmus said, the devil had broken loose in earnest. The Anabaptists, who had aspired to regenerate the world on an impossible

[1] *Ep.* mcclxxvi. [2] *Ep.* mcclxxx. May 31, 1535.

creed of love and equality — a creed which they were to propagate only by meekness and non-resistance — had been bitten by the madness of revolution, and had spread like a stream of fire over Western Germany and the Low Countries. They were stamped out with a ferocity like their own; but their rising intensified the passion of the Catholics, who regarded them as the natural offspring of Luther and Lutheranism, and were thus more opposed than ever to any kind of agreement. Francis took to burning heretics in Paris, rehearsing a prelude to St. Bartholomew, swinging the poor wretches in chains above the flames while he and the Court looked on. Darker news of another kind came from England. The country was on the eve of rebellion: half-a-dozen powerful nobles were ready to rise in the northern and eastern counties; the religious houses volunteering to pay the expense of an invading Catholic army. The Act of Supremacy was put into force to distinguish the loyal from the disloyal, and those who had given cause for suspicion were called on to take the oath of allegiance. The regular clergy we know, from the letters of Chapuys, were at heart disloyal to a man. Most of them took the oath with their lips; others, bolder, refused. Four centuries of immunity from the law had led them to regard themselves as sacred persons whom the secular arm could not reach. They were made to feel that their privileges could no longer protect them, and they suffered as traitors. "Cruel!" — we say — "inhuman! monstrous! such saintly men!" Yes, but civil war is cruel too. Many a home would have been laid in ashes, and many a hearth been desolate, if the Spaniards and the Catholic landknechts, whom these men were trying to bring upon our shores, had been let loose on the towns and villages of England.

We ought to think of this, and what it was that Henry's peremptory resolution saved us from. Paul, as was said, made overtures to him. Henry was in no hurry to respond. He said he had no wish to separate from Christendom if he and his realm were justly treated. Clement VII. had injured him. If Paul wished for a reconciliation, he had the remedy in his own hands. He might show it by his acts. There had been words enough.

The remedy, if there was one, lay in a free council. Henry wished for it. All wished for it who were not maddened by fanaticism, or, like the Roman Curia, terrified at the name of reform. Paul, however. seemed still in earnest, and began creating new cardinals as a preparation for the meeting. Among them he proposed to include Erasmus. Stronger proof of his sincerity it would have been impossible for Paul to give. Within a few months the Roman bigots would have consigned Erasmus to Phalaris's bull. Now, in his old age, the Pope desired to make him a prince of the Church. The only objection was his want of private fortune, and this could be easily remedied.

Unhappily for Paul — unhappily for the prospects which then seemed really brightening —he added a name to the list of promotions to the Sacred College less wisely chosen — that of Fisher, Bishop of Rochester. He protested that he knew Fisher only as a holy and learned man, a reformer of the old school, a notorious friend of Erasmus. He said that he required the assistance of some distinguished Englishmen at the council; and that he had made the appointment believing that he could have selected no one more agreeable to the King and the nation. It is hard to accept such an interpretation. The Imperial ambassador in England was in close and constant correspondence with Rome. Fisher had been named in his letters again and again as the leading spirit of the intended insurrection, as the most constant opponent of Henry's actions in everything that had been done. He had been imprisoned for many months in the Tower for having refused the succession oath. He had been sentenced for misprision of treason as having been concerned in the conspiracy of the Nun of Kent. It is impossible that the motive could have been as innocent as the Pope pretended. Perhaps it was no more than a pettish resentment at Henry's refusal of his overtures. But if it was a mistake, it was a fatal one. It was accepted in England as an act of defiance — a deliberate encouragement of the rebellion which Fisher had been so actively concerned in preparing. He was required to acknowledge the supremacy of the Crown. Sir Thomas More, as his dearest friend, was involved in the same fate and pressed with the same demand. They refused. Stern times required stern measures. They were both executed — both victims to the Pope's cunning or the Pope's folly.

This is not the place to discuss Henry's conduct in the matter. Erasmus was busy contemplating his own offered promotion, not without some natural pleasure; not, perhaps, without an intention of accepting it if his health would allow. The news from England was a terrible interruption of his meditations. Fisher had been among the warmest of his English friends. Sir Thomas More had been more than a friend — the most affectionate of his companions, the most constant of his defenders, the partner of his inmost thoughts. The fatal story first reached him as a rumour. "The King of England" (he writes to Damian à Goes)[1] "has been savagely punishing some of the monks. He

[1] *Ep.* mcclxxxiv.

has imprisoned the Bishop of Rochester and Sir Thomas More. News from Brabant report that they have been put to death. I trust it is but an idle tale."

If true, it was of ill omen for the council. Erasmus speaks of the rumour again in a letter to Latomus, as still unconfirmed, but, highly as he thought of Henry, as not necessarily incredible.

BÂLE, *August* 14, 1535.

My life has been long (he said [1]) if measured by years. Take from it the time lost in struggling against gout and stone, it has not been very much after all. You talk of the great name which I shall leave behind me, and which posterity is never to let die. Very kind and friendly on your part; but I care nothing for fame and nothing for posterity. I desire only to go home and to find favour with Christ. The French who fled hither from last winter's persecution have been allowed to return to Paris. The prophet says the lion roars and the people tremble. The other side are trembling now in England. Certain monks have been put to death as traitors. There is a constant report here, and probably enough a true one, that the King, when he heard that the Bishop of Rochester had been made a cardinal by Paul III., had him out of prison and cut his head off — a fine red hat for a bishop. More is said to have been executed too. This is not certain; but I wish he had not implicated himself in a dangerous business, and had left theology to the divines.

The Pope seems in earnest about a council, but I do not see how a council is to meet as the world now stands. Lower Germany swarms with Anabaptists; Münster, as you know, is taken; but there has been a dangerous riot in Amsterdam. At Lewis Bere's suggestion, I wrote to the Pope. His Holiness spoke of me in high terms, and mentioned me for a cardinalate.

[1] *Ep.* mcclxxxvi.

Health and fortune were the difficulties. It seems no one can be a cardinal who has not a private income of 3,000 ducats, but, alas! I can scarce put my head out of my room or draw a breath of air which has not been warmed artificially — and am I to be thinking of red hats? However, I am glad that the Pope wishes me well.[1]

Erasmus's health was now manifestly failing; the literary pirates chose the opportunity to prey upon him when he could not defend himself. His writings commanded an immense sale, and they were publishing his private letters, fragments of his early writings, and anything they could get hold of.

TO THE BISHOP OF CRACOW.[1]

BÂLE, *August* 31, 1535.

Whatever I may write, however carelessly, finds its way into type, and I cannot prevent it. Thus I am kept continually at work revising and correcting. They have even got hold of old exercises of mine at school, and publish them for what they can make by it. I was dangerously ill in the spring. I was ordered change of air, and was carried back to Bâle in a chair in which for several years I had driven about in Freyburg. The Bâle people had prepared a set of rooms which they thought would please me. The city which I left seven years back in revolution is now quiet and orderly. I have still ill-wishers here, but at my age, and with my experience, I am in no more danger at Bâle than elsewhere. I do not mean to stay long. I shall return to Freyburg when a house which I have bought there is ready for me. By-and-by, perhaps, I may go into Burgundy, the wine of that country being necessary for my health. The carriers spoil what they bring here by opening the casks and

[1] *Ep.* mcclxxxvii., abridged.

diluting what they leave with water. But, indeed, I cannot hope to be ever well again, either here or anywhere. I was delicate as a child. I had too thin a skin, and suffered from wind and weather. In my stronger days I did not mind my infirmities, but now that I am but skin and bone I feel them all again. I am worse or better according to the weather. My comfort is that the end cannot be far off. You are taken care of, and are not allowed to overwork yourself. I am kept for ever in the mill, do what I may to escape from it. Bonfires are blazing for the Emperor's victories in Africa. He is said to have stormed the Goletta. Münster is taken and the insurgents punished. The Anabaptists are crowding in hither from Holland. I am glad that the Emperor is doing well, wherever he may be; but I wish he had stayed in Germany and saved us from these creatures. These Anabaptists are no joke. They go to work sword in hand, seize towns, drive their creed down people's throats, set up new kings and queens, and make their own laws. Last winter there were troubles in Paris. Bills were posted threatening the King for persecuting what they called the Word of God. Four-and-twenty of the authors of these writings were executed. Many of the nobles fled. The King has recalled them, and promised them liberty of conscience if they will leave politics alone. Some say he was advised to be moderate by the King of England, some by the Pope. You will learn from a letter which I enclose the fate of Sir Thomas More and the Bishop of Rochester. They were the wisest and most saintly men that England had. In the death of More I feel as if I had died myself, but such are the tides of human things. We had but one soul between us. The Pope has created a few cardinals for the Synod, and proposed to make me one of them. Objections were made to my small fortune, my age and infirmities. Now they offer me other dignities, which I shall not accept. A poor, half-dead wretch such as I am cannot be tempted into grand idle company merely that I may end my life as a rich man. I am pleased by the Pope's letter to me, but the ox is not fit for the saddle.[1]

This was written on August 31, 1535, and it is the last which I shall have to read to you. Others followed, but of no particular moment, and in the autumn and winter his health gradually sank. Nothing happened to cheer his spirits. The red hat he might have had if he wished, but he did not wish. The Pope had no more thoughts of the council. His whole mind was bent on punishing the insolence of Henry of England. Kings and Popes had ceased to interest Erasmus. He lived long enough to hear of the fate of Anne Boleyn. He may have smiled if he knew that she was no sooner gone than the Emperor and Francis were both competing to secure Henry's vacant hand for one of their kinswomen. But popes and kings and Anne Boleyn were not important to a man like Erasmus, with the great change ever in sight of him. In early life death had seemed an ugly object to him. When his time came he received it with tranquillity. He died quietly at Bâle on July 12, 1536, and was buried in state in the cathedral.

I have left myself no time for concluding reflections, and I do not know that any reflections are necessary. I have endeavoured to put before you the character and thoughts of an extraordinary man at the most exciting period of modern history. It is a period of which the story is still disfigured by passion and prejudice. I believe that you will best see what it really was if you will look at it through the eyes of Erasmus.

[1] In another letter he says on the same subject: "Some of my friends at Rome wish to provide the income required for the red hat, and promote me whether I will or no. They mean it seriously. The Pope, six of the cardinals, and the Portuguese Ambassador are moving for me. I have written to say that I will not be provided for by benefice or pension."

INDEX.

Act of Appeals, 402, 407.
Act of Dissolution of Monasteries, 19.
Act of Succession (after birth of Elizabeth), 407, 409.
Act of Supremacy: a test of loyalty, 409, 414.
"Adagia" (Erasmus's work): specimens of its satire and wit, 50; its reception by the clergy, 51.
Adolf, son of the Lady of Vere, 74 *sq.*
Adrian of Utrecht (afterwards Pope Adrian VI.): a schoolfellow of Erasmus, 3; Charles V.'s tutor: made a cardinal, 287; elected Pope, 299; desires to reform the Roman Curia, 303; the mass of corruption that needed cleansing, 307; his position towards Erasmus, 308; pressing invitations to Erasmus to come to Rome: the latter's replies and counsel as to the treatment of Luther's movement, 309 *sqq.;* death of Adrian, 312.
Agricola, Rudolph: foretold Erasmus's fame, 4.
Albert, Cardinal. *See* Mentz, Archbishop of.
Aldington (Kent): Erasmus appointed to the benefice, and the sequel, 94.
Aldrich (master of Eton), a friend of Erasmus, 221.
Aleander (Papal Nuncio to Saxony), 215, 231 *sqq.*, 254, 269.
Ammonius (Papal agent in London), a friend of Erasmus, 112; the latter's advice to him on his elevation to dignity, 115.
Amsterdam in the fifteenth century, 1; Anabaptist riots there, 417.
Anabaptists: Erasmus's opinion of them, 336; spreading over Germany, 347; Charles V.'s edicts against, 355; account of their tenets, 357; one burnt as a heretic in Paris, 358; the rising at Münster, and its punishment, 413; their growth in the Low Countries, 417; Erasmus's account of their methods, 419.
Anderlac, Erasmus at, 291.
Anderlin, Faustus (poet-laureate): a friend of Erasmus at Paris, 21; suspected by some to have been the author of "Julius II. Exclusus," 135.
"Angelical Doctor," the, 68.
Antonia, a friend of Erasmus, 34.
Antwerp in the fifteenth century, 1.
Appeals, Act of, 402, 407.
Aquinas, Thomas: Dean Colet's opinion of him, 99.
"Arcanæ literæ," what Erasmus meant by, 67.
Arnoldus, a friend of Erasmus, 25.
Augsburg, Bishop of: letter of Erasmus to, 350; liberality towards the latter, 377; his efforts for peace between Catholics and Lutherans, 383 *sq.*
Augsburg, Confession of: drawn up by Philip Melanchthon, 379.
Augsburg, Diet of: summoned by Charles V. to consider the condition of the country, 373; description of the meeting, 379 *sqq.;* issues an edict commanding the restoration of Catholic worship, 386; some incidents of the discussion, 386; failure of an attempt to arrange a concordat, 387; impossibility of enforcing the edicts, 398.
Augustine (an associate of Erasmus), 71.
Augustine, Cardinal: letter of Erasmus to, on the libels uttered by Catholics against him, 395.
Augustinian Canons: Erasmus's life with, 14; their method of getting him into their order, 15; temporary success, 16; failure to get him back after he left them, 18, 170 *sqq.*
Aurotinus, Cornelius, a friend of Erasmus, 24.
Authors of books: their remuneration in Erasmus's days, 319.

"Babylonish Captivity" (Luther's work), 285.
"Bacalao," meaning of, 224.
Bâle: Erasmus's description of a journey thence to Louvain, 221 *sqq.;* Erasmus settled at, with Froben, 300; rapid spread of the Reformation doctrines there, 359; great destruction of images and wall paintings in churches, 359; Erasmus leaves the city, 360; his reasons for making the change, 360; his return to, 418; his death and burial there, 420.
Baptism: Erasmus's view as to the time for administering it, 336.
Baptista, Doctor: Erasmus's travelling companion to his sons, 83.
Barbara, Abbot of: letter of Erasmus to, 386.
Barbirius, Peter, 287.

Battus, Jacob, a faithful follower of Erasmus, 28 *sq.;* letter to Mountjoy about Erasmus, 49.
Bavaria, Duke of, 391.
Becket's tomb at Canterbury, 97, 221.
Berald, Nicholas, 281.
Bere, Lewis, 417.
Berne: a "pious fraud" practised there, 249.
Berquin, Louis (a friend of Erasmus): burnt at Paris, 361.
Bersala, Anna. *See* Vere, the Lady of.
Bible, the: neglect of its study in Erasmus's time, 119 *sq.;* Luther's translation into vernacular German, 299.
Bishops and monastic orders, contests between, 20.
Bishops: Erasmus's denunciation of their tyranny and evil lives, 121.
Boleyn, Anne: her marriage with Henry VIII., 408.
Bologna: Erasmus there (1504), 84; annexed to Papal territory, 85.
Bombasius, Paulus (Professor at Bologna), 217.
Book-trade, the, in Erasmus's time, 319.
Bruges in the fifteenth century, 1; Erasmus there, 259.
Brussels in the fifteenth century, 1; Erasmus's visit to, 180.
Burgundy, Duchy of, in the fifteenth century, 1.
Burlesquing Scripture: a trick of the monks, 123.

CAIN, Erasmus's imaginary legend of, 40.
Cajetan, Cardinal, 215, 232, 269, 399.
Calvin: his rise as a Reformer, 339.
Cambray, Bishop of: obtains Erasmus's release from the Augustinians, 18; treatment of him, 18 *sqq.;* sends him to study at Paris, 20; dissatisfaction with him, 55; makes inquiries into his manner of life, 62 *sq.;* Erasmus flatters him, 71.
Cambray: the Queens' conference at, 366: the Peace of, 367 *sq.*
Cambridge: Erasmus's lectures on Greek there in 1506, 83, 87; he returns there at Bishop Fisher's instigation, 110; his dislike for the place, 112 *sqq.;* his opinions on the junior teachers there, 118; the authorities forbid the reading or the sale of Erasmus's writings, 138.
Campegio, Cardinal: believed that Erasmus was the author of "Julius II. Exclusus," 136; told him that he was suspected of abetting Luther's movement by anonymous writings, 235; consults with him about Luther's case, 269; Erasmus's reply, 269; another consultation before the Diet of Worms, 274; Campegio's second mission to Germany, 315; sent as legate to settle Henry VIII.'s divorce case, 340, 368; at the Diet of Augsburg, 379.
Cantelius, a companion of Erasmus in his youth, 13.
Capito, Fabricius, a preacher at Bâle, 186.
Capnio (= Reuchlin), 2.
Carlstadt: his book, in German, on the Eucharist, 328; his advance from a denial of the sacraments to Anabaptism and social anarchy, 339.
Carpi, Prince of; dissatisfied with Erasmus's book against Luther, 331; Erasmus's reply, 332.
Catechism, the Lutheran, 313.
"Catena Aurea," the, 99.
Catherine of Aragon, Queen: anecdote of, 228; story of her marriage to Henry VIII., 367; the steps taken to get her assent to a divorce, 367; Erasmus's opinion of the case, 373, 406, 407.
Catherine of Sienna: her interviews with Christ, 13.
Catholics, English: made preparations to rebel against Henry VIII., 408.
Cavajal (Franciscan): a work of his condemned at Salamanca, 365.
Celibacy, clerical, Erasmus's denunciation of, 121, 126.
Centum Gravamina: the list of charges against the clergy drawn up by the German Diet, 371.
Ceremonies, use and abuse of, 351.
"Certainty" the pearl of price: Newman's and Luther's opposite views, 389.
Chapuys, Eustace (Imperial ambassador to England): proof of clerical disloyalty given in his despatches, 408, 414.
Charles, Archduke (afterwards King of Spain, etc.; later Emperor Charles V.): offers Erasmus a bishopric, 180. *See* Charles V.
Charles V., Emperor: elected in succession to Maximilian, 240; Erasmus's opinion thereon, 240; the election excites the fears of the Pope, France, and England, 338; the league formed against him, and what came of it, 313 *sq.;* Charles captures Rome and imprisons the Pope, 339; Erasmus's reply to the Emperor's request for his counsel, 340; Erasmus's fear that the Pope would become Charles's creature, 341; the Emperor's difficult position with regard to the Church in Spain, 345; he assents to the demand that Erasmus's writings should be examined by the Inquisition, 345; letter in reply to Erasmus's appeal to him, 345; summary of Charles's position after the capture of Rome, 346; makes peace with Clement, 347; opposed to the divorce of Henry VIII., 347; his edicts against Anabaptists, 355; policy of repression of the Reformers, 355; straitened finances, 362; position in regard to Henry VIII.'s divorce, 368, 371; goes to Italy to be crowned by the Pope, 368; at the Diet of Augsburg, 379; the pantomime produced before him, 380; a caricature of him published, 385; his position after Augsburg, 390 *sq.*

Charnock, Richard (Prior of St. Mary's College, Oxford), 40.
Chelsea: Erasmus with Sir T. More at, 97.
"Christian Knight's Manual, The" (work by Erasmus), 82, 119.
Christian religion: Erasmus's opinion of its condition in his day, 65 *sqq.;* what its practice consisted of at that time, 119.
Christianus, a friend of Erasmus, 23.
Christopher, a literary wine-merchant, 222.
Church courts, and their practices, in England, 371.
Clement VII., Pope, successor of Adrian VI., 312; asks the aid of Erasmus against Luther, 315; rewards Erasmus for the "De Libero Arbitrio," 328; urges Charles V. to extreme action against the Lutherans, 383; desirous of making terms with Henry VIII., 402; wavering about the proposed council, 409, 411; his death, 412.
Clergy: how they received Erasmus's New Testament, 127; depraved private lives, 236; the powers they claimed for the priesthood since the twelfth century, 256 *sq.;* ludicrous instance of ignorance, 354; immunities from common law in England, 371; made a trade of saying masses, 376; Erasmus's position towards those who married, 401.
"Cœna Pontificalis," Erasmus's interpretation of, 50.
Colet, Dean: Erasmus introduced to, 39; the latter's esteem for him, 40, 43; Colet's theological lectures censured by a bishop, 48; made Dean of St. Paul's: Erasmus's letter of congratulation, 86; Colet helped by Erasmus to found St. Paul's School, 97; the latter's sketch of his life and character, 97 *sq.;* Colet's low opinion of the morality of priests and monks, 98 *sq.;* opinions on education, 100; attack of the bishops on him, and the result, 101 *sqq.;* his opinion of Sir Thomas More, 107; reproves Erasmus for his carelessness in regard to money, 117; his death, 241.
Collationary Fathers: Erasmus and his brother placed under their care, 7; his account of their system and personal character, 7; their arguments to get him into their order, 12 *sq.*
"Colloquies," the (Erasmus's work), 220; Spanish translation widely read in Spain, 344.
Columbus, Christopher, 1.
"Commentary on the Psalms," Luther's: met with Erasmus's approval, 234.
Comunidades (Spain), revolt of the, 240.
Confession of Augsburg, the, 379.
Confession of sins to priests: Erasmus's opinion thereon, 245 *sq.*, 247, 336; the secrets of the confessional notoriously betrayed, 351; anecdote of a sleepy confessor, 353; confession abused by priestly villany to extort money, 364; and especially by mendicant friars, 401.
Coronellus, Ludovicus, a friend of Erasmus, 303.
Council, General: general demand for, 409; the Pope's objections, and their reasons, 409 *sq.*
Courtier's life, a: Erasmus's letter of counsel to friends at the Emperor's Court, 297 *sq.*
Cracow, Bishop of, letter of Erasmus to, 418.
Cranmer, Archbishop: continued Warham's pension to Erasmus, 94; pronounced the decree divorcing Henry VIII. and Catherine, 407.
Cranvelt, Francis, Councillor of Bruges, 274.
Cromwell, Thomas, 179.
Croy, Cardinal of, 243.
Curia, the Roman: Pope Adrian's desire to reform it, 303; a mass of corruption and personal profligacy, 307.

Dalbon, Abbot, letter of Erasmus to, on the wrong-headedness of the Catholic authorities, 393.
Darcy, Lord (afterwards leader of the Pilgrimage of Grace): drew up the attainder of Wolsey, 371.
Denmark, King of, 288.
Denmark, spread of Lutheranism in, 384.
Deventer, Erasmus at school at, 3.
Diet, the German: their list of wrongs (the *Centum Gravamina*) against the clergy, 371.
Dissolution of Monasteries, Act of, 19.
Dorset, Marquis of (uncle of Lady Jane Grey), 26.
Dunstable: Henry VIII.'s divorce decreed there, 407.

Eastminster, an old name of St. Paul's, 101.
Eck, a Dominican enemy of Luther, 260; writes an insolent letter to Erasmus, 386.
Edmond, Prince, 46.
Education, the meaning of, 321.
"Educational Institute," an: a work written by Erasmus for Prince Charles, 181.
Educational institutions of England: Colet's opinion of, 100.
Egmond, Nicholas (a Carmelite): attacks the writings of Erasmus, 196, 227, 265; Erasmus's description of a scene which occurred between him and Egmond, 275 *sqq.*
Egnatius: letter of Erasmus to, on his position before and after the "battle of the dogmas," 392.
Eirenicon: Erasmus's sketch of one he had planned, 318 *sq.*
Eltham, Erasmus at, 46.
"Encheiridion Militis Christiani," a

work by Erasmus, 82; his account of how he came to write it, 82.
"Encomium Moriæ." *See* Erasmus: *His Writings.*
England: its condition at the close of the fifteenth century, 37; Erasmus's reception there, 39; his delight with the country, 45; the exportation of specie forbidden, 48; Erasmus's visits in 1501 and 1506, 83, 87; his disappointment with his treatment, 115; his continued affection for the country, 193; his final departure from it, 127, 169; considers the people justly proud of their country, 342; the steps which led to the abolition of the authority of Rome, 370 *sqq.;* its state after the decree of Henry VIII.'s divorce, 408.
Epigram of Erasmus on Sir T. More's belief in the Real Presence, 326.
Epimenides, the story of, applied by Erasmus, 69 *sq.*
Epiphanius, St.: had personal experience of the Gnostic love feasts, 34.
"Epistolæ obscurorum Virorum" (Von Hutten's work), 103; Erasmus's opinion of the book, 194.
Erasmus: origin of his names ("Desiderius" and "Erasmus"), 2; story of his father and mother and his birth, 2; some details of his school life, 3; Erasmus and his brother left orphans, 4; their guardians propose to send them into a monastery, 5; Erasmus's early passion for learning, 7; his account of the lives of the Collationary Fathers, with whom the boys were placed, 7; their guardians endeavour to make monks of them, 10; Peter yields, but Erasmus holds out, 11; persistent efforts to induce him to yield, 12; as a compromise he becomes a boarder in a house of Augustinian Canons, 14; his life with them, 14; he becomes a novice, 15; the manner of life of these monks, 16 *sq.;* how he was induced to take the final vows, 16; disgust at his position, 16; the Bishop of Cambray obtains his nominally temporary release, 18.
Erasmus: *Youth:* his desire to see more of the world, 20; ordained priest, 21; the Bishop of Cambray makes him an allowance for study in Paris, 21; student life at the University, 21; he acquires, and teaches, Greek, 22; glimpses of his life and habits given in his letters, 23 *sq.;* admiration for Laurentius Valla, 24; accused of irregularities of life, 25; desires to take a degree at Bologna, 25; distinguished men among his pupils: Lord Mountjoy, Mr. Thomas Grey, 26; sketch of the character of the Lord of Vere, 26; visit to his castle (Tournehem) and introduction to the Lady of Vere, 28; the latter, for a time, his tutelary spirit, 29; description of her, 29; specimen of his mocking humor, 30; weak health and pecuniary difficulties, 30; period of despondency, 31; signs that his habits were not strictly in accordance with his profession, 34; invited to England by Mountjoy, 34; Erasmus's knowledge of languages, 35; character of his intellect, 35.
Erasmus: *First Visit to England* (1497): introduction by Mountjoy to Thomas More, Colet, Grocyn, Linacre, 39; his first impressions of the country and the society, 39; at Oxford: description of a symposium there, 40; example of Erasmus's improvising power, 41 *sqq.;* his opinion of Colet, 44; admiration of English country life, 45; and of the custom of ladies saluting guests with a kiss, 45; introduced to Henry VII.'s family at Eltham, 46; composes a laudatory poem on the King and his family, 46; disappointed in his expectations of making a position in England, 47; opinion on Colet's attempt to improve theology, 48; leaves England: misadventure with Custom-house officials at Dover, 48 *sq.;* publishes the "Adagia," 50; liberality of Archbishop Warham toward Erasmus, 51 *sq.;* hankering for Rome and Bologna, 53; the Lady of Vere offers him a benefice in reply to his appeal to her for pecuniary help, 53.
Erasmus: *In the Netherlands and France:* engaged in examining libraries, 55; death of the Lord of Vere, 56; Erasmus again begging of his widow, 56; his determination to be free from servitude to anyone, 57; his close study of Greek, and translations from Greek authors, 58; writes flattering letters to his three chief patrons, 58; his carelessness in money matters, 60; relations with the Bishop of Cambray, 62; flies to Orleans from the plague in Paris, 62; his work at Orleans, 63; saves a heretic from punishment, 64; his readiness to advise those who consulted him, 65; object of the work he was busy over: the destruction of the gross abuses which had overgrown true Christianity, 65 *sqq.;* preparing his edition of the New Testament and of the works of Jerome, 67; his desire to depose scholastic theology: studies Duns Scotus and the "Angelical Doctor," 67; description of Scotism, 69; Erasmus seeks pecuniary aid by flattering letters, 71; instructions to Battus for the same purpose, 74 *sqq.;* appeal to the Lady of Vere, 78; translation of Lucian's Dialogues, 81; the "Encheiridion Militis Christiani," 82.
Erasmus: *Visits to England and to Italy:* date of his second visit to England, 83; journey to Italy, 83 *sq.;* introduced to Julius II. at Bologna, 84; wrote a pamphlet at his request,

85; lectures at Sienna: his pupils there, 85; gratifying reception at Rome, 85; his delight with the city: rejects the efforts made to retain him there, 86; returns to Paris, 86; third visit to England: lectures at Cambridge, 87; intimacy with Prince Henry (afterwards Henry VIII.), 87 *sq.;* friendship with Archbishop Warham, 89; leaves England and goes again to Rome: his intention to remain there, 89; Mountjoy presses him to return to England, 90.

Erasmus: *Fourth Visit to England:* Henry VIII. invites Erasmus to come to his Court, 91; the King's offers and Erasmus's expectations, 93; Warham gives him a benefice, but changes it to a pension, 94; Erasmus's income at this time: Mountjoy's liberality, 94; disappointed in his expectations, Erasmus hankers after Rome, 95; association and journeys with Dean Colet, 97; Erasmus helps him in founding St. Paul's School, 97; his portrait of Colet, 97; Erasmus charged with being the author of the "Epistolæ obscurorum Virorum," 103; his portrait of Sir Thomas More, 103 *sqq.*; Erasmus his guest at Chelsea, 108; comparison of their characters, 108; Erasmus's epigram on More's belief in the Real Presence, 109; lectures at Cambridge, 110; pecuniary straits, 111; details of his life, 112 *sq.;* an attack of stone, 113; irksomeness of his life in England, 115 *sqq.;* Colet's conditional offer of pecuniary help, 117; intercourse with Cambridge dignitaries, 118; last interviews with Bishop Fisher and Sir T. More, 128; the King's endeavor to detain him in England, 169; his final departure, 169; another difficulty with Customhouse officers, 169.

Erasmus: *In the Netherlands:* the Augustinians demand his return to his old convent, 170; his reply, 170 *sqq.;* he appeals to the Pope, 173; his letter to Lambert Grunnius enforcing his appeal, 173 *sqq.;* denunciation of the immoral lives and methods of monks, 174; Erasmus obtains his freedom, 179; at Brussels: introduced to Archduke Charles (afterwards Emperor Charles V.), 180; offered ecclesiastical promotion, 180; supports Reuchlin in the battle of the languages, 181; Erasmus at Louvain, 183; reasons for his hopes of a peaceful Reformation, 186.

Erasmus: *Period of Contest:* virulent antagonism of the religious orders towards him, 190; his works denounced to Rome, 191; Leo X. decides in favour of Erasmus, 192; troubles arising from the violence of his own and Reuchlin's friends in Germany, 194; attack of Pfeffercorn's party, 195 *sq.;* and of the Carmelite Egmond, 196; Erasmus's friends at this period, 198.

Erasmus: *Luther's Rebellion:* Luther's and Erasmus's methods compared, 201; Erasmus's first opinions of the outbreak, 205; his dread that it would only generate another dangerous form of intolerance, 206; he keeps quite aloof from Luther and from his writings, 207; the Louvain monks attribute the outbreak to Erasmus, 208; he writes to Cardinal Wolsey explaining his position, 209 *sq.;* indignation at the Pope's method of treating Luther's movement: letter thereon to Abbot Volzius, 213; renewed bitterness of the clerical party, 215 *sqq.;* Erasmus longs to be back in England, 217; his manner of life at this period, 219; amusing description of a journey from Bâle to Louvain, 221 *sq.;* absurd charges against his New Testament, 226 *sq.;* Luther's appeal to him, 229; Erasmus's hesitation: its causes, 229 *sqq.;* the reply, 233; letter to Henry VIII., 236; estimate of that king's character, 238; the election of Maximilian's successor, 238 *sqq.*

Erasmus: *After Charles V.'s Election:* Erasmus's opinion of the new emperor, 240; raised to the dignity of Imperial Councillor, 241; attacked by Hochstrat, Egmond, and Edward Lee, 242; his own statement of his position towards Luther, 244; and of the latter's position towards the Church, 245; Erasmus's protest against injustice to Luther, 245; Philip Melanchthon's appeal to Erasmus, 250; the reply, 251; signs of the working of Erasmus's mind on the matter, 253; he foresees what a struggle is impending, 258; letter to Leo X. explaining his position towards Luther, 263; Erasmus's protest against Egmond's denunciation of him from the pulpit, 265; conference of Imperial Councillors, 267; Erasmus's letter to Campegio, attributing the whole convulsion to the religious orders, 269; Luther should not be condemned before he has been heard in his defence, 270; account of a curious scene between Erasmus and Egmond, 275 *sqq.;* Erasmus's aid sought for by both sides before the Diet of Worms, 278; his view of episcopacy in the early Church, 279 *sq.;* he is attacked by both sides, 281.

Erasmus: *After the Diet of Worms:* Erasmus condemns the unyielding position Luther assumed towards the Diet, 284; goes to Bruges to escape the Louvain Carmelites, 287; some specimens of the methods of the latter, 291; numerous friends of Erasmus press him to write against Luther, 293; his hesitation to comply, 295 *sq.;* the futility of disputations upon

Christian dogmas, 296; he believed that Luther was constructing a Protestant theology which might be as intolerant and dangerous as the Catholic, 297; Erasmus's interpretation of the moral of Lucian's Φιλοψεύδης, 300.

Erasmus: *After the Election of Adrian VI.:* Erasmus has renewed hopes of reform, 302; letter to Adrian, giving his views of what should be done, 304; letter to Duke George of Saxony on Luther's "excellent cause," and deprecating the use of force to put him down, 305; Adrian invites Erasmus to Rome, 309; the reply: Erasmus's advice to the Pope, 309; Hutten's attack on Erasmus, and the reply, 316.

Erasmus: *After the Election of Clement VII.:* Erasmus's sketch of a projected "Eirenicon," 317; the treatise "De Libero Arbitrio:" why Erasmus chose this subject against Luther, 320 *sqq.;* "Hyperaspistes," 326; strenuous efforts to bring about a peace, 326; Clement's remuneration for Erasmus's work, 328; discontent of the Catholic party with the work, 329, 331; Erasmus's reply to this discontent, 329 *sqq.;* Sir T. More and Faber desire him to repeat the attack, 333; his reply to the latter, 334; his sketch of the reforms he desired, 335 *sq.*, 340; how Erasmus regarded the breach between the Emperor and the Pope, 341; the confusions in Germany: the folly of monks and theologians the real danger, 343; Erasmus's works submitted to the examination of the Inquisition, 345; the Emperors' edict against the Reformers' followers, 347; Erasmus pleads for moderation, 347 *sq.;* denounces the abuse of the confessional, 351; the vicious lives of monks, friars, and nuns, 351 *sqq.;* the crass ignorance of the clergy, 354; yet he determines not to forsake the Church, 356; denounces Anabaptists, but would not have them burnt, 357; his belief that Henry VIII. was really the writer of the work against Luther, 358.

Erasmus: *His later Years:* iconoclasm of the Reformers at Bâle, 359; Erasmus removes to Freyburg, 360; interview with Œcolampadius, 360; denounces the punishment of heretics, 361; irregularity of Erasmus's income, 362; liberality of the Fuggers (Augsburg bankers) towards him, 363; his picture of the overstrained rope (the condition of modern Church doctrine): strand by strand giving way, 364; his expectations from the Peace of Cambray, 368; opinion about Henry VIII.'s proposed divorce, 373; Erasmus out of favour with the authorities at Rome, 374; letter in self-defence to the Papal Secretary, 375; on the futility of arguments about the Real Presence, 376; abuses of the Mass by priests, 376; the number and diverse rank of Erasmus's correspondents, 377; the advance of education among the higher classes, 378.

Erasmus: *The Diet of Augsburg:* the representation of Erasmus's character in the pantomime presented to the Emperor, 380; his great desire for toleration and concession, 381; criticisms on the work of the Diet, 382 *sqq.;* headstrongness on both sides, 385; Erasmus attacked by the Dominican Eck, 386; some details of the Diet, 387; what religion meant to Erasmus, 391; he foresees that force will be of no avail against the Lutheran movement, 391; he complains that he is "shot at from all sides," 393; his extensive correspondence with literary men on matters concerned with scholarship, 394; his influence with some of the more moderate Protestants, 396 *sq.*

Erasmus: *His last Days:* he receives offers of high promotion from Prince Ferdinand and from Clement VII., 399 *sq.;* his denunciation of the degeneracy of the sons of St. Francis, 400; immorality of travelling monks, 401; a joke on the marriage of widows, 402; defence of Sir T. More's treatment of heretics, 403; death of Erasmus's dearest English friend, Warham, 406; further expressions of opinion on Henry VIII.'s proposed divorce, 406, 408; Erasmus's reply to the charge that he had encouraged Henry VIII. to shake off the Pope's authority, 407; Erasmus consulted about the coming council, 410; attack on him by Nicholas Herborn (Franciscan), 412; Paul III., successor of Clement VII.: Erasmus again in favour at Rome, 412; a serious illness, 413; his reception of the news of the execution of More and Fisher, 416 *sq.;* the proposal to make Erasmus a cardinal, 419; his death and burial at Bâle, 420.

Erasmus: *His Writings:* the "Adagia:" the lash applied to ecclesiastics and ecclesiasticism, 50 *sqq.;* reception by the clergy, 51; its success, 52; his object in preparing his edition of the New Testament, and of the works of Jerome, 67; what he meant by *arcanæ literæ*, 67; translation of Lucian's Dialogues, 81; the "Encheiridion Militis Christiani:" occasion of writing it, 82 *sq.;* the publication of his New Testament, 119; description of the work, and specimens of his charges of degradation of religion against the bishops, seculars, and monks, 121 *sqq.;* enormous circulation of the work, 127; reception by the clergy, 127; the "Encomium Moriæ" ("Praise of Folly")—suggested by Sir T. More, 105, 129; the title a play on More's name, 129; description of Folly, 129; satire on theologians and their vain disputations, 130; on the *Religiosi et Monachi*, 132; on the evil conduct and character of mendicant friars, 132; on princes and courtiers, popes, cardinals, and bishops, 133; on priestly and monastic absurdity of ignorance, 134; great repute of the work, 137; a burst of clerical wrath, 138; an outcry against the study of Greek, 138 *sqq.;* an "Educational Institute" (written for Prince Charles), 181; production of the edition of Jerome's works, 184 *sq.;* Leo X. accepts the dedication, 185; publication of the Paraphrases on the New Testament books, 192; his "Apology," 196; publication of the "Colloquies," 220; object and character of the work, 220 *sq.;* edition of St. Augustine's works, 262; "Spongia" (Erasmus's reply to Hutten's attack on him), 316; "De Libero Arbitrio" (work against Luther), 320 *sqq.;* "Hyperaspistes" (rejoinder to Luther's "De Servo Arbitrio"), 326.

Erasmus: Letters of, to—
- Adrian VI., Pope, 304, 307, 309 *sqq.*
- Æmilius ab Æmilio, 362.
- Ammonius (Papal agent in London), 112, 115, 180, 191.
- Anderlin, Faustus, 45, 52.
- Andomar, 396.
- Anonymous, 25, 34, 44, 51, 55, 60, 65, 68, 181, 197, 252, 278, 285 *sq.*, 292, 297, 298, 301, 316, 317, 320, 335, 351, 354, 400.
- Arnoldus, 25.
- Augsburg, Bishop of, 350.
- Augustine, Cardinal, 395.
- Aurotinus, Cornelius, 24.
- Barbara, Abbot of, 386.
- Barbirius, Peter, 287.
- Battus, James, 53, 59, 61, 63 *sq.*, 70, 75.
- Ber, Lewis, 356 *sq.*
- Berald, Nicholas, 281.
- Bertin, the Abbot of, 71, 114, 116.
- Bombasius, Paulus, 217.
- Botzemus, 363.
- Cæsarius, 194 *sq.*
- Campegio, Cardinal, 136 *sq.*, 269, 383 *sq.*
- Cann, Nicholas, 342.
- Capito, Fabricius, 186.
- Carpi, Prince of, 332.
- Chisigat, Francis, 261.
- Christianus, 23.
- Colet, Dean, 44, 48, 86, 111, 117, 226.
- Coronellus, Ludovicus, 303.
- Cochlæus, 358.
- Cracow, Bishop of, 418.
- Cranvelt, Francis, 274.
- Dalbon, Abbot, 393.
- Egnatius, 392.
- Erfurt, the Rector of the school at (Luther's), 207.
- Everard, Nicholas (President of Holland), 232.
- Faber (Dominican), 334.
- Faber, John, 403.
- Falco, 30.
- Fisher, Bishop, 193, 242.
- Fisher, Robert, 39.
- Gauden, William, 31.
- George of Saxony, Duke, 305, 329, 342, 347 *sq.*, 393.
- Gerard of Nimegen, 260.
- Giles, Peter, 189.
- Goclenius, Conrad, 259.
- Godschalk, 265.
- Goes, Damian à, 407, 416.
- Grey, Mr. Thomas, 27, 68.
- Grunnius, Lambert, 5, 173.
- Grymanus, Cardinal, 95.
- Guildford, Sir Henry, 235.
- Henry, Prince (afterwards Henry VIII.), 88, 236.
- Herman, Elector (Archbishop), 348.
- Hildesheim, Bishop of, 376.
- Hutten, Ulrich von, 103.
- Jonas, Jodocus, 284.
- Kretzer, 391.
- Latomus, 417.
- Laurinus, Marcus, 216.
- Leonardi, 395.
- Leo X., 263.
- Lipsius, Martin, 354.
- Luther, Martin, 233.
- Marlianus, Bishop Louis, 253.
- Mechlin, President of Senate at, 304.
- Melanchthon, Philip, 250, 327, 381.
- Mentz, Archbishop of (Cardinal Albert), 241, 243.
- Mexia, 377, 411.
- More, Sir Thomas, 212, 275, 369.
- Mountjoy, Lord, 28 *sq.*, 44, 295, 370.
- Nanetensis, Cardinalis, 115.
- Nassau, the Secretary of Prince of, 293.
- Pace, Dr., 193, 285.
- Palencia, Bishop of, 303.
- Palermo, Archbishop of, 296.
- Peutinger, Conrad, 267.
- Pflug, Julius, 397.
- Pirkheimer, 183, 196, 260, 300 *sq.*, 359.
- Raphael, Cardinal, 182.
- Rhenanus, Beatus, 221.
- Rinckius, 382.
- Sadolet, 375.
- Schudelin, John, 291.
- Servatius (Augustinian), 170.
- Sixtinus, Joannes, 40.
- Spalatin, George, 240, 259.
- Trent, Bishop of, 385, 399.
- Tunstall, Cuthbert, 218, 374.
- Utenhove, Charles, 361, 400.
- Vere, the Lady of, 78.
- Volzius, Abbot, 213.
- Warham, Archbishop, 285, 288, 341.
- Wolsey, Cardinal, 209, 218.

Eucharist: Erasmus's opinion of the doctrine of the Real Presence, 336; gross abuses of the administration of the Sacrament, 337.

Europe: in 1467, 1; the position of its

military power after the Peace of Cambray, 366.
Evangelicals: name given to the Reformers, 396.
Everard, Nicholas (President of Holland), 232.

Faber (Dominican monk): urges Erasmus to write more fully against Luther, 334; Erasmus's reply, 334.
Faber, John, letter of Erasmus to, in defence of Sir T. More, 403 *sq.*
Falco, letter of Erasmus to, 30.
Fasting, extravagant importance attached to, 351.
Ferdinand, Archduke, 189, 350 *sq.*, 360, 369, 379, 399.
Fisher, Bishop (Rochester): induces Erasmus to go to Cambridge, 110; opposes Church reform in England, 372; Erasmus's high opinion of his character, 378; Fisher endeavours to procure a Catholic invasion of England, 408; committed to the Tower, 409; made cardinal by Paul III., 415; refuses to acknowledge the supremacy of the Crown, 416; executed, 416.
Fisher, Robert, a friend of Erasmus, 39.
Fitzjames, Bishop (London): his endeavour to put down Dean Colet, 101; what came of it, 102.
Flodden Field, battle of, 103.
Florence, the name under which Erasmus described his case to the Pope, 8 *n.*, 173, 178.
France, Henry VIII.'s war with, 93; instigated by Julius II., 102.
France, Queen of: arranged preliminaries of peace at Cambray, 366.
Francis of Assisi, Erasmus's dream of, 400.
Francis I.: invited Erasmus to Paris, 189; taken prisoner at Pavia, 338; gets dispensed by the Pope from his obligations under the Treaty of Madrid, 363; watched the burning of heretics in Paris, 413.
Franciscans: their persistent hatred of Erasmus, 365; denunciations of him by the friars in Spain, 377; his reply, 377.
Free cities, German: spread of Lutheranism in, 384.
Free will: what is really meant by the term, 320; the absolute rule of right of Catholic theologians, 322; Luther's theory, 323; Erasmus's opinion, 381.
Frewin Hall, Oxford, 40.
Freyburg: Erasmus removes thither from Bâle, 360.
Friars: their insolence towards bishops, 20; how they obtained their influence among the people, 66; their evil conduct and character, 132.
Friesland: spread of Lutheranism in, 384.
Froben, the famous printer, 181; Erasmus takes up his abode with him, 300.
Fuggers (bankers at Augsburg): their liberality to Erasmus, 363, 377, 395.

Gattinarius (secretary to Charles V.): letter to Erasmus conveying the Emperor's views regarding the healing of the Lutheran schism, 337.
Gauden, William, a friend of Erasmus, 31.
George of Saxony, Duke: opposed equally to Luther and to monks and bishops, 305; not satisfied with Erasmus's book against Luther, 328; letter of Erasmus to, 347; his desire that Erasmus should write against Luther again, 369.
German: Erasmus's ignorance of, 306.
Germany: Luther called upon to organise the Church, 313; its liturgy, ministers, and Catechism, 313; religious confusions following on Luther's movement, 339, 343; the reformed States refuse to comply with the Augsburg edict, 395.
Gerrard (father of Erasmus): story of his marriage, 2 *sq.*; his death, 4.
Gerrard, Margaret, mother of Erasmus, 2; her care for him, 3; death, 4.
Gerrard, Peter, brother of Erasmus, 4; consultation with his brother about joining the Collationary Fathers, 9; Peter joins their body, 11; his wretched life and death, 11.
Ghent in the fifteenth century, 1.
Giles, Peter, a pupil of Erasmus, 189.
Glapio, Alexander, a friend of Erasmus, 318.
Goclenius, Conrad, 259.
Godschalk, Moderator of the University of Louvain, 265, 275.
Goes, Damian à, letter of Erasmus to, stating his position of neutrality in regard to Henry VIII.'s divorce, 407.
Goude, 4.
Grace: Erasmus's opinion on, 381.
Græcized German names, 2.
Greek language: a rare acquisition in the fifteenth century, 22; monks' objection to the study of the language, 68; the study of it denounced at Oxford, 138; Sir T. More's defence of classical studies, 139 *sqq.*
Grey, Mr. Thomas, a pupil of Erasmus, 26; pecuniary liberality to his master, 30.
Grocyn, Erasmus introduced to, 39.
Grunnius, Lambert (Prothonotary at Rome): Erasmus's appeal to the Pope through him, 5, 173 *sqq.*; his reply, 179.
Grymanus, Cardinal, 95.
Guildford, Sir Henry, 235.

Hammes Castle (Calais Pale), 169.
Henry VII.: state of England under his rule, 37 *sq.*; his family at Eltham, 46.
Henry VIII.: Erasmus introduced to him when Prince Henry, 46; letter to Erasmus, 88; his accession to the throne, 90; desires to attach Erasmus to his Court, 90; autograph letter to him, 91; what the letter meant, 92;

his war with France, 93; his treatment of the bishops' charges against Dean Colet, 102; interview with the Dean, 102; high opinion of Sir T. More, 107; progress of the French war, 110; Erasmus's opinion of Henry's character, 236 *sq.;* Henry's answer to Luther, which gained him the title of Defender of the Faith, 306; the reasons for his seeking a divorce from Catherine, 338; was he really the writer of his book against Luther? 358; end of the war with France, 366; position of the divorce question, 366 *sq.;* he determines to have the question settled at home, in defiance of the Pope, 402; date of the beginning of the agitation for a divorce, 406 *n.;* the final sentence of Cranmer's court at Dunstable, 407; Henry's reply to Paul III.'s overtures for a reconciliation, 415; the execution of Bishop Fisher and Sir T. More, 416.

Herborn, Nicholas (Franciscan): antagonist of Erasmus, 412.

Heresy, fifteenth century notions of, 248; heresy-hunting in the Low Countries, 64; many heretics burnt in Paris, 414.

Herman, Elector, Archbishop of Cologne (afterwards a Lutheran), 348 *sq.*

Hildesheim, Bishop of: letter of Erasmus to, on the Real Presence and Transubstantiation, 376.

Hochstrat (Hebrew scholar): an enemy of Erasmus, 242; and of Luther, 260.

Holidays, Church, excessive number of, 351.

Holland, President of, 232.

Horace, Erasmus's youthful liking for, 3.

Hungary: overrun by the Turks, 347.

Hutten, Ulrich von: author of the "Epistolæ obscurorum Virorum," 103, 241, 243, 255; his attack on Erasmus, and the latter's reply, 316; his death, 316.

"Hyperaspistes," Erasmus's rejoinder to Luther, 326.

IGNORANCE, clerical: ludicrous instance of, 354.

Images: their removal from churches by Luther's followers, 313; Erasmus's opinion of their use, 335; great destruction of them in Bâle, 359.

Immaculate Conception: doctrine disputed between the Franciscans and the Dominicans, 249 *n.*

In Cœna Domini, the Bull: Luther included by name in it, 282.

Indulgences, the Papal doctrine of, 203; the sale of, as a subsidy for St. Peter's at Rome, 204; Erasmus's view on the doctrine, 364.

Inquisition, Spanish: Erasmus threatened by the, 345, 354.

Invocation of Saints: Erasmus's view on the practice, 364.

Irish rebellion against Henry VIII., 408.

JEROME, Erasmus's edition of, 110, 112; printed at Bâle by Froben, 181; dedicated, by permission, to Leo X., 185.

Jonas, Jodocus, a friend of Luther, 283.

Julius II., Pope, 83; description of him, 84; instigated the war of Henry VIII. with France, 102; his death (1513) ends the war, 117.

"Julius II. Exclusus" (a satire on the Pope): its production in Paris, 135; question of its author, 128; was it Erasmus? 135 *sq.*, 146; translation of the Dialogue, 149 *sqq.;* Erasmus's denial of being its author, 195.

Justification by faith only: Erasmus's view of the theory, 336, 381.

KIDNAPPING boys and girls for religious orders, 5.

Kissing, frequency of, as a salutation by English women, noted by Erasmus, 45.

Knight, William, 406.

Kretzer, letter of Erasmus to, 391.

LATIN, the common tongue of literary men in Erasmus's time, 35; Erasmus's objection to its use in Church service, 122.

Latomus, letter of Erasmus to, 417.

Laurinus, Marcus, Canon of Bruges, 216.

"Lax religion," meaning of, 367.

Laymen, English; their domestic conversation compared with that of monks, 38.

League, Protestant, 386, 390.

Lee, Edward (afterwards Archbishop of York): a violent opponent of Erasmus, 242, 259, 287.

Leo X.: successor of Julius II., 117; approved Erasmus's work on the Greek Testament, 120; accepted the dedication of Erasmus's Jerome, 185; recommended him to Henry VIII. for an English bishopric, 185; decided in Erasmus's favour against the Louvain theologians, 192; the great sale of indulgences for St. Peter's, and what came of it, 203 *sqq.;* Leo is said to have called the Church system a profitable fable, 211; determines on a fresh crusade against the Turks, 212; action against Luther, 214 *sq.;* issues a Bull against him, 260 *sq.*

"Libero Arbitrio, De" (Erasmus's work against Luther): why Erasmus chose this subject, 320.

Linacre, Dr. (afterwards Henry VIII.'s physician): Erasmus introduced to, 39; Linacre's advice to him about money matters, 118.

Lipsius, Martin, 354.

"Literæ humaniores:" meaning of the term, 36.

London: Erasmus's visit in 1497, 38.

Louis XII. (France): the Empire, Spain and England combined with the Pope against, 112; Scotland takes his side, 112; the end of the war, 117.

Louvain: Erasmus at, 18 *sq.;* conspiracy of monks against him, 192; continuous attacks of preachers on him, 192; the Louvain theologians attribute the origin of Luther's outbreak to Erasmus, 208 *sq.;* their indignation against Luther and Erasmus, 243 *sqq.;* attack renewed after the sentence on Luther, 286.

Low Countries, the, in the fifteenth century, 1.

Loyola, Ignatius: his dislike of Erasmus's New Testament, 122.

Lucian: Erasmus's translation of his Dialogues, 81; the Περὶ τῶν ἐπὶ μισθῷ συνόντων, 81; the Φιλοψευδὴς: Erasmus's application of it to his own times, 300; the fondness of mankind for lies, 300.

Luther, Martin: his early life, 200; becomes an Augustinian monk, 200; his visit to Rome compared with that of Erasmus, 200 *sq.;* teacher and preacher at Wittenberg, 202; the sale of indulgences: his challenge to Tetzel, 205; how Luther followed this up, 205 *sq.;* Erasmus's position in regard to Luther, 205; action of Leo X. against him, 214 *sq.;* Luther's letter to Erasmus, 228; the latter's reply, 233; his views on Luther's teaching, 243 *sqq.;* Luther's attack upon the system of spiritual domination of the priesthood, 256; burn's Leo X.'s Bull and the Papal Decretals, 265; the Diet of Worms, 281; Luther unflinching, 282; outlawed, 283; concealed by the Elector in the Castle of Wartburg, 283; Erasmus's letters on the result of the trial, 284 *sqq.;* Luther's translation of the Bible into German begun at Wartburg, 299; rapid growth of the number of his supporters, 306; dissolution of religious houses, 313; destruction of images, saints' shrines, and relics, 313; Luther recalled from Wartburg by the Elector to reorganise the Church, 313; estimate of his income, 319; his doctrine on the will, 324; and on predestination, 324; "De Servo Arbitrio," his reply to Erasmus, 326; his works, chiefly in German, had only a limited circulation, 343; Erasmus's belief in his persistence, 355; Luther not present at the Diet of Augsburg, 379; his defence of the position taken up there by his followers, 387; his condemnation of "Erasmian theology," and of Papal "doctrines and practices which are outside Scripture or against Scripture," 389.

MADRID Treaty of (Charles V. and Francis I.), 363.

Magical practices, curious story of, 72,

Maldonado, Juan: on the methods and manners of Spanish monks, 344.

Margaret, Princess (afterwards Queen of Scotland), 46.

Margaret, Queen Regent of the Netherlands, 350, 396.

Marlianus, Louis, Bishop of Tuy, in Gallicia, 253.

Mary, Princess (afterwards Queen of France and Duchess of Suffolk), 46, 117.

Mary, Queen, Regent of the Netherlands: a good friend to Erasmus, 396.

Mass, the: abuses of it by stupid and vagabond priests, 364; many of the clergy made a trade of saying masses, 376.

Matteo, Cardinal (Sedunensis): publicly accused the Dominicans of murder, 175, 178.

Maximilian, Emperor: Erasmus endeavours to obtain assistance from him, 116; defends Reuchlin, 182; his death, 233; how much depended on the choice of his successor, 238 *sq.*

Mechlin, President of the Senate at, 304.

Medici, Cardinal de' (afterwards Pope Leo X.), a friend of Erasmus, 86. *See* Leo X.

Melanchthon (= Swartzerde), 2; consults Erasmus, 250; stood by Luther at Worms, 283; letter of Erasmus to him, on Luther's tendency to cause more harm than he cured, 327 *sq.;* Melanchthon drew up the Confession of Augsburg, 379; Erasmus's letter to him about the Diet, 381; his reply to Erasmus, deprecating the violence and fury of the papal advocates, 383; his desire for peace, 383.

Mentz, Archbishop of: his share in the sale of indulgences, 204; made a cardinal, 226; Erasmus appeals to him for justice to Luther, 243 *sqq.*

Merit, the doctrine of, 324; Erasmus's opinion on, 381.

Μητραγύρται (Lucian's), mendicant friars compared to, 51.

Mexia, a friend of Erasmus, 377, 411.

Miltitz, 215, 232.

Miracles: lying stories set about by crafty knaves, 351.

Monasteries: the manner of life of their inmates, 16; treatment of rebellious monks, 17, evidences of their degradation in England, 19, 38; summary of the pernicious principles on which they were based, 68; monkish habit of burlesquing Scripture, 123; Erasmus's account of their depraved lives, 174; their continuous endeavours to prevent the circulation of his works, 343; his statement of disgusting details of their lives, 354.

More, Sir Thomas: on the beginning of monastic degradation, 19; Erasmus introduced to him, 39; More introduces Erasmus to the royal children at Eltham, 46; More's admiration of the "Epistolæ obscurorum Virorum," 103; Erasmus's description of his character, 103 *sqq.;* his domestic life, 105; dislike of Court life, 106; writings and religious principles, 107 *sq.;* his house at Chelsea, 108; his belief in the Real Presence in the Eucharist, 109; final parting with Erasmus, 128; More's opinion on the authorship of "Julius II. Exclusus," 136; letter of rebuke to Oxford for the opposition to the study of Greek, 139; passionate and indignant defence of Erasmus, 143; ambassador to the Low Countries, 190; warns Erasmus of a conspiracy of monks against him, 191; on the Carmelite Egmond, 197; More's conviction that spiritual insurrection must be put down with fire, 289; he urges Erasmus to follow up his attack on Luther, 333 *sq.;* representative of England at Cambray, 366, 368; appointed Chancellor in place of Wolsey, 370; advocated moderate reform of the Church, 372; his hatred of Lutheranism, 372; joke about marrying widows, 402; his position in regard to Henry VIII.'s proposed Church reform, 402; detestation for Lutheran demagogues, 402; Erasmus's defence of him to John Faber, 403; More boasted of his enmity to heretics, 403; his defence of his way of treating them, 404 *sq.;* refuses to take the oath enjoined by the Act of Succession, and is committed to the Tower, 409; refuses to acknowledge the supremacy of the Crown, 416; executed, 416.

Morton, Cardinal, 19: his visitation of religious houses in England, 38.

Mountjoy, Lord: his son a pupil of Erasmus, 26; his death, 61.

Mountjoy, Lord (son of the above): a pupil of Erasmus, 26; pecuniary liberality to his master, 30; invites him to England, 34; introduces him to distinguished Englishmen, 39; succeeds to the title and estates of his father, 61; letter to Erasmus inviting him to the Court of Henry VIII., 90; conferred a pension on Erasmus, 95; made Governor of Hammes Castle, 169; begs Erasmus to write against Luther, 293; Erasmus's reply, 295.

Music, modern Church, Erasmus's objection to, 122, 364.

Nanetensis, Cardinalis, a friend of Erasmus, 115.

Netherlands, the: Erasmus returns there after his visit to England, 127.

Netherlands, Queen Regent of the; arranged preliminaries of peace at Cambray, 366.

New Eagle, Count of, 223.

Newman, Cardinal: on Protestant tradition on the state of the Church before the Reformation, 365; his view of "certainty" the pearl of price, 389.

New Testament: Erasmus's edition (Greek text and Latin translation), 110, 119 *sqq.;* Leo. X. approved the undertaking, 120; specimens of the notes in it: on clerical celibacy, 121; conduct of popes and bishops, 121; honour paid to relics, 121; on the use of an unknown tongue in Church services, 122; Church music, 122; burlesquing of Scripture by monks, 123; vain disputations in theology, 124; profligacy of the clergy, 126; enormous circulation of the work, 127; Sir T. More's opinion of it, 143; Leo X. sanctioned the work, 185; Erasmus's Paraphrases on the New Testament, 192; Comments on the Apostolic Epistles, 226; specimens of ignorant objections to Erasmus's work, 227.

Norfolk, Duke of: succeeded Wolsey as Henry VIII.'s Prime Minister, 372.

Nun of Kent, the, 94, 416.

Nuns, Convents of: Erasmus denounces the immoral lives of inmates, 352.

Obedience: what monks mean by, 68.

Œcolampadius: interview with Erasmus at Bâle, 360.

Origen, Erasmus's opinion of, 87.

Orleans, Erasmus's literary work in, 63.

Oxford: Erasmus at (1498), 39; his description of a symposium there, 40; clamour against his writings, 138; consequent opposition to the study of Greek, 138; letter to the University from Sir T. More on the subject, 139.

Pace, Dr., a friend of Erasmus, 193, 217.

Paintings on church walls: whitewashed by the Reformers, 359.

Palencia, Bishop of, a friend of Erasmus, 303.

Palermo, Archbishop of: letter of Erasmus to, against vain theological disputes, 296.

Pantomime, the, acted before Charles V. at Augsburg, 380.

Papal authority: its abolition in England, 373.

Papal revenues: the sources of, 202.

Paraphrases of the New Testament, Erasmus's, 192, 194, 262.

Paris: student life of Erasmus at, 21; picture of a student's lodging-house, 23.

Parliament, the (English) of 1529: its work of legal revolution, 371 *sq.*

Patrons of literature, Erasmus's opinion of, 51.

Paul III. (successor of Clement VII.): hopeful signs in the first acts of his reign, 412; invites Erasmus to help him in the coming council, 413; overtures to Henry VIII., 415; Paul proposes to make Erasmus a cardinal, 415; raises Bishop Fisher to that rank, and the result, 415; Erasmus's reception of the proposal to make him a cardinal, 417 *sqq.*

Peasant wars in Germany, 355.

Peutinger, Conrad, Councillor of the Empire, 267.

Pfeffercorn, a converted German Jew: his denunciation of Hebrew books, 182 *sq.*; Erasmus's opinion of him, 195.
Pflug, Julius: his appeal to Erasmus to aid the cause of Church reform, 396; the reply, 397.
Philip, King (of Castile): correspondence of Erasmus and Prince Henry (Henry VIII.) on his death, 88 *sq.*
Pilgrimage of Grace, the, 371.
Plague, the, in England, 112 *sq.*
Pole, Cardinal Reginald, 238.
Prague, Erasmus invited to, 235.
"Praise of Folly, The." *See* "Encomium Moriæ."
Predestination, the Lutheran conception of, 323 *sq.*; Erasmus's opinion on, 381.
Priesthood, Erasmus's opinion of, 381.
Protestant dogmas, 324.
Protestant League, 386, 390.
Protestants, origin of the name, 383.
Purgatory: Erasmus's advice regarding the doctrine, 336.

Raphael, Cardinal, a friend of Erasmus, 89.
Real Presence, the: Erasmus's epigram on More's belief in, 109; his view of the Church's belief, 356, 381; Luther at first orthodox in this belief, 376; Erasmus's opinion of the doctrine, 376.
Reformation: its beginnings in England, 370 *sqq.*; the authority of Rome abolished there, 373.
Reform, Church: what kind Erasmus desired and hoped for, 186 *sqq.*, 336, 340.
Relics: Erasmus's denunciation of the exaggerated honour paid to them, 122; destruction of them by Luther's followers, 313.
Religious houses: speedy dissolution of, by Lutherans in Germany, 313.
Religious orders, their manner of entrapping recruits, 6.
Reuchlin (= Capnio), 2; account of his life and learning, 182; denounced to the Inquisition by the Dominicans, 182; defended by Emperor Maximilian, and by Erasmus, 182.
Rhodes: captured by the Turks, 347.
Ritual: Erasmus's protest against the excess of, 349.
Romans, King of the, 399.
Rome: Erasmus's visits to, 85, 89; his love for the city, 115; admiration of life there, 95; invited to reside there, with a handsome income, 309.
Rotterdam, the birthplace of Erasmus, 1.

Sacraments: the Catholic and the Lutheran theories about, 323; gross abuses in their administration, 353.
Sadolet (Secretary to the Pope): letter of Erasmus to, condemning the manner in which Luther's protest and attack had been met, 375.
Saint-worship: Erasmus's protest against its extravagances, 349; his satire on the saints' forbearance under the insults of iconoclasts, 359 *sq.*
Savonarola, 249.
Saxony, (Frederick) Elector of: his position in Luther's movement, 204, 215; seeks counsel from Erasmus, 231; procures the election of Charles (King of Spain) as Emperor, 240; calls upon Luther to organise the German Church, 313.
Scholastic theology, 68; specimens of the vain disputations of, 123 *sq.*
Scotists: their reply to Laurentius Valla, 24; Dean Colet's opinion of them, 99.
Scotland: takes the side of Louis XII. in the French war, 112.
Scotus, Duns: Erasmus's treatment of his theological system, 68 *sq.*
Septuagint, the, 145 *sq.*
Servatius, Father (Augustinian): seeks to recall Erasmus to his order, 170.
Shrines of saints: destroyed by Luther's followers, 313.
Sienna: Erasmus lectures there, 85.
Simony in the Church in England, 371.
Sin: the Catholic and the Lutheran conceptions of, 322 *sq.*
Sixtinus, Joannes, a friend of Erasmus, 40.
Solyman, Sultan (Turkey), 289.
Sorbonne doctors, the, and their system, 69; they procure the burning of an Anabaptist, 358.
Spain: wide circulation of Erasmus's works in; 344; intense hatred of the monks towards him, 344; failure of the attack against him, 355.
Spalatin, George, 240, 259.
Speyer, Diet of, 369.
"Spongia," Erasmus's pamphlet against Hutten, 316.
St. Albans, Abbey of: its state in the fifteenth century, 19.
St. Andrews, Archbishop of (natural son of James II. of Scotland): a pupil of Erasmus, 85.
St. Angelo, Cardinal of: liberality to Erasmus, 412.
St. Augustine: Erasmus's edition of his works, 262; the saint's opinion of monks, 352.
St. Bertin, Abbot of (brother of Bishop of Cambray), a good friend to Erasmus, 31, 58, 64 *sq.*, 71.
St. George, Cardinal of, a friend of Erasmus at Rome, 85 *sq.*
St. Mary's College, Oxford, in 1498, 40.
St. Paul's School, the foundation of, 97; Erasmus's description of it, 98.
St. Peter's, Rome: subsidy for its building obtained by sale of indulgences, 203.
Stokesly, a learned linguist and theologian, 218.
Students' life in the University of Paris, 21 *sqq.*
Study, Erasmus's counsel in regard to, 65.

Subsidy Act (Henry VIII.), 93.
Succession, Act of (after birth of Henry VIII.'s daughter Elizabeth), 407, 409.
Superstition: persistence of its characteristics, 300.
Supremacy, Act of, 409, 414.
Swartzerde (= Melanchthon), 2.
Switzerland: spread of Lutheranism in, 384.
Synaxis (in scholastic theology): meaning of the term, 124, 130.

TERENCE, Erasmus's youthful liking for, 3.
Tetzel (Dominican monk): his open sale of indulgences, 204.
Theodoric, a printer at Louvain, 225.
Theological controversies: Erasmus's protest against, 296.
Tournehem Castle (Lord of Vere's estate), 28; Erasmus's first visit to, 29.
Transubstantiation: Erasmus's opinion on the doctrine, 376.
Trent, Bishop of: Erasmus's letter to, pleading for prudence and judgment in dealing with the Lutherans, 385.
"Trojans," a faction (at Oxford) opposed to the study of Greek, 138.
Tunstall, Cuthbert (Master of the Rolls, afterwards bishop), 218; opposed to Church reform in England, 372; Erasmus's high opinion of his character, 377.
Turks: advance on Vienna, 347, 363.
"Tyrannicida," Lucian's: Sir T. More's answer to, 107.

UNIVERSITIES: Oxford and Cambridge forbid the reading or sale of Erasmus's writings, 138; a faction (the "Trojans") formed at Oxford against the study of Greek, 138; Sir Thomas More's letter on the subject, 139.
Utenhove, Charles: letter of Erasmus to, denouncing the degeneracy of the Franciscans, 400; vicious lives of mendicant friars, 401.
"Utopia" (Sir T. More's), 107.

VALLA, LAURENTIUS: character of his writings, 24; Erasmus's admiration for him, 24.
Vere, the Lady of, 26 *sq.;* for a time Erasmus's tutelary spirit, 29; his enthusiasm for her, 29, 54; his endeavours to obtain pecuniary help from her, 53; his unsuccessful visit to her, 56; letter of Erasmus to her, 78; her liberality to him, 81.
Vere, the Lord of: Erasmus's description of him, 27; his death, 56.
Vestments, Erasmus's protest against the abuse of, 349.
Vienna: threatened by the Turks, 347, 363.
"Vinum Theologicum:" Erasmus's interpretation of, 50.
Volzius, Abbot (afterwards a Calvinist): letter of Erasmus to, 213.
Vows, monastic: Erasmus's arguments against, 176.

WALSINGHAM, Our Lady of, 97, 221.
Warham, Archbishop: Chancellor and Master of the Rolls, 38; his admiration of the "Adagia" and of Erasmus, 51; Erasmus's indebtedness to him, 52; offers Erasmus a benefice in England, 89; other tokens of his esteem, 91; offer of a benefice repeated, and what came of it, 94; settles a pension on Erasmus, 94; Erasmus's estimate of his character, 96; jocular letter to Erasmus about the latter's complaint of the stone, 114; "gold is a good medicine," 114; opposed to Church reform in England, 372; died of grief, 373; Erasmus's high opinion of his character, 378; died very poor, 406.
Wartburg, Castle of: Luther concealed there by the Elector, 283.
Wicelius, George: appeals to Erasmus to take part in the expected council, 410.
Wickliff and his followers: contrasted by Erasmus with Luther and the Lutherans, 311; driven into schism by wicked monks and clergy, 356.
Wittenberg: scene of the beginning of the Reformation, 205.
Wolsey, Cardinal, 89, 169, 172; Erasmus's letter to him about Luther's movement, 209; dismissed from office by Henry VIII., 370; number of his bishoprics and benefices in England, 371; his attainder drawn up by Lord Darcy, 371.
Worms, Diet of, 281.

ZEALAND, Erasmus in, 55.
Zinthius, 4 *n*.
Zwingle, the Reformer, 339.
Zwinglians: refused a hearing at Augsburg, 386.

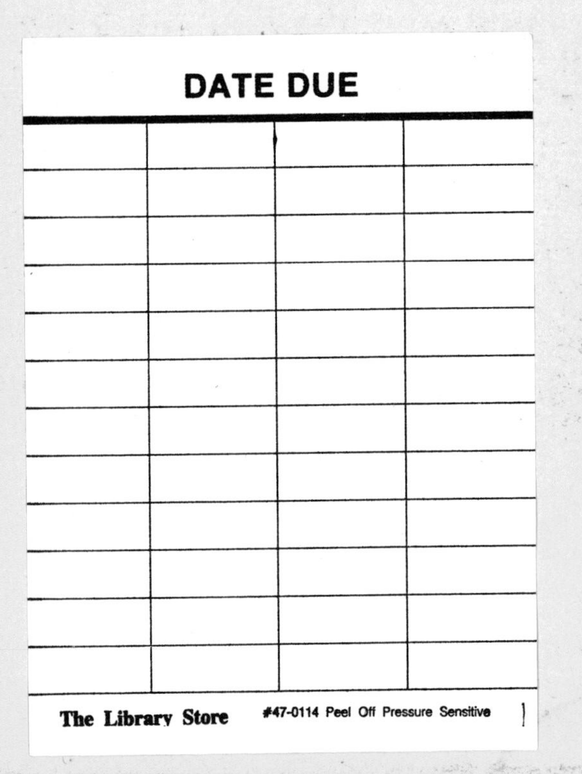